GUIDE TO THE MANDATORY DISCLOSURE RULE

Issues, Guidelines, and Best Practices

Report of the Task Force on
Implementation of the Contractor Code of
Business Ethics and Conduct and
Mandatory Disclosure Rule

© 2010 American Bar Association

Preparation of this Guide was a collaborative effort and the views expressed herein do not necessarily reflect the views of each of the authors. In addition, the views expressed should not be attributed to the authors' employers and should not be construed to be the action of either the American Bar Association or the ABA Section of Public Contract Law.

The Task Force acknowledges the assistance of the Government employees listed on the Acknowledgments page who, in their personal capacities only, participated in Task Force meetings and commented on drafts of this Guide. The views expressed in this Guide are those of the Task Force only, and do not necessarily represent the views of the Government or of these individuals.

Nothing contained in this Guide is to be considered as the rendering of legal advice for specific cases as readers are responsible for obtaining such advice from their legal counsel. This Guide is intended for educational and informational purposes only.

This publication is available through the ABA Service Center and may be ordered by calling 800-285-2221 and requesting Product Code 539-0276.

ISBN: 978-1-60442-782-0

TABLE OF CONTENTS

	Page
ACKNOWLEDGMENTS	xi
ACRONYMS	xiii
INTRODUCTION	1
GUIDE TO THE GUIDE	5
OVERVIEW OF THE MANDATORY DISCLOSURE RULE	9
I. Introduction	9
II. Summary of the Mandatory Disclosure Rule	10
A. New Contractor Code of Business Ethics and Conduct Clause	10
B. New Ground for Suspension or Debarment	16
C. New Definition of "Principal"	16
D. New Requirements for Contractor Responsibility and Past Performance	17
II. Background of the Mandatory Disclosure Rule	17
A. The FAR Councils Propose a Contractor Code of Ethics and Business Conduct Without a Mandatory Disclosure Requirement	17
B. The Department of Justice Requests Mandatory Disclosure	19
C. The First Proposed Mandatory Disclosure Rule	21
D. Comments on the First Proposed Mandatory Disclosure Rule	22
E. The Second Proposed Mandatory Disclosure Rule	25
F. The "Close the Contractor Fraud Loophole Act"	26
G. Comments on the Second Proposed Mandatory Disclosure Rule	26
H. The Final Rule and Its Preamble	28
SECTION 1: IDENTIFYING TYPES OF REPORTABLE CONDUCT	31
I. Introduction	31

TABLE OF CONTENTS

Page

- II. Meaning of "In Connection With the Award, Performance, or Closeout" of a Government Contract or Subcontract 32
  - A. Reporting Another Contractor's Possible Violation 34
  - B. Violations Arising from Indirect Costs 35
  - C. Direct Costs Under a Fixed Price Contract 35
  - D. A Supplier With No Direct Sales to the Government 36
  - E. A Supplier With Minimal Sales to the Government 36
  - F. Reportable Conduct in the Absence of Award 37
- III. Reportable Criminal Conduct 37
  - A. Background 38
  - B. Conflict of Interest, Bribery, and Gratuity Violations Under Title 18 39
  - C. Fraud Violations Under Title 18 40
  - D. Violations Not Found in Title 18 44
- IV. Reportable Violations of the Civil False Claims Act 46
  - A. Overview 46
  - B. Types of FCA Violations 48
- V. Significant Overpayments 56
  - A. Definition of "Significant Overpayment" 58
  - B. Overpayments and the False Claims Act 61
- VI. Conclusion 61

SECTION 2: THE "CREDIBLE EVIDENCE" STANDARD 63

- I. Introduction 63
- II. The Meaning of Credible Evidence 64
  - A. Guidance Found in the Preamble 65

TABLE OF CONTENTS

		Page
B.	The Use of the Term "Credible Evidence" in Other Contexts	67
C.	Interpretation Based on the Regulatory History	69
D.	The Role of Affirmative Defenses in Making a "Credible Evidence" Determination	70
E.	Relationship of "Credible Evidence" to "Reasonable Grounds to Believe" and "Preponderance of the Evidence"	71

III. Guidelines for Applying the Credible Evidence Standard 72

SECTION 3: CONTRACTOR OBLIGATIONS WITH RESPECT TO "PRINCIPALS" 75

I. Introduction 75

II. Meaning of "Principal" 75

III. Practical Considerations..78

SECTION 4: DISCLOSURES REGARDING SUBCONTRACTORS AND AGENTS 83

I. Introduction 83

II. Key Issues Relating to Subcontractors and Agents...................................85

    A. The Definition of "Subcontractor" or "Agent" 85

    B. Verification of Subcontractor Codes, Compliance Programs, and Internal Controls..86

    C. Obligation to Train Subcontractors and Agents "As Appropriate" 88

    D. Other Obligations a Contractor May Want to Impose on Its Subcontractors..90

    E. Mandatory Reporting Requirements...90

    F. Implications of the "Credible Evidence" Standard and Potential Liability for Erroneous Reports..91

    G. Subcontractor Disclosure to the Government 93

III. Best Practices for Implementing Subcontractor and Agent Provisions...94

iii

TABLE OF CONTENTS

		Page
SECTION 5:	OBTAINING INFORMATION REGARDING POTENTIALLY REPORTABLE EVENTS	97
I.	Introduction	97
II.	Key Concepts and Best Practices	97
III.	Sources of Information for Potentially Reportable Events	101
	A. Employees' Role in the Reporting Process	102
	B. Managers' Role in the Reporting Process	108
	C. Hotline Reports	113
	D. Internal Audits, Testing and Monitoring, Periodic Surveys, and Certifications	113
IV.	Keeping Track of Allegations of Potential Misconduct	113
	A. Use of a Registry	114
	B. Access to the Registry	116
	C. What Should Not Be on the Registry	117
	D. Monitoring and Updating the Registry	118
SECTION 6:	"TIMELY DISCLOSURE" AND "LOOK-BACK" REQUIREMENTS	119
I.	The Sources of the Timely Disclosure Obligation	119
II.	The Meaning of "Timely" Disclosure	120
	A. No Definition	120
	B. How Soon Reporting Is Required	120
	C. How a Contractor Should Determine Whether an Investigation Is Necessary	121
	D. What Is a Reasonable Amount of Time to Investigate	123
III.	The "Look-Back" Requirement	125
	A. Possible Scrub of All Contracts Within Three Years of Closeout	127

TABLE OF CONTENTS

				Page
		B.	Reasonable Good Faith Efforts	127

SECTION 7: THE FORM, CONTENT, AND RECIPIENTS OF DISCLOSURES 129

    I. Form of Disclosures 129

    II. Content of Disclosures 130

        A. Government Agency Expectations As to the Content of Disclosures 130

        B. Contractor Considerations in the Content of Disclosures 132

        C. FOIA Markings 133

        D. Disclaimers 134

    III. Recipients of Disclosures 134

        A. Reporting to the Agency Inspector General 135

        B. Multiple Contracts, Multiple Agencies, Multiple Contracting Officers 136

    IV. What to Expect Upon Making Disclosure 137

SECTION 8: VOLUNTARY DISCLOSURES 139

    I. Introduction 139

    II. Three Circumstances in Which Voluntary Disclosure May Be Appropriate 140

        A. "Abundance of Caution" Disclosures 141

        B. Pre-Internal Investigation Disclosures 142

        C. Disclosure of Determination That No Credible Evidence Exists 143

    III. Factors to Consider in Deciding Whether to Make a Voluntary Disclosure 144

    IV. Recommended Contents of a Voluntary Disclosure 145

    V. Recipients of a Voluntary Disclosure 146

TABLE OF CONTENTS

		Page
VI.	Conclusion	146

SECTION 9: "FULL COOPERATION" 147

    I. Introduction 147

    II. Frequently Asked Questions 149

SECTION 10: PRESERVING CONFIDENTIALITY AND PRIVILEGE AND PREVENTING DISCLOSURES TO THIRD PARTIES 165

    I. Introduction 165

    II. Potential Government Disclosures Under FOIA 165

        A. Government Contractual Commitment to Protect Disclosures From Disclosure Under FOIA 165

        B. Potential Limitations on the Government's Protection of Contractor Mandatory Disclosures Under FOIA 166

    III. Potential Waivers of the Attorney-Client Privilege and Work Product Protection 174

    IV. Practical Internal Steps That Contractors May Take 178

        A. Contractor Steps in Conducting Internal Investigations That May Protect Disclosures from Release 178

        B. Employee Steps to Help Protect Disclosures from Release 179

    V. Practical External Steps That Contractors and the Government May Take 180

        A. Contractor Steps When Making Submissions that May Protect Disclosures from Release 180

        B. Government Steps That May Help Protect Contractor Proprietary and Confidential Information 181

    VI. Considerations from the Government's Perspective 182

SECTION 11: DEALING WITH COMPANY EMPLOYEES AND OFFICERS 183

    I. Introduction 183

TABLE OF CONTENTS

Page

    II.   When Attorneys Conduct Inquiries: Rules of Professional Responsibility 183

        A.   Identify the Client 183

        B.   Additional Disclosure Obligation in Light of the Mandatory Disclosure Rule 185

        C.   Questions That May Arise 186

    III.   When Non-Attorneys Conduct Inquiries 187

SECTION 12: PAST PERFORMANCE AND CONTRACTOR RESPONSIBILITY DETERMINATION REQUIREMENTS 189

    I.   Introduction 189

    II.   Methods of Collecting Past Performance Information 190

    III.   Evaluation of Past Performance 193

        A.   The Rule Does Not Diminish Agencies' Discretion to Determine How Past Performance Will Be Evaluated 193

        B.   Practical Considerations and Limits on Agency Discretion in the Evaluation of a Contractor's Record of Integrity and Business Ethics 195

    IV.   Present Responsibility 198

    V.   Practitioner Guidelines 200

SECTION 13: STRUCTURING ETHICS AWARENESS PROGRAMS AND INTERNAL CONTROL SYSTEMS 203

    I.   Ethics Awareness Programs 203

        A.   Background 203

        B.   Company Values 204

        C.   Code of Business Ethics 204

        D.   Inquiry and Reporting Mechanisms 204

        E.   Information and Awareness Program 205

TABLE OF CONTENTS

Page

   F. Program Assessment and Evaluation 205

   G. Leadership Commitment 205

   H. DII Guidance on Creating and Maintaining an Effective Ethics and Business Conduct Program 206

 II. Internal Control Systems 206

   A. Regulatory Requirements 206

   B. Guidance for an Effective System 208

   C. Action Items for Consideration 211

   D. Potential Impact of the Rule on External Audits and Financial Reporting 211

   E. Disclosures and Accruals in Company Financial Statements Under Current FAS 5 212

   F. Disclosures and Accruals in Company Financial Statements Under the Proposed Amendments to FAS 5 213

   G. Factors the DCAA Will Likely Examine When Evaluating Internal Controls 215

SECTION 14: NONPROCUREMENT TRANSACTIONS 219

 I. Introduction 219

 II. The Recovery Act Disclosure Requirement 221

   A. The Recovery Act Disclosure Requirement 222

   B. Similarities and Differences Between the Recovery Act and FAR Mandatory Disclosure Rule Requirements 223

   C. Identifying the "Other Persons" for Whom a Grantee Must Disclose Violations 224

   D. Types of Violations to Be Disclosed 226

   E. Absence of Time Limitation on Disclosing Past Violations 228

   F. Application of Disclosure Requirement to Recovery Act Funding Received from State Grants 229

TABLE OF CONTENTS

		Page
G.	Enforcement of the Recovery Act's Disclosure Obligation	229
III.	The Potential Common Rule Disclosure Requirement	230
A.	Differing Definitions of "Principal"	230
B.	Time Limitations and Looking Back	232
IV.	Identifying Areas of Risk and Mitigating Damages	233
V.	Making a Disclosure	234

APPENDICES

A.	Mandatory Disclosure Rule: FAR 3.1003	A-1
	FAR 9.406-2	A-2
	FAR 9.407-2	A-3
	FAR 52.203-13	A-4
B.	Preamble: 73 Fed. Reg. 67,064 (Nov. 12, 2008)	B-1
C.	72 Fed. Reg. 7,588 (Feb. 16, 2007)	C-1
D.	Department of Justice Comments (May 23, 2007)	D-1
E.	72 Fed. Reg. 64,019 (Nov. 14, 2007)	E-1
F.	72 Fed. Reg. 65,873 (Nov. 23, 2007)	F-1
G.	Department of Justice Comments (Jan. 14, 2008)	G-1
H.	ABA Section of Public Contract Law Comments (Jan. 18, 2008)	H-1
I.	73 Fed. Reg. 28,407 (May 16, 2008)	I-1
J.	ABA Task Force on Attorney-Client Privilege Comments (June 20, 2008)	J-1
K.	"Close the Contractor Fraud Loophole Act," Pub. L. 110-252 (June 30, 2008)	K-1
L.	Department of Justice Comments (July 15, 2008)	L-1
M.	Council of Defense and Space Industry Associations Comments (July 15, 2008)	M-1
N.	ABA Section of Public Contract Law Comments (July 15, 2008)	N-1

TABLE OF CONTENTS

		Page
O.	Example of DCAA Request for Information	O-1
P.	"Template" for Notice to Employees of Internal Reporting Obligation	P-1
Q.	Defense Industry Initiative "Template" for Notice to Employees	Q-1
R.	James Graham, U.S. Department of Justice, "The New FAR Disclosure Rule" (Dec. 3, 2009)	R-1

ACKNOWLEDGMENTS

**Task Force Co-Chairs
and Principal Editors**

Robert K. Huffman, Akin Gump Strauss Hauer & Feld LLP
Frederic M. Levy, McKenna Long & Aldridge LLP

Contributors

Anthony Alexis, Mayer Brown LLP
Jonathan Aronie, Sheppard Mullin Richter & Hampton LLP
Peter D. Balch, Lockheed Martin Corporation
Joseph A. Barsalona, PricewaterhouseCoopers LLP
Richard J. Bednar, Crowell & Moring LLP
John T. Boese, Fried Frank Harris Shriver & Jacobson LLP
Alan Chvotkin, Professional Services Council
Robert W. Cobb, former NASA Inspector General
Anne M. Donohue, SRA International, Inc.
Michael C. Eberhardt
Allison Feierabend, Holland & Knight LLP
Stephanie Pontzer Gilson, Johnson & Johnson
Robert K. Huffman, Akin Gump Strauss Hauer & Feld LLP
Laura K. Kennedy, SAIC
Stephen D. Knight, Smith Pachter McWhorter LLC
Frederic M. Levy, McKenna Long & Aldridge LLP
Marcia G. Madsen, Mayer Brown LLP
Kevin M. McCall, Northrop Grumman Corporation
Peter A. McDonald, Navigant Consulting, Inc.
Michael D. McGill, Hogan & Hartson LLP
Richard Meene, PricewaterhouseCoopers LLP
Robert F. Meunier, Debarment Solutions Institute LLC
James C. Mifsud, Lockheed Martin Corporation
Kathryn T. Muldoon, Smith Pachter McWhorter PLC
Stuart B. Nibley, Dickstein Shapiro LLP
Lawrence Oliver II, The Boeing Company
William L. Olsen, Bechtel National, Inc.
Rebecca B. Ransom, Raytheon Company
Ronald A. Schechter, Arnold & Porter LLP
David Stewart, Debarment Solutions Institute LLC
Stanley R. Soya, Pepper Hamilton LLP
Gunjan Talati, Crowell & Moring LLP
Robert L. Vogel, Vogel, Slade & Goldstein, LLP
Martin P. Willard, Wiley Rein LLP

Government Participants on Task Force

W. Dan Blalock, Department of the Navy
Patricia Davis, U.S. Department of Justice
David A. Drabkin, General Services Administration
James Graham, U.S. Department of Justice
Rodney A. Grandon, Department of the Air Force
Richard K. Levi, General Services Administration
Frances Lynn McCormick, Department of Defense
Steven A. Shaw, Department of the Air Force
Michal L. Tingle, U.S. Department of Justice

Editorial Assistance

Peter B. Hutt II, Akin Gump Strauss Hauer & Feld LLP
Veronica Makell, Akin Gump Strauss Hauer & Feld LLP
Duncan N. Stevens, Akin Gump Strauss Hauer & Feld LLP

ACRONYMS

The following is a partial list of the acronyms used in this Guide:

CID	Civil Investigative Demand
CPARS	Contractor Performance Assessment Reporting System
CPS	Contractor Performance System
DII	Defense Industry Initiative on Business Ethics and Conduct
DOD	Department of Defense
DOJ	Department of Justice
FAR	Federal Acquisition Regulation
FCA	False Claims Act
FERA	Fraud Enforcement and Recovery Act of 2009
FOIA	Freedom of Information Act
FRE	Federal Rule of Evidence
GAO	Government Accountability Office
OFPP	Office of Federal Procurement Policy
OIG	Office of Inspector General
OMB	Office of Management and Budget
ORCA	Online Representations and Certifications Application database
PPDB	Past Performance Database
PPIRS	Past Performance Information Retrieval System
PRE	Potentially Reportable Event
SDO	Suspension and Debarment Official

INTRODUCTION

By Michael W. Mutek
2008-2009 Chair, ABA Section of Public Contract Law

The publication of this Guide to the Mandatory Disclosure Rule continues the tradition of the American Bar Association Section of Public Contract Law providing the contracting community with valuable resources to assist in addressing new regulatory regimes.

The FAR Mandatory Disclosure Rule represents a significant change in contractor governance. Since 1986, contractors have operated under a principle of voluntary disclosure. At that time, the concept of voluntary disclosure was instituted as an element of contractor self governance found in a recommendation of the Packard Commission[1] and adopted by many contractors through involvement with the Defense Industry Initiative on Business Ethics and Conduct,[2] better known as the "DII." The DII provides six principles to foster business ethics and conduct, including the fourth principle, which addresses the adoption of procedures within companies to make voluntary disclosures of violations of federal procurement laws. In 1986, the Section wrote to the Packard Commission to support the concept of contractor self-governance.[3]

In 1986, the Department of Defense instituted a Voluntary Disclosure Program, and the Public Contract Law Section of the American Bar Association formed a committee comprised of representatives from the public and private sectors to promote a better understanding of the "issues relating to voluntary disclosures under the DOD Program" and to "issue a report

---

[1] President's Blue Ribbon Commission on Defense Management, *A Quest for Excellence* 101, 110-111 (1986).

[2] Available at http://www.defenseethics.org/charter.html.

[3] Public Contract Law Section letter (March 18, 1986), found as Exhibit 1 to American Bar Association, Section of Public Contract Law, *Report by the Special Committee on Voluntary Disclosure* (Aug. 1994).

containing practical guidelines, which could be used as a framework for contractor and Government representatives in dealing with voluntary disclosures." In November 1987, the Public Contract Law Section published the committee's final report as a monograph on voluntary disclosure and updated the monograph a few years later.[4]

Not surprisingly, the 2008 FAR Mandatory Disclosure Rule generated a great deal of interest and raised many questions. The Section stepped up to help address the interest and questions through timely programs, which pulled together experts from both the public and private sectors to facilitate discussion of the Rule, its purpose, and compliance. The Section's Procurement Fraud and Debarment and Suspension Committees held meetings on the new Rule, and well-attended Section-sponsored programs provided valuable information.

Part of the Section's response to the new Rule involved the creation of a Task Force comprised of representatives from Government, industry, and law firms. This is similar to the Section's response in 1986 to the Voluntary Disclosure Rule. I asked Robert Huffman and Frederic Levy to serve as co-chairs of this Task Force. My invitation included two requests. First, I asked that this Task Force be comprised of individuals from the public and private sectors so that the stakeholders to this new process would be represented. Second, I asked that this Task Force seek to promote a better understanding of the issues to be faced during the Rule's implementation through the creation of a work product to assist in the compliance process.

Bob and Fred exceeded expectations. They sought out competent and knowledgeable individuals to serve on the Task Force. They served as able and strong leaders and understood the value of the task to all the stakeholders in the public procurement process. Finally, they marshaled and managed the collection of working group efforts in order to achieve the

---

[4] *See* American Bar Association, Section of Public Contract Law, *Report by the Special Committee on Voluntary Disclosure*, 1-1 (Aug. 1994).

completion of this Guide to the Mandatory Disclosure Rule. It is through the dedication of many people who served on the Task Force that this Guide came to be. Their efforts are appreciated by all who have a stake in the public procurement process.

It should be noted that the Section's involvement with this new Rule preceded the issuance of the final Rule. The first proposed disclosure Rule was issued on November 14, 2007.[5] The Section submitted comprehensive comments that addressed key issues including the issue of statutory authority.[6] Several of the Section's comments were discussed in the commentary section of the second proposed Rule, which was issued on May 16, 2008.[7] During the comment period, Congress addressed the lack of statutory authority through enactment of the Close the Contractor Loophole Act.[8] In its comments, the Section noted that the second proposed Rule represented "a substantial modification of the rule first proposed." The Section focused on the second proposed Rule's expansion of the reporting requirement and the addition of the grounds for suspension or debarment.[9] In addition, the American Bar Association Task Force on Attorney-Client Privilege submitted comments on the second proposed Rule. Fred Levy served as the Section's liaison to this task force and contributed to the comments, which

---

[5] Appendix E, FAR Case 2007-006, Contractor Compliance Program and Integrity Reporting, 72 Fed. Reg. 64,019 (Nov. 14, 2007).

[6] Appendix H, Public Contract Law Section letter (Jan. 18, 2008). Available in PDF format at http://www.abanet.org/contract/federal/regscomm/home.html under the topic "Ethics."

[7] Appendix I, FAR Case 2007-006, Contractor Compliance Program and Integrity Reporting (Second Proposed Rule), 73 Fed. Reg. 28,407 (May 16, 2008).

[8] Appendix K, Pub.L. No. 110-252. This statute mandates that the FAR include provisions "that require timely notification by Federal contractors of violations of Federal criminal law or overpayments in connection with the award or performance of covered contracts or subcontracts, including those performed outside the United States and those for commercial items."

[9] Appendix N, Public Contract Law Section letter (July 15, 2008). Available in PDF format at http://www.abanet.org/contract/federal/regscomm/home.html under the topic "Ethics."

addressed the Rule's impact on the attorney-client privilege, the proposed "reasonable grounds to believe" standard for mandatory disclosure, and the "full cooperation" requirement of the proposed FAR Rule.[10]

The involvement of the Section in reviewing the proposed rules was an effort to provide the Section's collective experience and expertise to aid the drafters. The publication of this Guide is an effort to bring together the public procurement community's experience and expertise to aid in the implementation of the Rule and in compliance efforts.

I want to close by expressing my sincere thanks to all who contributed to this Guide, and to personally thank Bob Huffman and Fred Levy for their dedication in leading this effort.

---

[10] Appendix J, ABA letter (June 20, 2008.) Available as an attachment to the Section's comments on the second proposed rule in PDF format at http://www.abanet.org/contract/regscomm/home.html under the topic "Ethics."

GUIDE TO THE GUIDE

By Robert K. Huffman and Frederic M. Levy
Task Force Co-Chairs

Why should anyone need a 400-page Guide to a four-page Rule? It is true that the Rule is short and that its mandatory disclosure requirement is shorter still. But it would be a mistake to confuse the Rule's brevity with simplicity. First, the Rule uses extremely broad and undefined terms to establish the scope of the mandatory disclosure requirement. Second, the Rule ties the mandatory disclosure requirement to broad and complicated statutes and regulations, including the civil False Claims Act and the myriad fraud-related provisions of Title 18 of the United States Code. Finally, even if the Rule were straightforward, its implementation will require contractors and agencies alike to apply its terms to numerous complex factual situations. What is often said of laws and regulations is particularly true of this one: "The devil is in the details."

In recognition of the Rule's complexity, the drafters of the Rule included a lengthy Preamble. This Preamble provides important insights into the sources of the Rule's key terms and the drafters' expectations as to how those terms should be applied in certain instances. Anyone interested in understanding the Rule must carefully read the Preamble. However, the Preamble does not begin to answer all of the questions raised by the Rule, let alone provide a practical roadmap for its implementation. Thus, anyone looking for guidance on how the Rule will or should be implemented must look to sources in addition to the Rule and its Preamble.

This Guide is an effort to gather in one place the information necessary to understand and implement the Rule. This information includes, of course, the Rule and its Preamble. It also includes regulations and case law from other areas of the law that shed light on the meaning of the Rule's key terms. Another source of information — one that is particularly hard to get from official sources — is the knowledge and experience of individuals in the contracting community with extensive background in creating, administering, and overseeing contractor compliance programs and with disclosures made under those programs. This knowledge and experience was provided by the individual members of the Task Force that created this Guide. These Task Force members were drawn from all segments of the contracting community, including Government agencies, contractors, private law firms, and consulting and accounting firms. Collectively, these individuals have many decades of relevant experience.

It is particularly fortunate in this regard that the Task Force participants included numerous Government officials charged with administering and enforcing the Rule. While each of these individuals participated on the Task Force in his or her individual capacity, and did not speak for his or her agency, they provided helpful insights into the Government's expectations regarding how the Rule should be interpreted and implemented by contractors and agencies. These insights include the following:

- Government officials want and expect the Rule to encourage disclosures by contractors. Accordingly, if a contractor is in doubt regarding whether there is "credible evidence" of a covered violation or a significant overpayment, Government officials prefer the contractor to err on the side of disclosure. Government officials fully expect to receive disclosures that are expressly made in an "abundance of caution."

- Government officials expect contractors to disclose facts, not the contractors' legal characterization of those facts. Accordingly, contractors' disclosures do not have to include analysis or discussion of what statute or regulation the disclosed conduct might violate. Contractor disclosures also do not have to address whether the disclosed facts constitute a significant overpayment as opposed to a criminal or civil FCA violation.

- Government officials expect that the "credible evidence" standard for mandatory disclosure will allow contractors sufficient time to conduct a reasonable internal inquiry and to evaluate the facts and potential defenses developed in that inquiry before making a disclosure. However, contractors are not required to conduct any inquiry before making a disclosure. Furthermore, if a contractor chooses to conduct an internal inquiry, Government officials expect a prompt disclosure once the contractor has determined that credible evidence of a violation exist even if the contractor has not conducted or completed a full investigation.

- Government officials expect contractors to disclose whenever they have credible evidence of *any* violation of the civil False Claims Act or the criminal statutes identified in the Rule in connection with a Government contract, no matter how small the amounts that may be involved. In other words, Government officials do not recognize a *de minimis* exception to the Mandatory Disclosure Rule for criminal or civil False Claims Act violations.

- By contrast, a contractor will not be exposed to potential suspension or debarment for failure to timely disclose an insignificant overpayment. The Rule plainly limits the scope of its suspension and debarment provision to knowing failure to timely disclose overpayments that are "significant."

The Government participants, again speaking only in their capacity as individual members of the Task Force, also provided helpful insight into the details of how and to whom contractor disclosures should be made and the disposition of such disclosures. These insights include:

- Government official's expectation that all disclosures involving DOD agencies will be made to the DOD Disclosure Program within the DOD Office of Inspector General ("DOD OIG"), and not to the OIG of the relevant DOD agency, such as the Army OIG or Navy OIG.. (The National Reconnaissance Office does not concur with this position, however.)

- Government officials' expectation that contractors will make disclosures using the electronic forms provided by the DOD OIG and other agency OIGs, but that use of such forms is not required.

- Government officials' expectation that all disclosures will contain sufficient information, including the identity of the affected contracts, contracting officer(s), and the employees or other individuals involved in the conduct, to enable the Government to decide whether the matter warrants further investigation. Some DOJ officials have expressed the position that the failure of a contractor to disclose relevant information may raise a "red flag" that would make the Government more likely to investigate the underlying facts.

- The expectation of some Government officials that significant overpayments be disclosed not only to the Contracting Officer, but also to the applicable agency Office of Inspector General in order to avoid possible suspension and debarment for knowing failure to timely disclose such overpayments.

- The expectation of some DOJ officials that if a contractor chooses to make a disclosure of a potential criminal or civil violation to the Contracting Officer rather than to the OIG, such a choice could be viewed as an improper attempt to avoid or conceal the contractor's contractual obligations or to avoid potential liability under the False Claims Act or various criminal statutes.

- The expectation of some Government officials that the Government will process disclosed matters more quickly than it has in the past and will notify the contractor if and when it has decided not to take any criminal or civil action against the contractor with respect to the disclosed conduct. Some DOJ officials have also suggested that any criminal prosecutions are more likely to involve only individuals if the contractor has made a disclosure. *See, e.g.*, Appendix R.

Government officials also expect that the Mandatory Disclosure Rule will assist its (and *qui tam* relators') enforcement efforts. DOJ has been contacted on more than one occasion by whistleblowers who state they told their management that the Rule required disclosure of certain conduct or who participated in discussions between senior company officials regarding whether to disclose. DOJ officials also report that *qui tam* complaints are beginning to reference the Rule and to allege failure to comply with the Rule. DOJ officials regard these developments as positive, because they may further encourage contractors to err on the side of disclosure.

It is important to remember that the expectations referenced above, as well as the other information contained in this Guide, do not represent the official position of any Government agency, private company, law firm, or other entity, including the American Bar Association or its Section of Public Contract Law.

This Guide begins with an Overview that provides a summary and regulatory history of the Mandatory Disclosure Rule. The Guide then analyzes the Rule and its implementation in fourteen separate Sections, each devoted to a particular issue or topic related to the Rule. Although many of these Sections cross reference related portions of other Sections, anyone interested in understanding how the Rule will work should consult all relevant Sections as well as the regulatory summary and background to gain an understanding of the Rule as a whole.

OVERVIEW OF THE MANDATORY DISCLOSURE RULE

I. INTRODUCTION

The Mandatory Disclosure Rule grew out of the dissatisfaction of the Department of Justice ("DOJ") with the DOD's Voluntary Disclosure Program.[11] A February 2007 proposed amendment to the Federal Acquisition Regulation ("FAR") implementing a new Contractor Code of Ethics and Business Conduct rule did not include a mandatory disclosure requirement. DOJ objected to the lack of such requirement, asserting that the DOD Voluntary Disclosure Program had become ineffective and, moreover, that the defense industry, once a leader in compliance programs, had fallen behind a trend to mandatory disclosure in the healthcare, banking, and securities industries. The Civilian Agency Acquisition Council and the Defense Acquisition Regulation Council (the "FAR Councils") followed DOJ's lead and in November 2007 proposed to adopt a mandatory disclosure requirement in the FAR. DOJ objected to the proposed rule on the grounds, *inter alia*, that it exempted commercial item contracts and contracts performed abroad and that it failed to require contractors to disclose violations of the civil False Claims Act. The FAR Councils proposed a second Mandatory Disclosure Rule in May 2008 that accepted most of DOJ's comments.

In the meantime, Congress began focusing on the proposed rulemaking and, in particular, the proposed exemption for commercial item contracts and contracts performed abroad. On June 30, 2008, Congress enacted the "Close the Contractor Fraud Loophole Act" as part of Pub. L. No. 110-252. That statute required the FAR to be revised within 180 days to require timely notifications by contractors of violations of criminal law or overpayments in connection with the

---

[11] The DOD Voluntary Disclosure Program is described in American Bar Association, Section of Public Contract Law, *Report by the Special Committee on Voluntary Disclosure* (Aug. 1994).

award or performance of covered contracts or subcontracts, including those for commercial items and those performed outside the United States. On November 12, 2008, the FAR Councils published a Mandatory Disclosure Rule that reflected the requirements of the Close the Contractor Fraud Loophole Act and DOJ's concerns and proposals, and also addressed some of the comments filed by other parties during the rulemaking process. 73 Fed. Reg. 67,064 (attached as Appendix B). This Rule and its related requirements took effect on December 12, 2008.

II. SUMMARY OF THE MANDATORY DISCLOSURE RULE

The FAR Mandatory Disclosure Rule and its Preamble are published at 73 Fed. Reg. 67,064 (November 12, 2008). *See* Appendices A & B. The Rule is comprised of two components: (1) a new business ethics and conduct FAR clause applicable to certain covered contracts and requiring, *inter alia*, disclosure of potential wrongful conduct; and (2) a new definition of "present responsibility" providing that federal contractors and subcontractors, regardless of whether they are subject to the new business ethics and conduct clause, can be suspended or debarred for failure to timely disclose potential wrongful conduct or significant overpayments. In addition, the Rule includes a new definition of "principal" and other ancillary changes to the FAR. This Section summarizes the key changes made by the Rule. Throughout this Guide, the Task Force will refer to the entire set of changes to the FAR collectively as the "Mandatory Disclosure Rule" or simply the "Rule."

A. New Contractor Code of Business Ethics and Conduct Clause

The Mandatory Disclosure Rule revises FAR 52.203-13, the "Contractor Code of Business Ethics and Conduct" clause, to impose significant new requirements on contractors who will become subject to the clause, *i.e.*, contractors who enter into contracts or contract modifications with a value in excess of $5 million and a period of performance in excess of 120 days ("covered contractors").[12] As amended by the Rule, the clause imposes certain requirements on *all* covered contractors. These include:

- A requirement to have a written code of business ethics and conduct and make a copy of the code available to each employee engaged in the performance of the contract;

- A requirement to exercise due diligence to prevent and detect criminal conduct;

- A requirement to promote an organizational culture that encourages ethical conduct and a commitment to compliance with the law; and

- A requirement to timely disclose in writing, to the agency Office of Inspector General ("OIG"), with a copy to the Contracting Officer whenever the contractor has "credible evidence" that a principal employee, agent, or subcontractor has committed a violation of Federal criminal law involving fraud, conflict of interest, bribery, or gratuity violations found in U.S.C. Title 18, or a violation of the civil False Claims Act, in connection with the award, performance, or closeout of the contract in which the clause appears or any subcontract thereunder.

FAR 52.203-13(b); *see* Appendix B, 73 Fed. Reg. at 67,091.[13]

With respect to the mandatory disclosure requirement identified above, the clause states that "to the extent permitted by law and regulation, [the Government] will safeguard and treat information obtained pursuant to the Contractor's disclosure as confidential where the information has been marked 'confidential' or 'proprietary' by the company." Appendix A, FAR 52.203-13(b)(3)(ii); *see* Appendix B, 73 Fed. Reg. at 67,091. Furthermore, "to the extent permitted by law and regulation, such information will not be released by the Government to the

---

[12] GSA has adopted the position the $5 million threshold is determined for GSA Schedule contracts by looking to the total estimated value of *all* contracts on the particular Schedule. This means that, as a practical matter, every Schedule contract will likely meet the threshold.

[13] The clause also states that if the violation required to be disclosed relates to an order against a Government-wide acquisition contract, a multi-agency contract, a multiple award schedule contract such as the Federal Supply Schedule, or any other procurement instrument intended for use by multiple agencies, the contractor "shall notify the OIG or the ordering agency and the IG of the agency responsible for the basic contract." Appendix A, FAR 52.203-13(b)(3)(iii).

public pursuant to a Freedom of Information Act request, 5 U.S.C. Section 552, without proper notification to the Contractor." Appendix A, FAR 52.203-13(b)(3)(ii). However, the clause provides that "the Government may transfer documents provided by the Contractor to any department or agency within the Executive Branch if the information relates to matters within the organization's jurisdiction." *Id.*

In addition to these basic requirements applicable to all covered contractors, the clause requires covered contractors other than small business concerns or commercial item contractors to have an "ongoing business ethics awareness and compliance program" and an "internal control system." Appendix A, FAR 52.203-13(c). The clause imposes the following minimum requirements for an acceptable business ethics awareness and compliance program:

- "This program shall include reasonable steps to communicate periodically and in a practical manner the Contractor's standards and procedures and other aspects of the Contractor's business ethics awareness and compliance program and internal control system, by conducting effective training programs and otherwise disseminating information appropriate to an individual's respective roles and responsibilities." FAR 52.203-13(c)(1)(i).

- "The training conducted under this program shall be provided to the Contractor's principals and employees, and as appropriate, the Contractor's agents and subcontractors." FAR 52.203-13(c)(1)(ii).

The clause also establishes minimum requirements for internal control systems. Appendix A, FAR 52.203-13(c)(2). Such systems must:

- Establish standards and procedures to facilitate timely discovery of improper conduct in connection with Government contracts; and

- Ensure corrective measures are promptly instituted and carried out.

In addition, FAR 52.203-13(c)(2)(ii) provides that the contractor's internal control system must include the following minimum features:

(A) Assignment of responsibility at a sufficiently high level and adequate resources to ensure effectiveness of the business ethics awareness and compliance program and internal control system.

(B) Reasonable efforts not to include an individual as a principal whom due diligence would have exposed as having engaged in conduct that is in conflict with the Contractor's code of business ethics and conduct.

(C) Periodic reviews of company business practices, procedures, policies, and internal controls for compliance with the Contractor's code of business ethics and conduct and the special requirements of Government contracting, including —

(1) Monitoring and auditing to detect criminal conduct;

(2) Periodic evaluation of the effectiveness of the business ethics awareness and compliance program and internal control system, especially if criminal conduct has been detected; and

(3) Periodic assessment of the risk of criminal conduct, with appropriate steps to design, implement, or modify the business ethics awareness and compliance program and the internal control system as necessary to reduce the risk of criminal conduct identified through this process.

(D) An internal reporting mechanism, such as a hotline, which allows for anonymity or confidentiality, by which employees may report suspected instances of improper conduct, and instructions that encourage employees to make such reports.

(E) Disciplinary action for improper conduct or for failing to take reasonable steps to prevent or detect improper conduct.

(F) Timely disclosure, in writing, to the agency OIG with a copy to the Contracting Officer, whenever, in connection with the award, performance, or closeout of any Government contract performed by the Contractor or a subcontractor thereunder, the Contractor has credible evidence that a principal, employee, agent, or subcontractor of the Contractor has committed a violation of Federal criminal law involving fraud, conflict of interest, bribery, or gratuity violations found in Title 18 U.S.C. or a violation of the civil False Claims Act (31 U.S.C. 3729-3733).

(G) Full cooperation with any Government agencies responsible for audits, investigations, or corrective actions.

Mandatory disclosure obligations for contractors subject to the internal control systems requirements (paragraph F above) are broader than the mandatory disclosure obligation applicable to all covered contractors, in that the former requires the contractor to make the requisite disclosures regarding *any* of its Government contracts, whereas the latter requires disclosure only of violations in connection with a contract that includes the clause.[14]

FAR 52.203-13(c)(2)(ii)(F)(3) further provides that "the disclosure requirement for an individual contract continues until at least 3 years after final payment on the contract." Thus, the contractor must disclose any credible evidence of a covered violation on a contract subject to the clause *even if the violation occurred prior to the date the clause became applicable to the contractor*. Further, contractors subject to the internal controls requirements must have a system in place to report covered violations on any of their federal contracts or subcontracts, unless final payment on the contracts occurred more than three years before the internal control system requirement first became applicable to the contractor. This requirement is part of the so-called "look-back" requirement imposed by the Rule on all contractors.

The Rule requires all covered contractors, including those required to have internal control systems, to make any disclosure involving multiple-agency procurement contracts to the ordering agency OIG and the OIG of the agency responsible for the basic contract, as well as to the respective agencies' contracting officers. Appendix A, FAR 52.203-13(c)(ii)(F)(2). The clause also provides that the Government will safeguard such disclosures from release under FOIA to the same extent as it protects disclosures by covered contractors without required internal control systems, *i.e.*, "to the extent permitted by law and regulation." FAR 52.203-13(c)(ii).

---

[14] As described herein, however, the Rule creates a ground for suspension and debarment for the "knowing failure to timely disclose" that applies to all contracts regardless of whether the clause is included. *See* Section B below. Thus, all contractors are effectively subject to a mandatory disclosure requirement with respect to all their Government contracts regardless of whether the clause appears in any given Government contract or subcontract.

In addition to requiring mandatory disclosure, the clause requires a covered contractor's internal control system to provide for "full cooperation" with any Government agencies responsible for audits, investigations, or corrective actions. Appendix A, FAR 52.203-13(c)(ii)(G). The clause defines "full cooperation" to mean "disclosure to the Government of the information sufficient for law enforcement to identify the nature and extent of the offense and the individuals responsible for the conduct," including "providing timely and complete response to Government auditors' and investigators' request for documents and access to employees with information." FAR 52.203-13(a)(1). The clause states that "full cooperation" does not "foreclose any Contractor rights arising in law, the FAR, or the terms of the contract"; that it "does not require [the] Contractor to waive its attorney-client privilege or the protections afforded by the attorney work product doctrine; or [a]ny officer, director, owner, or employee of the Contractor, including a sole proprietor, to waive his or her attorney client privilege or Fifth Amendment rights"; and that it "[d]oes not restrict a Contractor from [c]onducting an internal investigation; or [d]efending a proceeding or dispute arising under the contract or related to a potential or disclosed violation." FAR 52.203-13(a)(2)-(3). While the Rule discusses full cooperation only in the context of internal control systems, these same standards likely will be applied to all contractors and subcontractors making disclosures.

Finally, the clause states that the contractor "shall include the substance of this clause, including [this flow-down requirement] in subcontracts that have a value in excess of $5,000,000 and a performance period of more than 120 days." Appendix A, FAR 52.203-13(d).[15] This provision will subject all subcontractors (and their subcontractors) whose subcontracts meet the

---

[15] The clause states that "[i]n altering this clause to identify the appropriate parties, all disclosures of violation of the civil False Claims Act or of Federal criminal law shall be directed to the agency Office of the Inspector General, with a copy to the Contracting Officer."

$5 million/120 day threshold to all of the basic requirements discussed in this section, as well as the requirements for an internal control system and business ethics awareness and compliance program if they are other than small businesses or commercial item contractors.

B.   New Ground for Suspension or Debarment

The Rule creates a new cause for suspension and debarment for the:

> Knowing failure by a principal, until 3 years after final payment on any Government contract awarded to the contractor, to timely disclose to the Government, in connection with the award, performance, or closeout of the contractor or a subcontract thereunder, credible evidence of —
>
> (A)   Violation of Federal criminal law involving fraud, conflict of interest, bribery, or gratuity violations found in Title 18 of the United States Code;
>
> (B)   Violation of the civil False Claims Act (31 U.S.C. 3729-3733); or
>
> (C)   Significant overpayment(s) on the contract, other than overpayments resulting from contract financing payments as defined in 32.001.

Appendix A, FAR 9.406-2, 9.407-2. The Rule makes clear that a contractor may be suspended or debarred for failure to timely disclose "whether or not the clause at 52.203-13 is applicable" to the contractor. Appendix A, FAR 3.1003(a)(2).

C.   New Definition of "Principal"

The Mandatory Disclosure Rule adds a definition of "Principal" to Section 2.101(b)(2) of the FAR:

> "Principal" means an officer, director, owner, partner, or a person having primary management or supervisory responsibilities within a business entity (*e.g.*, general manager; plant manager; head of a subsidiary, division, or business segment; and similar positions).

Appendix B, 73 Fed. Reg. at 67,090. The Rule also adds an identically-worded definition to FAR 52.203-13(a) and FAR 52.209-5(a)(2). *Id.* at 67,091-92.

D. **New Requirements for Contractor Responsibility and Past Performance**

The Rule amends FAR Part 9, "Contractor Qualification," to require that the contractor "have a satisfactory record of integrity and business ethics (for example, see Subpart 42.15)." Appendix B, 73 Fed. Reg. at 67,091. The Rule also amends FAR Part 42, "Contract Administration and Audit Services," to state that a contractor's "past performance" for purposes of evaluating bids and proposals includes, *inter alia*, the "contractor's record of integrity and business ethics." *Id.* Thus, the Rule expressly makes a contractor's record of integrity and business ethics part of the agency's determination of its qualifications and responsibility and the agency's evaluation of its past performance.

II. BACKGROUND OF THE MANDATORY DISCLOSURE RULE

A. The FAR Councils Propose a Contractor Code of Ethics and Business Conduct Without a Mandatory Disclosure Requirement

On February 16, 2007, the Civilian Agency Acquisition Council and the Defense Acquisition Regulation Council proposed a new rule under FAR Case 2006-007, Contractor Code of Ethics and Business Conduct. Appendix C, 72 Fed. Reg. 7,588. The FAR Councils proposed to establish a new Subpart 3.10 of FAR Part 3 entitled "Contractor Code of Ethics and Business Conduct." Proposed Subpart 3.1002 ("Policy") stated that "Government contractors must conduct themselves with the highest degree of integrity and honesty" and "should have a written code of ethics and business conduct." 72 Fed. Reg. at 7,589. Furthermore, in order to promote compliance with such code of ethics and business conduct, proposed Subpart 3.1002 provided that:

> contractors should have an employee ethics and training program and an internal control system that —
>
> (a) Are suitable to the size of the company and extent of its involvement in Government contracting;

(b) Facilitate timely discovery and disclosure of improper conduct in connection with Government contracts; and

(c) Ensure corrective measures are properly instituted and carried out.

72 Fed. Reg. at 7,589. The FAR Councils also proposed a new FAR clause that would be inserted in contracts in excess of $5 million and with periods of performance greater than 120 days that would require the contractor to have a written code of ethics and business conduct within 30 days of contract award and to establish an employee ethics and compliance training program and an internal control system within 90 days of award. 72 Fed. Reg. at 7,590. The proposed clause would also require such contractors to prominently display agency-approved hotline posters in common work areas within business segments performing under the contract. Contractors subject to this clause would be required to include the clause in all subcontracts that exceeded $5 million and 120 days. The FAR Councils proposed to exempt from these requirements all commercial item contracts and subcontracts and all contracts and subcontracts to be performed outside the United States.

The proposed clause imposed certain minimum requirements for a covered contractor's or subcontractor's internal control system. First, the internal control system must "facilitate timely discovery and disclosure of improper conduct in connection with Government contracts." Appendix C, 72 Fed. Reg. at 7,590. Second, the internal control system must "ensure corrective actions are promptly instituted and carried out." Id. In addition, the proposal provided "examples" of what an effective internal control system should contain, including "timely reporting to appropriate Government officials of any suspected violations of law in connection with Government contracts or any other irregularities in connection with such contracts" and "full cooperation with any Government agencies responsible for either investigation or corrective action." *Id.* However, these "examples" were merely suggestions; the proposed Rule did not require that they actually be included in the covered contractor's internal control system.

B.   The Department of Justice Requests Mandatory Disclosure

On May 23, 2007, the Assistant Attorney General for the Criminal Division, Alice Fisher, wrote a letter to the Administrator of the OMB Office of Federal Procurement Policy requesting "some additions and modifications to the Federal Acquisition Regulation (FAR) that the Department of Justice believes are consistent with the purpose of the FAR System, while maintaining the public's trust and fulfilling public policy objectives." *See* Appendix D. Specifically, DOJ proposed that the FAR be modified to require that contractors "establish and maintain internal controls to detect and prevent fraud in their contracts, and that they notify contracting officers without delay whenever they become aware of a contract overpayment or fraud, rather than wait for its discovery by the Government."

DOJ's letter asserted that:

> [T]he 1980's witnessed significant innovations in the federal procurement system. Many of those reforms, including corporate compliance programs and corporate self-governance, were adopted with industry cooperation, and were later incorporated into evolving regulatory schemes in other business sectors and industries. In fact, the United States Sentencing Guidelines' treatment of corporations, adopted in 1991, borrowed heavily from reforms that were first instituted for government contractors in 1986. However, since that time, our government's expectations of its contractors has not kept pace with reforms in self-governance in industries such as banking, securities and healthcare.

The letter also asserted that:

> While we recognize that many government contractors have taken steps to establish corporate compliance programs, our experience suggests that few have actually responded to the invitation of the Department of Defense (DOD) that they report or voluntarily disclose suspected instances of fraud. Moreover, unlike healthcare providers or financial institutions, there is at present no general requirement that contractors alert the government immediately as a matter of routine when overpayments or fraud are discovered. We believe that if the FAR were more explicit in requiring

such notification, it would serve to emphasize the critical importance of integrity in contracting. In deference to the expertise of the Office of Federal Procurement Policy ("OFPP"), the attached outline prepared by our prosecutors merely suggests the recommended language and possible locations in the FAR for these proposed changes.

Appendix D. DOJ recommended the following changes:

1. Modify FAR Part 3 or 9 to provide that as part of a contractor's obligation to maintain "a satisfactory record of integrity and business ethics," all contractors with more than $5 million in federal contracts in the prior two consecutive calendar years are required to have a compliance program or other internal controls to detect and prevent fraud and other criminal violations as described in the *United States Sentencing Guidelines*, Section 8B2.1 Effective Compliance and Ethics Program, Attachment A. We intend to propose similar language in our written comments to FAR case 2006-007, which currently is pending at OMB.

2. Expand on FAR Part 3 or Part 9 with a new section "Contractor Integrity Reporting" requiring that all responsible contractors:

    a) notify the contracting officer in writing whenever the contractor becomes aware of an event affecting its initial or continuing right to receive any payment(s) under the contract. *{modeled on existing requirements for healthcare providers found at 42 U.S.C. 1320a-7b(3), Attachment B. Essentially, this provision would require a contractor to disclose any overpayments without waiting for government discovery. To limit the scope of this provision, it may be necessary to include a materiality requirement. Currently, it appears that the FAR only requires notification of overpayments for acquisition of commercial items, see FAR 52.212-4(i)(5)).*

    b) notify the contracting officer in writing whenever the contractor has reasonable grounds to believe an officer, director, employee, agent, or subcontractor of the contractor may have committed a violation of federal criminal law in connection with the award or performance of any government contract or subcontract. *{modeled on Suspicious Activity Reports required by the Office of the Comptroller of the Currency found at 12 CFR 21.11, Attachment C, the Anti-kickback disclosures currently required by FAR 3.502-2(g) and Sarbanes-Oxley reporting requirements, Section 302(a)(5), Attachment D. To limit the scope of this provision, it may be necessary to include guidance that defines terms such as "reasonable grounds".}*

3. Modify FAR 9.406-2, Causes for Debarment and 9.407-2 Causes for Suspension to include "knowing failure to timely disclose an overpayment or violation of federal criminal law as described above."

4. The contracting officer shall insert a clause at FAR 52.203 reflecting these requirements in all its solicitations and contracts.

5. The above language requiring notification of overpayments and fraud should be included in all subcontracts valued over $1 million.

Appendix D.

C. The First Proposed Mandatory Disclosure Rule

On November 14, 2007, the FAR Councils opened a new FAR case (Case 2007-006) and proposed a Mandatory Disclosure Rule in response to DOJ's request. Appendix E, 72 Fed. Reg. 64,019. The FAR Councils modified their previously proposed clause to include a requirement that the contractor notify the agency Office of Inspector General, with a copy to the contracting officer, whenever the contractor had "reasonable grounds to believe that a violation of criminal law has been committed in connection with the award or performance of the Government contract or subcontract." 72 Fed. Reg. at 64,023. The FAR Councils also proposed to modify the previously proposed clause to require that the contractor's internal control system require "full cooperation" by the contractor with any Government agencies responsible for audit, investigation, or corrective actions. *Id.*

Also in response to DOJ's request, the FAR Councils proposed to create a new cause for suspension or debarment for a "knowing failure to timely disclose an overpayment on a Government contract or violation of Federal criminal law in connection with the award or performance of any Government contract performed by the contractor or any subcontract thereunder." Appendix E, 72 Fed. Reg. at 64,022. The FAR Councils did not propose to exempt commercial item contractors or contracts performed abroad (or small businesses) from this new cause for suspension or debarment.

The proposed mandatory disclosure rule stated that the FAR Councils intended shortly to adopt the originally proposed clause without the mandatory disclosure and other requirements that were being proposed for the first time on November 14. Thereafter, on November 23, 2007, the FAR Councils amended the FAR to add two separate clauses, FAR 52.203-13 ("Contractor Code of Business Ethics and Conduct") and FAR 52.203-14 ("Display of Hotline Poster"). Appendix F, 72 Fed. Reg. 65,873. FAR 52.203-13, which was required to be included in all contracts over $5 million and greater than 120 days (except for commercial item contracts and contracts performed outside the United States), required the contractor to have a written code of business ethics and conduct, provide copies of the code to each employee engaged in performance of the contract, and promote compliance with the code. 72 Fed. Reg. at 65,882. In addition, unless the contractor was a commercial item contractor or the contract was to be performed outside the United States, the clause required the contractor to have an ongoing ethics and business conduct awareness program and internal control system that had certain specified features. *Id.* These required features did not include "full cooperation" with Government audits and investigations.

D. Comments on the First Proposed Mandatory Disclosure Rule

The DOJ Criminal Division submitted comments on the proposed Mandatory Disclosure Rule on January 14, 2008. *See* Appendix G. DOJ applauded the "fine work performed by the defense and civilian agencies in expeditiously evaluating and publishing our proposed FAR changes." Appendix G at 1. DOJ stated that it "continues to believe that mandatory disclosure of material overpayments and fraud is necessary and appropriate, and that government contractors should be held to the same disclosure standards as those in the healthcare and banking industries." *Id.* DOJ proposed several modifications of the proposed Mandatory Disclosure Rule, including:

- <u>Extending the proposed clause to contracts performed overseas.</u> While DOJ stated its agreement with the proposed exclusion of Part 12 commercial item contracts from the proposed clause, it urged the FAR

Councils to apply the clause to contracts performed overseas. "[T]hese types of contracts, which in many cases support our efforts to fight the global war on terror, need greater contractor vigilance because they are performed overseas where U.S. government resources and remedies are more limited." Appendix G, Attachment A at 1.

- Extending the proposed clause to require disclosure of overpayments. "In our view, the duty to disclose overpayments is just as important as the disclosure of a criminal violation and also relieves the contractor from having to decide whether there is an actual criminal violation before deciding to disclose." DOJ suggested that "a materiality requirement is appropriate" to limit the scope of the requirement to disclose overpayments. DOJ also suggested that the FAR Councils "may want to consider defining 'overpayments.'" Appendix G, Attachment A at 1.

- Standard for disclosure. "[I]n order to avoid contractor concern that the proposal would require disclosure of every allegation of a criminal violation or overpayment without regard to merit, we suggest inserting either 'reasonable grounds to believe,' found elsewhere in the proposed rule or 'credible information of . . .' found at DFARS 252.246-7003 governing reports of Potential Safety Issues." Appendix G, Attachment A at 2.

- Scope of reportable criminal violations. "Contractors may reasonably complain that requiring disclosure of any 'violation of Federal criminal law' is too broad, even when limited by the phrase 'in connection with the award or performance of any Government contract or subcontract.' We would not object to including the following additional limiting language: 'involving fraud, conflict of interest, bribery, or gratuity violations found in Title 18, United States Code.'" Appendix G, Attachment A at 2.

- Obligation to disclose potential violations of the civil False Claims Act. "We recommend that the grounds for suspension and debarment also include the knowing failure to disclose potential violations of the False Claims Act . . . . Given the importance of the civil False Claims Act to the federal contract fraud enforcement effort, contracts should also be required to include in their 'business ethics awareness' obligation reflected in the proposed Rule . . . , 'training on the False Claims Act' as is currently required of healthcare providers in § 6033 of the Deficit Reduction Act." Appendix G, Attachment A at 2.

- Time limit for disclosures. "To avoid imposing a duty to disclose matters occurring many years ago, we suggest limiting the mandatory disclosure of overpayments or criminal violations to matters discovered by the contractor within three years of the contract completion." Appendix G, Attachment A at 3.

- Grounds for suspension and debarment. "In response to the concern that suspension or debarment is too severe a remedy for merely failing to disclose an overpayment or federal criminal violation, we would add to the proposed rule on grounds for suspension or debarment 'for the purpose of defrauding the United States.' See 42 U.S.C. § 1320a-7b(a)(3). In the Preamble, the Councils may want to be clear that the intent standard found described here, namely, 'for the purpose of defrauding the United States,' has no application to the False Claims Act." Appendix G, Attachment A at 3.

- FOIA exemption. "For a variety of reasons, not the least of which is to encourage contractors to submit information pertaining to overpayments or violations of federal law even if such occurrences have not yet been confirmed, the Councils may wish to recommend to agencies that the submitted information be maintained confidentially to the extent permitted by law. The Councils may further wish to remind agencies that any decision by agencies to make a discretionary disclosure of information protected under the FOIA should be made only after full and deliberate consideration of the institution, commercial, and personal privacy interests that could be implicated by such a disclosure. In particular, agencies should be mindful that the Trade Secrets Act operates as a prohibition on the discretionary disclosure of any information covered by Exemption 4 of the FOIA, unless such disclosure is otherwise authorized by law." Appendix G, Attachment A at 3.

- Subcontractors. "While we believe it is important to flow the disclosure obligation down to subcontractors, some subcontractors may not be comfortable making the disclosure to the government through the prime contractor. Accordingly, the mechanism through which a subcontractor makes a disclosure to the government may need to be addressed in any final rule." Appendix G, Attachment A at 3.

- Contractor internal investigation. "The final rule preamble should make clear that nothing in the rule is intended to preclude a contractor from continuing to investigate after making its initial disclosure to the government. In fact, much like the DOD Voluntary Disclosure Program, in most cases, we would expect that the Inspector General or the Contracting Officer will encourage the contractor to complete its internal investigation and make a full report of its findings." Appendix G, Attachment A at 3.

The ABA Section of Public Contract Law also submitted comments on the first proposed rule. See Appendix H. These comments challenged DOJ's assertions that the Voluntary Disclosure Program was ineffective and that the declining number of disclosures under that

Program evidenced that mandatory disclosure was necessary, and asserted that DOJ should be required to offer factual support for its rationale for mandatory disclosure before any rule was adopted. Appendix H at 3-5. The Section also pointed out that mandatory disclosure could undermine existing incentives for voluntary disclosure such as those found in the U.S. Sentencing Guidelines. Appendix H at 7-8. The Section also pointed out that the FAR treated overpayments as a matter of contract administration and that it was therefore inappropriate to make the failure to disclose such overpayments a ground for suspension and debarment. Appendix H at 11-12. Finally, the Section argued that the vagueness of the proposed Rule would cause implementation problems and raise possible constitutional concerns. Appendix H at 19-22. Other commentators asserted similar objections. *See* Appendix B. In all, 43 comments were received on the first proposed Mandatory Disclosure Rule.

E. The Second Proposed Mandatory Disclosure Rule

The FAR Councils promulgated a second proposed Mandatory Disclosure Rule on May 16, 2008. Appendix I, 73 Fed. Reg. 28,407. The Councils proposed to modify the first proposed Mandatory Disclosure Rule by, *inter alia*: (1) requiring inclusion of the proposed contractor code of business ethics and conduct clause in contracts and subcontracts to be performed outside the United States; (2) requiring inclusion of the proposed clause in contracts and subcontracts for the acquisition of commercial items; and (3) adding a new cause for suspension or debarment for the knowing failure to timely disclose a violation of the civil False Claims Act in connection with the award or performance of any Government contract or subcontract thereunder. 73 Fed. Reg. at 28,407-08. The Councils noted that the civil False Claims Act "would also be added as a required disclosure in the [proposed] contract clause." *Id.* at 28,408.

F. The "Close the Contractor Fraud Loophole Act"

On June 20, 2008, Congress enacted the "Close the Contractor Fraud Loophole Act," Pub. L. 110-252, Title VI, Chapter 1, as part of the Supplemental Appropriations Act for FY 2008. *See* Appendix K. This statute required the FAR Councils to revise the FAR within 180 days of enactment pursuant to FAR case 2007-006 or any follow-on FAR case "to include provisions that require timely notification by Federal contractors of violations of Federal criminal law or overpayments in connection with the award or performance of covered contracts or subcontracts, including those performed outside the United States and those for commercial items." The statute defined a covered contract or subcontract as "any contract in an amount greater than $5,000,000 and more than 120 days in duration."

G. Comments on the Second Proposed Mandatory Disclosure Rule

The Civil Division of DOJ submitted comments on the second proposed Rule on July 15, 2008. *See* Appendix L. The Civil Division stated that the FAR Councils' proposal to require disclosure of civil False Claims Act violations "would ensure that a contractor whose underlying conduct falls short of a criminal violation, but is more than a mistake or negligence, cannot avoid the effect of the proposed rule by failing to disclose that it has received government funds to which it knows it is not entitled." Appendix L at 1. DOJ asserted that the disclosure of such information "will enhance the government's civil enforcement efforts, which are a critical component of the government's overall scheme for combating government contract fraud." *Id.*

The DOJ Civil Division also asserted that "requiring the disclosure of False Claims Act violations would complement the disclosure provisions of the False Claims Act, which permit a court to reduce the government's recovery of damages where a person makes a timely disclosure and complies with other applicable requirements." Appendix L at 2. Specifically, DOJ noted:

> [T]he FCA provides that a court may impose only double, rather than treble, damages if a person reports an FCA violation within 30 days of obtaining information about the violation, fully cooperates with the government's investigation, and was not previously aware of the existence of any such investigation. . . . Adding the civil FCA to the mandatory disclosure provision in the FAR should enhance the effectiveness of these provisions because a person that meets these requirements would receive the dual benefit of qualifying to seek reduced damages under the FCA and avoiding the potential for suspension and debarment under the FAR.

Appendix L at 2.

Other commenters also focused on the proposed extension of the proposed rule to civil False Claims Act violations. The Council of Defense and Space Industry Associations ("CODSIA") noted that the FCA "presents many difficult legal and factual issues, such as whether a submission constitutes a 'claim;' whether a statement is 'false;' and whether the person making the statement or submitting the claim acted with requisite knowledge." Appendix M at 5. CODSIA also noted that case law concerning these elements "continues to evolve," and "sometimes differs from jurisdiction to jurisdiction." *Id.* Thus, CODSIA argued, extending the mandatory disclosure requirement to potential civil False Claims Act violations would impose a "vague, if not impossible, standard considering the complexities of the [FCA] and the evolving case law in this area." *Id.* at 2. CODSIA warned that "[r]equiring contractors to report 'violations' of the civil FCA before any legal determination is made as to the sufficiency of allegations would not promote the exposure of fraud. It would more likely be a disincentive for contractors to enter, or remain, in the government contract marketplace." *Id.* at 5.

Comments submitted by the ABA Section of Public Contract Law also focused on the complexities and risks associated with requiring disclosure of potential civil False Claims Act violations. *See* Appendix N. The Section stated that "[g]iven the multiple elements required to establish a civil FCA violation, and the numerous and sometimes conflicting court decisions interpreting those elements, it is unreasonable and oppressive to demand that contractors undertake to determine whether there are 'reasonable grounds to believe' that one or more of its employees, principals, or agents may have violated the civil FCA." Appendix N at 4. The Section pointed out that those concerns were exacerbated by the False Claims Act's *qui tam* provisions, which allow private entities to bring suits against contractors alleging violations on behalf of the Government. The Section stated that requiring disclosure of potential False Claims Act actions "would, as a practical matter, require contractors to guess what theories of liability a *qui tam* relator might conceivably argue and whether those arguments would survive a motion to dismiss." *Id.* at 5. The Section pointed out that a contractor that guessed incorrectly "could be subject to potential suspension and debarment for failure to timely disclose a situation where a *qui tam* relator might allege a potential civil FCA violation," even if the contractor regarded that situation as a matter of contract administration. *Id.*

The ABA Task Force on Attorney-Client Privilege also submitted comments on the proposed Rule. *See* Appendix J. The Task Force expressed its concern that the Rule would be used by federal officials to pressure contractors to waive their attorney-client privilege or work product protections or to take unfair punitive actions against their employees during an audit, investigation, or corrective action. The ABA Task Force proposed specific changes to the proposed Rule to prevent these abuses. *See* Appendix J, attachment.

In all, 25 companies, groups, or individuals submitted comments on the second proposed Mandatory Disclosure Rule.

H. The Final Rule and Its Preamble

The final Mandatory Disclosure Rule was published in the Federal Register on November 12, 2008. *See* Appendix A. The Rule was accompanied by an extensive Preamble setting forth the FAR Councils' responses to many of the comments on the second proposal. *See* Appendix B. The requirements of the Rule are analyzed in the following sections of this Guide.

The relevant portions of the Preamble to the Rule are also discussed in each of these sections. Readers seeking guidance on implementation of the Rule are encouraged to begin by reading the Rule (Appendix A) and its Preamble (Appendix B) and then proceeding to one or more of the relevant sections below.[16]

---

[16] The case law surrounding the issue of the weight that should be given to the Preamble is complicated (and beyond the scope of this Guide). A recent Supreme Court case, however, gives some guidance. In *Wyeth v. Levine*, 129 S. Ct. 1187 (2009), the Court rejected a statement on the pre-emptive effect of an FDA regulation that was contained within the Preamble to the FDA's regulation. The Court noted (at 1201) that the Preamble was not subject to notice and comment rulemaking. Further, according to the Court, the Preamble was at odds with the evidence of Congress's purpose, and reversed the FDA's own longstanding position. Consequently, the Court accorded the FDA's statements in the Preamble no weight at all. *Id.* at 1203. *Wyeth*'s direct application may be limited here. Nevertheless, *Wyeth* does serve as a helpful reminder that while the Preamble can provide helpful interpretive guidance, because the Preamble is not subject to notice and comment rulemaking, it cannot alter the meaning of the text of the regulation.

SECTION 1: IDENTIFYING TYPES OF REPORTABLE CONDUCT

I. INTRODUCTION

The nature and scope of activity considered "reportable conduct" under the FAR Mandatory Disclosure Rule are set forth in two separate sections of the FAR:

- FAR 52.203-13: A clause entitled "Contractor Code of Business Ethics and Conduct" must be included in certain new contracts awarded after December 12, 2008 and identifies the type of conduct that must be reported.

- FAR 9.406-2 (Debarment) and FAR 9.407-2 (Suspension): The debarment and suspension rules include reportable conduct requirements as a factor that agency suspension and debarment officials ("SDOs") must consider when evaluating the present responsibility of a contractor.

Appendix A. As set forth in the FAR contract clause and the clause's requirement for internal controls, a contractor must timely disclose certain types of listed "reportable conduct," namely where the contractor has credible evidence of:

- A "violation of Federal criminal law involving fraud, conflict of interest, bribery, or gratuity violations found in Title 18 of the United States Code"; or

- A "violation of the civil False Claims Act."[17]

Also, as set forth in the debarment and suspension provisions, a contractor can face suspension or debarment for a failure to timely report the above types of violations or the failure to report:

- "Significant overpayment(s)," "other than overpayments resulting from contract financing payments as defined in 32.001."[18]

---

[17] On May 20, 2009, several amendments to the FCA became law, and these changes include a significant overhaul of the liability provisions of the FCA. This chapter will discuss these revised liability provisions, most of which apply only to conduct after May 20, 2009, as well as the former liability provisions.

[18] The reporting of "significant overpayments" is covered only in the debarment/suspension provisions. The new FAR clause does not require reporting of overpayments because the obligation to report overpayments is already included in other FAR clauses, including the prompt payment clauses.

Importantly, the Rule limits the type of reportable violations to those violations occurring "in connection with the award, performance, or closeout" of a Government contract or subcontract.

This Section will not address a number of issues covered elsewhere in this Guide, such as what is a covered contract (except for the "in connection with the award, performance, or closeout" requirement), what constitutes "credible evidence," or what "timely disclosure" means. Rather, this Section will explore the meaning of the limiting phrase "in connection with the award, performance, or closeout" of a Government contract or subcontract and what types of conduct are reportable under the Rule. While in the normal case these questions may be readily answered, the application of the Rule at the margins likely will prove to be more difficult.

Moreover, practitioners should understand that many events may be reportable as more than one type of violation. For example, discovery of an overcharge scheme on a Government contract may be reportable both as a criminal violation as well as a civil False Claims Act ("FCA") violation. The improper retention of a "significant overpayment" could be a civil FCA violation or a criminal violation, or both, depending on whether the contractor had the requisite "knowledge" or intent when the claim was submitted or the overcharge was retained. This Section, however, will deal separately with each type of reportable conduct. Practitioners are cautioned to consider the potential for events to be reportable as more than one type of "reportable conduct."

II. MEANING OF "IN CONNECTION WITH THE AWARD, PERFORMANCE, OR CLOSEOUT" OF A GOVERNMENT CONTRACT OR SUBCONTRACT

Under the Mandatory Disclosure Rule, not every criminal violation or False Claims Act violation needs to be disclosed (although nothing prohibits a contractor from doing so).[19] The

---

[19] The Government certainly would encourage voluntary disclosures even if not required by the FAR Rule, and, as stated later in this Section, it might be in the contractor's best interests to make such disclosures. *See* Section C.4 below.

FAR contains an important limit to mandatory disclosure. The Rule requires disclosure and authorizes suspension or debarment only if the violations identified therein are *"in connection with the award, performance, or closeout"* of a Government contract or a subcontract thereunder. Whether certain conduct should be deemed to be "in connection with the award, performance, or closeout" of a contract or subcontract is the starting point for practitioners trying to determine whether they have credible evidence requiring the disclosure of a criminal or False Claims Act violation. (Note that contractors have contractual obligations to report and/or return all overpayments, whether or not significant, under the FAR prompt payment clauses and other FAR clauses.)

The FAR Rule itself does not elaborate on the meaning of the phrase "in connection with," other than to limit the required connection to the "award, performance, or closeout" of a Government contract or subcontract. Therefore, the first task is to find the commonly understood meaning of "in connection with," and courts have generally given this phrase a broad interpretation. "Related" is a word commonly used in liability insurance policies that has been held to mean "in connection with" or "associated with." *See, e.g., Westport Ins. Co. v. Coffman*, 2009 WL 243096 (S.D. Ohio Jan. 29, 2009). Many federal courts have held that the common understanding of "related" covers "a very broad range of connections, both causal and logical." *Id.* at *7. In *Morrison v. Zangpo*, 2008 WL 4449585 (N.D. Cal. Sept. 30, 2008), the court noted that the phrase "in connection with this agreement" has been construed to include every dispute between the parties having a significant relationship to the contract and all disputes having their origin or genesis in the contract. *Id.* at *5 (quotation marks omitted). *See also BNY AIS Nominees Ltd. v. Quan*, 609 F. Supp. 2d 269, 277-78 (D. Conn. 2009) ("related" means connected by reason of an established or discoverable relation).

The explanatory Preamble provided by the FAR Councils makes clear that the phrase "in connection with the award, performance, or closeout" is important and is used to create limits on what conduct is to be reported. While any wrongful conduct may be of interest to prosecutors or investigators, the FAR Councils made clear that only conduct with a causal or logical link to the contract must be reported. The most reasonable interpretation would be that "in connection with" applies to any conduct that bears a nexus or relationship to the award, performance, or closeout of a Government contract or subcontract.

In fact, the Preamble emphasizes that the touchstone for the FAR Rule was that "in all cases the reportable violations are linked to the performance of Government contracts." Appendix B, 73 Fed. Reg. at 67,073. It does not appear as though the FAR Councils intended the Mandatory Disclosure Rule to apply more broadly to require disclosure of conduct merely because the perpetrator is a Government contractor or because the conduct has some tangential relationship to a Government contract. It is the nexus of the reportable conduct to a contractor's Government contract or contracts, and not merely the contractor's status as a Government contractor, that triggers the Mandatory Disclosure Rule. As the Preamble explains: "If there is no connection to a Government contract performed by the contractor, or a subcontract thereunder, then [the violation] need not be disclosed." 73 Fed. Reg. at 67,075.

Some examples may provide context for this analysis.

A. Reporting Another Contractor's Possible Violation

Whether or not the reporting obligation is contained in a contract clause, the Preamble makes clear that the obligation applies only to performance of a contractor's own contracts or the subcontracts thereunder: "It was not the intent of the proposed rule to require contractors to report on violations of other contractors under contracts unrelated to their own contracts." Appendix B, 73 Fed. Reg. at 67,073.

B. Violations Arising from Indirect Costs

One question that arises is whether a contractor's reporting obligations apply to matters involving "indirect" costs (*e.g.*, overhead and "general and administrative" costs) or to direct contract costs only. A direct cost is defined as a cost that relates to a single cost objective (usually a contract), while an indirect cost relates to more than one cost objective (often a group of contracts).

Although the regulation does not specifically address indirect costs, the phrase "in connection with the award, performance, or closeout" likely means that violations involving indirect costs charged to a Government contract or subcontract fall within the scope of the Mandatory Disclosure Rule. Thus, if a contractor's indirect charges result in a false invoice relating to a Government contract, there is little doubt that this conduct (assuming that it could be pursued under the False Claims Act or Title 18 or led to a significant overpayment) is "in connection with" the Government contract. On the other hand, if the same contractor charges time or costs only to an unallowable cost pool or the time or costs are otherwise clearly not charged to any Government contract, that conduct is likely not "in connection with" a Government contract. That said, whether any action would be considered "in connection with" a Government contract or subcontract within the meaning of the Mandatory Disclosure Rule needs to be analyzed carefully on a factual and legal basis.

C. Direct Costs Under a Fixed Price Contract

Altering slightly the example above, suppose that a contractor employee who works on a Government contract leaves early and charges a full day, and that the contract is a fixed price contract. In this case, the conduct is technically "in connection with" the performance of a Government contract, even though the federal Government has suffered no harm as a result. The conduct is likely not reportable under the Rule, however, because it would not appear to be a violation of Title 18 or the civil False Claims Act, nor lead to any overpayment, even if the conduct might harm the contractor and violate company policy.[20]

D. A Supplier With No Direct Sales to the Government

There might be other situations in which conduct ultimately affects Government contracts or subcontracts without being "in connection with" them. Suppose an energy firm is accused of a conspiracy under the antitrust laws to fix certain fuel prices, and that it has no sales to the federal Government through a contract or subcontract. The conspiracy results in higher prices paid by the Government under its contracts with other energy suppliers. Although the unlawful conduct eventually could affect the prices the Government pays, the wrongful conduct is not "in connection with" a Government contract because the offender has no Government contracts.

E. A Supplier With Minimal Sales to the Government

One can change the result by altering the example above just slightly. Suppose the same energy firm is engaged in a conspiracy to fix prices, but 5% of its sales are to the federal Government. If, in connection with the award of its Government contracts, the contractor has also executed a certificate stating that it has not engaged in the types of conduct it has, in fact, engaged in, and if the conduct otherwise could be pursued under the False Claims Act or Title 18, that conduct would now most likely be considered "in connection with" a Government contract and disclosure would be required under the Rule. That is, if a criminal charge or a False Claims Act claim is cognizable under a company's Government contracts, the "in connection with" requirement of the Rule is likely met.

---

[20] If, however, the costs charged on that fixed price contract are the basis for the amounts charged on a follow-on contract, the false charges may result in an FCA violation. For this reason, it is critical that each situation be analyzed on its own.

F. Reportable Conduct in the Absence of Award

The price-fixing hypothetical raises another set of issues under the Rule — when in the procurement process is a violation "in connection with the award" of a contract? In short, when does the reporting obligation begin? The Rule refers to "the award" of a contract, not just its performance, but it does not define "award." What if the energy firm decides not to compete before the solicitation is formally issued? What if it drops out after the Government issues the solicitation? What if it competes but loses the award? Given the FAR Councils' overarching intent to protect the integrity of the procurement process, the most prudent way for contractors and potential contractors to read the Rule's reference to "the award" of a contract or subcontract would encompass the entire award process, and not just the successful award and awardee. In other words, bidders that decide to drop out of the bidding process, or who are not awarded contracts, cannot be sure that the Government will view misconduct in connection with their unsuccessful bids as falling outside the scope of the Mandatory Disclosure Rule.[21]

As with much of the Rule, the "in connection with" language in the disclosure requirement is heavily dependent on the facts and circumstances of each case. What is clear from the explanation by the FAR Councils is that not every violation needs to be reported and that the key criteria is some direct relationship to the "award, performance, or closeout" of a Government contract or subcontract.

III. REPORTABLE CRIMINAL CONDUCT

The Rule requires disclosure whenever there is credible evidence of criminal violations "involving fraud, conflict of interest, bribery, or gratuity violations found in Title 18 of the

---

[21] On the other hand, dropping out before award will eliminate some grounds for disclosure. Without an award, there is probably no False Claims Act liability and no possibility of overpayment. To trigger the mandatory disclosure requirement, the violation would necessarily require criminal conduct in violation of a statute which does not require a contract award (*e.g.* conspiracy, bid rigging, Ethics in Government Act, Procurement Integrity Act, Economic Espionage Act, etc.). *See* Subsection III below.

United States Code." Appendix A, FAR 52.203-13(b)(3)(i)(A). This limitation to certain types of criminal conduct found in Title 18 reflects a clear attempt by the FAR Councils to limit the scope of reportable criminal conduct under the Mandatory Disclosure Rule. How this limitation works in practice is far less clear than the seemingly straightforward reference to certain crimes in Title 18 of the United States Code.

A. Background

In defining the scope of criminal violations subject to the Mandatory Disclosure Rule, it clearly was the Councils' intention to narrow the range of conduct requiring disclosure. The initial proposed Rule broadly required disclosure of "violations of Federal criminal law" in connection with the award or performance of a Government contract or subcontract. Appendix E, 72 Fed. Reg. at 64,019. This phrasing was targeted by commenters as overly broad, which both the Department of Justice ("DOJ") and the Councils recognized and attempted to remedy. In a letter commenting on the proposed rule, the DOJ acknowledged that contractors "may reasonably complain that requiring disclosure of any 'violation of Federal criminal law' is too broad, even when limited by the phrase 'in connection with the award or performance of any Government contract or subcontract.'" Appendix G, Attachment A at 2. In the Preamble accompanying the final Rule, the Councils indicated that they had adopted a "more specific description of criminal law suggested by DOJ as responsive to many of the concerns expressed by the respondents." Appendix B, 73 Fed. Reg. at 67,075.

Specifically, in the Preamble, the Councils described their intent when incorporating the final language of the Rule as follows:

> Numerous respondents stated that the rule fails to specify what constitutes a "criminal violation" "in connection with contract award or performance." Some of these respondents made the following comments:
>
> . . . .

> The [initial proposed] provision is vague in regard to the type of "criminal violation" covered, leaving open application of the rule to non-procurement related offenses. If an employee commits a criminal violation while driving on Federal lands in the course of performing a contract, must the traffic violation be reported to the agency OIG? Also, the agency OIGs may receive reports about violations of Federal tax law or Occupational Safety and Health laws that occur in connection with the performance of the contract, over which the OIGs do not have jurisdiction. This can result in unnecessary or inappropriate reports.
>
> The proposed rule does not elaborate on the nexus between the perceived criminal conduct and the Federal contract so as to trigger the reporting requirement. A contractor's silence could be alleged to be a false statement where the employer had "reason to believe" that one of its employees, agents, or subcontractors had violated criminal law in connection with a contract. . . .
>
> DOJ also suggested tightening the standard for disclosure by adding the phrase "involving fraud, conflict of interest, bribery, or gratuity violations found in Title 18 of the United States Code."
>
> *Response:* The Councils have adopted the more specific description of criminal law suggested by DOJ as responsive to many of the concerns expressed by the respondents. As to nexus with the contract, the clause stipulates in paragraph 52.203 13(b)(3)(i) that the violation should have occurred "in connection with the award, performance, or closeout of this contract, or any subcontract thereunder." If there is no connection to a Government contract performed by the contractor, or a subcontract thereunder, then it need not be disclosed.

Appendix B, 73 Fed. Reg. at 67,075.

B.   Conflict of Interest, Bribery, and Gratuity Violations Under Title 18

FAR 52.203-13(b)(3)(i)(A) sets forth four distinct types of Title 18 violations subject to the Mandatory Disclosure Rule: violations involving (1) fraud, (2) conflict of interest, (3) bribery, and (4) gratuity. Conflict of interest, bribery, and gratuity violations are expressly defined and covered by Chapter 11 of Title 18. *See* 18 U.S.C. §§ 201-226. While these three types of violations frequently overlap in these sections (*e.g.*, gratuities offered as a bribe), these criminal statutes specifically define the covered conduct.

Specific conflict of interest prohibitions can be found in Title 18 with respect to advocacy by Government officials upon retirement (§ 207) and involvement by Government officials in matters where they have a personal financial interest (§ 208).

Bribery is addressed generally by 18 U.S.C. § 201, where it is described as offering or promising "anything of value to any public official . . . to influence any official act." Other sections, meanwhile, deal more specifically with bribery as it relates to Government appointments (§ 210), loan procurement (§ 215), sporting events (§ 224), and port security (§ 226). Section 666 of Title 18 also addresses bribery in programs involving federal funds.

Gratuities are defined generally at 18 U.S.C. § 201(c)(1) and are discussed specifically with regard to gifts to Members of Congress (§ 203), receipt of non-Governmental salary by Government officials (§ 209), and improper inducements to financial examiners (§ 212).

Thus, on the whole, determining whether alleged conduct would constitute a conflict of interest, bribery, or gratuities violation under Title 18 is not particularly vexing; it simply requires a close review of the crimes enumerated in Chapter 11 of Title 18.

C. Fraud Violations Under Title 18

It is in considering violations "of fraud under Title 18" that the limits on reportable conduct become less clear. "Fraud" is defined generally as "a knowing misrepresentation of the truth or concealment of a material fact to induce another to act to his or her detriment."[22] While common law elements of fraud vary by jurisdiction, in general a finding of fraud requires (1) an act of misrepresentation or concealment, (2) that is knowing [scienter], (3) to another's harm or detriment. The most obvious criminal provisions involving fraud are those found in Title 18,

---

[22] Black's Law Dictionary (8th ed. 2004). "Criminal fraud" has a somewhat circular definition: "Fraud that has been made illegal by statute and that subjects the offender to criminal penalties such as fines and imprisonment." *Id.* at 686.

Chapter 47, "Fraud and False Statements." 18 U.S.C. §§ 1001-1040. Two particularly relevant statutes are Section 1001, which authorizes up to five years' imprisonment for making "any materially false, fictitious, or fraudulent statement or representation," and Section 1031, which authorizes up to ten years' imprisonment for contractors engaging in "major fraud against the United States."

FAR 52.203-13 covers violations involving fraud beyond those found in Chapter 47, however. Violations of Chapter 15, "Claims and Services in Matters Affecting Government," arising in the context of the award, performance, or closeout of a Government contract or subcontract, also must be included within the ambit of the FAR Rule. For example, 18 U.S.C. §§ 286-287, which prohibit making or conspiring to make criminal false or fraudulent claims to the Government, are the quintessential form of fraud in connection with a Government contract and are clearly within the scope of the FAR Rule.

Problems may arise, however, in determining whether other criminal violations should be deemed as "involving fraud" for purposes of the Mandatory Disclosure Rule. There are as many as eighty criminal statutes "found in Title 18" that arguably "involv[e] fraud."[23] *See* Table 3.1 below. Violation of certain of these provisions often could arise in the context of a federal procurement. For example, 18 U.S.C. § 1516 involves obstruction of a federal audit, and the Economic Espionage Act, 18 U.S.C. § 1831, would cover situations where a contractor illegally obtains and utilizes a competitor's proprietary data in connection with a federal procurement. The question the practitioner must decide is whether a violation of some of the more obscure sections of Title 18 that expressly involve fraud or fraudulent conduct arise "in connection with the award, performance, or closeout" of any Government contract or subcontract. Where a

---

[23] Table 3.1 represents all Title 18 sections expressly prohibiting "fraud," attempts to "defraud," or "fraudulent" conduct.

contractor has credible evidence of such a violation of one of these provisions and the violation is connected to the contractor's Government contract or subcontract, the contractor risks suspension and/or debarment if the contractor applies too narrow an understanding of what constitutes a reportable criminal fraud violation.

<u>Table 3.1</u>
<u>Title 18 Sections Involving Fraud</u>

38	(fraud involving aircraft or space vehicle parts in interstate or foreign commerce)
113a	(telemarketing fraud)
152	(concealment of assets; false oaths and claims)
153	(embezzlement against estate)
155	(fraudulent fee agreements in cases under Title 11)
157	(bankruptcy fraud)
201	(in bribery of public officials and witnesses)
226	(bribery affecting port security)
286	(conspiracy to defraud U.S. with respect to claims)
287	(false claims)
288	(false claims for postal losses)
289	(false claims for pensions)
331	(mutilation, diminution, and falsification of coins)
332	(debasement of coins, alteration of scales, or embezzlement of metals)
371	(conspiracy to commit offense or defraud U.S.)
472	(sale of counterfeit obligations or securities)
479	(sale of counterfeit foreign obligations or securities)
480	(possessing counterfeit foreign obligations or securities)
481	(in counterfeiting foreign obligations or securities)
482	(forgery of foreign bank notes)
483	(sale of counterfeit foreign bank notes)
484	(connecting parts of different notes)
485	(forgery of coins or bars)
490	(forgery of minor coins)
491	(fraudulent use of tokens or paper as money)
495	(fraudulent contracts, deeds, and powers of attorney)
499	(forgery of official military pass or permit)
500	(forgery of money orders)
501	(forgery of postage stamps)
506	(forgery or misuse of seals of departments or agencies)
507	(forgery of a ship's documentation)
542	(entry of commercial goods to U.S. by means of false statements)
545	(smuggling goods into the U.S.)
548	(removing or repacking goods in warehouses)
550	(false claim for refund of duties)
551	(concealing or destroying invoices or other papers)

554.1 (smuggling goods from the U.S.)
666 (theft or bribery concerning programs receiving federal funds)
706a (fraudulent display of Geneva distinctive emblems)
707 (fraudulent use of 4-H Club emblem)
831 (in prohibited transactions involving nuclear materials)
915 (impersonation of foreign diplomat)
917 (fraudulent impersonation of Red Cross agent)
1001 (false statements or entries generally)
1002 (possession of false papers to defraud U.S.)
1003 (fraudulent demands against the U.S.)
1005 (false reports intending to defraud banks)
1006 (false reports intending to defraud federal credit institutions)
1012 (false reports intending to defraud HUD)
1013 (concerning farm loan bonds)
1015 (naturalization, citizenship, or alien registry)
1017 (wrongful use of government seals)
1023 (insufficient delivery of money for military or naval service)
1025 (false pretenses on high seas and other waters)
1028 (in connection with ID documents, authentication features, and information)
1028a (aggravated identify theft)
1029 (in connection with access devices)
1030 (in connection with computers)
1031 (major fraud against U.S.)
1035 (false statements relating to health care matters)
1036 (entry by false pretenses to U.S. property or secure area of any airport or seaport)
1037 (in connection with electronic mail)
1039 (in connection with obtaining confidential phone records of covered entity)
1115 (misconduct or neglect of ship officers)
1341 (mail fraud)
1343 (by wire, radio, or television)
1516 (in obstruction of federal audit)
1591 (in sex trafficking of children)
1708 (theft or receipt of stolen mail matter)
1712 (falsification of postal returns to increase compensation)
1726 (fraudulent collection of postage)
1728 (weight of mail increased fraudulently)
1732 (fraudulent certificate of bond or sureties by postmaster)
1831 (economic espionage)
1832 (theft of trade secrets)
1920 (to obtain federal employees' compensation)
1923 (fraudulent receipt of payments of missing persons)
2073 (false entries and reports of moneys or securities)
2261 (interstate domestic violence)
2262 (interstate violation of protection order)
2314 (transportation of stolen goods, securities, moneys)
2315 (sale or receipt of stolen goods, securities, moneys, or fraudulent State tax stamps)

Moreover, it should also be noted that some criminal violations enumerated in Title 18 may be considered fraudulent in nature even where "fraud" is not expressly mentioned in the statute. For example, 18 U.S.C. § 641 prohibits the unlawful conversion or embezzlement of United States property. A violation of Section 641 would seem to qualify as fraud, though the word "fraud" itself is absent from the statutory text, under the common law definition of knowing misrepresentation to another's detriment. In short, the range of unlawful conduct under Title 18 that may be considered "fraud" is considerable. In reviewing the statutory applicability of potential acts of fraud, a practitioner's cursory review of select provisions may prove insufficient.

D. Violations Not Found in Title 18

While the FAR Rule does not explicitly so require, contractors must also consider whether to disclose credible evidence of potential criminal violations even where the implicated statute is not found in Title 18. Statutes of particular relevance to Government contractors that might be considered include the Foreign Corrupt Practices Act,[24] the Procurement Integrity Act,[25] the Arms Export Control Act[26] (and its implementing regulations, the International Traffic in Arms Regulations[27]), the Trade Agreements Act,[28] and the Buy American Act.[29] None of the above statutes are found in Title 18, and some of them do not carry with them any possible criminal penalties of their own and are therefore outside the express definition of criminal

---

[24] 15 U.S.C. § 78dd-1 *et seq.*

[25] 41 U.S.C. § 423.

[26] 22 U.S.C. § 2778.

[27] 22 C.F.R. § 120.1 *et seq.*

[28] 19 U.S.C. § 2501 *et seq.*

[29] 41 U.S.C. § 10a-10c.

conduct warranting mandatory disclosure. Nondisclosure of a known criminal violation, however, may be unwise for a contractor seeking to guard its present responsibility status, even where the violation is not expressly included in the FAR's Mandatory Disclosure Rule.

Moreover, violations that appear to fall outside Title 18 may also include or give rise to secondary criminal violations found in Title 18. An act made unlawful by statutes other than Title 18 could easily involve a conspiracy under 18 U.S.C. § 371, for example. Other criminal violations that fall outside of Title 18 may also lead to secondary criminal violations involving a false statement punishable under 18 U.S.C. § 1001 or a false claim punishable under 18 U.S.C. § 287, or they may give rise to communications resulting in mail fraud or wire fraud chargeable under 18 U.S.C. §§ 1341-1343. Where this occurs, the conduct could be covered under FAR 52.203-13 (or FAR 9.406-2 or 9.407-2) even when the primary statute implicated by the conduct is found outside Title 18. In addition, where the violation of any criminal statute may involve the violation of a contract clause, the violation could result in liability under the False Claims Act, another source of "reportable conduct" that will be discussed below.

When implementing the Rule, therefore, it is important that practitioners keep in mind that the Councils intended to limit the scope of criminal conduct subject to the Rule's application to violations "in connection with the award, performance, and closeout" of a Government contract or subcontract and clearly did not intend the Rule to be an enforcement tool for other statutory regimes having virtually nothing to do with the award, performance, or closeout of those contracts or subcontracts. The Councils' focus in implementing the Rule was on the connection the violation has to the award, performance, or closeout of a Government contract or subcontract.

IV. REPORTABLE VIOLATIONS OF THE CIVIL FALSE CLAIMS ACT

A. Overview

The False Claims Act ("FCA") is often said to be the Government's primary tool for recovering monies lost as the result of fraud against the Government. *See* S. Rep. No. 345, 99th Cong., 2d Sess. at 2 (1986), *reprinted in* 1986 U.S.C.C.A.N. 5266. The FCA provides, among other things, that persons who knowingly submit or cause the submission of false claims for payment, or who knowingly make or use false records or statements material to false or fraudulent claims, are liable for treble damages plus civil penalties of between $5,500 and $11,000 per false claim. 31 U.S.C. § 3729.[30] Originally passed into law in 1863, the FCA can be enforced by the Government or by an individual "*qui tam*" plaintiff, known as a "relator," who files a lawsuit as a private attorney general. *See United States ex rel. Williams v. NEC Corp.*, 931 F.2d 1493, 1496-98 (11th Cir. 1991). If there is a successful recovery in a *qui tam* case, the relator is normally entitled to a percentage of the Government's recovery.

The liability provisions of the FCA were recently amended in Section 4 of the Fraud Enforcement and Recovery Act of 2009 ("FERA"), Public Law No. 111 21, 123 Stat. 1617, which was signed into law on May 20, 2009. While most of the amended liability provisions are not retroactive, the amendments will have an immediate impact on some mandatory disclosure decisions because contractors may have to decide whether there is credible evidence that conduct violates the FCA under the current (*i.e.*, post-FERA) version of the law.

The liability provisions of the FCA have always been dynamic provisions that can potentially encompass a broad range of misconduct. A claim for payment can be "false" because

---

[30] The False Claims Amendments Act of 1986 provided that the range of civil penalties was between $5,000 and $10,000 per false claim. However, this range was raised to between $5,500 and $11,000 per false claim for conduct which occurred on or after September 29, 1999. *See* 64 Fed. Reg. 47,099, 47,104 (Aug. 30, 1999).

a party seeks payment for goods or services that the party either did not provide or provided in a manner falling short of contractual specifications as to quantity or quality. *See, e.g., United States v. Bornstein*, 423 U.S. 303 (1976); *United States v. Aerodex, Inc.*, 469 F.2d 1003 (5th Cir. 1972). Claims might also be considered "false" where a contractor or subcontractor seeks payment for goods or services that were provided as required, but the contractor or subcontractor failed to comply with some other law, rule, or contractual condition. *See, e.g., Mikes v. Straus*, 274 F.3d 687 (2d Cir. 2001). In these latter situations, involving what might be termed "legally false claims" or "false certifications," courts have struggled to develop workable boundaries between situations where the violation of a law, rule, or contract provision triggers liability under the FCA and where the violation does not trigger liability. *See, e.g., United States ex rel. Hopper v. Anton*, 91 F.3d 1261 (9th Cir. 1996). FCA liability also requires that a false claim or statement be "material," although the courts have struggled with the definition of that term. *Compare United States v. Southland Mgmt. Corp.*, 326 F.3d 669 (5th Cir. 2003) (en banc) *with United States v. Bourseau*, 531 F.3d 1159 (9th Cir. 2008). *See also United States ex rel. Longhi v. Lithium Power Techs., Inc.*, 575 F.3d 458 (5th Cir. 2009).[31]

Against that background, the Mandatory Disclosure Rule requires a contractor to report instances where there is "credible evidence" that the contractor or one of the specified persons has committed a violation of the FCA in connection with the award, performance, or closeout of a contract. Often, deciding whether certain conduct constitutes a violation of the FCA will be relatively straightforward. In other instances, however, making that judgment may prove to be

---

[31] This debate ended, at least for actions occurring after May 20, 2009, with the passage of FERA. This legislation, discussed below, provided the following definition of "material" for the FCA: "having a natural tendency to influence, or be capable of influencing, the payment or receipt of money or property." 31 U.S.C. § 3729(b)(4).

more difficult. Knowledgeable attorneys may disagree on whether a set of facts represents a violation of the FCA.

In responding to this critique, the FAR Councils noted the following in the Preamble to the Rule:

> The Councils do not agree that the requirements of the civil FCA cannot be reasonably ascertained and understood by contractors, and expect that contractors doing business with the Government are taking appropriate steps to ensure their compliance with the statute and all other applicable laws. The most recent amendments to the statute were made in 1986, and a significant body of case law interpreting the statute, and the 1986 amendments in particular, has developed in that time period. These cases interpret the various elements of a civil FCA violation, including the definition of a claim, falsity, knowledge, and damages.
>
> Although the Councils recognize that some issues concerning the proper application of the civil FCA remain unsettled and subject to further judicial interpretation, this is not unique to the civil FCA.
>
> Moreover, the disclosure requirement applies only where the contractor has "credible evidence" that a violation of the civil FCA has occurred. The contractor is subject to suspension and debarment for failure to timely disclose the violation only where the contractor does so knowingly. Genuine disputes over the proper application of the civil FCA may be considered in evaluating whether the contractor knowingly failed to disclose a violation of the civil FCA.

Appendix B, 73 Fed. Reg. at 67,081. This final observation by the Councils has taken on more meaning in light of the May 2009 amendments to the FCA, because there may be genuine disputes over the meaning of these amendments.

B. Types of FCA Violations

Although there are currently seven subsections of 31 U.S.C. § 3729(a) which address substantive FCA liability, virtually all modern FCA cases involve conduct that falls under four of those subsections, as described in sections 1-4 below.

1. **False Claim, § 3729(a)(1) (now § 3729(a)(1)(A))**[32]

In the pre-2009 amendment version of the FCA, subsection 3729(a)(1) imposed liability on any person who "knowingly presents, or causes to be presented, to an officer or employee of the United States Government or a member of the Armed Forces of the United States a false or fraudulent claim for payment or approval." The new provision, subsection 3729(a)(1)(A), which was enacted on May 20, 2009 and is applicable to conduct on or after that date, imposes liability on any person who "knowingly presents, or causes to be presented, a false or fraudulent claim for approval." The new provision expressly defines the term "claim" as follows:

> [T]he term 'claim' —
>
> (A) means any request or demand, whether under a contract or otherwise, for money or property and whether or not the United States has title to the money or property, that —
>
>   (i) is presented to an officer, employee, or agent of the United States; or
>
>   (ii) is made to a contractor, grantee, or other recipient, if the money or property is to be spent or used on the Government's behalf or to advance a Government program or interest, and if the United States Government —
>
>   (I) provides or has provided any portion of the money or property requested or demanded; or
>
>   (II) will reimburse such contractor, grantee, or other recipient for any portion of the money or property which is requested or demanded; and
>
> (B) does not include requests or demands for money or property that the Government has paid to an individual as compensation for Federal employment or as an income subsidy with no restrictions on that individual's use of the money or property.

31 U.S.C. § 3729(b)(2).

---

[32] The amendments to the FCA in FERA renumbered the FCA's liabilities provisions. While this Guide will use the old numbers for ease of reference, we will cite at the beginning the new numbering system.

The FCA's first liability provision, *i.e.*, for knowingly presenting, or causing to be presented, a false claim, is the one that is most commonly used in FCA cases. In its most straightforward application, it can impose liability on a contractor that directly deals with a Government agency or any Government agent, contractor, or grantee. For example, suppose someone is paid by the hour to provide computer services to a Government research laboratory. If the person performs four hours of work, but knowingly submits to the Government a claim stating that he performed eight hours of work, the person violates this provision. In another example, consider a subcontractor that provides devices to a prime contractor, where the Air Force contract and the subcontract explicitly require that these devices work in particular conditions and that the supplier performs tests to verify this. If the subcontractor knowingly provides defective devices or falsifies test results, the subcontractor may be liable for knowingly "causing" the prime contractor to submit false claims.

It is important to note that the FCA (both pre- and post-amendment) expressly defines the term "knowingly" to encompass actual knowledge, reckless disregard for the truth, or deliberate ignorance of the truth. 31 U.S.C. § 3729(b)(1). Whether a contractor is acting with the requisite "knowledge" to violate the FCA is a complex topic beyond the scope of this Guide. However, it is clear that mere negligence is not a basis for FCA liability.

2. False Statement, § 3729(a)(2) (now § 3729(a)(1)(B))

Subsection 3729(a)(2) of the pre-2009 version of the FCA imposed liability on any person who "knowingly makes, uses, or causes to be made or used, a false record or statement to get a false or fraudulent claim paid or approved by the Government." Amended subsection 3729(a)(1)(B) which, by the terms of the May 20, 2009 amendments, is supposed to be effective as if enacted on June 7, 2008 and apply to all claims under the FCA pending on or after that date, imposes liability on any person who "knowingly makes, uses, or causes to be made or used, a false record or statement material to a false or fraudulent claim."[33]

There is frequently an overlap between cases involving violations of this subsection and cases involving violations of subsection 3729(a)(1). In *Allison Engine Co. v. United States ex rel. Sanders*, 128 S. Ct. 2123 (2008), a case decided on June 9, 2008, the Supreme Court held that a significant difference between the two subsections involves the issue of to whom the false claim was presented. By its plain language, old subsection 3729(a)(1) required that a claim be presented to "an officer or employee of the United States Government," while old subsection 3729(a)(2) did not have such a requirement; on the other hand, old subsection 3729(a)(2) required that the person knowingly make a false record or statement "to get" a false or fraudulent claim paid or approved by the Government. The Supreme Court interpreted the language of the previous subsection 3729(a)(2) to require that the defendant must have "intended" that his false record or statement be used to get a claim paid or approved by the United States. *Allison Engine Co.*, 128 S. Ct. at 2126. This interpretation led Congress to enact the amended version of the "false statement" provision, which no longer includes the language that the Court interpreted as incorporating an "intent" requirement.

As a practical matter, this "false record or statement" provision has been used to impose liability on a person who, while not himself submitting a false claim for payment or causing

---

[33] The first two courts to address the retroactivity issue have found that the term "claim" has the same meaning as in the FCA itself. The courts in both *United States v. SAIC*, 2009 WL 2929250 (D.D.C. Sept. 14, 2009) and *United States ex rel. Sanders v. Allison Engine Company, Inc.*, 2009 WL 3626773 (S.D. Ohio Oct. 27, 2009) (on remand from the Supreme Court) held that the clear language of the amendments required that the revisions to section 3729(a)(1)(B) applied only to "claims," not "cases," pending on July 7, 2008. The *Allison Engine* decision went on to state that, if the language did apply to "cases," then retroactive application would be unconstitutional. These decisions are likely to be appealed and other courts are likely to rule on this issue, so the practitioner must analyze prevailing law in determining whether the FCA applies to the facts.

someone else to submit a false claim, creates a false record in order to assist someone else in submitting a false claim. For example, suppose a Government contractor that is being reimbursed by a Government agency for the costs of building a boat asks a supplier to provide a false invoice inflating the amount of an important component, explaining that this will help the contractor get paid more money by the Government, and the supplier provides the inflated invoice. In this situation, the supplier could be liable under subsection 3729(a)(2). *See United States v. O'Connell*, 890 F.2d 563 (1st Cir. 1989).

3. Conspiracy, § 3729(a)(3) (now § 3729(a)(1)(C))

In the pre-amendment version of the FCA, subsection 3729(a)(3) imposed liability on any person who "conspires to defraud the Government by getting a false claim allowed or paid." The new provision, subsection 3729(a)(1)(C), applicable to conduct on or after May 20, 2009, imposes liability on anyone who "conspires to commit a violation of [any of the other substantive liability provisions of the FCA]." There is frequently an overlap between this section and former subsection 3729(a)(2): a person who knowingly creates a false record, in order to assist someone else in getting a false claim paid, is often also engaging in a conspiracy. Although the newly enacted subsection 3729(a)(1)(B) may not require any showing of specific intent to defraud the Government, which the Supreme Court in *Allison Engine* held to be a requirement for an FCA conspiracy (*see* 128 S. Ct. at 2130-31), the newly enacted conspiracy provision likely still requires a showing of intent to enter into a conspiracy to violate the FCA, as that is one of the traditional elements of any conspiracy claim.

4. Reverse False Claims, § 3729(a)(7) (now § 3729(a)(1)(G))

In the pre-amendment version of the FCA, subsection 3729(a)(7) imposed liability on any person who "knowingly makes, uses, or causes to be made or used, a false record or statement to conceal, avoid, or decrease an obligation to pay or transmit money or property to the

Government." The new provision, subsection 3729(a)(1)(G), applicable to conduct on or after May 20, 2009, imposes liability on anyone who "knowingly makes, uses, or causes to be made or used, a false record or statement material to an obligation to pay or transmit money or property to the Government, or knowingly conceals or knowingly and improperly avoids or decreases an obligation to pay or transmit money or property to the Government . . . ."

This subsection, which imposes liability for so-called "reverse false claims," has typically applied in situations where certain types of contracts or statutes require a party to pay money to the Government (hence, the "reverse" of the typical false claim). Common examples are royalty contracts where those who extract materials from federal lands (for oil, gas, coal, timber, etc.) are required to pay a percentage to the Government; those who falsely state the amount due would be liable under this subsection. While countless other examples could be provided, in general anyone who creates false documentation that decreases a payment otherwise due to be made to the Government would incur similar FCA liability.

This subsection has been substantially rewritten by the 2009 amendments to the FCA. Under the "reverse false claims" provision of the pre-2009 amendment FCA, the FCA imposed liability on a person who knowingly made, used, or caused to be made or used, a false record or statement to conceal, avoid, or decrease an obligation to pay or transmit money to the Government. Thus, the event that triggered liability was the making or using of a false record or statement. The amended version of the FCA, however, unlike its predecessor, also imposes liability on a person who "knowingly conceals or knowingly and improperly avoids or decreases an obligation to pay or transmit money or property to the Government." Moreover, the term "obligation" is now defined to include "an established duty, whether or not fixed, arising from . . . the retention of any overpayment." 31 U.S.C. § 3729(b)(3).

Thus, there are now two new potential triggering events under the FCA: (1) a person's *knowing concealment of* an obligation to pay or transmit money to the Government or (2) a person's *knowing and improper avoidance* of an obligation to pay or transmit money to the Government. Whereas under the prior version of the FCA, someone had to knowingly do something in order to trigger reverse false claims liability, under the new version of the FCA, one only has to knowingly and improperly *fail to do something* in order to be liable.

The ramifications of this change are significant with respect to the FAR Mandatory Disclosure Rule. Under the Rule, a contractor's failure to report "significant overpayments" could potentially result in suspension or debarment. Now, given the new "reverse false claims" provision of the FCA, a contractor's failure to report and return a known overpayment (whether "significant" or not) could subject the contractor not only to potential suspension or debarment but also to liability under the FCA.

5. Special Issues in FCA Cases Involving Noncompliance With Regulatory or Contractual Requirements

There is much litigation and unsettled law in the application of the FCA to cases involving claims that, while accurate on their face, may nonetheless be considered "false" because of the contractor's noncompliance with a law, regulation, rule, or contract term.

Such noncompliance is frequently analyzed in terms of materiality; namely, was the contractor's noncompliance with certain laws, regulations, or rules "material" to the Government's decision to pay the contractor. Under the old FCA, courts in various jurisdictions were divided on how to conduct this sort of materiality analysis. Some would ask whether the contractor's noncompliance would have had a tendency to influence the Government's decision whether to pay the claim, *United States ex rel. Berge v. Bd. of Trustees of Univ. of Ala.*, 104 F.3d 1453 (4th Cir. 1997), while others would ask whether the contractor's noncompliance actually determined the outcome of the payment question, *United States ex rel. Costner v. URS Consultants, Inc.*, 317 F.3d 883 (8th Cir. 2003). This question has probably been resolved by the 2009 amendments to the FCA, which rewrote subsection 3729(b)(4) to define "materiality" under the FCA as follows: "[T]he term 'material' means having a natural tendency to influence, or be capable of influencing, the payment or receipt of money or property." This definition had been utilized by several courts. *See United States ex rel. Longhi v. Lithium Power Techs., Inc.*, 575 F.3d 458 (5th Cir. 2009).

Finally, many courts have categorized cases involving "legally false claims" as "false certification" cases. Some cases — those where a contractor must actually certify compliance with one or more specific conditions as part of a claim — are called "express false certification" cases. Other cases, those where a contractor does not actually certify anything, are called "implied false certification" cases. The reasoning behind the use of the term "implied false certification" is that a contractor that is under a legal or contractual obligation to fulfill certain conditions when performing a Government contract "impliedly certifies" its compliance with those conditions by the mere act of submitting a claim for payment for goods or services provided under the contract.

In these false certification cases, whether the certification is express or "implied," courts generally focus on the connection, if any, between the so called "certification" and the Government's decision to pay. Where the Government's decision to pay for services is contingent upon the contractor's fulfillment of certain specific conditions, courts have held that the contractor's failure to fulfill those conditions can render its claims for payment "false." On the other hand, where the Government would clearly pay for the goods or services regardless of the contractor's compliance with a specific condition, the courts tend to hold that a false statement of compliance does not render the claim for payment false under the FCA.

6. "Inconsequential" FCA Violations

One question that has generated significant debate is the necessity to report inconsequential FCA violations. A good example is the employee working on a Government contract who spends two hours shopping on his or her computer yet bills those hours to the Government contract. Most contractors, faced with such a situation, simply credit the contract on the next billing cycle (after disciplining the employee). While the contractor may not have a reportable FCA violation, the employee may have violated the FCA by causing his/her employer to bill for time not spent on the contract, depending on the employee's knowledge.

While there is no *de minimis* exception for FCA violations (and a famous FCA case, *United States v. Halper*, 490 U.S. 435 (1989), involved 65 false claims of $9 each), one rational interpretation of the Councils' intent would be that a company could reasonably decide that such *de minimis* violations need not be reported to the OIG unless the circumstances suggest a larger or more prevalent problem. No Government agency, however, has publicly supported this view. (Of course such violations could still be "overpayments" triggering other reporting or repayment obligations.) This "*de minimis*" issue, however, should not be confused with cases in which an FCA violation involving a small-value part results in larger damages to the Government. *Cf. United States ex rel. Roby v. Boeing Co.*, 302 F.3d 637 (6th Cir. 2002), cert. denied, 123 S. Ct. 2641 (2003).

V. SIGNIFICANT OVERPAYMENTS

As a threshold matter, it is important for all practitioners to recognize that Government contracts include standard FAR clauses that mandate reporting and/or return of all overpayments, whether or not "significant." *See, e.g.*, FAR 12.215; FAR 32.008; FAR 52.212-4(i)(5); FAR

52.232-25(d); FAR 52.232-26(c); FAR 52.232-27(l). Thus, unlike criminal violations and FCA violations, a significant overpayment is not a "reportable" event mandated by FAR 52.203-13. The failure to report a significant overpayment, however, may be a cause for debarment under FAR 9.406-2(b)(1)(vi) (Causes for debarment) or for suspension under FAR 9.407-2(a)(8) (Causes for suspension). These provisions make it grounds for debarment or suspension if there is a:

> [k]nowing failure by a principal, until 3 years after final payment on any Government contract awarded to the contractor, to timely disclose to the Government, in connection with the award, performance, or closeout of the contract or a subcontract thereunder, credible evidence of —
>
> . . .
>
> [s]ignificant overpayment(s) on the contract, other than overpayments resulting from contract financing payments as defined in 32.001.

Contractors should also be aware that the standard FAR clauses requiring return of overpayments also require that information concerning the overpayment be disclosed. For example, the standard Prompt Payment clause, FAR 52.232-25(d), provides:

> Overpayments. If the Contractor becomes aware of a duplicate contract financing or invoice payment or that the Government has otherwise overpaid on a contract financing or invoice payment, the Contractor shall —
>
> (1) Remit the overpayment amount to the payment office cited in the contract along with a description of the overpayment including the —
>
> > (i) Circumstances of the overpayment (*e.g.*, duplicate payment, erroneous payment, liquidation errors, date(s) of overpayment);
> >
> > (ii) Affected contract number and delivery order number, if applicable;
> >
> > (iii) Affected contract line item or subline item, if applicable; and
> >
> > (iv) Contractor point of contact.

(2) Provide a copy of the remittance and supporting documentation to the Contracting Officer.

A. Definition of "Significant Overpayment"

The term "significant overpayment" is nowhere defined in the FAR. In 2003, when the FAR Councils promulgated several FAR provisions that mandated reporting and/or return of overpayments, the Councils specifically refused to define "overpayment" fearing unintended consequences. *See* 68 Fed. Reg. 56,682 (Oct. 1, 2003). Nevertheless, an "overpayment," while not defined in the FAR, is generally considered an amount paid by the Government in excess of the amount that was, or should have been, paid to the contractor for goods or services provided. "Overpayments" can occur for a variety of reasons, including errors in quantity or billing or deficiencies in quality. *See* FAR 32.601(b)(12). Overpayments may have occurred where a contractor fails to comply with one of the Cost Accounting Standards and that noncompliance causes an overbilling. *See* FAR 32.607-2(g)(3).[34] Overpayments may also occur when a contractor is required to repay amounts to the Government in accordance with the GSA Price Reduction Clause. *See* GSAM 552.238-75.

Once a contractor has determined it has received an overpayment, it has an obligation to report or repay the overpayment. *See, e.g.*, FAR 12.215; FAR 32.008; FAR 52.212-4(i)(5); FAR 52.232-25(d); FAR 52.232-26(c); FAR 52.232-27(l). But not every overpayment is necessarily "significant." Because the FAR Councils modified the term "overpayment" with "significant," it seems certain that the Councils did not envision every unreported overpayment as being a basis for suspension or debarment. As the Councils explained in issuing the Rule:

---

[34] Recently, for example, the Federal Circuit concluded that a contractor's failure to perform a segment closing adjustment in accordance with CAS 413 and to credit the Government in accordance with CAS 413 meant that the contractor had received "overpayments" under its contracts. *Gates v. Raytheon*, No. 2008-1543 (Fed. Cir. Sept. 14, 2009).

> The Councils agree with the suggestion by the DOJ that it is appropriate to limit the application of suspension and debarment to cases in which the unreported overpayment is significant. . . . The Councils have revised the final rule to address only significant overpayments, which implies more than just dollar value and depends on the circumstances of the overpayment as well as the amount.

Appendix B, 73 Fed. Reg. at 67,080.

As a general rule, contracting officers rely on a contractor's accounting system and internal controls when approving invoices for payment (*see* FAR 32.503-4). The determination of whether a significant overpayment has occurred, however, is subjective. In this regard, the first Government official to make that determination will usually be the Government auditor (although the auditor's decision is only a recommendation because the authority to suspend or debar contractors rests with the agency suspension and debarment official). Of course, the FAR provisions associated with invoice and payment processes under Government contracts are intended to prevent a substantial overpayment (or underpayment) from arising. For example, FAR 42.704(c) allows billing rates to be revised as necessary during a contract. Similarly, subparagraph (g) of FAR 52.216-7 (Allowable Cost and Payment), which is also a required clause in cost-reimbursement contracts, establishes a mechanism in the audit process for overpayments to be routinely collected:

> *Audit.* At any time or times before final payment, the Contracting Officer may have the Contractor's invoices or vouchers and statement of costs audited. *Any payment may be —*
>
> (1) Reduced by amounts found by the Contracting Officer not to constitute allowable costs; or
>
> (2) *Adjusted for prior overpayments* or underpayments.

(Emphasis added.) Note that subparagraph (g) concerns *any* overpayments, not just significant overpayments. As a rule, Government auditors may initially suspect that overpayments were caused by overbilling, although in fact they may have been caused by other factors, such as inaccurate estimates or Government errors.[35]

The concept of "significance" when related to overpayments is highly fact-specific. Thus, the "significance" of an overpayment may depend on a number of factors, including:

- the value of the contract;
- any non-monetary affect on contract performance;
- the frequency of the overpayment;
- the impact on the program;
- the root cause of the overpayment; and
- the handling of prior similar overpayments.

In sum, whether an overpayment will be considered "significant" by the agency debarment official will depend on the amount and circumstances.

---

[35] Although the term "significant overpayment" is not defined anywhere in the FAR, the Defense Contract Audit Agency Contract Audit Manual ("CAM") sets forth general guidance in CAM 5-1100, *Audit of Billing System Internal Controls*, and CAM 6-1007, *Direct Submission of Interim Public Vouchers to Disbursing Offices (Direct Billing)*. More importantly, specific DCAA audit guidance is set forth in Section C-1(6)(c) of *Annual Testing of Contractor Eligibility for Direct Bill Program*, Activity Code 11015, Version 7.0 (October 2008), which states:

> c. Immediately notify the paying office, via memorandum, if a significant contractor overpayment is found (*$50 thousand [sic] on a single issue or on an individual contract*), and (1) the contractor has not notified the Government, and (2) the overpayment is over 30 days old and has not been returned.

(Emphasis added.) Although this might be read to provide a definition or example of "significant overpayment," three cautionary points should be kept in mind. First, the context is different, because the CAM here is on its face only providing guidance as to when the auditor should "immediately notify" the payment office of an overpayment. Second, the $50,000 amount stated in the guidance may be adjusted downward where an auditor deems it appropriate to do so. Finally, an auditor's subjective "significant overpayment" determination may be a function of the frequency of the overpayments as much as the amount of the overpayment. This may be particularly true where the auditor believes the contractor has been overbilling. Of course, as noted above, the Government auditor has no authority to impose sanctions against a contractor, as these matters are left to the agency suspension and debarment official.

B. Overpayments and the False Claims Act

It should also be noted that, under the 2009 amendments to the False Claims Act, a contractor that receives an overpayment and fails to repay it may not only face debarment or suspension but may also be subject to civil liability under the FCA. An FCA violation (which includes the knowing and improper retention of an overpayment) is a separate basis for a reportable event under FAR 52.203-13(b)(3), as discussed above.

VI. CONCLUSION

Determining whether conduct qualifies as "reportable conduct" under the FAR Mandatory Disclosure Rule is the beginning of the decisionmaking process. A contractor must analyze each situation carefully based on the unique facts and the law applicable. Bright line tests are not very useful.

SECTION 2: THE "CREDIBLE EVIDENCE" STANDARD

I. INTRODUCTION

This Section will explore the meaning and application of the term "credible evidence" under the Mandatory Disclosure Rule. While in many cases the determination of whether there is credible evidence of a specified violation may be clear, in others reasonable people may disagree. Even if there is no credible evidence of a specified criminal or False Claims Act violation, disclosure may still be required to avoid potential suspension or debarment if there is credible evidence of a significant overpayment under any of a contractor's Government contracts. The determination that there is credible evidence of a specified violation or a significant overpayment is the threshold at which timely disclosure is mandatory to avoid suspension or debarment. The Government encourages early disclosure, before the contractor has determined that there is credible evidence of a triggering event, even though disclosure under such circumstances is not mandatory. However, if the contractor does not make a disclosure when there is credible evidence, the Government can suspend or debar the contractor.

All Government contractors now are required to disclose "credible evidence" of certain federal criminal law violations, civil False Claims Act violations, or significant overpayments in connection with the award or performance of any of their Government contracts or subcontracts, or face suspension and debarment. This Mandatory Disclosure Rule flows from FAR 52.203-13 and from amendments to the debarment and suspension provisions in FAR 9.406-2 and 9.407-2. Under these provisions, a contractor can be debarred based upon a preponderance of the evidence, or suspended based upon adequate evidence, for the "knowing failure by a principal, until 3 years after final payment on any Government contract awarded to the contractor, to timely disclose to the Government, in connection with the award, performance, or closeout of the contract or a subcontract thereunder, credible evidence" of the specified violations or significant overpayments. Appendix A, FAR 9.406-2(b), 2(b)(vi), and 9.407-2(a), 2(a)(8).

Contract-specific requirements mandating disclosure of credible evidence of violations of specified federal criminal laws or the civil False Claims Act are also contained in the new Contractor Code of Business Ethics and Conduct clause, Appendix A, FAR 52.203-13, applicable to many Government contracts and subcontracts. The contract clause requires the contractor to make a written disclosure to the agency Office of Inspector General, with a copy to the contracting officer, whenever the contractor, in connection with the award, performance, or close out of the contract or any subcontract thereunder, has credible evidence that a principal, employee, agent, or subcontractor of the contractor has committed specified violations of federal criminal law or violations of the civil False Claims Act.

II. THE MEANING OF CREDIBLE EVIDENCE

Although the FAR does not define "credible evidence," the term has been used in numerous other contexts, ranging from Black's Law Dictionary to regulations to case law. As discussed below, the usage of "credible evidence" in those contexts appears consistent with the regulatory history concerning the term "credible evidence" in the Mandatory Disclosure Rule. This regulatory history, and the use of the term "credible evidence" in other disclosure regimes, also supports the conclusion that "credible evidence" turns on all the facts and circumstances developed by the contractor during its preliminary investigation, and not merely upon the credibility or incredibility of the information that may have prompted the investigation. In the end, the term "credible evidence" is a subjective standard that may lie somewhere between reasonable grounds to believe that a violation or significant overpayment has occurred and a preponderance of the evidence that such a violation or overpayment has occurred.

A.   **Guidance Found in the Preamble**

In finalizing the new regulations, the FAR Councils replaced the "reasonable grounds to believe" standard for mandatory disclosure, which was contained in the proposed Rule issued May 16, 2008, with the "credible evidence" standard. Appendix B, 73 Fed. Reg. at 67,073. The Preamble to the Rule states that the credible evidence standard "implies" a higher standard than the previously proposed "reasonable grounds to believe" standard and provides the contractor with the opportunity to take some time for preliminary examination of the evidence to determine its credibility before deciding to disclose to the Government. *Id.*

The first proposed Rule published on November 14, 2007, arguably would have required reporting of any allegation of a violation of criminal law or an overpayment. *See* Appendix E. "[I]n order to avoid contractor concern that the proposal would require disclosure of every allegation of a criminal violation or overpayment without regard to merit, [the DOJ Criminal Division] suggested inserting 'reasonable grounds to believe,' found elsewhere in the proposed rule or 'credible information of' found at DFARS 252.246-703 governing reports of Potential Safety Issues." Appendix G, DOJ Criminal Division Letter to the GSA Regulatory Secretariat (Jan. 14, 2008). The FAR Councils proposed the "reasonable grounds to believe" standard in the second proposed Rule issued May 16, 2008. Appendix I, 73 Fed. Reg. at 28,409. In the final Rule issued on November 12, 2008, the FAR Councils ultimately settled on "credible evidence" as the standard for required disclosure. Appendix B, 73 Fed. Reg. at 67,065.[36]

The Preamble states that the FAR Councils replaced the "reasonable grounds to believe" standard with "credible evidence" in response to comments that the "reasonable grounds"

---

[36] The FAR Councils stated that the "DOJ Criminal Division recommended this standard after discussions with industry representatives." Appendix B, 73 Fed. Reg. at 67,073. In fact, the DOJ did not recommend the "credible evidence" standard.

standard "is subject to varying interpretations, and may be viewed as an even lower standard than probable cause." Appendix B, 73 Fed. Reg. at 67,073. The Preamble states that credible evidence "indicates a higher standard [than reasonable grounds to believe], and that using the standard of 'credible evidence' rather than 'reasonable grounds to believe' will help to clarify 'timely' [disclosure] because it implies that the contractor will have the opportunity to take some time for preliminary examination of the evidence to determine its credibility before deciding to disclose to the Government." *Id.* at 67,074. The FAR Councils stated that "[u]ntil the contractor has determined the evidence to be credible, there can be no 'knowing failure to timely disclose.'" *Id.* The Preamble states, however, that the Rule does not direct the contractor to investigate. *Id.* at 67,087.

The Preamble's discussion of the requirement to disclose False Claims Act ("FCA") violations also provides clarification of the "credible evidence" standard. In this regard, the Councils recognized that some issues concerning the proper application of the civil FCA remain unsettled and subject to further judicial interpretation, and stated that genuine disputes over proper application of the FCA may be considered in evaluating whether a contractor knowingly failed to disclose a violation. Appendix B, 73 Fed. Reg. at 67,081. The Councils also noted that the mere filing of an FCA *qui tam* action is not sufficient to establish a violation under the statute, nor does it represent, standing alone, credible evidence of a violation. *Id.*[37] Similarly, the FAR Councils stated that the Government's decision not to intervene in an FCA *qui tam* action, standing alone, is not dispositive of whether the contractor has credible evidence of an FCA violation. *Id.*

---

[37] By similar logic, it would appear that a contractor's receipt of a Government subpoena or other request for information, and its attendant compliance with that subpoena or request, would not be sufficient to represent credible evidence of a violation.

The Preamble also states that the FAR Councils considered and "[did] not consider it necessary to add 'potential' to 'violation' because that preceding language already is in terms of 'credible evidence.' That does not necessarily mean that a violation has occurred, but the principals are looking for 'credible evidence' that a violation has occurred. 'Potential violation' would open it even wider and could result in too many unnecessary disclosures." Appendix B, 73 Fed. Reg. at 67,075.

B. The Use of the Term "Credible Evidence" in Other Contexts

Although the FAR does not define "credible evidence," the term has been used in numerous other contexts, ranging from Black's Law Dictionary to regulations to case law. Thus, for example, the dictionary definition of "credible evidence" is: "Evidence that is worthy of belief; trustworthy evidence" (*Black's Law Dictionary* 474 (abridged 8th ed. 2005)) and "[s]uch evidence as is sufficient to produce a belief that the thing is true" (*Black's Law Dictionary* 1342 (6th ed. 1990)). Similarly, "credible evidence" has been used in the banking context to define "[e]vidence of a material violation," namely evidence upon which "it would be unreasonable, under the circumstances, for a prudent and competent attorney not to conclude that it is reasonably likely that a material violation has occurred, is ongoing, or is about to occur." 17 C.F.R. § 205.2(e). Case law uses similar language. *See, e.g., Dupuy v. Samuels*, 397 F.3d 493, 497 (7th Cir. 2005) (credible evidence exists if "the available facts when viewed in light of surrounding circumstances would cause a reasonable person to believe that" something is the case).

Case law also indicates what would *not* be considered "credible evidence." Evidence is not credible if it consists of implausible factual assertions or frivolous claims, or if it is not worthy of belief. *See, e.g., Geiger v. Comm'r of Internal Revenue*, 279 F. Appx. 834, 835 (11th Cir. 2008). Thus, the critical question is the quality of the evidence, not its quantity. *LeFevre v.*

Sec'y, Dept. of Veterans Affairs, 66 F.3d 1191, 1200 (Fed. Cir. 1995). It has been stated that "[n]o better definition of these terms can be given," in holding that "satisfactory" and "credible" evidence mean "that evidence which is sufficient to produce a belief that the thing is true." *Walker v. Collins*, 59 F. 70, 74 (8th Cir. 1893).

The term "credible evidence" also appears in various HHS OIG Compliance Program Guidance documents, including the Guidance for Pharmaceutical Manufacturers. 68 Fed. Reg. 23,731, 23,742 (May 5, 2003). This HHS OIG Guidance states that "[w]here the compliance officer, compliance committee, or a member of senior management discovers *credible evidence* of misconduct from any source and, *after a reasonable inquiry*, believes that the misconduct may violate criminal, civil, or administrative law, the company should promptly report the existence of misconduct to the appropriate federal and state authorities within a reasonable period, but not more than 60 days, after determining that there is credible evidence of a violation." 68 Fed. Reg. at 23,742 (emphasis added). The phrase "credible evidence" is also mentioned in other HHS regulations. *See, e.g.,* 42 CFR 422.510(a)(4) & 42 CFR 423.509(a)(4) (CMS's termination of certain contracts justified when "[t]here is *credible evidence* that the [organization] committed or participated in false, fraudulent, or abusive activities affecting the Medicare program, including submission of false or fraudulent data.") (emphasis added).

In the HHS OIG Pharmaceutical Guidance, "credible evidence" is what prompts the contractor to conduct a "reasonable inquiry." In the FAR Rule, "credible evidence" is not necessarily what precipitates the contractor's preliminary inquiry, but that which may emerge from the inquiry. Therefore, unlike "credible evidence" under the HHS OIG Guidance, "credible evidence" under the FAR Rule allows an evaluation of all the facts and circumstances ascertained by the contractor during its preliminary inquiry. As we show below, this conclusion is reinforced by the regulatory history of the FAR Rule. (Of course, there may be circumstances where the initial information alone amounts to credible evidence without further inquiry.)

C. Interpretation Based on the Regulatory History

The regulatory history of the "credible evidence" standard supports the conclusion that a contractor may base its determination of whether there is "credible evidence" on an evaluation of all the facts and circumstances of which the contractor becomes aware during a preliminary investigation rather than on a single allegation or piece of information standing alone. The FAR Councils abandoned the "reasonable grounds to believe" standard in favor of the "credible evidence" standard in part because they wanted to ensure that the contractor "will have the opportunity to take some time for preliminary examination of the evidence to determine its credibility before deciding to disclose to the Government." Appendix B, 73 Fed. Reg. at 67,073. An obvious implication of the "opportunity to take some time for preliminary examination" is that such examination will unearth facts or circumstances either consistent or inconsistent with the allegation or condition that led the contractor to undertake the preliminary evaluation. It is fair to assume that the FAR Councils intended for the contractor to take such additional facts and conditions into account in determining whether "credible evidence" of a covered violation or overpayment exists.

Similar reasoning presumably underlies the FAR Councils' rejection of DOJ's proposed "credible information" standard based on DFARS 252.246-7003. DFARS 252.246-7003 requires a contractor to notify the Government within 72 hours whenever the contractor has "credible information" of nonconformances or deficiencies that may result in a system or part safety impact. The DFARS regulation defines "credible information" as "information that, considering its source and the surrounding circumstances, supports a reasonable belief that an event has occurred or will occur." DFARS 252.246-7003(a). This definition was presumably unacceptable to the FAR Councils at least in part because it includes the "reasonable belief" terminology that the FAR Councils had deemed inadequate.[38] The FAR Councils may also have concluded that "credible evidence" denotes a higher degree of reliability or certainty than does "credible information." Regardless, the FAR Councils' adoption of "credible evidence" rather than "credible information" supports the view that contractors should consider all available facts and circumstances developed during a preliminary inquiry in determining whether there is credible evidence of a violation or significant overpayment.

Nothing in the Rule, however, mandates that a contractor must undertake an investigation of every allegation that is made. There may be circumstances in which an allegation is so unlikely to be substantiated that a contractor may conclude that no investigation is warranted. In such circumstances, the contractor may want to document the reasons that an allegation does not warrant investigation.

D. The Role of Affirmative Defenses in Making a "Credible Evidence" Determination

Thus far, the discussion has focused on whether there is credible evidence of the violations specified in the Mandatory Disclosure Rule — i.e., what standard or level of evidence must exist before a contractor is under a duty to disclose. A related issue is how the existence of affirmative defenses to the underlying possible violation affects the contractor's determination of whether credible evidence of that violation exists. The Preamble to the Rule does not address the role that affirmative defenses may play in a credible evidence determination.

Examples of potential affirmative defenses include the statute of limitations, accord and satisfaction, estoppel, and waiver. A contractor may wish to consider these affirmative defenses

---

[38] The Councils may also have found the definition unacceptable because the underlying regulation required notification within 72 hours, which did not allow time for the investigation contemplated by the disclosure rule.

in making a "credible evidence" determination. The risk of relying on an affirmative defense as justification for not making a disclosure, however, will depend in large part on the nature and circumstances of the affirmative defense. For example, the statute of limitations might be extended if there is a conspiracy or a violation of the Major Fraud Act. The clearer the applicability of the defense, the less the risk will be. On the other hand, affirmative defenses are generally fact-intensive, and a creative affirmative defense, either factual or legal, may not be persuasive to the Government. As a best practice, contractors should be cautious about relying on affirmative defenses in deciding not to make a disclosure.

E. Relationship of "Credible Evidence" to "Reasonable Grounds to Believe" and "Preponderance of the Evidence"

Many persons affected by the Rule have asked what standard or amount of proof the "credible evidence" standard requires. Another way of asking the same question is "how much evidence of a violation must there be to constitute credible evidence that the violation occurred?" Unfortunately, there is no clear answer to this question because the meaning of the term "credible evidence" is inherently subjective, as discussed above.

However, the Preamble to the Rule, as well as some of the other authorities discussed above, suggest that "credible evidence" lies somewhere between "reasonable grounds to believe" that a violation occurred and a "preponderance of the evidence" that a violation occurred. As discussed above, the Preamble and the regulatory history suggest that the FAR Councils regarded "credible evidence" as a more demanding standard than "reasonable grounds to believe." On the other hand, the Preamble and regulatory history also suggest that the FAR Councils did not view "credible evidence" as requiring a conclusion that it was more likely than not that a violation had occurred. For example, the FAR Councils rejected a request to add the word "potential" before "violation" in the Rule because they found that the concept of "potential violation" was already present in the term "credible evidence." Appendix B, 73 Fed. Reg. at 67,075. The FAR Councils further stated that credible evidence "does not necessarily mean that a violation has occurred, but [rather that] the principals are looking for 'credible evidence' that a violation has occurred." *Id.* These statements appear to acknowledge that a contractor need not conclude that a violation has actually occurred in order to determine that there is "credible evidence" of such a violation.

A number of Task Force participants — including some Government participants — do not agree that the Preamble's reference to credible evidence as a "higher standard" should be interpreted to mean that "credible evidence" is a substantively more demanding standard than "reasonable grounds to believe." In the view of these participants, the Preamble's reference to credible evidence as implying a "higher" standard simply means that contractors can take some time to consider whether the evidence provides a reasonable ground to believe that a violation has occurred. Under this approach, there is no substantive difference between "credible evidence" and "reasonable grounds to believe" in terms of the level or amount of proof required to trigger the duty to disclose.

III. GUIDELINES FOR APPLYING THE CREDIBLE EVIDENCE STANDARD

To effectively apply the credible evidence standard, remember that credible evidence can be viewed as something more than reasonable belief based on allegation alone. However, care should be taken not to be overly legalistic. Failure to report credible evidence of a violation based on a defense or a conclusion that the evidence would not support a civil judgment or criminal conviction exposes the contractor to significant risk if the Government learns of and pursues the matter. The following guidelines may assist a contractor in identifying "credible evidence" as that term is used in the Mandatory Disclosure Rule.

- Conduct an appropriate evaluation and investigation of any allegation or concern.

- Consider whether an anonymous allegation has an impact on the determination. A vague anonymous complaint that does not provide any specific information that would permit the contractor to conduct an evaluation or investigation would not be credible. However, the mere fact that an allegation is anonymous is not likely to be a sufficient reason not to disclose if it otherwise provides specific credible information about a violation.

- Factors that may bear on credibility of the evidence include:

    (1) Background/reliability of the individual making the allegation.

    (2) Whether the individual was in a position to have direct knowledge.

    (3) Possible motivations.

    (4) Specificity of information provided.

    (5) Extent of corroboration, particularly of key details:

        (a) By documentation.

        (b) By other direct evidence, including photographic or audio/visual evidence.

        (c) By other witnesses.

        (d) By investigation.

    (6) Extent and type of contradictory information.

- Mere contract disputes or cost accounting disputes without more are not credible evidence of a violation.

- The filing of a *qui tam* action, standing alone, is not sufficient to establish that there is credible evidence of a violation. Conversely, the Government's decision not to intervene in a *qui tam* action is not dispositive of whether a contractor has credible evidence of a violation.

SECTION 3: CONTRACTOR OBLIGATIONS WITH RESPECT TO "PRINCIPALS"

I. INTRODUCTION

The Mandatory Disclosure Rule creates a new basis for either the suspension or debarment of a contractor for the knowing failure *by a principal* to timely disclose to the Government credible evidence of the specified misconduct or significant overpayments *known to the principal*. FAR 9.406-2 & 9.407-2.[39] In addition, the Rule requires that covered contractors establish internal control systems that make:

> Reasonable efforts not to include an individual *as a principal*, whom due diligence would have exposed as having engaged in conduct that is in conflict with the Contractor's code of business ethics and conduct.

FAR 52.203-13(c)(2)(ii)(B) (emphasis added).

This Section will address the meaning of "principals" and a contractor's obligations under the Rule with respect to its principals. This Section will provide general guidelines for determining who within a Contractor's organization falls within this definition of "principal," and will address some of the practical considerations to take into account in making this determination.

II. MEANING OF "PRINCIPAL"

The Rule provides the following definition of "principal," to apply throughout the FAR:

> Principal means an officer, director, owner, partner, or a person having primary management or supervisory responsibilities within a business entity (*e.g.*, general manager; plant manager; head of a subsidiary, division, or business segment; and similar positions).

---

[39] This provision is confusingly worded, but when read in context with the FAR payment clauses and the contract clause at FAR 52.203-13, it is clear that the suspension and debarment provisions should be interpreted as imposing the obligation to report on the contractor, not on the contractor's principals.

FAR 2.101(b)(2). A threshold consideration for every contractor under the Rule is determining which of its employees should be considered "principals." Neither the definition in the Rule nor the text of the Preamble provide clear guidance for determining who, exactly, is a principal.

The FAR Councils took the definition for "principal" from the existing definition of "principal" contained in the "Certification Regarding Responsibility Matters" at FAR 52.209-5.[40] Contractors are required to submit this certification along with their proposals in all procurements in excess of the simplified acquisition threshold. Consequently, the definition of principal is one that contractors have been grappling with for some time.

Nevertheless, the meaning of the definition is open to interpretation. The definition encompasses "a person with primary management or supervisory responsibilities within a business entity (*e.g.*, general manager; plant manager; head of a subsidiary, division, or business

---

[40] The Government-wide Debarment and Suspension (Nonprocurement) Rule (*i.e.*, the Common Rule) also contains a definition of Principal:

> The Principal means —
>
> (a) An officer, director, owner, partner, principal investigator, or other person within a participant with management or supervisory responsibilities related to a covered transaction; or
>
> (b) A consultant or other person, whether or not employed by the participant or paid with Federal funds, who —
>
> > (1) Is in a position to handle Federal funds;
> >
> > (2) Is in a position to influence or control the use of those funds; or,
> >
> > (3) Occupies a technical or professional position capable of substantially influencing the development or outcome of an activity required to perform the covered transaction.

2 C.F.R. § 180.995. On its face, the definition of principal used in the Mandatory Disclosure Rule (and the FAR) appears to be more limited than the Common Rule's definition of principal. However, because there is no evidence that the FAR Councils considered the Common Rule's definition of principal prior to using the definition of principal that already existed in the FAR at 52.209-5 ("Certification Regarding Responsibility Matters"), the interpretative value of the Common Rule's definition may be limited.

segment, and similar positions)." Does this mean that any employee with any supervisory responsibilities (even if only for one person) qualifies as a principal, or should only those employees who have "primary . . . supervisory responsibilities" be viewed as principals? Because the enumerated positions — general manager, plant manager, head of a subsidiary, etc. — are high-level positions, standard rules of statutory construction would suggest that an interpretation including every employee who supervises anyone is likely too broad.[41]

On the other hand, the Preamble to the Rule provides that "the Councils note that this definition should be interpreted broadly, and could include compliance officers or directors of internal audit, as well as other positions of responsibility." Appendix B, 73 Fed. Reg. at 67,079. This is the first time that the Councils have opined on the interpretation of principal, despite its long-standing existence in the FAR under FAR 52.209-5. However, while the Preamble may be relevant to the interpretation of the definition of principal, it cannot alter the written definition.[42]

---

[41] Alternatively, does the phrase "having primary management or supervisory responsibilities within a business entity" also modify "officer, director, owner, [or] partner" such that, for example, only officers who have primary management or supervisory responsibilities are principals? An Administrative Law Judge in the Department of Housing and Urban Development adopted such an interpretation, in dicta, of an earlier version of HUD Debarment and Suspension (Nonprocurement) Rule, 24 C.F.R. § 24.105. See In re Gonzales, HUDALJ 00-9165, 2002 WL 34228866 (HUD Jan. 22, 2002); see also United States v. Ali, 27 Fed. App. 728, No. 00-10165, (9th Cir. Oct. 2, 2001) (unpublished) ("operative definition of the term [principal in FAR 52.209-5] describes 'persons having primary management or supervisory responsibilities within a business entity.'"). However, the particular wording of the prior HUD Rule's definition may explain this interpretation and limit its applicability to the FAR definition.

[42] As explained in the Overview section of this Guide, the case law surrounding the issue of the weight that should be given to the Preamble is beyond the scope of this Guide. A recent Supreme Court case, however, gives some guidance. In *Wyeth v. Levine*, 129 S.Ct. 1187 (2009), the Court rejected a statement on the pre-emptive effect of an FDA regulation that was contained within the Preamble to the FDA's regulation. The Court noted (at 1201) that the Preamble was not subject to notice and comment rulemaking. Further, according to the Court, the Preamble is at odds with the evidence of Congress's purpose, and reverses the FDA's own longstanding position. Consequently, the Court accorded the FDA's statements in the Preamble no weight at all. *Id.* at 1203. *Wyeth*'s direct application may be limited here because Congress has been silent on the meaning of "principal," and although the definition is long-standing, the FAR Councils have not expressed a prior opinion. Nevertheless, *Wyeth* does serve as a helpful reminder that while the Preamble can provide helpful interpretive guidance, because the Preamble is not subject to notice and comment rulemaking, it cannot alter the definition contained in the body of the regulation.

In other words, a contractor employee who does not fit within the categories listed in the definition (*i.e.*, officer, director,[43] etc.) or a similar position cannot be transformed into a principal simply because the Preamble states the Rule "should be interpreted broadly."

Ultimately, contractors will need to identify principals in a way that is appropriate to their particular corporate structure.

III. PRACTICAL CONSIDERATIONS

The answer to the question of who is a principal will differ for every contractor because every contractor organization is structured differently. For some contractors, certain managers may be principals; for other contractors, managers in equivalent positions may not qualify as principals. Additionally, some employees may be principals not because of their supervisory responsibilities, but because they serve as officers of the contractor. While an interpretation that makes every supervisor a principal would minimize some after-the-fact questioning of the contractor, such an interpretation is not without risk. There are certain practical considerations that should be taken into account.

1. Whichever employees the contractor determines are covered by the definition of "principal" in the Rule are the same employees for whom the contractor must complete the "Certification Regarding Responsibility Matters" relating to suspension and debarment, certain

---

[43] However, it is not clear what is meant by the listed positions. For instance, does "director" refer to a member of the Board of Directors or someone with the managerial title of "Director"? Support can be found for both interpretations. In one matter, the HUD Board of Contract Appeals found the Director of the Patterson, New Jersey Department of Community Development to be a Principal based solely on her position as "Director." *In re: Jackson*, HUDBCA No. 05-K-112-D7, 2005 WL 3739729 (HUDBCA Oct. 13, 2005). On the other hand, the DOJ's Office of Legal Counsel ("OLC") has issued a series of opinions in the Government employee conflicts of interest arena that finds that the phrase "officer, director, trustee, general partner or employee" in 18 U.S.C. § 208 would prevent a federal employee from participating in a particular matter in which any entity on which she serves as a member of the Board of Directors has a financial interest. *See* Applicability of 18 U.S.C. § 208 to Proposed Appointment of Government Official to the Board of Connie Lee, 18 Op. Off. Legal Counsel 136 (1994); *see also* Op. Off. Legal Counsel, Financial Interests of Nonprofit Organizations (Jan. 11, 2006). While these OLC opinions do not interpret the definition of principal contained in the FAR, the positions covered in 18 U.S.C. § 208 and the FAR definition are quite similar.

tax delinquencies, and past or pending civil or criminal actions. *See* Appendix A, FAR 52.209-5. These certifications will also need to be updated annually in the Online Representations and Certifications Application database ("ORCA").

2. Whichever employees the contractor determines are covered by the definition of "principal" in the Rule are the same employees for whom the contractor, as part of its internal control system, must undertake reasonable efforts at due diligence prior to hiring (or promoting to a position as a principal) to ensure that these individuals have not engaged in conduct that is in conflict with the contractor's code of business ethics and conduct.

3. Although a contractor's obligations under the new suspension and debarment provision (and, thus, its "look-back" provision as well) are triggered by the knowledge of a principal, the contractor's disclosure obligations under the new contract clause (Appendix A, FAR 52.203-13) are not limited to misconduct known to the principal. Both the Rule and the Preamble explicitly limit the reach of the suspension and debarment provision and its look-back provision to misconduct or significant overpayments within the knowledge of the principal. *See* Appendix B, 73 Fed. Reg. at 67,076 ("The Councils concur that for suspension and debarment, a principal must have the requisite knowledge for mandatory disclosure to be applicable."); *id.* at 67,079 ("[t]he Councils . . . have revised [the suspension and debarment provisions] to make disclosure mandatory when a principal of the company has knowledge."). However, the contract clause requires a contractor to timely disclose to the OIG and the contracting officer (regardless of who has knowledge) whenever the contractor has credible evidence that a principal, employee, agent, or subcontractor has committed certain misconduct. In other words, the contractual disclosure obligation is not limited to misconduct within the knowledge of a principal.

4. While the new Rule has been appropriately described as a "sea change" in Government contracting, at least in the realm of suspension and debarment law, the Rule simply provides explicit notice of potential bases for suspension and debarment that, in large part, already existed. From a practical standpoint, the actions of a principal should create little additional exposure to adverse administrative action compared to what existed prior to the implementation of the Rule. The fraudulent, criminal, or other seriously improper conduct of principals, as well as many other individuals associated with a contractor, has long been a basis for imputing the improper conduct of the individual to the contractor. *See* Appendix A, FAR 9.406-5(a) ("The fraudulent, criminal, or other seriously improper conduct of any officer, director, shareholder, partner, employee, or other individual associated with a contractor may be imputed to the contractor when the conduct occurred in connection with the individual's performance of duties for or on behalf of the contractor, or with the contractor's knowledge, approval, or acquiescence."); FAR 9.407-5.

Thus, even prior to the Rule, if a principal knew of criminal misconduct, a violation of the False Claims Act, or a significant overpayment, but failed to act on such information, suspension and debarment officials could have concluded that the failure to act was of "so serious and compelling a nature that it affect[ed] present responsibility" and thereby created a basis for a debarment or suspension of the contractor and the principal. However, the Task Force is not aware of any cases where this interpretation has been applied.

5. It is important to note that the FAR does not mandate that a failure to timely disclose covered misconduct or significant overpayments known to a principal must result in an automatic suspension or debarment of the contractor or the principal. Rather, as has long been the case, the contractor's or principal's failure to disclose *may be* a cause for suspension or

debarment. Appendix A, FAR 9.406-1(a) ("[t]he existence of a cause for debarment, however, does not necessarily require that the contractor be debarred"); FAR 9.407-1(b)(2) ("[t]he existence of a cause for suspension does not necessarily require that the contractor be suspended"). The agency suspension and debarment official still must consider the "seriousness of the contractor's acts or omissions" and any "remedial measures or mitigating factors." FAR 9.406-1(a); FAR 9.407-1(b)(2).

SECTION 4: DISCLOSURES REGARDING SUBCONTRACTORS AND AGENTS

I. INTRODUCTION

The Mandatory Disclosure Rule has significant implications for subcontractors and agents, many of which find themselves subject to its provisions as a result of a flow-down provision that requires the new FAR clause to be included in all subcontracts valued in excess of $5 million that have a performance period of more than 120 days. The Rule also charges prime contractors with certain obligations related to the compliance of their subcontractors and agents with the provisions of the Rule. The Rule requires contractors:

- when they first determine that there is "credible evidence" of any violation of certain Federal criminal laws or of the civil False Claims Act, whether by their subcontractors or agents, to timely disclose the potential violation in writing both to the Contracting Officer and to the cognizant agency Office of Inspector General, FAR 52.203-13(b)(3)(i);[44]

- to establish and maintain an internal control system to detect, prevent, and disclose improper conduct in connection with the award or performance of a Government contract or subcontract, FAR 52.203-13(c)(2);[45]

- to maintain an on-going business ethics and compliance program that includes training their employees and, "as appropriate," training their agents and subcontractors on business ethics and compliance required under the Rule, FAR 52.203-13(c)(1)(ii)[46]; and

---

[44] Specifically, the FAR requires that: "The Contractor shall timely disclose, in writing, to the agency Office of the Inspector General (OIG), with a copy to the Contracting Officer, whenever, in connection with the award, performance, or closeout of this contract or any subcontract thereunder, the Contractor has evidence that a principal, employee, agent, or subcontractor of the Contractor has committed — (A) A violation of Federal criminal law involving fraud, conflict of interest, bribery, or gratuity violations found in Title 18 of the United States Code; or (B) A violation of the civil False Claims Act (31 U.S.C. 3729-3733)." FAR 52.203-13(b)(3)(i).

[45] This requirement does not apply to a contractor that has represented itself as a small business concern pursuant to the award of the contract or if the contract is for the acquisition of a commercial item as defined in FAR 2.101. See FAR 52.203-13(c).

[46] This requirement, likewise, does not apply to a contractor that has represented itself as a small business concern or to a commercial item contractor. See FAR 52.203-13(c).

- to include the substance of the Rule in all subcontracts with a value in excess of $5 million and a performance period of more than 120 days, FAR 52.203-13(d).

The Rule also provides that the prime contractor or subcontractor may be suspended or debarred for the knowing failure to make the mandatory disclosures identified above, including disclosures of subcontractor or agent wrongdoing, as well as for failing to disclose significant overpayments on a contract (other than overpayments resulting from contract financing payments as defined in FAR 32.001).

These new requirements bring into sharp focus the difficulties for a prime contractor when it is held responsible for the policies and training of, and for reporting the possible misconduct by, entities over which it does not exert direct control. With its flow-down provision, the Rule also imposes extensive obligations for ethics and compliance training, internal controls, and mandatory reporting directly on subcontractors, many of which may not have the existing infrastructure to comply with these new requirements. In the Preamble accompanying the Rule, the FAR Councils suggest that "[t]he same reasonable efforts the contractor may take to exclude from its organizational structure principals whom due diligence would have exposed as engaging in illegal acts are the same reasonable efforts the contractor should take in selecting its subcontractors." Appendix B, 73 Fed. Reg. at 67,084. However, the subcontractor and agent provisions quite probably will prove more complicated to implement than the FAR Councils have recognized.

As with the other provisions in the Rule, the provisions relating to subcontractors and agents raise many difficult questions of interpretation and application. The Preamble accompanying the Rule provides some guidance on these issues, but many open questions remain. This Section will highlight some of these questions and, where possible, provide practical guidance on possible approaches to resolving these issues.

II. KEY ISSUES RELATING TO SUBCONTRACTORS AND AGENTS

A. The Definition of "Subcontractor" or "Agent"

A threshold question for the subcontractor and agent provisions is definitional: Who qualifies as either a subcontractor or an agent under the Rule? Although the two categories of actors are grouped together in many of the provisions, they are, in fact, very different. Under the Rule, a subcontractor is "any supplier, distributor, vendor, or firm that furnishe[s] supplies or services to or for a prime contractor or another subcontractor." Appendix A, FAR 52.203-13(a). This definition suggests that a subcontractor is an entirely separate legal entity from the prime contractor, which interacts with the prime contractor through an independent, contractual relationship. Conversely, the Rule defines an agent as "any individual, including a director, an officer, an employee, or an independent Contractor, authorized to act on behalf of the organization." *Id.* In many instances, an agent will be an employee of the prime contractor. In all cases, the agent will be authorized to act on behalf of the organization. As a result, prime contractors have an obligation, irrespective of the new requirements, to take steps to ensure the compliance of their agents, whether or not the agent is an employee, with applicable laws and regulations.

Practically speaking, it will be easier for prime contractors to comply with the requirements as they relate to agents than as they apply to subcontractors. Because contractors exert greater control over their agents, often through a contractual employment relationship, it will be comparatively easy for them to conduct due diligence, to provide training, and to investigate any potentially reportable allegations of wrongdoing by agents that may arise. As described below, however, implementing these requirements with respect to subcontractors presents several practical challenges.

B. Verification of Subcontractor Codes, Compliance Programs, and Internal Controls

As discussed above, the Rule requires prime contractors to flow down the obligations of the Rule to their subcontractors in certain circumstances. The Preamble to the Rule provides:

> There is no requirement for the contractor to review or approve its subcontractors' ethics codes or internal control systems. Verification of the existence of such code and program can be part of the standard oversight that a contractor exercises over its subcontractors. The prime contractor is subject to debarment only if it fails to disclose known violations by the subcontractor.

Appendix B, 73 Fed. Reg. at 67,084. On its face, this guidance does not state that a contractor *must* verify the existence of its subcontractors' ethics codes and internal controls systems, but rather suggests that such verification *can* be part of the contractor's standard subcontract management. Moreover, the guidance indicates that a contractor has no obligation to review the adequacy of its subcontractors' codes and internal control systems. The Preamble and the Rule provide little insight, however, into the specific steps a contractor must take to ensure that it will later be considered by agency suspension and debarment officials or others to have acted reasonably in assuring implementation of the Rule by subcontractors.

As a practical matter, prime contractors may wish to provide written notice of the Rule's requirements, particularly to subcontractors that supply "commercial items" as defined at FAR Part 2.101 and to small business contractors, because neither of these types of businesses is likely to be as familiar with the obligations under the Rule as major subsystem suppliers. Prime contractors may also want to consider requiring certifications or representations that their subcontractors have the necessary ethics codes and internal controls and are in compliance with their obligations under the Rule. Because the Rule does not expressly require such certifications, however, subcontractors may be reluctant, or may even refuse, to provide such a certification. In these situations, prime contractors will need to reach an agreement with their subcontractors as to what information the subcontractors will be willing to provide to permit the prime contractors to fulfill their obligations under the Rule.

It is possible that the only stage at which a contractor will have the leverage to obtain verification is before it has selected a subcontractor. A prudent strategy, therefore, might be to require a certification as part of a subcontractor's bid submission. Because the Rule does not require a subcontractor to have the written code of ethics or internal controls systems until after contract award, however, post-award follow-up activities may be required by the prime contractor. Prime contractors should expect resistance at any stage from subcontractors whose only involvement in the Government procurement process is through sales of commercial item supplies or services to customers that happen to be federal prime contractors or subcontractors. Many of these companies will be surprised by these new requirements and may react negatively to requests for verifications of their codes of business conduct and ethics and internal controls.

Another question raised by the new Rule is whether there may be situations in which a contractor's reliance on a certification from a subcontractor is not enough. The Rule does not obligate contractors to do a qualitative analysis of a subcontractor's ethics program. But what if public reports or information from private sources suggest to a contractor that a current or prospective subcontractor's compliance program is inadequate? Is the mere existence of a signed certification, in the face of evidence that a compliance program is sub-par, enough to satisfy a contractor's duty under the Rule with regard to its subcontractors? Although the Rule and the Preamble do not address this scenario, contractors should be on notice of these risks. A contractor on notice of potential deficiencies in a subcontractor's compliance program may want to take steps to ensure the subcontractor's program is brought into compliance. Such steps might include informing the subcontractor of the potential deficiencies in its code or internal controls;

informing the subcontractor of a potential contract noncompliance that might suggest such deficiencies; and requiring the subcontractor to respond adequately. Such steps might help the contractor demonstrate its present responsibility.

C. Obligation to Train Subcontractors and Agents "As Appropriate"

The Rule requires that prime contractors provide to their agents and subcontractors, "as appropriate," the training they conduct under their business ethics awareness and compliance program and internal control system. Appendix A, FAR 52.203-13 ("The training conducted under this program shall be provided to the Contractor's principals and employees, and as appropriate, the Contractor's agents and subcontractors."). Neither the Rule nor the Preamble, however, contains guidance on when such training is "appropriate" or how contractors could effectively or efficiently train their lower-tier subcontractors. Periodic and practical training on a prime contractor's business ethics awareness and internal controls "standards and procedures" may not translate readily to subcontractors with different internal control models. There may be different standards of conduct in a subcontractor's written code of conduct, different channels to report violations of that code, and different means of investigating alleged violations of that code.

Though compliant with the spirit and letter of the Rule, a company's internal control system may vary by the adopting company's type, size, and degree of complexity. Suggesting that prime contractors provide "generic" training across what could be a very diverse pool of suppliers presents significant challenges. Without a doubt, prime contractors should train and certify their agents, who may be employees and who, by definition, are authorized to act on behalf of the organization. It is less clear, however, when it is appropriate for a prime contractor to provide training to its subcontractors, particularly given the considerations above. The discretionary nature of the requirement suggests that the Councils intended to impose a different training burden for different companies. If this is the case, prime contractors must determine what factors to consider when determining whether a subcontractor should be required to participate in the prime contractor's training program.

Large contractors, which may at times be primes and at other times subcontractors, would have training programs of their own and training imposed by another contractor would be unwelcome. Small businesses and commercial item suppliers, on the other hand, are exempt from the Rule's requirement to have formal training programs and internal controls systems.[47] It therefore may be appropriate and cost effective for a prime contractor to provide a standard training module only to a narrow segment of subcontractors that are neither too large nor too small and that lack formal training programs. Although some businesses may welcome such training from a prime contractor, others may not wish to expend the labor hours necessary for their employees to complete the training. Subcontractors that do business with multiple major prime contractors may face training requirements from multiple companies with which they contract. In such situations, must a subcontractor submit to the training programs of each prime contractor for which it is a requirement? And, if they do, what happens when the training programs of various prime contractors reflect differing philosophies or provide conflicting information?

Prime contractors may wish simply to ask their subcontractors whether they need assistance with training on the new FAR provision rather than requiring their participation in training. A contractor could offer resources, including an express offer of assistance with training, on the form it uses to ensure that its subcontractors are in compliance with the ethics

---

[47] Appendix A, FAR 52.203-13(c). The formal training and internal control systems requirements are inapplicable to small businesses, and the disclosure requirement is limited to known violations of federal criminal laws involving fraud, conflict of interest, bribery, or gratuity violations found in Title 18 of the U.S. Code, and violations of the False Claims Act.

and internal controls requirements.[48] Because the Rule contains the "as appropriate" qualifier, simply offering training, and allowing subcontractors to decide whether to take advantage of that offer, may be a practical way to comply with the Rule.

D. Other Obligations a Contractor May Want to Impose on Its Subcontractors

The Rule and the Preamble do not provide guidance concerning when it is appropriate for a subcontractor to inform a prime contractor of a potential violation. Prime contractors may want to consider requiring that their subcontractors notify them immediately of any potential problems to enable them to weigh in on the credible evidence determination. Because this may be met with resistance from subcontractors, prime contractors that wish to impose such a requirement should consider introducing it at the bid stage, when they have leverage over potential subcontractors. Prime contractors also should consider whether they want to require audit or investigation rights in their contracts with subcontractors. Doing so is not without significant risks, however, as the more involved a prime contractor becomes in a subcontractor's internal affairs, the more responsibility the Government is likely to find that the prime contractor has for that subcontractor's misconduct. Further, many subcontractors will balk at providing expanded audit rights to prime contractors. Regardless of what approach a contractor decides to take, each party must be careful to avoid any appearance of inviting collusion on nondisclosure.

E. Mandatory Reporting Requirements

The mandatory reporting requirements effected under the Rule include an obligation for prime contractors to report credible evidence of specified violations by their subcontractors and

---

[48] Prime contractors will also need to factor these costs into their cost proposals, especially for firm fixed price contracts.

agents.[49] In fact, a prime contractor faces possible debarment if it fails to disclose known violations by its subcontractor. This requirement raises questions about the "credible evidence" standard as it applies to subcontractors and the potential for liability arising from erroneous disclosures.

F. Implications of the "Credible Evidence" Standard and Potential Liability for Erroneous Reports

A key issue presented by the Mandatory Disclosure Rule as it relates to subcontractors is the "credible evidence" standard.[50] The Councils' decision to adopt this elevated standard resulted from their recognition of the practical need for contractors to "take some time for preliminary examination of the evidence to determine its credibility before deciding to disclose to the government." Appendix B, 73 Fed. Reg. at 67,063 ("This revision provides to the contractor sufficient opportunity to take reasonable steps to determine the credibility of any possible disclosure prior to disclosing it to the agency Inspector General and contracting officer."). It may be difficult, however, for a prime contractor to conduct the "preliminary examination" contemplated by the standard into alleged wrongdoing at a subcontractor. Prime contractors have only a small window, at best, into the inner working of their subcontractors, who are under no obligation to cooperate with an investigation by their prime contractors into allegations of wrongdoing. Without access to documents or employees, it may be difficult for a

---

[49] Specifically, the Rule requires prime contractors to timely disclose to the contracting agency's Office of Inspector General (providing a copy to the contracting officer) whenever, in connection with the award, performance, or closeout of a Government contract, the contractor has "credible evidence" that an agent or subcontractor has committed a violation of federal criminal law involving fraud, conflict of interest, bribery, or improper gratuity violations found in Title 18 of the U.S. Code, or a violation of the civil False Claims Act (31 U.S.C. §§ 3729-3733). This disclosure requirement applies until three years after final payment on the contract.

[50] The Rule does not define the term "credible evidence" but, as discussed in detail in Section 2 of this Guide, the FAR Councils made clear that the term is intended to be a higher standard than the "reasonable grounds to believe" standard initially included in the proposed regulations.

prime contractor to develop additional evidence, so the contractor may have to make a "credible evidence" determination based on very limited information.

Even though a contractor is not required by the Rule to make a disclosure absent credible evidence, the threat of debarment may counsel in favor of reporting alleged violations even where an investigation to determine whether there is credible evidence is practically impossible. There also may be situations where a contractor is contractually obligated or may feel ethically obliged to make a report, separate and apart from the Mandatory Disclosure Rule. For example, a prime contractor may become aware of alleged wrongdoing or other potential problems at a subcontractor through an anonymous letter or whistleblower complaint, or may learn of a quality issue with a subcontractor's products or services. In each of these scenarios, a prime contractor may lack the ability to investigate sufficiently to determine whether the evidence is credible, but it may still be appropriate for the contractor to alert the Government of the potential wrongdoing. Because there is no "good faith" safe harbor in the Rule, however, a prime contractor that makes such a disclosure may face significant liability if the allegations prove false.

The Councils fail to address adequately the risk of liability for erroneous disclosures inherent in a mandatory disclosure scheme. In response to concerns raised about this issue during the comment period, the Councils state that "the potential for erroneous disclosure is minimized by requiring the contractor to disclose only credible evidence of violations, thereby reducing the contractor's potential liability for damages associated with erroneously disclosing alleged violations which are not substantiated." Appendix B, 73 Fed. Reg. at 67,084. However, in many circumstances, ascertaining what is credible evidence is less than self-evident. Faced with the potential for debarment or with civil False Claims Act suits by the Government alleging reckless disregard on the one hand, and the potential of significant liability to the subcontractor if a disclosure is erroneous on the other hand, prime contractors must navigate their obligations carefully. Even prior to the Mandatory Disclosure Rule, contractors faced suits for defamation and economic harm resulting from erroneous disclosures. The threat of debarment, and the pressure this will put on contractors to make disclosures, only heightens this risk.

G. Subcontractor Disclosure to the Government

The Rule and the Preamble make clear that subcontractors need not make disclosures through prime contractors. Rather, all subcontractor mandatory disclosures should be directed to the agency OIG, with a copy to the contracting officer. Appendix A, FAR 52.203-13(d); Appendix B, 73 Fed. Reg. at 67,084. This may result in a "double disclosure" of the same conduct by both the prime contractor and the subcontractor, a result which some OIGs believe to be both logical and acceptable.

Nothing in the Rule or the Preamble indicates that a subcontractor is obligated to notify the prime contractor when it makes a disclosure to the Government. However, there may be contractual provisions that would on their face obligate a subcontractor to provide notice to a prime contractor of communications with the Government concerning matters pertaining to the subcontract. There may also be circumstances in which the subcontractor believes such notice to the prime contractor would be inappropriate or impermissible. For example, the principal of a subcontractor may have credible evidence that its employee has made an improper payment to the prime contractor's buyer in order to obtain business for the subcontractor, and reports the violation to the Contracting Officer of the prime contract and to the agency OIG. The prime contractor does not know of this violation or of the subcontractor's report of the violation. Is it permissible and appropriate for the subcontractor to notify the prime contractor that it has made such disclosure after its disclosure to the Government? What about before its disclosure to the Government? The subcontractor may feel the need to do so to maintain its relationship with the prime contractor, but the Government may feel that such disclosure to the prime will impede its investigation of the matter. One possible source of action would be for the subcontractor to contact the relevant OIG for guidance in such a situation.

A parallel issue is the permissibility of prime contractors informing subcontractors when they make disclosures of alleged subcontractor wrongdoing. In many cases, subcontractors will be aware of the issue as a result of a prime contractor's efforts to investigate the allegations of wrongdoing. It is unclear, however, whether the Government would object to a prime contractor notifying a subcontractor of its intent to disclose the allegations to the Government or, later, of the fact that a disclosure has been made. Again, one possible course of action would be for the prime contractor to contact the relevant OIG for guidance.

III. BEST PRACTICES FOR IMPLEMENTING SUBCONTRACTOR AND AGENT PROVISIONS

- As a threshold matter, companies must determine whether the new rules are applicable to them. Many subcontractors that previously were exempt from FAR requirements, such as those that do not sell directly to the Government or that sell only commercial items or services, will now find themselves subject to at least some of the new provisions. Similarly, prime contractors should bear in mind the applicability of these rules to this broader category of subcontractors.

- Any company subject to the new Rule needs to review its code of business conduct and ethics to determine whether its code meets the regulatory requirements. Subcontractors that do not have written codes will need to draft and implement them. Subcontractors with training programs and internal control systems will need to review and update them to incorporate the mandatory disclosure and full cooperation requirements.

- Contractors may wish to provide written notice of the Rule's requirements to their subcontractors, particularly to commercial item suppliers and small business contractors, who may not be as familiar with their obligations under the Rule.

- Contractors may need to develop a system for verifying their subcontractors' codes of business conduct and internal controls. They may wish to develop a certification or representation form to provide to their subcontractors that requires confirmation that the subcontractors are in full compliance with the FAR's requirements. Alternatively, they may wish to include verification in their bid solicitations.

- Contractors will need to evaluate to which of their subcontractors they should provide or offer their training, if any. Such training may be appropriate in situations where subcontractor personnel are performing on the prime contractor's or Government's site. Contractors also should be alert to subcontractors that, because of their status as a small business or a commercial item supplier, may be exempt from the requirement of having their own training programs.

- Contractors will need to ensure that FAR 52.203-13 is flowed down to subcontractors in all future contracts and to existing subcontractors when the new clause is added by a modification to an existing contract.[51]

---

[51] We do not address the situation where a subcontractor rejects a request to modify the subcontract even though the Government has modified the prime contract. However, prime contractors are advised to consider this possibility before agreeing to the Government's request to modify, especially with sole source or specially qualified subcontractors.

SECTION 5: OBTAINING INFORMATION REGARDING POTENTIALLY REPORTABLE EVENTS

I. INTRODUCTION

While FAR clause 52.203-13, Contractor Code of Business Ethics and Conduct, and the related provisions in FAR Part 9 imply that contractors must have controls in place to assure timely identification and investigation of potentially reportable events, neither the Mandatory Disclosure Rule nor its Preamble explicitly advise Government contractors how to accomplish this objective. This Section of the Guide explores best practices in this area that are designed to assure that counsel and, as appropriate, compliance personnel are informed of potentially reportable events in a manner that facilitates their expeditious and appropriate resolution.

II. KEY CONCEPTS AND BEST PRACTICES

In order to ensure compliance with the Mandatory Disclosure Rule, the contractor must be aware of all potentially reportable events ("PREs") that occur. Regardless of size, type, or industry, Government contractors must have internal controls in place to allow a competent and dedicated individual or group to capture all PREs and ensure that all such events are properly logged, investigated, evaluated, and disclosed to the Government as appropriate. Of course, the result of such reporting and investigations may prompt the organization to take other actions, including but not limited to remedial corrective action, disciplinary action, and changes in process.

In considering whether existing controls are adequate to meet this objective or whether additional controls may be needed, a contractor must first candidly evaluate the capabilities and effectiveness of any existing controls or compliance program. The following questions should be considered when evaluating the adequacy of an internal control system:

- Does the entity have a code of conduct in place?
- Does the entity have a hotline?
- What other reporting mechanisms are in place?
- Does the entity have a Compliance Officer?
- What training is conducted regarding business ethics and internal reporting?
- What happens to reports of PREs?
- Is there a consistent response for investigating PREs?
- Are the investigation results, corrective actions and recommendations documented?
- How does the entity ensure that instances of noncompliance are reported?
- To whom are they reported?
- How does the entity ensure that PREs are elevated to an appropriate person?
- Would existing controls be sufficient to support a determination of lack of credible evidence and nondisclosure to the Government? This question is perhaps the most important consideration in determining whether existing controls are adequate.

See also Section 13 regarding Internal Control Systems. When making this assessment, entities should consider that research conducted by the Compliance and Ethics Leadership Council showed that approximately 50% of observed misconduct is never reported by employees and 60% of the information that is reported to managers by their employees is not elevated for further investigation.

Equally alarming is the fact that the primary reason for failure to elevate compliance concerns is that managers do not know what to do with a noncompliance matter that is reported. Managers who attempt to resolve the issue themselves may compromise compliance with other obligations, such as identifying the root cause of the problem or the issuance of appropriate disciplinary action. These statistics underscore that many corporations may not have an effective compliance reporting mechanism or an effective compliance program.

After the Task Force canvassed an ad hoc sample of Government contractors, including large and small companies, defense contractors, health care companies, commercial item companies, and companies that sell both services and products, a few consistent themes emerged in terms of best practices for the reporting of internal PREs. In this context, "best practice" is defined by a process that:

- significantly increases the likelihood of issues being detected and appropriately reported and resolved;

- operates in a timely and resource efficient manner; and

- enables an entity to defend itself against allegations of failing to address a reported noncompliance.

A review of best practices indicates that the following processes should be considered for compliance with the Mandatory Disclosure Rule:

1. All employees are provided a clear definition, in terms that non-lawyers can understand, of what constitutes noncompliant conduct.

2. All employees are informed of their personal obligation to identify and report instances of potentially noncompliant conduct.

3. The personal obligation is disseminated through written/electronic communication, explained and reinforced through training, and refreshed through periodic communication from an appropriate source within the company (*e.g.*, Compliance Officer, staff meetings, bulletins, newsletters, company, or division management).

4. Multiple avenues for reporting noncompliance are made available to employees. These include a hotline, an individual's manager, the legal department, a compliance officer or organization, and/or internal audit. Employees are more likely to report matters of noncompliance when they have multiple avenues.

5. Managers are informed of their responsibility to act upon all instances of reported potential noncompliance in a timely manner. Managers should be trained on what this means, *i.e.*, reporting the PRE to designated

contacts as soon as possible to assure that the PRE is acted upon appropriately. Internal reporting must be done in a timely manner to assure the investigation is not compromised.

6. Meaningful, periodic, subject matter-appropriate training on regulatory, legal, and ethical requirements is essential to the functioning of the reporting process. Without such training (and associated procedures), individuals are unlikely to recognize non-compliant practices. Furthermore, the training is often a source of questions about noncompliant activities. Trainers should be alert for this possibility and ensure that questions regarding potential noncompliant activity are referred to the appropriate individual or group for follow-up.

7. A hotline is essential, as there will be some individuals who will not be comfortable reporting potential noncompliance directly to their management or the legal department. Some individuals will only report if they are assured of anonymity.

8. The company should have a clear policy that prohibits retaliation against any employee who reports a PRE or participates in an internal investigation. An explanation of the policy should be included in training.

9. All allegations of noncompliance should be reported into a single location, if possible, but no more than two locations. This could be a designated point of contact in the legal department, *i.e.*, the investigation section, or internal audit or compliance functions. If an entity is small, outside counsel could serve as the point person for evaluating these reports.

10. All reported PREs should be captured in some form of registry or log. The log should be controlled by the single point of contact and contain only the essential information necessary to track the status of a PRE investigation. A designated individual or group of individuals should be responsible for the review, triage, and resolution of all reported PREs.

11. Information on potential noncompliances from all reporting avenues should be added to the registry or log as appropriate. Potential sources include internal audits, results of testing and monitoring, periodic surveys or self-assessments, and internal certifications. This assures that all items, regardless of source, are tracked, evaluated, and resolved. It also facilitates the identification of trends and root causes. Not all audit findings or testing and monitoring results will be appropriate to include in the registry or log, but all such results or reports should be reviewed to determine whether any findings rise to the level that they should be reported as potential noncompliance. Experience has shown that many companies do not follow up and resolve audit findings in the same manner as they do other allegations of noncompliance or unethical conduct.

12. The review or triage process should be undertaken with frequency to assure that PREs receive a preliminary review in a timely manner. This review should be led by counsel. The review or triage process may result in some PREs being handled under the attorney-client privilege, whereas others may be returned to the business units or HR departments for further factfinding. The escalation and reporting process is designed to capture all instances of potential noncompliance and assure their appropriate resolution. Other processes for handling certain types of complaints may operate in parallel.

13. The status of all PREs should be reviewed on a periodic basis to assure that all are moving forward in a timely manner. Resolution of all matters should be appropriately documented.

These best practices must be tailored to the size and existing compliance protocols in place at an entity.

III. SOURCES OF INFORMATION FOR POTENTIALLY REPORTABLE EVENTS

Prudent Government contractors monitor all of the possible sources within their organization for PREs. The variety and range of sources that should be monitored naturally depend on an entity's unique structure and internal controls. In smaller organizations, the sources of PREs may be fewer in number, while in larger organizations there will be additional sources that should be monitored.

Regardless of the extent of a company's internal controls, for purposes of compliance with the Rule, contractors must be confident that all allegations of noncompliance are identified and acted upon in a timely manner. This means that companies and their management should be reviewing reports characterized as personnel complaints, quality issues, audit findings, and even compliance program "gaps" to determine whether there are issues that potentially could trigger a disclosure under the Rule upon further investigation. For example, complaints to an HR department may be based on charges of retaliation, but the retaliation claim may relate to underlying assertions of noncompliance with a policy, law, or regulation.

In most organizations, the greatest source of information about potential noncompliance is likely to be employees or their managers who identify concerns and raise them in the ordinary course of business. Whether a company is able to capture and appropriately handle the issues raised through these informal channels and whether an entity uses all of the information available to it to identify compliance trends are significant factors in the effectiveness of an entity's compliance program.

A. Employees' Role in the Reporting Process

Employees engaged in performing work on Government contracts or other Government funded activities are frequent sources of information related to potential noncompliant activity. Employees often have direct visibility to actions being taken on a contract or in connection with a contract.

1. Clear Definition of Noncompliant Conduct

If contractor employees are to be responsible for reporting instances of noncompliant conduct to company management or compliance officers, those employees must have a good understanding of what constitutes noncompliant conduct. It is not sufficient simply to tell employees that they must report whenever they have credible evidence of potential violations of the civil False Claims Act or those provisions of Title 18 of the United States Code relating to fraud, conflict of interest, bribery, or gratuities. Laypersons are unlikely to understand such legalistic terms, nor would it appear to be useful to attempt to educate thousands of lay person employees about the meaning of terms such as "credible evidence." Rather, guidance to employees regarding reportable conduct should be framed in terms of the principles enunciated in the contractor's code of ethics and conduct and by the contractor's contractual and other legal obligations.

Any guidance to employees should begin by defining reportable conduct as conduct inconsistent with the contractor's code of ethics and business conduct. Such conduct will likely be broader in scope than the conduct that the contractor is required to disclose by the Mandatory Disclosure Rule. Nevertheless, contractor employees should not be asked or expected to distinguish between violations of the contractor's code of ethics that are required to be disclosed to the Government and those that are not. Rather, employees should be encouraged to report to management or the contractor's compliance organization *any* conduct that they believe potentially fails to comply with the contractor's code of ethics and conduct.

The same is true of conduct that the employee believes may fail to comply with the contractor's statutory, regulatory, or contractual obligations. Compliance with such obligations may already be part of the contractor's code of ethics and conduct; to the extent it is not, employees should be expressly instructed to report instances of failure to comply with such obligations. Employees should not be asked to report only certain types of contractual or statutory violations (*i.e.*, violations of the civil False Claims Act or the fraud-related provisions of Title 18), as such instructions would only create confusion.

Finally, while employees should not be asked to decide what conduct could give rise to a mandatory disclosure obligation under the Rule, providing specific examples of such conduct may make employees more likely to report it. The following are illustrations of the types of conduct that employees could be instructed that they should report:

- Labor mischarging (*e.g.*, charging time to Government contracts or indirect cost accounts that was not actually spent on the activities described).

- False statements or certifications.

- Falsification of documents.

- Delivery of nonconforming product/product substitution.

- Failure to perform required testing.
- Soliciting, offering, receiving, or paying kickbacks.
- Conflicts of interest.
- Price reduction not extended to the Government (Schedule Contractors).
- Theft or misuse of Government property.
- Fraudulent SBA 8(a) certification.
- Failure to credit or return overpayments received from the Government.

This list is not intended to be exhaustive. Contractors may wish to tailor these examples to get their particular lines of business, Government contracts, and/or compliance experience.

The Task Force has created a representative "template" for contractors to consider using to notify employees of their internal reporting obligations. *See* Appendix P. In addition, the Defense Industry Initiative has also created a draft notice to employees concerning "Internally Reportable Events" (as an attachment to a document describing the Mandatory Disclosure Rule. *See* Appendix Q. Before using either of these documents, contractors should tailor them to reflect their own particular needs, and should seek legal advice.

2. Policies and Training in Functional Areas

One component of an effective internal control system for capturing concerns from employees is to establish a formal reporting mechanism that requires employees to identify and escalate their concerns about suspected noncompliant matters. For a reporting policy to be effective, it is critical that employees be informed of what constitutes compliant conduct for their particular job function. This is best accomplished through issuance of clear policies and procedures for each functional area, supplemented with periodic training.

Some training is likely to be widely applicable throughout an organization, such as that related to a code of conduct. Other training will be job specific. Without such policies and training, employees will be unable to identify misconduct or noncompliances, or may confuse compliant behavior as noncompliant.

3. "Reporting Up," or Escalation Policy and Procedure

In addition to functional area policies, processes, and training, a critical step in ensuring compliance is establishing a policy that requires employees to report all instances of potential noncompliance. This should cover reporting instances of observed misconduct as well as instances of misconduct in which the employee may have some role. Such policies may be referred to as "speaking-up" policies or "escalation policies."

Alternatively, a policy statement requiring that employees "speak up" or escalate issues of potential noncompliance may be embedded in other standards of business conduct or an entity's code of conduct. The critical issue here is that in some form or another, employees understand that they must ensure that potential noncompliant activity is escalated to the appropriate point of contact for further review.

Employees should be advised of all available internal reporting channels. These channels may include: (1) legal counsel; (2) compliance officers; (3) ethics officers; (4) human resources representatives; (5) managers; and (6) anonymous hotlines. Providing multiple reporting channels increases the likelihood that PREs will be reported and investigated. However, contractors should consider designating legal counsel as the primary recipients of reports in order to preserve the privileged nature of the communication, and also to avoid delays in the triage process. In implementing the internal reporting process, companies should consider available resources and train managers to receive and elevate reports in a timely manner. *See* Section B.2 below.

The review or triage process may result in some reports being treated as sensitive matters that are investigated under the attorney-client privilege, while others may be turned over to the HR or compliance departments for completion of fact finding.

Employees must be advised that they are obligated to report potentially noncompliant matters through one of the designated reporting avenues. They should also be advised that they are *not* to undertake their own investigation or comprehensive factfinding, except when there may be extenuating circumstances, such as a situation creating an immediate physical or security hazard. For some entities this will be a cultural shift. Companies may want to consider requiring reporting within a certain number of days after a concern arises to ensure that employees don't unnecessarily delay reporting. The rationale for this approach is to avoid compromising any subsequent investigation or the ability to issue appropriate disciplinary action.

All too often employees take matters into their own hands to resolve issues. When this occurs, disciplinary actions may be overlooked, documentation needed to support an HR action may not be created, patterns of incorrect or inappropriate conduct may not be detected, and root causes may not be identified or corrected. Training provided to employees in connection with the dissemination of the escalation or reporting policy should explain why employees are directed not to undertake comprehensive factfinding.

4. Employees May Engage in a Preliminary Discussion With Their Line Management

In many situations it will be appropriate for a lower level employee, such as an analyst, to report a matter to the employee's direct line management and possibly to collect some readily available data or documents to facilitate a discussion of the issue. The distinction is that more inexperienced or junior personnel often do not have the substantive expertise to distinguish between a potential noncompliance, meaning an activity that may be a violation of law, regulation, a contract clause, or company policy, and a factual situation that is contemplated in the ordinary course of business, such as preliminary billing rates which are adjusted as a routine matter.

Within most organizations, it is appropriate for individuals to raise issues of potential noncompliance with their direct line management to discuss whether the facts being raised are accurate and there is a potential compliance issue. If the individual or management believe there is still a potential or actual noncompliance at the conclusion of such a discussion, the matter should be escalated. This means that if the management believes there is no problem, yet the individual remains convinced that there is a problem, the employee should escalate the matter through available channels.

5. Techniques for Encouraging Employees to Report Misconduct

Once employees have been advised of and trained on an escalation policy, reports of alleged noncompliance will likely become more frequent. However, it is important to continually reinforce the internal reporting obligation to employees. This can be done through reminder communications related to the escalation policy and periodic communications related to specific high risk areas that affect the company or a functional area. Below are a few examples of communications to consider:

- Periodic communications relating to the requirements for properly completing timesheets, what would be considered mischarging, and the obligation to report mischarges.

- Periodic communications to individuals in sales and marketing functions who may interact with Government employees and officials reinforcing the rules related to gratuities, conflicts of interest, and employment restrictions imposed on former Government officials.

- Reminders of the obligation and avenues to report any misconduct.

6. Self-Reporting

Often employees are reluctant to report noncompliant conduct in which they may have been involved, or which they had a responsibility to oversee. Employees should be advised that it is better to self-report than to become the subject of someone else's allegation.

7. Non-Retaliation Policy

Non-retribution against reporting parties should be stressed. Companies should have formal non-retaliation policies and mandate training for management. For example, managers may not appreciate that giving an employee "the silent treatment" after the individual reports a concern might give rise to an allegation of retaliation.

At the same time, employees should be advised that speaking up will not necessarily insulate an individual from disciplinary action if the individual was involved in or responsible for the misconduct. It may, however, impact the quality or nature of any resulting disciplinary action. Companies may not want to make any promises in this regard.

8. Maintain Confidentiality or Anonymity for Reported Misconduct to the Extent Feasible and Appropriate

Some individuals will be more comfortable coming forward with a concern if their identity will not be shared with the target of any resulting investigation. While it is advisable that companies maintain the confidentiality of the identity of individuals reporting misconduct, individuals should be advised that absolute confidentiality may not be feasible during the course of an investigation in all instances.

B. Managers' Role in the Reporting Process

This section on managers as a source of reports of potential noncompliance should be viewed together with the prior subsection on employees. Managers should be held accountable for the following:

- Abiding by their individual obligation to follow the reporting or escalation policy for PREs. Managers should report PREs to designated contacts within the organization as soon as possible to enable them to act on them as necessary in a timely manner.

- Encouraging employees to speak up about their concerns.

- Responding appropriately to employee reports or concerns, which may mean escalating those concerns. This responsibility often receives little attention. Companies should strongly consider including language in their code of conduct that expressly communicates the company's expectations for managers in regard to receiving and managing employee concerns.

Companies should implement these protocols through a prepared tool for managers, such as a guide for handling reports of misconduct, or mandating training in this area when an individual first is given supervisory responsibilities.

1. Encouraging Employees to Speak Up

Managers should create an environment that encourages employees to raise questions and concerns. To accomplish this, managers may benefit from understanding why employees engage in misconduct. Many times employees are under the misconception that their conduct is desirable because the outcome will curry favor with an influential person in the organization. For example, they may believe that management expects the inappropriate conduct as a means of achieving a particular goal, such as maximizing revenue. Employees may also be afraid of what might happen if they do not engage in the misconduct. Finally, employees may believe the misconduct is either standard practice in their company or the industry, or that the misconduct will advance their career. An entity's code of conduct should be clear that these instances of misconduct represent misconceptions about what is expected within the company.

There are some general tips that managers should consider in connection with establishing an effective "speaking up" policy:

- Make sure employees understand what is, and is not, expected of them. This includes understanding how to perform their jobs properly and the laws and policies relating to their area. This also means making sure that employees understand that they are expected to perform in compliance with a company's code of conduct and to report noncompliant conduct.

- Recognize that it takes courage to speak up and value this courage.

- Find opportunities to demonstrate the importance of ethics and compliance, and seek ways to discuss these issues at staff meetings and other group functions.

- Recognize that how you say something is as influential as what you say.

- Recognize that how managers handle reports of misconduct is critical to the likelihood of receiving future reports of misconduct. Word travels fast when employees feel that managers are not addressing their concerns appropriately.

- Do not retaliate and do not tolerate retaliation by others. Employees who fear retaliation for raising allegations of misconduct are more likely to report their concerns to the Government or other organizations. This may result in a problem becoming more significant than if the problem was addressed early on. It may also result in damage to a company's reputation, problems with regulators, and expensive legal action.

2. Training Managers on How to Handle Employee Concerns

In addition to the general concepts above, a highly valuable tool for improving the likelihood that employees will speak up and that managers will appropriately act on reported misconduct is to create a guideline for the managers regarding what to do when they receive a report of misconduct. The following provides some possibilities to be considered for such a guideline for managers.

- When a concern is raised, abide by the following:

    - Show respect and care to employees who raise concerns;

    - Address concerns promptly;

    - Acknowledge every report made. Address employees' concerns as to the status of a reported matter, even though the response may be limited in substance due to sensitive issues or privilege issues. For example, the response may be as limited as: "the investigation is proceeding, closure is targeted for [date]"; and

- Avoid retaliation by continuing to communicate normally with employees who raise concerns, continuing to provide meaningful assignments, and sharing information needed for the employees to get their work done.

- When meeting with an employee to discuss a complaint, adhere to the following:

  - Provide privacy;

  - Give the employee your full attention;

  - Acknowledge (thank) the employee for having the courage to come forward;

  - Be prepared to answer questions the employee may ask, such as how long the investigation will take and what will happen next;

  - Listen actively and remain objective while the employee reports the facts. Do not cast doubt on the employee's version of the facts while they are being presented;

  - Take notes. This demonstrates your attention and your seriousness to the issue. It also avoids reliance on your memory when it comes time to evaluate whether the matter needs to be escalated in accordance with the company's policies and procedures;

  - Ask open-ended and probative questions (who, what, when, where and why);

  - Watch your manner, including body language, facial expression, and tone of voice;

  - Clearly identify and agree on the concern or allegation;

  - Avoid objecting during the discussion;

  - Determine what efforts the employee has already taken to report the concern, such as to a supervisor; and

  - Advise the employee to retain all documentation related to the allegation, including email.

- When concluding a meeting with an employee, take the following steps:

  - Explain the next steps in the process to the employee as stated in the company's escalation policy or procedure. Be cautious not to commit to any action that the employee is seeking, such as discipline of a colleague, because any actions may require further investigation and because of privacy concerns; and

- Explain the importance of confidentiality to the employee. Ask the employee not to speak to anyone about the matter, aside from any subsequent participation in the investigation.

- After a discussion with an employee on an allegation of noncompliance:

  - After reviewing the matter, act in accordance with the company's procedures for escalation. If applicable, forward all relevant information to the appropriate point of contact in the organization;

  - Thereafter, respond as directed by the legal or compliance officer; and

  - Keep all information confidential unless directed by counsel to handle the information in a different manner.

3. Consistent Application of Company Policies and Procedures

In applying the above guidelines, companies should ensure consistent application of policies and procedures, *i.e.*, no special treatment for individuals who may be in senior positions or who are viewed as highly valuable to the company. Company policies often are developed with the line employees in mind, including sales representatives, individuals who charge their time on a timesheet, or quality personnel. Training also tends to be targeted largely at these audiences.

However, research shows that this approach to training and awareness is poorly considered. The research shows that a large percentage of violations involve management, including senior management. These are the individuals who may be perceived to know what compliance is, to behave in a compliant manner, or in some cases, to be above the chain of compliance in an organization. While management, and senior executives especially, may have demanding schedules, targeted awareness training on the primary risk areas for their business is time well spent.

C. Hotline Reports

For most companies, hotline reports are an obvious source of information about potential noncompliance that must be investigated and evaluated to determine whether the underlying allegation may give rise to reporting under the Mandatory Disclosure Rule. For companies that do not currently have a hotline, the Task Force recommends that they implement a hotline if they intend to contract with the Government, receive money from the Government under the Recovery Act, or are otherwise subject to the False Claims Act as recently amended by FERA. *See* 31 U.S.C. § 3729.

D. Internal Audits, Testing and Monitoring, Periodic Surveys, and Certifications

Many larger Government contractors, and some mid-size Government contractors, have processes to conduct audits of various parts of their enterprise on a periodic basis. These may be performed by internal auditors or consultant auditors engaged for that purpose. Some audits are conducted "for cause," meaning in response to a particular allegation, whereas others are performed in the ordinary course of business. The findings of "for cause" and routine audits should be reviewed and evaluated in the same manner as calls into the hotline or the legal department. Results from routine testing and monitoring and other periodic surveys and certifications that a company may undertake should be evaluated in the same way.

The output of each of these compliance controls should serve as a potential source of information that is evaluated. Failure to connect the dots between the results of these controls and an established process for reviewing allegations of potential noncompliance may undermine a company's efforts to comply with its obligations under the Mandatory Disclosure Rule.

IV. KEEPING TRACK OF ALLEGATIONS OF POTENTIAL MISCONDUCT

As the prior Sections demonstrate, there are numerous sources within an organization that may bring a PRE to the attention of the appropriate company officials. Tracking all potential sources of information is critically important. A proven method to ensure that nothing is neglected is to utilize a registry, log, or case management system. There are infinite variations as to the form, level of sophistication, or automation of such tools. For convenience, we will refer to all of these variations as a "registry" throughout the remainder of this section.

A.   Use of a Registry

1.   Registry for All Potentially Reportable Events

When deciding on what type of registry is appropriate for your company for purposes of tracking allegations that may give rise to a reportable event under the Mandatory Disclosure Rule, a company should first consider what processes it has in place to track other types of potential violations, such as quality or ethics allegations. For example, if a company already has an established reporting system in place that tracks allegations of ethics violations, it may make the most sense for the company to add onto that existing process rather than creating an altogether new process. On the other hand, a reporting system designed to track quality issues may not be closely enough related to the types of issues that would give rise to a disclosure under the Rule such that a company could use one single system to track both types of issues. The key issue then becomes whether: (1) to establish a registry for all or some set of reported allegations of noncompliance if the company has a void in this area; (2) to set up a separate registry for allegations of noncompliance that may give rise to a disclosure under the Rule; or (3) to add on to an existing process that includes a registry of alleged noncompliant conduct. There is no "right" answer.

The main point is that regardless of the type or size of a company, some form of registry is necessary to track allegations of noncompliance. As a tool, a registry provides visibility to all open issues and helps assure that none "fall through the cracks." Moreover, without a registry, a company simply will not be able to assure itself, or the Government, that it did not have knowledge of a particular allegation that should have been disclosed. A company without a registry would also have difficulty in defending a decision not to report an alleged PRE.

When deciding on what type of approach will be most suitable, the following factors should be considered:

- Whether the individuals who will review the items on the registry — the review or triage group — have the breadth of knowledge and competence to properly evaluate the appropriate treatment of all of the items that may be reported. This does not mean that the review or triage group must have the substantive expertise to investigate an issue, but simply that they have enough familiarity with a subject matter to be able to distinguish high risk and time sensitive matters, such as those that present an immediate security or physical hazard or an ongoing noncompliance, from those that have less urgency or sensitivity.

- Whether the individuals who will maintain, triage, and review items on the registry will have sufficient time to dedicate to all of the matters that may be reported on the registry.

- Whether more than one registry should be maintained. For example, if a company is large, it may be appropriate to have different registries (and reporting processes) based on divisions or business units. However, a single registry for all noncompliances, regardless of the nature of the issue, may be the easiest to manage for a small or mid-size company.

Overall, the main focus should be manageability. The registry should be a tool that makes compliance with the Mandatory Disclosure Rule more manageable. The registry should be designed in a way that will be most manageable for a particular organization. If the registry becomes too complex, it will not serve its intended purpose.

2. Maintenance of the Registry

Registries should be maintained by legal, compliance, or audit individuals or units. In considering the best entity for the job, key considerations should be who or where allegations are naturally reported within an organization. For instance, if hotline calls are reported to a specific office, then that office should maintain the registry. The registry should also be maintained by a point person who is easily accessible, as it does not benefit the company if no one can ever reach the point person. Companies will need to decide what form is acceptable, but oral reports would have to be transcribed for preservation purposes.

The chore of maintaining the registry should not be underestimated in terms of the time or competency required. Thus, its maintenance and review is not a function that can or should be relegated to an administrative function. Rather, the task of maintaining the registry should fall upon the shoulders of an individual or business unit that is well respected and knowledgeable. While an administrative support staff may be helpful in tracking items on a registry that are missing target completion dates, support staff personnel are not likely to be able to review the registry to evaluate the nature of what has been reported.

3. Design of the Registry

Considerable thought must be given to the design of the registry. This includes: How information will be input into the registry; single user or multiple user access; standard phrases or free form text; what data fields will be captured; and what numbering or tracking reference will be used to distinguish the reported allegations. As with many other features of registries, the most important requirement is that the tool be compatible with the processes for reporting employed by the company.

B. Access to the Registry

Access to the registry should be limited, preferably only to a designee and a back-up. Alternatively, the registry can be made available to a key person responsible for maintaining the registry and all members of the review or triage committee. This objective is to ensure that information on the registry is treated in accordance with the sensitivity of the matters on the list, and also to assure there are no unsanctioned edits (or deletions) to items on the registry. Ideally, the registry would have a mechanism that would allow it to track who makes additions, deletions, or modifications.

There are systems available that allow for multiple individuals to input and access data in a single system, yet maintain firewalls between the data input by various individuals or groups. This allows users from various parts of an organization to view information pertinent to their part of the organization or function, but restricts their access to information from other parts of the organization. For some companies, this type of system may work well to log potential noncompliances, with a master user who can see and track the status of all entries. Other companies may use or choose a less sophisticated arrangement, whereby all PREs are orally or electronically submitted to a single point of contact who then enters the pertinent information manually into the registry. Each approach has its benefits (such as ease of access or control over entries) and its drawbacks (such as expensiveness or manually intensive process).

C. What Should Not Be on the Registry

Usually there is no need for extensive details of the reported allegation to be contained in the registry. The registry should contain only enough information to facilitate meaningful identification of an issue which enables the users of the registry to differentiate between matters, and to allow for appropriate metrics to be measured. It may help, for example, for each recorded allegation to track who is assigned to follow up or investigate the matter, whether the matter is at the preliminary stage, in an investigative stage, or closed, and whether the matter was disclosed or not. It may also be helpful to identify the location of any relevant files. Any other detailed information related to an allegation should be maintained in a manner consistent with an organization's practices for confidential files, such as in confidential legal or audit files.

Attorney-client privileged information should not be included in the registry. PREs being investigated under the attorney-client privilege should be identified as "Attorney-Client Privileged" with a notation indicating information related to the PRE is maintained by the legal department.

D. Monitoring and Updating the Registry

To be an effective tool, a registry needs to be something more than a place to record initial entries of alleged misconduct. The registry should be designed to capture updates relating to the progress of investigations and resolution of each matter, ideally on an event-driven basis. Recognizing that in practice this approach does not always work, a tickler system process is recommended for items in the registry. This might entail a standard, periodic (such as a monthly or quarterly basis) communication to all lawyers, auditors and compliance officers assigned responsibility for matters on the registry to provide updates by a set date.

In addition, the compliance officer, compliance committee, review or triage committee, or other designated individuals responsible for compliance in an organization should be held accountable for monitoring the status of all items in the registry on a regular basis and be proactive in moving matters along when it appears they are not progressing appropriately on their own. A breakdown in this process may result in a compromised investigation, delayed disciplinary action, or a failure to recognize that the threshold of "credible evidence" of a violation covered by the Mandatory Disclosure Rule has been met, resulting in an untimely disclosure or a failure to disclose.

SECTION 6: "TIMELY DISCLOSURE" AND "LOOK-BACK" REQUIREMENTS

I. THE SOURCES OF THE TIMELY DISCLOSURE OBLIGATION

The requirement for timely disclosure is located in three sections of the FAR. The first section is the debarment and suspension provisions of the FAR, which provide that a cause for debarment or suspension includes:

> Knowing failure by a principal, until three years after final payment on any Government contract awarded to the contractor, to timely disclose to the Government, in connection with the award, performance or closeout of the contract or a subcontract thereunder, credible evidence of—
> (A) Violation of Federal criminal law involving fraud, conflict of interest, bribery or gratuity violations found in Title 18 of the United States Code;
> (B) Violation of the civil False Claim Act (31 U.S.C. 3729-3733); or
> (C) Significant overpayment(s) on the contract, other than overpayments resulting from contracting financing payments as defined in 32.001.

Appendix A, FAR 9.406-2 (debarment); FAR 9.407-2 (suspension). The second section is the contract clause:

> The Contractor shall timely disclose in writing, to the agency Office of the Inspector General (OIG), with a copy to the Contracting Officer, whenever, in connection with the award, performance, or closeout of this contract or any subcontract thereunder, the Contractor has credible evidence that a principal, employee, agent or subcontractor of the Contractor has committed (A) A violation of Federal criminal law involving fraud, conflict of interest, bribery, or gratuity violations found in Title 18 of the United States Code; or (B) A violation of the civil False Claims Act (31 U.S.C. 3729-3733).

Appendix A, FAR 52.203-13(b)(3)(i). Third, for those contractors that are required to have a business ethics awareness and compliance program and internal controls system, such internal controls shall:

> (A) Establish standards and procedures to facilitate timely discovery of improper conduct in connection with Government contracts; and
> (B) Ensure corrective measures are promptly instituted and carried out.

Appendix A, FAR 52.203-13(c)(2)(i). These standards are also required to provide for timely disclosure to the agency OIG of credible evidence of a covered violation concerning *any* of the contractor's Government contracts:

> At a minimum, the Contractor's internal control system shall provide for the following: . . . (F) Timely disclosure, in writing, to the agency OIG, with a copy to the Contracting Officer, whenever, in connection with the award, performance, or closeout of any Government contract performed by the Contractor or a subcontract thereunder, the Contractor has credible evidence that a principal, employee, agent, or subcontractor of the Contractor has committed a violation of Federal criminal law involving fraud, conflict of interest, bribery, or gratuity violations found in Title 18 U.S.C. or a violation of the civil False Claims Act (31 U.S.C. 3729-3733).

FAR 52.203-13(c)(2)(ii)(F).

Conceptually, therefore, the timely reporting requirement emanates from three discrete sources — the suspension and debarment provisions, the contract clause, and the requirement for an internal control system. The Preamble to the final Rule discusses the implications of these sources, which are relevant to the "look-back" requirement discussed below. Appendix B, 73 Fed. Reg. at 67,075.

II. THE MEANING OF "TIMELY" DISCLOSURE

A. No Definition

The regulations do not define "timely" or "promptly." There is no statutory or regulatory prescription for determining the maximum length of time that may pass before a disclosure will no longer be considered "timely."

B. How Soon Reporting Is Required

To a significant degree, what is "timely" will depend on the facts, the complexity of the legal issues, and the effort involved to determine the existence of "credible evidence." The Preamble further explains, "[u]ntil the contractor has determined the evidence to be credible, there can be no 'knowing failure to timely disclose.'" Appendix B, 73 Fed. Reg. at 67,074. The regulation is clear that as soon as a contractor has determined that "credible evidence" of a reportable event exists, there is an obligation to communicate that information to the appropriate Government officials.

One question is how soon after a contractor determines the existence of credible evidence does the contractor have an obligation to report. Fairly read, the Rule contemplates that the obligation to report is triggered immediately upon the determination of credible evidence, and no delay in communication of the information should occur. As discussed elsewhere in this Guide, this determination presumes that a contractor has undertaken an analysis of whether particular events or allegations constitute "credible evidence." Before such an analysis, the contractor generally cannot know, within the meaning of the Rule, that "credible evidence" exists and no obligation to report is triggered. But if the contractor has reached a point where it believes "credible evidence" does exist, including credible evidence of a *"significant overpayment,"* then a disclosure must be made or the contractor risks suspension and debarment, as well as not receiving credit regarding any prosecutorial determination.

It would be reasonable for the Government to permit a contractor some period of time after the existence of credible evidence has been determined to prepare its submission of evidence to the Government. That said, contractors will be well advised to establish that the time taken to prepare their submission is no longer than necessary.

C.   How a Contractor Should Determine Whether an Investigation Is Necessary

Recognizing that contractors (except small businesses and commercial item contracts) are required to have in place a business ethics awareness and compliance program, as well as a system of internal controls that must establish standards and procedures to facilitate timely discovery of improper conduct and ensure corrective measures are promptly instituted, contractors will receive various reports of potentially improper conduct. A contractor will need a means to review the reports quickly and determine which require follow-up and in what order. Investigative resources will need to be allocated accordingly. Internal compliance officials and company counsel should be available to advise with respect to the potential gravity of reported allegations.

The initiation, extent, and nature of any investigation is necessarily dependent on the allegation and the facts available to the contractor. Given the allegation and the available facts, a contractor may make a decision that the allegation does not merit an investigation. With respect both to decisions not to investigate and decisions regarding the level of investigation, the contractor should document its decisionmaking process to guard against a later assertion that it failed to timely disclose. Appendix B, 73 Fed. Reg. at 67,087. Contractors should expect that the question "why was this not reported earlier" will be asked if a report appears to have been delayed. In cases where a report was not made, but the matter otherwise comes to light, the contractor likely will be on the spot to explain what information was known and why it was not reported. In either case, the contractor will need to demonstrate that appropriate procedures were in place and effective in the context of the particular facts. The company also should preserve such documentation until the period for disclosure and the relevant statute of limitations have expired.

1. Small Businesses and Commercial Item Contractors Should Take the Initiative to Institute Their Own Programs

Despite the ostensible exception in FAR 52.203-13(c) for small businesses and commercial item contracts, such companies also should undertake an ethics awareness and compliance program and develop a system of internal controls. The suspension and debarment provisions of FAR 9.406-2 and 9.407-2 make no exception for small business or commercial item contracts. The Preamble notes that an ethical company that learns of misconduct would investigate such information as a sound business practice. Appendix B, 73 Fed. Reg. at 69,086. This expectation shows why small businesses and commercial item contractors will need the protection of a business awareness ethics and compliance program and meaningful internal controls. As the Preamble states, "The Councils cannot establish a different suspension or debarment standard for small businesses," or presumably commercial item contactors." *Id.*, 73 Fed. Reg. at 67,087.[52]

D. What Is a Reasonable Amount of Time to Investigate

There was much discussion during consideration of the regulations about the time frame between receiving an initial report and the point at which a disclosure is required. As a result, the Preamble explains that implicit in the credible evidence standard is the "opportunity to take some time for preliminary examination of the evidence to determine its credibility before deciding to disclose to the Government." Appendix B, 73 Fed Reg. at 67,074. "Until the contractor has determined the evidence to be credible, there can be no 'knowing failure to timely disclose.'" *Id.*

Although the Rule allows contractors time to take reasonable steps to determine that evidence of wrongdoing is credible, it does not direct contractors to carry out any particular level or type of internal investigation. Appendix B, 73 Fed. Reg. at 67,086. The Preamble states expressly that the Government does not direct companies to investigate. *Id.* at 67,087. As the Preamble notes further, "In the normal course of business, a company that is concerned about ethical behavior will take reasonable steps to determine the credibility of allegations of

---

[52] It appears that the reason the Rule does not require an ethics program, training, and internal control systems was to avoid the impact of such burdens on these contractors and characterization as a major rule. That gap is illusory. Companies cannot meaningfully comply with the disclosure requirements without an ethics program and internal control systems.

misconduct within the firm. It is left to the discretion of the company what these reasonable steps may entail." *Id.*

The use of the phrase "preliminary examination" in the Preamble strongly suggests that while contractors are allowed some time to investigate, it is important to proceed diligently and in good faith, consistent with the nature of the allegations, *i.e.*, a timely effort to gather the necessary information. This is consistent with the requirement for an internal control system in FAR 52.203-13(c)2)(i)(A) to "facilitate timely discovery of improper conduct. . . ." Contractors should expect that if a disagreement later arises regarding how their investigation was conducted, it will be important, with the application of hindsight, to demonstrate that an investigation was launched promptly and pursued diligently. It also will be important to document these decisions in case of future review.

1. Circumstances Where Early Voluntary Reporting May Be Advisable

It has been suggested that a contractor should make a disclosure before it has determined whether credible evidence of a violation exists, if there are early indications of a serious problem. The Preamble notes the DOJ's comment that "nothing in the Rule is intended to preclude a contractor from continuing to investigate after making its initial disclosure to the Government." Appendix B, 73 Fed. Reg. at 67,074. It also is possible that upon further investigation, the contractor may determine that a problem which sounded serious is minor or not a problem at all. In this regard, some believe that there is no downside to early disclosures.

Contractors should consider whether an early heads-up to the Government is warranted in a particular case. That is a judgment which must be made on the facts and on the nature of initial reports. When the facts do not yet constitute credible evidence, but allegations suggest a substantial problem, it may be in the contractor's interest to report prior to making a determination of credible evidence. The contractor can then continue its own investigation.

Moreover, a practical consideration for a disclosing contractor is the concern that a delay in making a disclosure might result in a third party or the Government identifying the issue, thereby creating possible difficulties for the contractor in establishing that it was acting in good faith in the process of making an independent disclosure. This consideration suggests a preliminary notification may be prudent in many cases.

On the other hand, it is not necessarily correct that there is no downside to early reporting. If the Government believes that the contractor has a serious issue, it may require that the contractor take steps to protect the Government's interest before the facts are known — steps that ultimately may be proven unnecessary.

2. Establishing Good Lines of Communication

Contractors would be well advised to have good lines of communication with their points of contact in the Government, including in the OIG, to permit informal communication about potential disclosures. In most instances, if the OIG is satisfied that the contractor is aware of and attuned to the need to protect the Government's best interests and is proceeding diligently to identify misconduct, the contractor may be able, through coordination and cooperation, to retain substantial control of the development of facts through its own investigation.

III. THE "LOOK-BACK" REQUIREMENT

The new suspension and debarment provisions of FAR 9.406-2 and 9.407-2 contain a "look-back" provision that permits suspension or debarment for a failure to disclose misconduct or significant overpayments known to a "principal" that occurred prior to the date of the Rule. This look-back obligation is found in the suspension and debarment provisions because the contract clause and internal control system are not contained in contracts that predate the Rule. The look-back obligation exists until three years after final payment on "any Government contract awarded to the contractor" and is "in connection with the award, performance, or closeout of the contract or a subcontract thereunder." Appendix A, FAR 9.406-2(b)(i)(vi) and 9.407-2(a)(8). As a practical matter, this requirement can affect contracts that are quite old, but not yet closed out, or not yet closed out for three years. Given the Government's audit cycle, it may take several years after performance has been completed for a contract to be closed out and final payment made. The Rule then extends the period for reporting to three years after final payment.

Furthermore, once a contractor becomes subject to the contract clause, FAR 52.203-13, the provisions of that clause may also require the contractor to "look-back" to potential violations that occurred prior to the effective date of the Rule, December 12, 2008. That is because FAR 52.203-13(b) and (c) both provide that the duty to disclose credible evidence of violations of Title 18 or the False Claims Act remains in effect until three years after final payment has been received on the Government contract in connection with which the potential violation occurred. Thus, once the clause is in effect, a contractor needs to be aware of any credible evidence of a violation in connection with the Government contract in which the clause appears (if section (b) applies) or any of the contractor's other Government contract (if section (c) applies), so long as final payment was not received on that contract or those contracts more than three years before the date the clause took effect for the contractor. This look-back requirement differs from the look-back requirement in the suspension and debarment provision in that it is not limited to the knowledge of principals and does not encompass credible evidence of significant overpayments.

Recognizing that look-back requirements may apply to old contracts and that there may have been turnover among those with potential knowledge of violations, what processes should contractors reasonably employ to determine if violations prior to December 12, 2008, exist that must be disclosed?

A. Possible Scrub of All Contracts Within Three Years of Closeout

The regulation is not clear and could be read to require a top-to-bottom review of all open contracts and all closed contracts that have been closed within the past three years. However, such a comprehensive review of aged contracts, which would involve a potentially enormous expenditure of resources, should not reasonably be required. This raises the question of how much effort a contractor must undertake to examine files and documents regarding these contracts to be in a position to demonstrate that the contractor exercised good faith in attempting to identify reportable events.

B. Reasonable Good Faith Efforts

Some Government officials have expressed a view that the contractor should be expected to check events of which a contractor should reasonably have been expected to be aware, but not scrub each contract for occurrences prior to the effective date of the Rule. The challenge is that before the promulgation of the Mandatory Disclosure Rule, the contractor may not have performed an assessment of allegations or information to determine the existence of "credible evidence," but in other contexts, such as a contract dispute or an audit. Reasonable efforts should not involve a complete review of aged contracts, but, depending on the rigor of compliance programs previously in place, contractors may want to consider the following actions:

- Formation of a dedicated committee to perform the look-back, including representatives from the relevant areas of potential knowledge such as Legal, Ethics, Audit, Contracts, Finance and Billing, Human Resources, and Quality Assurance.

- Survey of management regarding events related to the contracts of which they may be aware.

- Areas for review:
    - Previous disclosures
    - Internal reports of ethics cases or internal investigations
    - *Qui tam* actions
    - Subpoenas or civil investigative demands
    - Contract close-out documents
    - Audit reports
    - Accounting reserves

With respect to overpayments, contractors should look particularly at situations where they may have made a credit or refund to the Government and determine whether the overpayment would be significant under the circumstances. Contractors should recognize that what constitutes a significant overpayment may vary based upon the facts (*e.g.*, on a small contract a relatively small dollar amount could be a significant percentage). If the contractor made a credit or refund, but did not disclose the underlying facts to the Government, the contractor will want to examine those facts to determine if a violation exists that should be disclosed.

In each instance, the contractor should document its efforts to determine whether a reportable event exists and be attuned to the possibility that it will be called upon to justify, after the fact, the diligence of its efforts.

SECTION 7: THE FORM, CONTENT, AND RECIPIENTS OF DISCLOSURES

I. FORM OF DISCLOSURES

The Mandatory Disclosure Rule does not set forth any required format for disclosures. However, the contract clause created by the Rule states that disclosures must be "in writing." Appendix A, FAR 52.203-13(b)(3)(i) & (c)(2)(f). The cause for suspension or debarment does not specify that disclosures must be in writing, *see* FAR 9.406-2, 9.407-2, but this requirement in the contract clause is a useful guide for contractors who are not covered by the clause. For record-keeping and precision purposes, written disclosures are all but indispensable.

Several Offices of Inspector General have established electronic forms on their web sites. Inspectors General with web-based forms include the General Services Administration, Department of Defense, and National Aeronautics and Space Administration.[53] Use of the Inspector General forms offers several advantages. The forms delineate the information to be reported, so there should be no dispute about the type of information to be submitted.[54] The electronic format makes for ease of use. Communication is instantaneous and delays caused by,

---

[53] OIGs that have published a form or instructions include the following:

DOD: http://www.dodig.mil/Inspections/IPO/voldis.htm
GSA: http://www.gsaig.gov/integrityreport.htm
NASA: http://oig.nasa.gov/contdiscw.html
USAID: http://www.usaid.gov/oig/hotline/contractor_complaint_frm2.html
Commerce: http://www.oig.doc.gov/oig/FAR_Disclosure_Req.html
National Archives: http://www.archives.gov/oig/contractor.html
Transportation: http://www.oig.dot.gov/far_reporting.jsp
Justice: http://www.usdoj.gov/oig/FOIA/ContractorReportingForm.pdf
Labor: http://www.oig.dol.gov/contractor_disclosure.php
Interior: http://www.doioig.gov/form/farcontract_form.php

[54] The GSA OIG also allows attachments to be uploaded to its form.

for example, screening of mail are avoided. Electronic receipts also can be provided to confirm submission of the material, or the OIG can provide an instantaneous return copy of exactly what was received. There is no legal requirement, however, to use these electronic forms. A disclosing contractor should feel free to use a non-electronic means of disclosure if the contractor believes that this is the best way to ensure that the Government receives all relevant information. The language of the Rule is satisfied as long as the information is submitted in writing to the required OIG and contracting officer.

In making a disclosure to an agency which has no published form for disclosure, contractors should contact the agency OIG beforehand to ensure that they are aware of that agency's expectations as to the form and content of the disclosure.

The Task Force encourages Government-wide standardization of reporting forms and procedures if possible.

II. CONTENT OF DISCLOSURES

The issue of what should be the content of a disclosure should be examined from two perspectives. First, the expectations of the Government agency receiving the disclosure must be recognized so that the disclosing contractor is not regarded as deficient and thereby exposed to potential suspension and debarment. Second, the disclosing contractor may have special considerations — both legal and practical — which it needs to address in the disclosure.

A. Government Agency Expectations As to the Content of Disclosures

Before addressing the "normal" expectations of Government agencies with respect to the content of disclosures under the new Rule, the "exceptions" are worth noting. Historically, even under the earlier voluntary disclosure programs, Inspectors General consistently have cautioned contractors with respect to the need to make "immediate" reports when certain types of conduct are detected or suspected by contractor personnel. Some of the more notable examples are situations involving bribery of federal officials, extortion by federal officials, subcontractor kickbacks, or potential violations that could affect health or safety. Each of these situations presents circumstances where immediate law enforcement intervention is an option, and therefore contractors must not delay in orally reporting such allegations. The "content" of this type of disclosure is not the primary concern; rather, it is the timeliness of the report to OIG or law enforcement personnel. A contractor reporting in these circumstances can subsequently submit a report under the provisions of the new Rule and follow the reporting guidelines otherwise established by the receiving agency. A subsequent written report under circumstances such as these, where expedience has required an immediate oral report, should not jeopardize a contractor in terms of any assessment as to whether it has properly disclosed a matter required by the new Rule. This conclusion should apply in any situation where a contracting officer or higher level agency official is implicated in the conduct being disclosed.

Aside from these types of exceptions, the expectations of at least three federal agencies already have been provided, at least to some extent. As set forth in Section I, the OIGs at GSA, NASA, and DOD each have posted a disclosure form on their respective websites. Those forms illustrate the scope and detail that OIGs are seeking in contractor disclosures. All three forms identify certain required basic information, including data on the following:

- The official submitting the disclosure;
- The contractor;
- The affected contracts;
- Amount of loss;
- Complete description of the facts and circumstances surrounding the reported activities;
- Evidence forming the basis of the report;

- Names of the individuals involved;
- Dates and location;
- How the matter was discovered;
- Potential witnesses and their involvement; and
- Any corrective action taken by the company.

In addition to this general information, the DOD form asks if a contractor investigation has been conducted and requests that the contractor "[d]escribe the scope of the investigation (records reviewed, number and positions of employees interviewed, etc.)." The DOD form also asks whether there was an overpayment, and if so, the estimated amount. The DOD form also asks whether the company is "willing to provide a copy of its investigative report."

From the forms posted by the GSA, NASA, and DOD, it seems apparent that Government agencies expect the disclosure of facts and evidence, and do not expect (or invite) legal characterizations of the facts and evidence. Thus, for example, a contractor would not be expected to characterize the disclosed facts as constituting evidence of a criminal violation, a violation of the civil False Claims Act, or a significant overpayment.

B. Contractor Considerations in the Content of Disclosures

Apart from the obvious interest in trying to be responsive to agency expectations, a disclosing contractor may have additional concerns.

First, contractors may feel the need to make a "preliminary report" in order to announce, prior to Government or third party identification of a potentially reportable matter, that the contractor has an active review underway but that the review is only in its preliminary stages. If this "preliminary report" approach is undertaken, the contractor should clearly announce that fact to the receiving federal agency, but also attempt to provide as much information as is available.

Certainly information about the contractor, affected contracts, corrective action to date, and the general nature of the matter could be included in preliminary reports.

Second, contractors desiring to assure that their reports are not construed as admissions of liability may wish to include a disclaimer as noted in subsection II.D below.

Third, contractors also may have concerns relating to the protection of company proprietary information from disclosure under the Freedom of Information Act ("FOIA") or other disclosure, which is addressed in more detail elsewhere in this Guide. Those concerns also must be specifically addressed as discussed in subsection II.C below.

Fourth, contractors may also be interested in addressing certain "legal" issues in disclosures. These issues may include concerns such as specifically naming "involved employees" where allegations are less than conclusive, statute of limitations issues which may bar prosecution, and the quality of the supporting evidence as part of an assessment of whether "credible evidence" exists. While the disclosure report perhaps should not be used as a form of legal brief, a disclosing contractor should not be constrained from identifying relevant legal issues as part of its disclosure provided it also is meeting the expectations of the receiving agency with respect to the relevant facts.

C. FOIA Markings

Disclosures made to the Government may be subject to FOIA requests. While disclosures may be exempt under the investigative records/law enforcement exemption of FOIA, 5 U.S.C. § 552(b)(7), if there is an open investigation, contractors cannot be certain that the Government will invoke this exception. Accordingly, contractors should mark as appropriate all information submitted under the disclosure as proprietary, confidential, and not subject to disclosure under the trade secrets/confidential commercial information exemption of FOIA, 5 U.S.C. § 552(b)(4).

D. Disclaimers

Submission of a disclosure under the new Rule does not necessarily mean that a violation has occurred. Contractors should include a disclaimer in a disclosure stating that the disclosure does not constitute an admission that a violation or overpayment has occurred or that the contractor or its employees have violated the law.

III. RECIPIENTS OF DISCLOSURES

There are three separate sources of disclosure requirements under the Mandatory Disclosure Rule: (1) the suspension and debarment provisions of FAR 9.406-2 and 9.407-2; (2) the contract clause requirement of FAR 52-203-13(b)(3)(i); and (3) the contractor code of business ethics and conduct requirements of FAR 52.203-13(c)(2).

The contract clause requirement and the requirements for contractor codes of business ethics and conduct clearly specify that disclosures of criminal and False Claims Act violations are to be made to the agency's OIG with a copy to the contracting officer. Appendix A, FAR 52.203-13(b)(3)(i); FAR 52.203-13(c)(2)(ii)(F). By contrast, the suspension and debarment provisions indicate that they may be triggered by a contractor's knowing failure to disclose to "the Government." Though the word "Government" might suggest that a contractor could make disclosures of criminal or False Claims Act violations to persons other than the OIGs and face no prospect of suspension or debarment, the Task Force discourages any such interpretation. To begin with, some OIG and DOJ officials interpret the term "Government" to mean the relevant OIG, which would require even significant overpayments to be reported to the OIG. Furthermore, because the contract clause and code of conduct provisions specifically require reporting to OIGs, with copies to contracting officers, the DOJ and some agency suspension and debarment officials will at a minimum expect that all reports of potential civil and criminal violations should be made to the OIG with a copy to the contracting officer. Indeed, to the extent the contractor chooses to make such disclosures to a Government official other than the Inspector General, the DOJ may assert that such disclosure was an improper attempt to avoid or conceal the contractor's contractual obligations or to avoid potential liability under the False Claims Act or even a criminal violation.[55]

However, for conduct that occurred and was reported prior to the adoption of the Mandatory Disclosure Rule, there appears to be a reasonable basis to interpret the word "Government" to include the OIG, contracting officer, or any other person in the Government with a sufficient degree of responsibility or oversight to address the reported conduct in accordance with then-existent practices. Thus, if a contractor already disclosed conduct to a recipient other than the OIG prior to adoption of the Rule, it would not appear reasonable to interpret such a disclosure as a failure to disclose to the "Government."[56] However, as stated above, for a criminal or civil FCA violation disclosed after the effective date of the Rule, disclosure to a Government official other than the agency OIG could be seen by the Government as the basis for an FCA allegation of a reverse false claim, or conceivably a criminal violation.

A. Reporting to the Agency Inspector General

Who is the Inspector General? Inspectors General are not all the same. Inspectors General at the larger departments and agencies are appointed by the President and confirmed by the Senate. Other Inspectors General, commonly at boards and commissions, are designated by the heads of the agencies. The military departments and many defense agencies have their own

---

[55] One DOJ participant on the Task Force opined that anyone who makes a disclosure of an overpayment to a contracting officer to conceal fraud or a violation of the FCA would be exposed to a concealment charge under 18 U.S.C. § 1001, and that anyone who receives an overpayment and fails to repay is exposed to 18 U.S.C. § 641.

[56] However, some Government participants on the Task Force opined that if the contractor had not made a complete disclosure of the relevant facts regarding the violation or significant overpayment to the Government recipient prior to the Rule's effective date, a second, more complete disclosure of the violation or overpayment to the relevant OIG would be required.

appointed Inspectors General. Furthermore, the offices vary widely in size and geographic scope. Some have a very few employees in a single office; others have hundreds of employees and Special Agents in offices around the world. The best practice for reporting is to report in the manner preferred by the Office of the Inspector General involved. In the case of DOD, reporting to the DOD Office of Inspector General with respect to defense contracts is the best practice. A disclosure to a field representative or special agent rather than to the prescribed point for reporting will likely not be viewed as compliant by the receiving Inspector General.

As noted above, a number of federal agencies have electronic reporting tools available on their respective websites. Even with the limitations inherent in using these electronic tools, using these forms for reporting assures the reporting party that the form is submitted where the receiving Inspector General wants the reporting to take place.

B. Multiple Contracts, Multiple Agencies, Multiple Contracting Officers

Where only a single agency is affected by a contractor disclosure, and a single contracting officer is responsible for that contract, the reporting responsibilities discussed above are straightforward. With more complicated situations, this is not the case. The regulations on contractors' codes of business ethics and conduct state:

> Multiple agencies: "If a violation relates to more than one government contract, the Contractor may make the disclosure to the agency OIG and Contracting Officer responsible for the largest dollar value contract impacted by the violation." *See* FAR 52.203-13(c)(2)(ii)(F)(1).

> Government-wide acquisition contracts: "If the violation relates to an order against a Government-wide acquisition contract, a multi-agency contract, a multiple-award schedule contract such as the Federal Supply Schedule, or any other procurement instrument intended for use by multiple agencies, the contractor shall notify the OIG of the ordering agency and the IG of the agency responsible for the basic contract, and the respective agencies' contracting officers." *See* FAR 52.203-13(c)(2)(ii)(F)(2).

However, there are additional reporting scenarios that require attention and clarification, such as where only a single agency is involved but there are multiple affected contracting officers within that agency. In such a case, the contractor should consider including in the comments section of the report a statement that more than one contracting officer within the agency could be affected. The agency OIG, in coordination with the appropriate agency acquisition official, should be able to coordinate the review within that agency. But the reporting party should confirm with the OIG that the OIG can or will undertake this coordination.

A disclosure also might affect more than one agency and contracting officers in more than one agency. While the Rule recommends that disclosure be made to the agency with the greatest relationship to the disclosure, the contractor should consider filing identical reports with all agencies, with notations in the report that a disclosure on the same matter has been filed with the other agencies. Alternatively, when in doubt about where to make the appropriate disclosure, the contractor should consult one of the relevant OIGs.

Finally, it is important to note that the Mandatory Disclosure Rule does not supplant or modify other reporting requirements a contractor may have to an agency in connection with its contracts.

IV. WHAT TO EXPECT UPON MAKING DISCLOSURE

A contractor should expect to receive confirmation that its disclosure has been received by the agency. If a contractor does not receive such confirmation promptly, it should follow up to ensure that the OIG and contracting officer (or other recipients) have received the submission. For any number of reasons, a disclosure can go unanswered for quite some time. Silence by the OIG should not be viewed as "good news" or "bad news." A disclosing contractor should draw no inference from a delayed response, or no response, following an acknowledged disclosure submission.

Generally, the Rule does not require that a disclosing contractor supplement an adequate initial disclosure. If the initial disclosure revealed "all pertinent information" about the conduct, such that auditors or investigators can determine (a) the nature and extent of the conduct, and (b) the individuals responsible for the conduct, then it is reasonable to await further word from the Government before submitting additional information. Nonetheless, some within the Government expect that an initial disclosure will be supplemented as new material facts come to light even if the full cooperation requirement initially was met. Others, generally outside the Government, disagree, and argue that the Rule does not require supplementation. In light of this disagreement, a contractor would be well served to consult legal counsel should this issue arise. In any event, a disclosing company should remain vigilant to the potential discovery of new facts that reveal credible evidence of a broader or different covered event. Such new evidence, if not fairly encompassed by the initial disclosure, could create a new disclosure obligation.

At some point, the OIG may contact a disclosing company with a request for additional information, or with a request that it interview company personnel with relevant knowledge. As discussed below in Section 9, the Rule requires that a company provide "full cooperation" to the Government in response to such requests.

All disclosures to OIGs are referred to a group of Government officials for review that includes representatives of the DOJ Criminal Division and the civil fraud section of the Civil Division. This group, in consultation with the affected OIG and agency "stakeholders," determines whether the matter warrants further investigation or possible criminal or civil action by DOJ. If DOJ decides not to prosecute the contractor or pursue an investigation under the FCA, the contractor may be notified of that decision, at least by DOD. The matter could then be "closed out" or transferred to other agency personnel for administrative action.

SECTION 8: VOLUNTARY DISCLOSURES

I. INTRODUCTION

Prior to adoption of the Rule, Government departments and agencies routinely accepted voluntary disclosures by contractors of potential contract-related fraud or criminal violations. The Department of Defense ("DOD"), the Department of State, and the Department of Commerce were among the few departments that published written procedures for accepting, processing, investigating, and resolving such voluntary disclosures. The DOD Voluntary Disclosure Program was the subject of an earlier ABA Report. *See* American Bar Association, Section of Public Contract Law, *Report by the Special Committee on Voluntary Disclosure* (Aug. 1994).

The DOD Voluntary Disclosure Program did not require that a voluntary disclosure be of actual fraud. All that was needed was a suspicion or possibility of fraud or a violation of criminal law. Also, under the DOD Program and the Department of State's program, the disclosing company could (and in most cases did) conduct an internal inquiry and follow up its initial disclosure with a report to the Government of the results of its internal inquiry. The Government often elected not to initiate an investigation until it had received the report of the company's internal investigation. The company would then cooperate with the Government's verification investigation.

Following the effective date of the Mandatory Disclosure Rule on December 12, 2008, the DOD Office of Inspector General ("DOD OIG") formally replaced the DOD Voluntary Disclosure Program with the "Contractor Disclosure Program." DOD OIG officials have noted on several occasions that the DOD OIG Contractor Disclosure Program is not limited to disclosures required by the Rule (mandatory disclosures), but is intended to cover *all* disclosures whether mandatory or voluntary. DOD OIG officials have also stated that they do not intend to require contractors to characterize their disclosures as mandatory or voluntary or with respect to the type of violation (*e.g.*, criminal or civil FCA violation) that may be involved. Finally, DOD OIG officials have stated that the Rule is intended to encourage disclosures and that the Government wants contractors to err on the side of disclosure. Representatives of other Government agencies have made similar statements. These statements, as well as the absence of any statement in the Rule that precludes voluntary disclosure, support the conclusion that voluntary disclosure remains a viable option for Government contractors.

This Section identifies three circumstances in which voluntary disclosure may be particularly appropriate. It analyzes the benefits and risks of voluntary disclosure in each of these circumstances. It then examines the factors that contractors may wish to consider in determining whether to make a voluntary disclosure and, in the case of Government agencies, whether and to what extent the contractor should be given credit for such disclosures. Finally, this section provides some recommended best practices regarding the form and content of voluntary disclosures and to whom in the Government they should be made.

II. THREE CIRCUMSTANCES IN WHICH VOLUNTARY DISCLOSURE MAY BE APPROPRIATE

There are at least three circumstances in which voluntary disclosure to the Government may be particularly appropriate. They are: (1) circumstances in which, following an internal investigation, the contractor is uncertain whether the conditions for mandatory disclosure exist ("abundance of caution disclosures"); (2) circumstances in which the contractor has not yet completed (or perhaps even begun) an internal investigation, but wishes to provide early notification to the Government of the conditions or allegations that prompted an investigation ("early warning disclosure"); and (3) circumstances in which the contractor has definitively concluded that the conditions or allegations do not require mandatory disclosure, but that the conditions or allegations should nevertheless be disclosed to the Government for business relations or other reasons ("no credible evidence disclosures"). Each of these three types of voluntary disclosure has its own potential benefits and risks.

A. "Abundance of Caution" Disclosures

Voluntary disclosures made by a contractor "in abundance of caution" are perhaps the most common type of voluntary disclosure. In fact, DOD OIG officials have stated on several occasions that they fully expect, and that they have no objection to, such disclosures. These statements implicitly acknowledge that many of the Rule's key terms, such as "credible evidence" and "significant overpayment," are undefined and susceptible to multiple interpretations, and that contractors may therefore reasonably find themselves unable to conclude with reasonable certainty that the conditions requiring mandatory disclosure exist.

Voluntary disclosure provides such contractors a way to accomplish the Government's stated goal of encouraging disclosure while at the same time avoiding some of the disadvantages of mandatory disclosure. For example, by accompanying its disclosure with the disclaimer that it was made "in an abundance of caution" or similar language, a contractor may be able to prevent the disclosure from being viewed by agency suspension and debarment officials as an "admission" by the contractor of adequate evidence of a criminal violation, FCA violation, or significant overpayment. In fact, contractors making any type of disclosure — voluntary or mandatory — may wish to consider affirmatively disclaiming any such "admission." *See* Section 7.

There are other significant advantages to an "abundance of caution" disclosure. As explained in Section 10, some courts have applied a more lenient standard under FOIA Exemption Four for information that is voluntarily provided to the Government than for information that is required to be provided. In order to establish that voluntarily-provided information is exempt from disclosure, a contractor need show only that it does not customarily make such information available to the public, whereas in the case of information required to be provided by statute, regulation, or contract, the contractor must demonstrate that release of the information would likely cause it substantial competitive harm or significantly impair the agency's ability to obtain similar information in the future. Thus, a contractor making a voluntary disclosure could reasonably expect the information it disclosed would probably not be released under FOIA if it can demonstrate to the agency's satisfaction that it did not customarily make this type of information available to the public.

"Abundance of caution" disclosures are not without risk, however. First, such disclosures may unnecessarily involve the OIG and DOJ in matters where there is, in fact, no credible evidence of a violation of criminal law or the FCA. Second, such disclosures could give rise to a *qui tam* action against the disclosing company under the False Claims Act if the disclosure results in a *qui tam* relator finding out about the condition or conduct disclosed by the contractor. Finally, a contractor that chooses to make a voluntary disclosure concerning actions of a terminated employee could risk a suit or labor grievance proceeding by that employee alleging that the disclosure violated an obligation that the contractor owed the employee under the contractor's labor agreement or federal, state, or local labor laws. For these and other reasons, contractors contemplating a voluntary "abundance of caution" disclosure should carefully consider both the recipient and content of the contemplated disclosure.

B.   Pre-Internal Investigation Disclosures

Another circumstance in which a voluntary disclosure may be appropriate is where a contractor receives some information or allegation suggesting a criminal or False Claims Act violation (or receipt of a significant overpayment), but has not yet had the opportunity to conduct an internal investigation of the information or allegation. The primary benefits of such a disclosure would be: (1) to minimize the possibility that the Government would later assert that the mandatory disclosure (if it turned out that one was required) was "untimely," (2) to avoid the possibility of the Government or a *qui tam* relator launching its own investigation or proceeding before the contractor makes a mandatory disclosure; and (3) to demonstrate the contractor's good faith to the Government. The primary disadvantages of an "early" voluntary disclosure are: (1) involving the OIG and DOJ in matters that turn out not to involve credible evidence of a criminal violation or a violation of the FCA; (2) losing control of the internal investigation if the OIG or the DOJ become actively involved at a very early stage; and (3) risking an action by an employee, agent, or subcontractor for violation of some obligation of privacy or fiduciary or contractual duty. In addition, an early disclosure, even if voluntary, could trigger the contractor's obligations to make other disclosures, including financial reporting disclosures.

C. Disclosure of Determination That No Credible Evidence Exists

A third possible scenario where voluntary disclosure may be appropriate is where the contractor has completed an internal investigation and concluded that no credible evidence exists of a criminal violation or civil False Claims Act violation warranting mandatory disclosure. The advantage of making a voluntary disclosure in such circumstances would be to prevent the Government from subsequently "second-guessing" the contractor and asserting a suspension and debarment proceeding based on the theory that the contractor had an obligation to disclose the information it had to the relevant OIG. On the other hand, voluntary disclosure by the contractor of its decision that no credible evidence exists could precipitate the involvement of the OIG or DOJ in matters that do not reasonably involve the possibility of a criminal or civil FCA violation. Moreover, as was the case with other voluntary disclosures, a voluntary disclosure that no credible evidence exists could precipitate a *qui tam* FCA suit or trigger a requirement to disclose to the contractor's accountants or in connection with its financial statements, or possibly result in an action against the contractor by an employee, agent, or subcontractor.

In conclusion, the fact that certain disclosures are now mandatory does not preclude a company, out of an abundance of caution or simply a desire to inform its contracting partner of its ongoing compliance reviews, from voluntarily notifying an agency of a potential violation of law or the receipt of an overpayment.

III. FACTORS TO CONSIDER IN DECIDING WHETHER TO MAKE A VOLUNTARY DISCLOSURE

The company official(s) with responsibility for determinations as to whether mandatory disclosures should be made should also be responsible for determining whether voluntary (*i.e.*, non-mandatory) disclosures should be made, and, if so, what information should be furnished to the Government. Factors that a contractor should consider when deciding whether to make a voluntary disclosure include:

- What type of working relationship does the company have with the contracting officer and the buying agency's investigators? Does the contracting officer trust company officials, or does the agency view reports from the company with suspicion such that the disclosure might be viewed as an attempt to paper over serious problems? Companies should also consider that an agency's investigators may have views that differ from the views of the procurement office and its personnel.

- Does the company typically report early signs of problems to the appropriate contracting officer and follow up initial reports with status reports until the problems are resolved, or does the company typically address contract-related problems internally without notifying the Government's contract administration officials? If the company has a policy of making status reports to the Government, what types of issues does it report?

- What is to be gained from a disclosure? Will the company avoid an appearance of nonchalance or an appearance that it has not timely investigated or taken the matter seriously by notifying the Government early on? Will the Government defer to the company to conduct an inquiry before it assigns investigators and auditors? The company should also be able to invoke the fact that it filed a report to support its claim of present responsibility, should its integrity be challenged in a suspension or debarment action.

- What will the contracting officer or OIG do with the disclosure? Although the executive branch agencies have not announced how they would deal with voluntary disclosures, it is reasonable to expect such disclosures will be referred to the office (investigative, audit, or contract administration) that has responsibility for the matter disclosed.

- Finally, what is the likelihood that the agency would release the information provided by the company when faced with a Freedom of Information Act request, especially where the information is disclosed out of an abundance of caution and might not be deemed law enforcement sensitive?

IV. RECOMMENDED CONTENTS OF A VOLUNTARY DISCLOSURE

Once a company elects to make a voluntary disclosure and considers the likelihood that the information it provides to the Government will be released to the public, it must decide what facts to disclose. The Government routinely seeks a complete recitation of the facts to assure itself that there was no misconduct or overpayments. When investigators, auditors, or contract administrators are put in a position of having to request additional information, suspicions might be instinctively aroused. Companies therefore may want to err on the side of more complete disclosure to forestall Government requests for further information. The disclosure should tell Government officials:

- When and how the company was alerted to the possibility that there was a problem;

- The issues the company examined;

- The contracts involved;

- The facts discovered to date and whether additional inquiry is necessary; and

- How management is responding to the issue and what corrective action the company intends to take.

Careful consideration should be given in the context of a voluntary disclosure before disclosing the names or contact information of the individuals involved.

V. RECIPIENTS OF A VOLUNTARY DISCLOSURE

There is no guidance of which the Task Force is aware that indicates to whom a voluntary disclosure should be made. The DOD has formally disbanded its Voluntary Disclosure Program, so the rules that formerly applied to voluntary disclosures are no longer applicable. However, it would seem that in most circumstances, a contractor that elects to make a voluntary disclosure would be prudent to make the disclosure to the same entities that are the required recipients of a mandatory disclosure under the Rule — that is, the OIG with a copy to the contracting officer. Thus, if the Government subsequently concludes that the contractor should have viewed the disclosure as a mandatory disclosure, the contractor will not face suspension or debarment or other sanctions for any alleged failure to provide information to the proper authority.

VI. CONCLUSION

To demonstrate a commitment to integrity in contractual relations with the Government, companies have the option of making voluntary disclosures of possible misconduct, as opposed to disclosures now mandated by the FAR relaying credible evidence of criminal fraud, violations of the civil False Claims Act, or significant overpayments. This option is not based upon any statute or regulation. Rather, it is a natural element of the contractual relationship between companies and the Government, and should be used after careful considerations of all potential risks and benefits. Because such disclosures are generally not governed by established procedures, agencies may not respond to such voluntary disclosures in a consistent fashion. The company making the disclosure should take upon itself the responsibility for seeking periodic status reports from the Government.

SECTION 9: "FULL COOPERATION"

I. INTRODUCTION

The Mandatory Disclosure Rule contract clause requires that certain contractors establish an internal control system, and mandates that such internal control systems provide for "full cooperation" with Government agencies responsible for audits, investigations, or corrective actions.

The "full cooperation" mandate flows from a single element of the Contractor Code of Business Ethics and Conduct contract clause created by the Rule, FAR 52.203-13. Specifically, in the context of setting out the mandatory elements of an internal control system, the clause requires contractors to:

> establish the following within 90 days after contract award, unless the Contracting Officer establishes a longer time period: . . . (2) An internal control system. . . . (ii) At a minimum, the Contractor's internal control system shall provide for the following . . . (G) Full cooperation with any Government agencies responsible for audits, investigations, or corrective actions.

Appendix A, FAR 52.203-13(c). The definition section of the clause defines "full cooperation" as:

> disclosure to the Government of the information sufficient for law enforcement to identify the nature and extent of the offense and the individuals responsible for the conduct. It includes providing timely and complete response to Government auditors' and investigators' request for documents and access to employees with information.

Id. The definition goes on to explain what the term does not mean. Specifically, the definition provides that the term:

> (2) Does not foreclose any Contractor rights arising in law, the FAR, or the terms of the contract. It does not require —
>
> (i) A Contractor to waive its attorney-client privilege or the protections afforded by the attorney work product doctrine; or

(ii) Any officer, director, owner, or employee of the Contractor, including a sole proprietor, to waive his or her attorney client privilege or Fifth Amendment rights; and

(3) Does not restrict a Contractor from —

(i) Conducting an internal investigation; or

(ii) Defending a proceeding or dispute arising under the contract or related to a potential or disclosed violation.

Appendix A, FAR 52.203-13(a).

The clause's "full cooperation" requirement applies only to other-than-small businesses selling other than commercial items. FAR 52.203-13(c). Regardless of the applicability of this element of the clause, contractors may be subject to other statutory, regulatory, or contractual provisions requiring cooperation with Government auditors and investigators. Moreover, the Government expects cooperation from all companies with which it does business, and as a practical matter is unlikely to apply a different standard for cooperation to commercial item contractors or small businesses than to other contractors.

Beyond the definition set forth above, the clause itself offers no guidance as to the meaning and scope of the term "full cooperation." The Preamble accompanying the Rule, however, does offer some further discussion, and identifies the following drafters' expectations concerning the meaning of "full cooperation":

- "Cooperation must be both timely and thorough."

- "Contractors are not expected to block Government auditors and investigators' access to information found in documents or through its employees in furtherance of a contract fraud or corruption investigation."

- Contractors are expected to "encourage employees both to make themselves available and to cooperate with the Government investigation."

- Contractors are expected to encourage employees to cooperate with "reasonable Government requests for documents."

- Contractors are expected not to "ignor[e] or offer[] little attention to detail in responding to auditor or investigator requests or subpoenas for documents or information."

- Cooperation should include "all information requested as well as all pertinent information known by the contractor necessary to complete the investigation, whether the information helps or hurts the contractor." (Obviously, this would not include privileged information.)

Appendix B, 73 Fed. Reg. at 67,078. These expectations set forth in the Preamble were intended to help contractors understand the Rule's intent. What weight a court will give to the Preamble likely will depend upon the specific factual context in which a given issue arises.[57] Nonetheless, the foregoing expectations do reflect the Government's interpretation of the Rule.

In addition, even though the "full cooperation" requirement imposed by the new contract clause is applicable only to contractors obligated to have an internal control system, this does not mean that the Government does not expect such cooperation from other contractors. Government suspension and debarment officials, for example, generally expect that all contractors appearing before them will "cooperate fully" with any Government investigator, and the extent of a contractor's cooperation will usually be a critical factor in the determination of a contractor's present responsibility. *See generally* FAR 9.406-1(a)(4) (debarment); FAR 9.407-1(b)(2) (suspension).

II. FREQUENTLY ASKED QUESTIONS

While most people are well equipped to identify conduct at the extremes of the "cooperation spectrum" — *i.e.*, clear examples of cooperation and clear failures to cooperate —

---

[57] As noted in the Overview section of this Guide, a recent Supreme Court case gives some guidance regarding the weight of a Preamble in some factual contexts. In *Wyeth v. Levine*, 129 S. Ct. 1187 (2009), the Court rejected a statement on the pre-emptive effect of an FDA regulation that was contained within the Preamble to the FDA's regulation. The Court noted that the Preamble was not subject to notice and comment rulemaking, and, thus, under the specific facts of that case, accorded the Agency's statements in the Preamble no weight at all. *Id.* at 1201, 1203.

most situations in real life don't take place at the extremes. Nonetheless, contractors and Government officials are responsible for abiding by the new Rule in all situations. The following "Frequently Asked Questions" are intended not only to address the Rule's requirements, but also to pick up where the text of the Rule left off. To that end, these FAQs identify ways to help facilitate compliance in those situations where the new Rule is silent or unclear.

TABLE OF CONTENTS

Topic	Question(s)
Access to documents	8, 28
Access to employees	9, 10, 28
Attorney-client privilege	20, 21, 22, 23, 24, 25
Attorney work product doctrine	20, 21, 22, 23, 24, 25
Counsel, participating in interviews	17
Counsel, providing to employees	18
Disclosure, sufficiency of	4, 5, 7
Employees rights	12, 13, 14, 15, 16
Fifth Amendment	4, 10, 11, 26
Indemnification of employees	19
Labor/employment issues	12, 13, 14, 15, 16, 19
On-line forms	3
Scope of Rule	1, 2, 27
Supplement, duty to	6
Timeliness of full cooperation	8
Union rights	15, 16

Question 1. How does the Rule define "full cooperation"?

Answer. The Mandatory Disclosure Rule contract clause, FAR 52.203-13, requires that companies subject to that clause implement an internal control system that provides for "full cooperation with any Government agencies responsible for audits, investigations, or corrective actions." Appendix A, FAR 52.203-13(c). The clause defines "full cooperation" as "disclosure to the Government of the information sufficient for law enforcement to identify the nature and extent of the offense and the individuals responsible for the conduct. It includes providing timely and complete response to Government auditors' and investigators' request for documents and access to employees with information." FAR 52.203-13(a). The clause states that "full cooperation" does *not*:

- Foreclose any contractor rights arising in law, the FAR, or the terms of the contract;

- Require a contractor to waive its attorney-client privilege or the protections afforded by the attorney work product doctrine;

- Require any officer, director, owner, or employee of the contractor, including a sole proprietor, to waive his or her attorney client privilege or Fifth Amendment rights;

- Restrict a contractor from conducting an internal investigation; or

- Restrict a contractor from defending a proceeding or dispute arising under the contract or related to a potential or disclosed violation.

Id.

Question 2. Who has to "cooperate fully" in federal audits or investigations following a mandatory disclosure?

Answer. The Rule requires "full cooperation" only as part of the business ethics awareness and compliance program and internal control system requirement, which applies only to "large" businesses holding non-commercial federal prime contracts or subcontracts. Appendix A, FAR 52.203-13(c). Nonetheless, the Government expects cooperation from all companies with which it does business. Thus, all companies, regardless of size and contract type, have an interest in cooperating with federal auditors and investigators acting within the scope of their authority.[58] Additionally, taking steps that obstruct an audit or investigation, such as destroying documents, pressuring witnesses not to cooperate, or the like, could be viewed by the Government as obstruction of justice.

Question 3. I've seen that several OIGs have posted on-line disclosure forms on their web sites. Does the FAR's new "full cooperation" Rule require that I use those forms to make my initial disclosure?

Answer. No, you are not required to use the OIGs' on-line forms to disclose conduct covered by the new Rule. The OIGs characterize the on-line

---

[58] *See* Appendix B, 73 Fed. Reg. at 67,078 ("That also applies to responding to reasonable Government requests for documents. Ignoring or offering little attention to detail in responding to auditor or investigator requests or subpoenas for documents or information may, in some circumstances, be obstruction of justice and, if established, certainly would not be deemed full cooperation.").

forms as a "convenience" to allow contractors to comply with their reporting requirements.[59] Government officials have explained that reasons for using the on-line form may include assurance of instant notification and receipt, convenience of electronic tracking, compliance with OIG preferences and information requests, and ease of further transmittal. The on-line forms, however, call for information that, for some cases or disclosures, may go beyond that required by the Rule, and there may be legitimate reasons why you do not want to use the on-line form. For instance, statements included in the on-line form may be construed as "admissions" that could be used as evidence against you in a later proceeding. It is best to consult your attorney before deciding if and how to make a disclosure under the new Rule. Whether or not you use the on-line form to make your initial disclosure, however, the OIG will expect that you ultimately provide the same or similar information to the Government.[60]

Question 4. Does the concept of "full cooperation" require that I include all the details of the event in my initial disclosure?

Answer. Since the promulgation of the new Rule, two schools of thought have emerged regarding how much information the Rule requires a contractor to provide in connection with an initial mandatory disclosure. Some view the Rule as requiring the disclosure of the actual credible evidence forming the basis for the disclosure. Others view the Rule as requiring only the disclosure of *the existence* of such credible evidence in the initial disclosure, the details of which later are to be provided. The text of the Rule itself does not definitively resolve this ambiguity with regard to the initial disclosure.[61] To the extent you fall within the "only disclose the existence of such credible evidence" school of thought, however, you should be aware that some OIGs and DOJ attorneys may expect additional detail in your disclosure, and likely will view a threadbare offering as insufficient even to qualify as a "disclosure" within the meaning of the Rule.

However, there may be reasons why you do not want initially to disclose unsupported information in your possession. For example, you may not have sufficient facts to determine whether the evidence is "credible," or

---

[59] *See, e.g.,* http://oig.gsa.gov/integrityreport.htm.

[60] *See* Section 7, note 53, for a list of the agency on-line reporting forms that have been made available as of the date of this Guide.

[61] The ambiguity stems from the use of different phrases in the Rule to describe a contractor's disclosure obligation. The new language of FAR Part 9 requires the contractor "to timely disclose . . . credible evidence. . . ." FAR 9.406-2. In contrast, the new language of FAR 52.203-13 requires the contractor to "timely disclose . . . whenever . . . [it] has credible evidence. . . ."

you may be making a preliminary disclosure out of an abundance of caution. In any event, the definition of full cooperation does not require you to waive the protections afforded by the attorney-client privilege or work product doctrine nor does it require waiver of the Fifth Amendment. It also does not restrict you from performing an internal investigation to determine what allegations are supported by credible evidence. Accordingly, it is best to consult legal counsel before making an initial (or subsequent) disclosure under the Rule.

Of course, whether or not your initial disclosure provides sufficient detail to identify "the nature and extent of the offense and the individuals responsible for the conduct," such information will have to be provided to the Government later, for example, in response to subsequent Government requests. As discussed in Question 5 below, full cooperation means disclosure of sufficient information for law enforcement to identify the nature and extent of the offense and the individuals responsible for the conduct.

Question 5. How much detail do I have to share with the Government after my initial disclosure?

Answer. The Preamble to the Rule suggests that the Government ultimately expects to receive "all pertinent information known by the organization." Appendix B, 73 Fed. Reg. at 67,078. The Preamble further suggests that a useful measure of whether you have disclosed "all pertinent information" is to ask yourself whether the information you have provided is sufficient for the auditors or investigators to determine (a) the nature and extent of the offense, and (b) the individual(s) responsible for the conduct. *Id.* This Preamble is consistent with the definition of "full cooperation" in the Rule. Appendix A, FAR 52.203-13(a). A review of the on-line reporting forms established by the various OIGs suggests that the Government expects companies to provide a complete description of the facts and circumstances surrounding the reported incident, including names of individuals involved, dates, locations, how the matter was discovered, potential witnesses and their involvement, estimated monetary loss to the United States, and any corrective action taken by the company.[62]

The on-line forms, however, call for information that, for some cases or disclosures, may go beyond that required by the Rule, and there may be legitimate reasons why you do not want to use the on-line form or respond to all the questions on the form. In addition, information may be protected by the attorney-client privilege or work product doctrine. Moreover, such disclosure and "full cooperation" may as a practical matter make internal investigations more difficult for contractors to conduct. Contractors will

---

[62] *See, e.g.,* http://oig.nasa.gov/contdiscw.html; http://oig.gsa.gov/integrityreport.htm.

need to conduct internal investigations and make disclosures carefully to avoid waiver of privileges. Finally, you may not have sufficient facts to provide such information, and speculation may not be in the best interest of the company or its employees. Thus, you may want to consult legal counsel before making a disclosure under the new Rule, and to make sure that every statement, whether made using the on-line form or not, is supported by sufficient facts at the time of disclosure.[63]

Question 6. What if the OIG doesn't contact me after I make my initial disclosure? Do I have an obligation to contact the OIG with additional information?

    Answer. Generally, the Rule does not require that you supplement an adequate initial disclosure. Accordingly, if your initial disclosure revealed "all pertinent information" about the underlying event, such that the auditors or investigators can determine (a) the nature and extent of the offense, and (b) the individual(s) responsible for the conduct, then it is reasonable that you await further word from the Government before submitting additional information. The converse applies if your initial disclosure is *not* adequate to meet this standard.

    Nonetheless, some within the Government expect that an initial disclosure be supplemented as new material facts come to light even if the full cooperation requirement initially was met. Others, generally outside the Government, disagree, and argue that the Rule does not require this. In light of this disagreement, you would be well served to consult legal counsel should this issue arise. In any event, you should remain vigilant to the potential discovery of new facts that reveal credible evidence of a broader or different covered event. Such new evidence, if not fairly encompassed by the initial disclosure, could create a new disclosure obligation.

    Finally, keep in mind that, for any number of reasons, an initial disclosure can go unanswered for quite some time.

Question 7. When I make disclosures in the course of "full cooperation," do I have to identify people other than those responsible for the conduct?

    Answer. No. The Rule requires only that you identify the "individual(s) responsible for the conduct." Nonetheless, the Government subsequently may request additional information. For example, auditors and investigators often request the names of potential witnesses. Some OIGs may view a company that knowingly refuses to provide such information in response to specific Government requests as non-cooperative. In

---

[63] For a description of what the Department of Defense views as "sufficient information" in the context of its Voluntary Disclosure Program, *see The Department of Defense Voluntary Disclosure Program, A Description of the Process* ¶ C.3.b.

responding to such requests, you should keep in mind that the new Rule defines "full cooperation" as "providing timely and complete response to Government auditors' and investigators' request for" . . . "access to employees with information."

Question 8. How quickly do I need to respond to an auditor's or investigator's request for access to documents?

Answer. The Rule states that full cooperation includes "timely and complete" responses to requests for access to documents. This does not mean, however, that documents must be produced on day one. Government auditors and investigators understand that companies need time to search for, review, and process requests for documents. Therefore, you should agree upon a production schedule with the Government that facilitates the production of responsive materials as promptly as possible under the circumstances, and make reasonable efforts to stick to that schedule.

Question 9. What does the FAR clause mean when it says that I must provide Government auditors and investigators "access to employees with information"?

Answer. FAR 52.203-13 requires that companies subject to the clause implement an internal control system that provides for "full cooperation with any Government agencies responsible for audits, investigations, or corrective actions." The clause defines "full cooperation" as, among other things, "providing . . . access to employees with information . . . ." Appendix A, FAR 52.203-13(a). This does not mean, however, that you must compel your employees to speak to auditors and investigators. Employees may have reasonable and lawful reasons not to speak to the Government. A reasonable course of action in most situations would be to advise your employees that the company intends to fully cooperate in any audit or investigation, but that you recognize that whether they want to meet with the Government is up to them, and that they will not be disciplined for either speaking or not speaking to the Government. You must not in any way, implicitly or otherwise, indicate to your employees that you would prefer they not talk to the Government. You should consider making any statements to employees regarding their meeting with the Government in writing or having a second person with you when you have such conversation to preclude any future dispute regarding what you said or how you said it.

Notwithstanding the above, some Government officials may request that employees be required to personally tell the auditor or investigator that the employee will not speak to them. You should consult legal counsel before agreeing to such a request. The Rule does not define what is meant by "access to employees," and the meaning and scope of the phrase is untested and the subject of ongoing debate. While there are potential advantages to acceding to such a request (*e.g.*, acceding to such a request may help insulate your company from a charge by Government auditors and investigators that your company discouraged your employees from cooperating), there also are potential disadvantages (*e.g.*, running afoul of a collective bargaining agreement by improperly coercing an employee into submitting to an interview to which they did not consent).

Question 10. How quickly do I need to respond to a request for access to employees?

Answer. You need to respond to such requests in a "timely" fashion. This does not mean that you must provide access immediately, however. The Government recognizes that in order to preserve the attorney-client privilege, the work product doctrine, and your employees' Fifth Amendment rights, you likely will need some time to ensure that your employees are aware of their rights and the rights of the company before providing access to employees. Nevertheless, auditors and investigators will expect to be provided with access as soon as possible. It is best that after receiving a request for access to employees, the contractor contact the Government auditor or investigator to establish a reasonable schedule for providing "access to employees." *See* Question and Answer 9 above. What is reasonable will depend on the circumstances, including the promptness and completeness of any disclosure. You should make reasonable efforts to live up to whatever schedule is established.

Question 11. If I require my employees to speak to the Government, or put pressure on them to speak to the Government (*i.e.*, with threat of termination of employment) do I violate the Fifth Amendment?

Answer. The Fifth Amendment protects individuals from being forced to incriminate themselves. The Fifth Amendment restricts only Government conduct and will constrain a private entity only insofar as its actions are found to be "fairly attributable" to the Government. Action by a private entity is fairly attributable to the Government where there is a sufficiently close nexus between the Government and the challenged action of the private entity so that the action may be fairly treated as that of the Government itself. In one recent case, because a company had such a close connection to Government officials during an investigation, and because it threatened an employee with termination if he did not speak with the Government investigators, the employee's statements were ultimately suppressed because they were deemed "coerced" and his Fifth Amendment rights were violated.[64] Thus, although an employer does not itself face legal exposure under the Fifth Amendment, under certain limited circumstances an employee's Fifth Amendment rights may be violated if he is coerced by his employer into speaking with the

---

[64] *Stein v. KPMG LLP*, 2006 WL 2060430, *16 (S.D.N.Y. July 28, 2006).

Government and, as a result, the statements could be suppressed in any ensuing litigation.[65]

However, you should keep in mind that your employees may have a reasonable and lawful basis not to speak to the Government, and coercing those employees could expose your company to legal risk; for example, you may be violating a Collective Bargaining Agreement. *See* Question 14.

Question 12. Will my company be penalized for an employee's decision not to speak to the Government?

Answer. No. Unless you actually *discourage* your employees from cooperating with the Government, either explicitly or implicitly, you will not be penalized for an employee's independent decision not to cooperate. The Preamble to the Rule makes clear that cooperation is measured by the actions of the company itself, not by the actions of the individuals within the company. Employees may have reasonable and lawful reasons not to speak to the Government. You must not, however, in any way discourage your employees from speaking to the Government. Discouraging your employees from speaking to the Government — even with a "wink and a nod" — may be viewed by the Government as a lack of cooperation, or in some circumstances as obstruction of justice.

A reasonable course of action in most situations would be to advise your employees that the company intends to fully cooperate in any audit or investigation, but that you recognize that whether they want to meet with the Government is up to them, and that they will not be disciplined for either speaking to or not speaking to the Government. You should consider making such statements in writing or having a second person with you when you have such conversations to preclude any future dispute regarding what you said or how you said it.

It is conceivable, however, that there may be some circumstances in which an employee's or officer's decision not to speak to the Government might cause the Government to undertake a broader or more thorough investigation.

Question 13. Do I have to discipline employees who refuse to talk to the Government?

Answer. No. It is up to your employees whether they want to talk to the Government, and it would not necessarily be misconduct to decline to speak to the Government. Moreover, the Rule makes clear that an

---

[65] For a thorough discussion of what may constitute "state action" in the "full cooperation" context, *see, e.g., United States v. Stein*, 541 F.3d 130 (2d Cir. 2008).

employee's decision not to speak to the Government will not be viewed as the company's failure to cooperate.

Although employers may certainly choose to take disciplinary action against employees for "improper conduct" (including, but not limited to, suspension and/or termination), employers must be careful not to take any adverse disciplinary action against employees for their personal decision to talk to the Government or not, as this could expose the company to legal risk for a retaliation or wrongful termination claim under applicable state law.

Question 14. Do I have to worry about running afoul of any labor/employment issues if I encourage my employees to speak to the Government?

Answer. Possibly. Since your labor/employment obligations will vary depending upon your state, it is prudent to consult legal counsel or your Human Resources specialist in this regard.

In any event, keep in mind that employees may have reasonable and lawful reasons not to speak to the Government. A reasonable course of action in most situations would be to advise your employees that the company intends to fully cooperate in any audit or investigation, but that you recognize that whether they want to meet with the Government is up to them, and that they will not be disciplined for either speaking to or not speaking to the Government. You must not in any way, implicitly or otherwise, indicate to your employees that you would prefer they not talk to the Government. In this regard, it would also be prudent for employers to update all internal policies, procedures, and handbooks to reflect this "no reprisal" position. You may want to have a second person with you when you have such conversations to preclude any future dispute regarding what you said or how you said it.

Question 15. Are my employees entitled to bring their union representative with them to interviews conducted by company counsel relating to a mandatory disclosure?

Answer. Depending upon the terms of the specific collective bargaining agreement, union employees may be entitled to request that their union representative be present at any "investigatory-disciplinary" interview. This could include company interviews. Denial of a request for union representation in such a context may constitute an unfair labor practice in violation of the National Labor Relations Act. You should consult Human Resources and/or your employment lawyer before initiating employee interviews.

Question 16. Are my employees entitled to request that a union representative accompany them to interviews conducted by Government auditors or investigators relating to a mandatory disclosure?

    Answer. Employees may request that a union representative, or anyone else for that matter, including personal or company counsel, attend an interview with them. While the Government has the right to deny a request for representation by anyone other than the employee's counsel, the employee likewise has the right to decline to be interviewed.

Question 17. Can the company's attorney participate in the Government's interviews of company personnel?

    Answer. Company counsel usually will seek to participate in Government interviews of current employees. Although some Government investigators or auditors may react negatively to such participation, generally company counsel will insist on participating in such interviews. Participation of company counsel in employee interviews is important (1) to protect the company's privileged information, and (2) to stay aware of the types of information that the employee discloses to the Government in order to allow the company to further investigate any alleged wrongdoing. Appendix A, FAR 52.203-13(c).

    The Government's practice regarding non-employees is different. The Government takes the position that its investigators have the right to contact and meet with unrepresented former employees without the company's consent or participation. While many investigators will honor a request that company counsel participate in such meetings, many will not. One possible solution is to offer to coordinate such interviews for the Government in exchange for being permitted to participate. In any event, while the new Rule does not require the company to provide access to former employees, the company should not in any way discourage anyone from meeting with the Government.

Question 18. Can I provide my employees with counsel, at company expense, to represent them in any meetings with Government auditors and investigators?

    Answer. Yes. In a break with previous policy, the Department of Justice has made clear that it would not view the provision of counsel to company employees as a sign of non-cooperation, as long as counsel is provided consistent with the company bylaws and the laws of the state.[66]

---

[66] *See* Memorandum from Mark R. Filip, Deputy Attorney General to Heads of Department Components and United States Attorneys (Aug. 28, 2008) at 13. Previously, the DOJ took the position that companies that provided counsel to their employees would be viewed as not fully cooperating with the Government. *See* Memorandum of Deputy Attorney General Larry Thompson (Jan. 20, 2003). The DOJ position was held unconstitutional in *United States v. Stein*, 495 F. Supp. 2d 390 (S.D.N.Y. 2007).

Question 19. Can I indemnify my employees without running afoul of the requirement to "fully cooperate" in a Government audit or investigation?

    Answer. Yes. The Preamble to the Rule makes clear that a company decision to indemnify employees for legal costs will not be viewed by the Government as a lack of full cooperation.[67]

Question 20. Does the requirement to "fully cooperate" with auditors and investigators require that I provide the Government with material protected by the attorney-client privilege or the attorney work product doctrine?

    Answer. No. The Mandatory Disclosure Rule explicitly provides that a company need not waive the protections of the attorney-client privilege or the attorney work product doctrine.[68] Your decision not to share privileged information with auditors and investigators will not be viewed by the Government as a lack of full cooperation. Of course, it is important to keep in mind that facts are not protected by the attorney-client privilege or

---

[67] The Preamble to the Rule offers a thorough discussion of the FAR Councils' view of indemnification in the "full cooperation" context:

> With regard to indemnification of employees for legal costs, State law — not Federal — controls. Just as full cooperation cannot mean a company forfeits its attorney-client privilege, there is no reason to think it means employees forfeit their right to indemnification from their employers. On December 12, 2006, DOJ addressed this issue in a memorandum sent to all DOJ attorneys by Deputy Attorney General Paul McNulty ("McNulty Memorandum"), stating:
>
> > Prosecutors generally should not take into account whether a corporation is advancing attorneys' fees to employees or agents under investigation and indictment. Many state indemnification statutes grant corporations the power to advance the legal fees of officers under investigation prior to a formal determination of guilt. As a consequence, many corporations enter into contractual obligations to advance attorneys' fees through provisions contained in their corporate charters, bylaws or employment agreements. Therefore, a corporation's compliance with governing state law and its contractual obligations cannot be considered a failure to cooperate.

Appendix B, 73 Fed. Reg. at 67,077.

[68] The Preamble to the Rule states as follows in this regard: "It is doubtful any regulation or contract clause could legally compel a contractor or its employees to forfeit these rights. However, the Councils have revised the final rule to provide such assurance. To address concern that cooperation might be interpreted to require disclosure of materials covered by the work product doctrine, the Councils have added a definition of 'full cooperation' at 52.203–13(a) to make clear that the rule does not mandate disclosure of materials covered by the attorney work product doctrine." Appendix B, 73 Fed. Reg. at 67,077.

work product doctrine.[69] At the same time, if facts are learned through a privileged communication, the line between privileged and non-privileged material may become blurred. Your attorney can help you determine whether material is privileged.

Question 21. Can I choose to produce to the Government material covered by the attorney-client privilege or attorney work product doctrine?

Answer. Yes. In some cases, a company may choose to waive the attorney-client privilege and counsel may choose to waive the protections of the attorney work product doctrine, even though this is not required by the Rule. However, there are numerous issues to consider before making this decision.

In addition, the privileges are personal to the "holder," and may be waived only by the holder. Thus, only an authorized representative of the company may decide to waive the attorney-client privilege. Further, the company should advise employees that the company is the "holder" of the privilege, and should remind them to protect the confidentiality of attorney-client privileged communications. A voluntary disclosure of privileged communications between an attorney and client may waive the privilege as to all communications between them on the same subject. Careful consideration should be given regarding the scope of the material disclosed and the subjects covered by the disclosure. *See* Question 24.

The work product doctrine protects an attorney's mental impressions, opinions, conclusions, and theories.[70] Disclosure of materials protected by the attorney work product doctrine should be discussed with counsel.

---

[69] In this context, the Preamble provides as follows: "Any limitation in this rule should not be used as an excuse by a contractor to avoid disclosing facts required by this rule. Facts are never protected by the attorney-client privilege or work product doctrine." Appendix B, 73 Fed. Reg. at 67077. For additional discussion regarding the attorney-client privilege and work product doctrine, *see generally* United States Attorneys' Manual § 9-28.700. For the view that these protections do not extend to *facts* concerning allegations of misconduct, *see id.* § 9-28.720.

[70] The Restatement (Third) of The Law Governing Lawyers § 90 has the following to say regarding the invocation of the Lawyer Work-Product Immunity:

> (1) Work-product immunity may be invoked by or for a person on whose behalf the work product was prepared. (2) The person invoking work-product immunity must object and, if the objection is contested, demonstrate each element of the immunity. (3) Once a claim of work product has been adequately supported, a person entitled to invoke a waiver or exception must assert it and, if the assertion is contested, demonstrate each element of the waiver or exception.

Question 22. What should I do to protect information from an auditor or investigator on the basis of the attorney-client privilege or attorney work product doctrine?

Answer. To facilitate a determination of whether materials are privileged, a company with the assistance of counsel should create a "privilege log" that contains the following information to the extent it does not reveal privileged information:[71]

(1) the identity and position of the author;
(2) the identity and position of the recipient(s);
(3) the date the document was prepared or written;
(4) the title and description of the document;
(5) the subject matter addressed;
(6) the purposes for which it was prepared or communicated;
(7) the document's present location; and
(8) the specific privilege or other reason the document is being withheld.

The log may later be provided to the Government auditor or investigator to support nondisclosure of privileged materials. Documents withheld based on privilege should be retained and preserved by the company.

Question 23. Will I get "extra credit" if I waive the attorney-client privilege?

Answer. No. Neither the Rule nor DOJ guidance states that any benefit will be given for waiving the attorney-client privilege. In addition, a decision not to waive the attorney-client privilege will *not* be viewed by the Government as a failure to cooperate. Finally, waiver with respect to one communication may operate as a waiver for all communications on the same subject matter. *See* Question 24.

Question 24. Will my intentional partial waiver of the attorney-client privilege operate to waive the privilege for all communications on the same subject matter under Federal Rule of Evidence ("FRE") 502?

Answer. Not necessarily. According to FRE 502(a), the intentional waiver of privilege applies to undisclosed information only if it concerns the same subject matter as material over which the privilege has been waived and the other material "ought in fairness" be considered together with the voluntarily disclosed material. The Advisory Notes explain that the purpose of this rule is to "prevent a selective and misleading presentation of the evidence to the disadvantage of the adversary." When waiving privilege over particular information, a corporation should be careful to avoid this perception so as not to "open[] itself to a more complete and

---

[71] For a thorough discussion of privilege logs, *see, e.g., Knight v. Nimrod*, No. C 00-00290 (N.D. Cal. Jul. 27, 2007) (order regarding discovery procedures); Fed. R. Civ. P. 26(b)(5).

accurate presentation" that requires revealing related information the corporation did not wish to disclose.[72]

Question 25. Can I still conduct a privileged internal investigation even after making a disclosure?

Answer. Yes. The Rule specifically states that full cooperation does not restrict your right to conduct an internal investigation. Appendix A, FAR 52.203-13(a)(3)(i). In addition, other parts of the Rule require you to establish practices and procedures to detect and prevent criminal conduct. FAR 52.203(b)(2), (c)(2). That obligation does not end simply because the contractor has made an initial disclosure to the Government. The rule also states that disclosure and full cooperation do not prevent a contractor from defending against a proceeding related to a disclosed violation. In order to adequately defend against a proceeding of that kind, it may be in the best interest of the contractor to continue its internal investigation after making an initial disclosure.[73] As a practical matter, disclosure and "full cooperation" may make internal investigations more difficult for contractors to conduct. Contractors will need to conduct internal investigations and make disclosures carefully to avoid waiver of privileges.

Question 26. I am a sole proprietor; do I have to waive my Fifth Amendment rights?

Answer. No. Whether you are a sole proprietor or the CEO of a major cooperation, nothing in the Rule requires that you waive your Fifth Amendment rights. The explicit text of the Rule makes clear that "it does not require . . . [a]ny officer, director, owner, or employee of the Contractor, including a sole proprietor, to waive his or her attorney client privilege or Fifth Amendment rights." Appendix A, FAR 52.203-13(a)(2).

Question 27. Does full cooperation mean I cannot dispute the allegation?

Answer. No. The Rule does not restrict your right to defend against a proceeding or dispute arising under the contract or related to a potential or disclosed violation. Appendix A, FAR 52.203-13(a)(3)(ii). Likewise, the Rule does not prevent you from advancing a defense or an explanation for the alleged misconduct. However, you should be aware that statements made in your disclosures to the Government could be construed as "admissions" that could be used as evidence against you in a later proceeding. As a result, when making the disclosure, you should make sure that your

---

[72] For the full rationale and supporting decisional law behind this rule, *see* the Advisory Notes to Federal Rule of Evidence 502.

[73] *See* Question 6 for further discussion of the circumstances under which you may need to supplement your initial disclosure.

language is considered and precise, and that every statement is supported by sufficient facts at the time of disclosure.

Question 28. Does the Rule create expanded Government audit rights?

Answer. According to the drafters, it does not. Outside of the context of a mandatory disclosure, the Rule has no application to or impact on the Government's exercise of its audit and access to records rights. For example, the Government may not use the Rule to expand its rights in the context of a routine contract administration audit. With respect to audits and investigations relating to mandatory disclosures, however, the Rule does suggest an expansion of the Government's rights. Specifically, the Rule requires contractors to provide auditors and investigators with "access to" employees with information.[74]

Whether or not the "access to employees" provision of the Rule is viewed as expanding the Government's audit rights, it is important to note that other regulatory and statutory changes seemingly do provide the Government with expanded audit rights.[75]

---

[74] *See* Questions 9 and 10 above. It is notable also that, on December 19, 2008, DCAA issued guidance on "Denial of Access to Records Due to Contractor Delays" (08-PAS-042(R)), available at http://www.dcaa.mil/mmr/08-PAS-042.pdf. DCAA indicated that contractor documentation responsive to DCAA requests should be readily available and any delay not accompanied by an appropriate explanation will be deemed a formal denial of access to records and reported to appropriate Government personnel. DCAA stated that if necessary, DCAA will exercise its right to subpoena the requested documents.

[75] For example, on March 31, 2009, the FAR Councils issued interim rules implementing the Duncan Hunter National Defense Authorization Act for Fiscal Year 2009 (Pub. L. 110-417) ("Defense Authorization Act") and the American Recovery and Reinvestment Act (Pub. L. 111-5) ("Recovery Act"). The interim rule issued under the Defense Authorization Act amends FAR clauses 52.215-2 (Audit and Records - Negotiation) and 52.214-26 (Audit and Records - Sealed Bidding) to provide GAO with the right to interview current employees regarding transactions being examined during an audit of contracting records. That rule applies to all solicitations and contracts, except commercial item contracts, awarded on or after March 31, 2009.

The interim rule issued under the Recovery Act adds FAR clauses 52.212-5(d) (Commercial Items); 52.214-26(c) (Sealed Bidding); and 52.215-2(d) (Negotiation). The rule applies to all contracts and solicitations that are funded in whole or in part by Recovery Act funds. It provides: (1) GAO and the OIG with authority to review any records of contractors or subcontractors regarding Recovery Act funds; (2) GAO and the OIG authority to interview employees of prime contractors regarding Recovery Act funds; and (3) GAO authority to interview employees of subcontractors regarding Recovery Act funds. *See* 74 Fed. Reg. at 14,649-51.

SECTION 10: PRESERVING CONFIDENTIALITY AND PRIVILEGE AND PREVENTING DISCLOSURES TO THIRD PARTIES

I. INTRODUCTION

Contractors facing the prospect of a mandatory disclosure will often be concerned about the confidentiality of the information they disclose. Such information may be subject to release to third parties under the Freedom of Information Act ("FOIA"), 5 U.S.C. § 552. Moreover, if contractors have conducted an internal investigation before making the disclosure, they may also be concerned about possible waiver of the attorney-client privilege and work product protection.

This Section will address the legal rubric of FOIA and the standards the Government employs in determining whether to release information under FOIA. It will also address briefly some of the privilege and work product considerations that contractors should understand when making a disclosure. Finally, the Section will identify practical steps that contractors can take to minimize the possibility of waivers of privilege or the release of information by the Government to third parties in response to FOIA requests.

II. POTENTIAL GOVERNMENT DISCLOSURES UNDER FOIA

A. Government Contractual Commitment to Protect Disclosures From Disclosure Under FOIA

In its comments on the Proposed Rule issued in November 2007, the Department of Justice ("DOJ") suggested that the FAR Councils should "recommend" that agencies protect contractor disclosures "to the extent permitted by law."[76] The FAR Councils responded to DOJ's

---

[76] *See* Appendix G, Attachment A at 3 ("FOIA Exemption. For a variety of reasons, not the least of which is to encourage contractors to submit information pertaining to overpayments or violations of federal law even if such occurrences have not yet been confirmed, the Councils may wish to recommend to agencies that the submitted information be maintained confidentially to the extent permitted by law. The Councils may further wish to remind agencies that any decision by agencies to make a discretionary disclosure of information protected under the FOIA should be made only after full and deliberate consideration of the institutional, commercial, and personal privacy interests that could be implicated by such a disclosure. In particular, agencies should be mindful that the Trade Secrets Act operates as a

suggestion by adding the following provision to FAR clause 52.203-13, indicating that the Government will safeguard information "to the extent permitted by law and regulation," including FOIA, 5 U.S.C. § 552:

> The Government, to the extent permitted by law and regulation, will safeguard and treat information obtained pursuant to the Contractor's disclosure as confidential where the information has been marked "confidential" or "proprietary" by the company. To the extent permitted by law and regulation, such information will not be released by the Government to the public pursuant to a Freedom of Information Act request, 5 U.S.C. Section 552, without prior notification to the Contractor.

Appendix A, FAR 52.203-13(b)(3)(ii). In the Preamble, the FAR Councils indicated that the addition was intended to "provide appropriate assurance to contractors about the Government's protection afforded to disclosures" and stated that it was based on a similar provision employed by the DOD Voluntary Disclosure Program (DOD Directive 5106.01, April 23, 2006) in "XYZ" agreements with contractors under the DOD Voluntary Disclosure Program Guidance (IGD 5505.50, CIPO, April 1990) (*see* http://www.dodig.mil/ Inspections/vdprogram.htm). Appendix B, 73 Fed. Reg. at 67086.

B. Potential Limitations on the Government's Protection of Contractor Mandatory Disclosures Under FOIA

1. Government Disclosure Obligations Under FOIA

The Government's commitment to safeguard contractor proprietary information contained in disclosures is quite helpful and contractors should take appropriate steps when submitting disclosures to benefit from the Government's commitment. However, contractors should be aware that the Government's contractual commitment to protect information under

---

prohibition on the discretionary disclosure of any information covered by Exemption 4 of the FOIA, unless such disclosure is otherwise authorized by law.").

FAR 52.203-13 may be limited by its statutory obligation under FOIA to disclose certain agency records.

The Freedom of Information Act, 5 U.S.C. § 552, generally provides that any person has a right, enforceable in court, to obtain access to federal agency records, except to the extent that such records (or portions of them) are protected from public disclosure by one of nine exemptions. There are two exemptions that might protect some or all of a contractor's submissions under the Mandatory Disclosure Rule: Exemptions 4 and 7.

2. Exemption 7 of FOIA

Exemption 7 of FOIA protects from disclosure "records or information compiled for law enforcement purposes, but only to the extent that the production of such law enforcement records or information (A) could reasonably be expected to interfere with enforcement proceedings. . . ." 5 U.S.C. § 552(b)(7). The Government is likely to consider investigations into potential criminal violations or violations of the civil False Claims Act to qualify as "law enforcement" activities.[77] Thus, the Government can be expected to invoke Exemption 7 to protect the content of disclosures from disclosure under FOIA, as well as its related investigatory records and information, when it has an ongoing law enforcement investigation into the subject of the disclosure. Less clear is whether the Government would continue to assert protection after an investigation is concluded. It might elect to do so on the ground that such information "(E) would disclose techniques and procedures for law enforcement investigations or prosecutions, or would disclose guidelines for law enforcement investigations or prosecutions if such disclosure could reasonably be expected to risk circumvention of the law." 5 U.S.C.

---

[77] The DOJ Guide on FOIA provides that the "'law' to be enforced within the meaning of the term 'law enforcement purposes' includes both civil and criminal statutes, as well as those statutes authorizing administrative (*i.e.*, regulatory) proceedings." *See* http://www.usdoj.gov/oip/exemption7.

§ 552(b)(7). But the Government may not continue to seek to protect either the content of disclosures, or its own investigative files, after an investigation is concluded.

Thus, there are circumstances in which the Government may elect not to protect information based on Exemption 7. Moreover, contractors have no control over, or say in, the Government's assertion of Exemption 7 in response to a FOIA request. Therefore, a contractor's more likely source of guarding against the Government's release of information provided in a disclosure is Exemption 4.

3. Exemption 4 of FOIA

FOIA Exemption 4 precludes the Government from disclosing "trade secrets and commercial or financial information obtained from a person and privileged or confidential." 5 U.S.C. § 552(b)(4).[78] To fit within Exemption 4, the information in question must be: (1) information obtained from a person that constitutes a trade secret or financial or commercial information; and (2) privileged or confidential. As to the first element, the term "financial" is given its ordinary meaning. *Public Citizen Health Research Group v. FDA*, 704 F.2d 1280, 1290 (D.C. Cir. 1983). "Commercial" means "pertaining to or relating to or dealing with commerce." *American Airlines, Inc. v. Nat'l Mediation Board*, 588 F.2d 863, 870 (2d Cir. 1978). Consequently, whether the information satisfies the requirements of Exemption 4 depends primarily on the second element, that is, whether the information is "confidential."

---

[78] Congress designed Exemption 4 to prevent use of FOIA to inflict competitive harm. *See* Senate Report No. 813, 89th Cong., 1st Sess. 9 (1965); *see also* House Report No. 1497, 89th Cong., 2d Sess. 10 (1966) ("[T]he purpose of Exemption 4 is to "protect the confidentiality of information which is obtained by the Government . . . but which would customarily not be released to the public by the person from whom it was obtained."). The courts have similarly recognized that a principal purpose of Exemption 4 is to protect parties that submit information to the Government from suffering competitive disadvantage as a result of a disclosure. *See Nat'l Parks & Conservation Ass'n v. Morton*, 498 F.2d 765, 767-68 (D.C. Cir. 1974).

Federal courts interpreting Exemption 4 for some time have focused heavily on the issue of whether or not the information at issue was provided *voluntarily* or by *mandate* (*i.e.*, mandatory disclosure). If the agency receives the information on a voluntary basis, the information is considered "confidential" if the person from whom it was obtained would customarily not release the information to the public. *Critical Mass Energy Project v. Nuclear Regulatory Comm'n*, 975 F.2d 871, 879 (D.C. Cir. 1992); *see also McDonnell Douglas Corp. v. National Aeronautics and Space Administration*, 180 F.3d 303, 304 (D.C. Cir. 1999) (citing *Critical Mass*). This test is often referred to as the *Critical Mass* test.

By contrast, if the agency's receipt of the information was compelled by a legal obligation, the information is considered "confidential" only if disclosure would likely either: (1) impair the Government's ability to obtain necessary information in the future; or (2) cause substantial harm to the competitive position of the person from whom the information was obtained. *Nat'l Parks & Conservation Ass'n v. Morton*, 498 F.2d 765, 770 (D.C. Cir. 1974). A showing of actual competitive harm is not required. Rather, there need only be actual competition and a likelihood of substantial competitive injury if the information were disclosed. *NPCA v. Kleppe*, 547 F.2d 673, 679 (D.C. Cir. 1976); *see also Gulf Western Indus., Inc. v. United States*, 615 F.2d 527, 530 (D.C. Cir. 1979). This test is often referred to as the *National Parks* test.[79]

---

[79] The court in *National Parks* remanded the case to the district court emphasizing that the provider of the information had been required by mandate to provide the information to the Government, and therefore the release under FOIA could not have a chilling effect on the voluntary provision of such information to the Government:

> On the record before us the Government has no apparent interest in preventing disclosure of the matter in question. Some, if not all, of the information is supplied to the Park Service pursuant to statute. *Whether supplied pursuant to statute, regulation or some less formal mandate, however, it is clear that disclosure of this material to the Park Service is a mandatory condition of the concessioners' right to operate in*

Accordingly, in determining the protection accorded mandatory disclosures under Exemption 4, the first issue to consider is whether information submitted under the contractual obligation will be considered a voluntary or an involuntary submission. The mandatory nature of the contractual disclosure obligation could affect the Government's ability to protect the information under Exemption 4. The new FAR clause 52.203-13(b)(3)(i) dictates that a contractor subject to the clause "shall" disclose covered violations.[80] It seems quite possible that courts will consider a contractor's decision to submit information to the Government in compliance with a contract clause that mandates disclosure to be an *involuntary* act.

If that is the case, the appropriate legal standard to apply to the FOIA request would appear to be the *National Parks* test. *See Critical Mass*, 975 F.2d at 880 (limited reach of *National Parks*-style competitive impact analysis "to the category of cases to which it was first applied; namely, those in which a FOIA request is made for commercial or financial information a person was obliged to furnish the Government."); *see also Center for Auto Safety v. NHTSA*, 244 F.3d 144, 149 (D.C. Cir. 2001) (holding that only "actual legal authority, rather than parties' beliefs or intentions" can render a submission to the Government mandatory). Significantly, the *Critical Mass* court emphasized the fact that *National Parks* involved information that had been

---

> national parks. Since the concessioners are required to provide this financial information to the Government, there is presumably no danger that public disclosure will impair the ability of the Government to obtain this information in the future.

498 F.2d at 770 (emphasis added; footnote omitted).

[80] *See* Appendix A, FAR 52.203-13(b)(3)(i) ("The Contractor *shall* timely disclose, in writing, to the agency Office of the Inspector General (OIG), with a copy to the Contracting Officer, whenever, in connection with the award, performance, or closeout of this contract or any subcontract thereunder, the Contractor has credible evidence that a principal, employee, agent, or subcontractor of the Contractor has committed — (A) A violation of Federal criminal law involving fraud, conflict of interest, bribery, or gratuity violations found in Title 18 of the United States Code; or (B) A violation of the civil False Claims Act (31 U.S.C. 3729-3733)") (emphasis added).

submitted pursuant to a *statutory or regulatory requirement*.[81] *Critical Mass*, 975 F.2d at 873, 878. Therefore, when FAR 52.203-13 is prescribed by regulation and included in a contract, the *National Parks* analysis would seem to apply to a disclosure made under the contractual obligation.[82]

Under the *National Parks* test, confidential information can be protected even if it was submitted involuntarily (*i.e.*, compelled). Therefore, even if FAR 52.203-13 disclosures are considered "mandatory" for purposes of Exemption 4, the disclosures could still be protected under the *National Parks* test if the contractor can demonstrate that release would likely either: (1) impair the Government's ability to obtain necessary information in the future; or (2) cause substantial competitive harm. *National Parks*, 498 F.2d at 770. The second prong of this test will usually be more relevant in protecting contractor disclosures. Meeting the *National Parks* standard for Exemption 4 protection first requires the contractor to demonstrate the presence of actual competition. *Gulf & Western Indus. v. United States*, 615 F.2d 527, 530 (D.C. Cir. 1979). The second element of the *National Parks* test requires the contractor to establish that in the face of actual competition, release of the information at issue would likely cause the contractor substantial competitive harm. *See McDonnell Douglas Corp. v. U.S. Dept. of the Air Force*, 375

---

[81] In *Center for Auto Safety*, the D.C. Circuit stressed the objective nature of the voluntary / involuntary test, stating: "We reject the argument that, in assessing submissions for the purpose of Exemption 4 analysis, we should look to subjective factors, such as whether the respondents believed that the Information Request was voluntary, or whether the agency, at the time it issued the request for information, considered the request to be mandatory. Focusing on parties' intentions, for purposes of analyzing submissions under Exemption 4, would cause the court to engage in spurious inquiries into the mind. On the other hand, linking enforceability and mandatory submissions creates an objective test: regardless of what the parties thought or intended, if an agency has no authority to enforce an information request, submissions are not mandatory." 244 F.3d at 149.

[82] Even absent the contractual obligation under FAR 52.203-13 and the FAR provisions that mandate disclosure or return of overpayments, a contractor's decision to submit information to avoid potential suspension and debarment under FAR 9.406-2 and 9.407-2 could be considered an involuntary submission.

F.3d 1182 (D.C. Cir. 2004) (finding that "National Parks I, of course does not require the party invoking Exemption 4 to prove disclosure certainly would cause it substantial harm, but only that disclosure would 'likely' do so").

The D.C. Circuit's decision in *Canadian Commercial and Orenda Aerospace Corporation v. Department of the Air Force*, 514 F.3d 37 (D.C. Cir. 2008), reinforces the view that courts will protect involuntarily submitted information if the contractor can demonstrate that disclosure would cause substantial competitive harm. In its decision, the Court did not focus on the voluntary/mandatory distinction. Rather, in affirming the principles it had previously articulated in two *McDonnell Douglas* decisions, it linked Exemption 4 closely to the Trade Secrets Act, 18 U.S.C. § 1905. The Court ruled that line-item prices are covered by Exemption 4 and that if a company can demonstrate there is a reasonable chance that their release would result in competitive harm, the Trade Secrets Act prohibits the Government from releasing the line-item pricing.

Therefore, the cases suggest that a contractor may be able to protect its FAR 52.203-13 submission or at least portions of its submission. However, as a practical matter, the mandatory nature of the disclosure will put a heightened burden on the contractor and make protecting the information from disclosure more difficult.

Some practitioners have suggested that contractors should lace their "mandatory" disclosures with proprietary data and possibly thereby cloak the disclosures in *Canadian Commercial's* strong Trade Secret Act protections. However, this approach might backfire because a reviewing court might find that the *Canadian Commercial* decision had no impact on the *National Parks* test, and might release the proprietary data. Taking that risk into consideration, the opposite approach might be warranted — that is, contractors should place no proprietary information in their disclosures, as the disclosures may be released under the *National Parks* test. Another approach to consider is to submit a mandatory disclosure that omits proprietary information, and to submit a "voluntary" addendum that contains competition-sensitive information. Finally, as discussed in Section 8 of this Guide, another approach is to submit a disclosure as a voluntary disclosure made in an "abundance of caution," which may cause a reviewing court to conclude that the submission is voluntary and therefore subject to review under the more lenient *Critical Mass* test.

4.   Discretionary Government Limitations

The Government may also reconsider the extent to which it wishes to use FOIA exemptions to protect contractor information contained in disclosures. The FOIA policies adopted by the Obama Administration raise some doubts on this issue. In a Memorandum for the Heads of Executive Departments and Agencies issued during his first day in office, President Obama stated that: "[t]he Freedom of Information Act should be administered with a clear presumption: In the face of doubt, openness prevails." Based on the President's direction, Attorney General Eric Holder issued a memorandum on March 19, 2009 with new FOIA guidelines for the heads of agencies.[83] The memorandum provided two primary directives:

- "[A]n agency should not withhold information simply because it may do so legally. . . . An agency should not withhold records merely because it can demonstrate, as a technical matter, that the records fall within the scope of a FOIA exemption."

- "[W]henever an agency determines that it cannot make full disclosure of a requested record, it must consider whether it can make partial disclosure."

---

[83] Available at http://www.dod.mil/pubs/foi/docs/foia-memo-march2009.pdf.

Importantly, the Holder Memorandum states that DOJ will defend an agency's denial of a FOIA request if (1) the agency reasonably foresees the disclosure would harm an interest protected by one of the statutory exemptions, or (2) disclosure is prohibited by law.

The impact of the Administration's position on FAR 52.203-13 disclosures is not yet clear, but it suggests that the Administration will apply closer scrutiny before relying on Exemption 4 or Exemption 7 to protect contractor information. Still, it would seem that if a contractor can convince agencies that specific information is subject to the Trade Secrets Act, or if there is an open investigation, agencies will safeguard the information pursuant to the Holder Memorandum.

III. POTENTIAL WAIVERS OF THE ATTORNEY-CLIENT PRIVILEGE AND WORK PRODUCT PROTECTION

One issue contractors should examine carefully when contemplating a disclosure is the possibility that the disclosure will require, or be deemed to result in, a waiver of the attorney-client privilege or the work product protection that might otherwise protect information from disclosure. Contractors that have conducted an internal investigation typically consider the written documentation developed as a result of that investigation, such as interview memoranda and analyses, to be protected by the work product doctrine. If attorneys are involved in conducting or directing an investigation, the documents reflecting advice concerning the conduct at issue, or the transmission of facts to the attorneys so that advice could be rendered, are protected by the attorney-client privilege. A full analysis of the subtleties of privilege and work product considerations is beyond the scope of this Guide, and contractors contemplating a disclosure should consult legal counsel. However, the following provides some guidance regarding a number of the important privilege and work product considerations that contractors may wish to consider when contemplating a disclosure.

First, the disclosing contractor should be aware that all information disclosed will almost certainly be deemed to waive any attorney-client privilege or work product protection that otherwise might have attached to the disclosed information itself. Thus, disclosing contractors will likely be unable to resist, on the basis of privilege or work product protection, third party requests for the disclosed information (whether directed to the contractor or to the Government). To the extent that the contractor discloses only factual information, it would appear that no waiver should be deemed to occur, because facts are generally not protected by the attorney-client privilege or work product protection. However, to the extent that the contractor discloses analytical information that otherwise would have been subject to a claim of privilege or protection (such as, for example, an analysis of the impact of the disclosed conduct on contract cost or price), then it may be difficult for the contractor to claim subsequently that such information retains any protection against disclosure.

Disclosing parties have argued that disclosures to the Government do not waive privilege and work product protections as against third parties, but such arguments have generally not met with success. In *In re Martin Marietta Corp.*, 856 F.2d 619 (4th Cir. 1988), for example, the company argued that its disclosure of privileged materials to the Government with the expectation of confidentiality did not operate as a waiver as to third parties. The Fourth Circuit rejected this "limited waiver" theory and held that disclosure to the Government waived any attorney-client privilege or work product protection that attached to the disclosed material. Similarly, in *In re Subpoenas Duces Tecum*, 738 F.2d 1367 (D.C. Cir. 1984), the D.C. Circuit permitted a grand jury to subpoena materials a company had submitted to the SEC voluntarily that disclosed illegal payments to foreign officials, finding that attorney-client and work product protections were waived by the disclosure.[84]

Second, the disclosing contractor should also consider whether the disclosure will be deemed to serve as a "subject-matter waiver" as to undisclosed information and communications. For example, the contractor should consider whether the disclosure will result in a waiver of privilege or work product that otherwise would protect undisclosed information such as: interview memoranda of interviews with employees; emails concerning the results of employee interviews; summaries of documents reviewed; and analyses of impact of noncompliances on Government contract costs or prices.

If a contractor discloses only facts, and not any information that is arguably covered by the attorney-client privilege or work product doctrine, then it would seem that there should be no waiver of any privilege or work product claim. However, if the contractor discloses information that is covered by the attorney-client privilege or work product doctrine, then Federal Rule of Evidence ("FRE") 502(a) will govern the scope of the waiver, at least in subsequent federal proceedings. In general, FRE 502(a) (promulgated in September 2008) addresses the scope of the waiver as a result of an intentional disclosure of privileged information or work product that is made in a federal proceeding or to a federal office or agency. The rule provides that a waiver of the privilege or protection as to specific information generally does not effect a broad subject

---

[84] Most other courts have followed suit. *Compare In re Qwest Communications Intern. Inc.*, 450 F.3d 1179 (10th Cir. 2006) (rejecting selective waiver as to work product and attorney-client privileged material); *In re Columbia/HCA Healthcare Corp. Billing Practices Litigation*, 293 F.3d 289 (6th Cir. 2002) (same); *United States v. Mass. Inst. of Tech.*, 129 F.3d 681, 686 (1st Cir. 1997) (same); *Westinghouse Elec. Corp. v. Republic of the Phil.*, 951 F.2d 1414, 1422 (3d Cir. 1991) (same); *In re Chrysler Motors Corp.*, 860 F.2d 844, 845 (8th Cir. 1988) (no selective waiver as to work product material) *In re John Doe Corp.*, 675 F.2d 482, 489 (2d Cir. 1982) (no selective waiver for attorney-client privileged material) *with Diversified Indus., Inc. v. Meredith*, 572 F.2d 596, 607 (8th Cir. 1977) (en banc) (permitting selective waiver of attorney-client material).

matter waiver. Instead, the waiver extends to undisclosed communications or information only if three conditions are met:

    (1)   the waiver was intentional;

    (2)   the disclosed and undisclosed communications or information concern the same subject matter; and

    (3)   the disclosed and undisclosed communications or information "ought in fairness to be considered together."

FRE 502(a).

Thus, an intentional, selective disclosure will effect a waiver of privilege or work product as to materials with the same subject matter only if those materials "ought in fairness to be considered" with the disclosed documents. This is the same language found in FRE 106, which requires that when partial or portions of documents or recordings are introduced into evidence, related writings or recordings may be introduced if they "ought in fairness" to be considered together. Presumably, courts will look to decisions interpreting the language in FRE 106 in construing FRE 502(a). Such circumstances might include (for instance) situations where the disclosed material would be misleading without the undisclosed information, or situations where the disclosing party uses disclosed materials in support of an "advice of counsel" defense, and the undisclosed information is also relevant. The Explanatory Note promulgated by the Judicial Conference Advisory Committee on Evidence Rules accompanying FRE 502 clarifies that "subject matter waiver is limited to situations in which a party intentionally puts protected information into the litigation in a selective, misleading and unfair manner." Explanatory Note at 6. Accordingly, a contractor that has made a mandatory disclosure and is deemed to have selectively and misleadingly disclosed privileged information may be held to have waived its privilege claims as to other information under FRE 502(a), with respect to either the Government or third parties.

Finally, disclosing contractors may be concerned that they will be expected by the Government to waive attorney-client privilege or work product protections. However, as discussed in detail above in Section 9, Questions 20-25, the Mandatory Disclosure Rule explicitly provides that a company need not waive the protections of the attorney-client privilege or the attorney work product doctrine to meet the Rule's requirement for "full cooperation" with the Government.[85]

IV. PRACTICAL INTERNAL STEPS THAT CONTRACTORS MAY TAKE

A. Contractor Steps in Conducting Internal Investigations That May Protect Disclosures from Release

There are several specific steps that contractors can consider taking to help protect their disclosures from release by the Government to third parties. The following provides some guidance as to mechanisms that contractors may want to employ, based on prior experience with steps that have withstood legal challenges.

- **Give an *Upjohn warning*** to all pertinent employees in the investigation explaining what steps the corporation must take to assure privilege protection when initiating internal corporate investigations. *See, e.g., Upjohn Co. v. United States*, 449 U.S. 383 (1981); *Seibu Corp. v. KPMG LLP*, 2002 WL 87461, *2-3 (N.D. Tex. Jan. 18, 2002). Further details about *Upjohn* warnings are set forth in Section 11 below.

- **Limit the disclosure and circulation of the information** within the corporation to necessary parties. This will, in turn, limit comments and

---

[85] The Preamble to the Rule states as follows in this regard: "It is doubtful any regulation or contract clause could legally compel a contractor or its employees to forfeit these rights. However, the Councils have revised the final rule to provide such assurance. To address concern that cooperation might be interpreted to require disclosure of materials covered by the work product doctrine, the Councils have added a definition of 'full cooperation' at 52.203-13(a) to make clear that the rule does not mandate disclosure of materials covered by the attorney work product doctrine." Appendix B, 73 Fed. Reg. at 67,077.

responses to individuals and parties inquiring about reported matters and investigations absent a "need to know." *See Strougo v. BEA Assoc.*, 199 F.R.D. 515, 519-520 (S.D.N.Y. 2001).

- **Limit the involvement of people** who are not necessary to the investigation. *See Cruz v. Coach Stores, Inc.*, 196 F.R.D. 228, 230-31 (S.D.N.Y. 2000).

- If it is necessary to distribute documents to senior management, **request the return of the documents** after they have been reviewed.

- **Retrieve the protected information** at the conclusion of any disclosure of information.

- **Assign a single person** to oversee the distribution and collection of information and ensure the preservation of the attorney-client privilege.

- **Assign investigations to in-house or outside specialists,** not to transactional or multiple-role attorneys. The day-to-day business advice is the responsibility of human resources and other ethics employees. *See* Fed. R. Evid. 501; *In Re: Horowitz*, 482 F.2d 72 (2d Cir. 1973).

- Except where safety and/or security are concerned, **delay Human Resources and other collateral investigations** until after the internal investigation has been completed by counsel. *In Re: Horowitz*, 482 F.2d 72 (2d Cir. 1973).

B. **Employee Steps to Help Protect Disclosures from Release**

Employees can also take the following steps that might help protect information from unwanted release.

- **Attend training** regarding the creation and handling of documents or communications that are attorney-client privileged, proprietary, or confidential.

- **Understand the difference between privileged and non-privileged materials,** *i.e.*, documents created as regular business documents versus documents created at counsel's request.

- **Appropriately mark** documents and e-mails.

- **Maintain confidentiality** of internal investigations.

V. PRACTICAL EXTERNAL STEPS THAT CONTRACTORS AND THE GOVERNMENT MAY TAKE

A. Contractor Steps When Making Submissions that May Protect Disclosures from Release

There are several steps that contractors should consider taking when making their mandatory disclosure submissions to the Government that may help protect the content of the disclosures from release.

- **Mark all confidential, proprietary, and Trade Secret material** as such, and "exempt from FOIA." Note that while such markings are suggested, the markings alone do not guarantee that the Government will safeguard the information from disclosure to third parties.

- **Prepare and submit "White Paper" disclosures that include only facts.** Such papers should be drafted under the protection of the attorney-client privilege until you have determined what should be included in the submission. Characterizations of the facts or witnesses and attorney opinion should be avoided if possible in the disclosed white paper, as it may be deemed to waive the privilege. Companies will typically not want to mark produced information as "subject to attorney-client privilege and attorney work product doctrine," as such marking will likely result in a conclusion that the company has waived such protections and create the possibility that they will be deemed to have effectuated a subject-matter waiver.

- **Consider attempting to enter into a Confidentiality Agreement with the Government** after the initial disclosure, but before further data is provided in order to protect further confidential information. This Agreement should include the protection of presentations, documents, notes, electronic communications, and other documents. It is not yet known whether the Government will entertain such agreements in connection with mandating disclosures. Be aware that the request for a Confidentiality Agreement, in certain circumstances, could be seen as noncooperative or obstructionist.

- **Be aware that a Confidentiality Agreement may not protect information from disclosure.** In *United States v. The Williams Companies*, 2009 WL 1025338, (D.C. Cir. April 17, 2009), the D.C. Circuit ruled that documents produced by the company pursuant to an agreement between the company and the United States were not exempt from disclosure. The parties had agreed that the documents were being produced with the express understanding that the company was not waiving any privileges with respect to any other documents in its possession related to the subject matter, and that the Government would assist the company in preserving the confidentiality of the produced documents. The court held this agreement was not sufficient to prevent the disclosure of the documents by court order if the documents would constitute Brady material or Criminal Rule 16 materials. In *Williams*, the target company had produced some documents, including attorney notes of witness interviews and summaries to the grand jury pursuant to Federal Rule of Criminal Procedure 6(e). In addition, the company voluntarily produced some documents to the Commodity Futures Trading Commission which was conducting a parallel civil investigation into the company's conduct. The case, which turned in part on the fact that D.C. does not permit selective waiver, focused on the factors of preserving the confidentiality of the materials balanced against the need for the defense to obtain access to the information to prepare its defense and for use at trial if the documents were impeaching or exculpatory to the defendant.

B. Government Steps That May Help Protect Contractor Proprietary and Confidential Information

The Government, to the extent permitted by law and regulation, must safeguard and treat information obtained pursuant to a contractor's disclosure as confidential where the company has marked the information "confidential or proprietary." *See* Appendix A, FAR 52.203-13(b)(3)(ii); Appendix B, 73 Fed. Reg. at 67,078. Moreover, Government employees are covered by the Trade Secrets Act, a criminal statute which prohibits the discretionary disclosure of any information covered by Exemption 4 of FOIA, unless disclosure is otherwise authorized by law. 5 U.S.C. § 1905; *Canadian Commercial*, 514 F.3d at 39. Accordingly, an agency's release of records covered by Exemption 4 could violate the Trade Secrets Act. *See, e.g., Chrysler Corp. v. Brown*, 441 U.S. 281 (1979); *McDonnell Douglas Corp. v. Widnall*, 57 F.3d 1161 (D.C. Cir. 1995); *CNA Fin. Corp. v. Donovan*, 830 F.2d 1132 (D.C. Cir. 1987). The following represent steps that the Government can take to meet these obligations.

- Either collect and safeguard, or else destroy, all information at the conclusion of consideration of a disclosure.

- Follow agency guidelines and rules regarding protection of contractor proprietary information.

VI. CONSIDERATIONS FROM THE GOVERNMENT'S PERSPECTIVE

- Generally, a contractor's disclosure of privileged material to a third party, including the Government, will operate to waive the attorney-client privilege. Accordingly, the contractor's attorney-client privilege is waived once a Government contractor discloses information voluntarily to an OIG or in response to an OIG Subpoena.

- With respect to a Civil Investigative Demand ("CID"), 31 U.S.C. § 3733(b) provides protection against the disclosure of information in response to a CID.

- The Federal Rules of Criminal Procedure governing Grand Jury proceedings provide a somewhat higher degree of protection of privileged material from dissemination, although there is no guarantee that information revealed in connection with a Grand Jury proceeding will remain confidential. *See, e.g.*, Fed. R. Crim. P. 6(e).

SECTION 11: DEALING WITH COMPANY EMPLOYEES AND OFFICERS

I. INTRODUCTION

The Mandatory Disclosure Rule provides that contractors must disclose certain types of conduct in connection with the award, performance, or closeout of a contract or subcontract.

- Conduct is reportable if there is "credible evidence" of a violation of federal criminal law involving fraud, conflict of interest, bribery or gratuity violations, or a violation of the civil False Claims Act.

- A significant overpayment must also be reported by other FAR rules, and now a failure to report can be the basis for suspension or debarment.

In order to determine whether "credible evidence" of a violation exists, the contractor will, in most cases, have to talk to employees and company officers who have knowledge of the matters at issue. When questioning these individuals, consideration must be given to:

- Who will conduct the inquiry, *i.e.*, whether an attorney or non-attorney; and

- What warnings should be given to the employees and officers in light of the Mandatory Disclosure Rule in the event credible evidence is found.[86]

II. WHEN ATTORNEYS CONDUCT INQUIRIES: RULES OF PROFESSIONAL RESPONSIBILITY

A. Identify the Client

A lawyer for the company represents the company and does not usually represent the employees as well. Representation of both the company and the employee presents significant potential conflicts of interest, particularly when a contractor is obligated to disclose "reportable conduct." It may not be in the employee's interest for the company to disclose the information that the employee may provide.

---

[86] Company investigators should be aware, of course, that the Government may conduct its own investigation of the conduct at issue. Such investigations, and companies' responses to them, are beyond the scope of this Guide.

Hence, employees should be given *Upjohn* warnings to apprise them that they are being questioned to provide the corporation with the information needed for the rendition of legal advice. The basic message that counsel needs to communicate to an employee in an *Upjohn* warning before an interview commences is: (1) counsel represents the company, not the employee being interviewed; (2) the information learned during the interview is covered by a privilege held by the company, and it is the company's decision alone whether to disclose the information to the Government or other parties; and (3) the information in the interview is to be kept confidential so that the company's privilege can be preserved. The privilege does not attach if the attorney does not take these steps. *Upjohn*, 449 U.S. 383.

In accordance with *Upjohn*, any communications between a contractor and its employees should clearly explain the potential legal implications of the investigation without revealing possible strategy, *i.e.*, primarily that the company may find it appropriate or necessary to share findings with the Government. Employees being interviewed should be made aware that the communications are confidential and needed for the rendition of legal advice to the contractor.

Furthermore, it is important to recognize that the attorney-client privilege extends only to communications, not to facts, *see Philadelphia v. Westinghouse Elec. Corp.*, 205 F. Supp. 830 (E.D. Pa. 1962), and that the title of an employee's position is irrelevant to the applicability of the privilege. *Upjohn*, 449 U.S. 383 (1981). Anyone in the corporate hierarchy can have the facts an attorney needs to advise the corporate entity. The attorney-client privilege covers communications to and from any corporate employee who meets the requisite standards irrespective of the individual's position in the corporate hierarchy.

Many employees interviewed will be unrepresented. Under the Model Rules of Professional Responsibility, when dealing with an unrepresented person the attorney must explain the identity of the client and has an obligation to correct any misunderstanding regarding the lawyer's role "when the lawyer knows or reasonably should know that the unrepresented person misunderstands the lawyer's role in the matter." Model Rule 4.3. An attorney for an organization must explain the identity of the client when the attorney knows or reasonably should know that the organization's interests are adverse to those of the constituents with whom the lawyer is dealing. Model Rule 1.13(f).

In the recent case of *United States v. Nicholas*, 606 F. Supp. 2d 1109 (C.D. Cal. 2009), the federal court in Los Angeles suppressed as evidence statements made by a company officer in an interview with company counsel that counsel had provided to the Government. The court found that the attorneys had not clearly disclosed that they represented only the company and not the individual officer when they interviewed him. The court found that an attorney-client relationship in fact existed with the officer, that his statements were thus privileged, and that counsel violated that privilege when they disclosed the statements to the Government. The court referred the attorneys to the State Bar for discipline.

B. Additional Disclosure Obligation in Light of the Mandatory Disclosure Rule

Depending on the information learned by the company during the interview or learned at some other point in the investigation, the company may be required by law or its Government contract to disclose the information to the Government.

Because of the Mandatory Disclosure Rule, it is important to advise the employee that the information provided may be disclosed to a third party, including the Government. Prosecutors have recently used obstruction of justice theories to indict employees who make false statements to company counsel who are conducting an internal investigation when the employee knows or has reason to know that the results of the investigation will be shared with the Government. *United States v. Kumar*, 2006 U.S. Dist. LEXIS 96142 (E.D.N.Y. 2006).

Providing these warnings in writing is not a common practice, although there may be circumstances when a written warning may be appropriate based on counsel's evaluation of the employee's reaction to the oral warning. Investigating counsel must walk a very fine line when dealing with employees. While counsel must advise the employee as described above, counsel does not want to frighten the employee so the employee does not want to cooperate, which will only serve to make it more difficult to determine whether there is "credible evidence." However, counsel must be clear about whether counsel is or is not representing the employee.

C. Questions That May Arise

1. Do I need a lawyer?

Counsel should advise the employee that counsel cannot provide advice on that issue, except to tell the employee that the employee has the right to have separate counsel. If applicable to the circumstances, counsel may also consider advising the employee about the corporation's policy of paying for an employee's counsel.

2. Is there a conflict of interest?

Related to the preceding question, it may be necessary for counsel to discuss whether a conflict of interest exists between the corporation and the person being interviewed. If conflicts of interest are discussed, counsel should emphasize that facts and circumstances can change, that the interests of the employee and the corporation could come into conflict with each other, that counsel will alert the employee of such a conflict if and when counsel learns of one, and that the employee should do the same.

3. What if employees refuse to cooperate in this investigation?

In cases where the employee inquires about the consequences of not cooperating in the investigation, the employee should be informed of the pertinent corporate policies applicable to internal investigations. In particular, most corporate policies will discipline employees who refuse to cooperate in internal investigations, and such discipline can include termination of employment.

III. WHEN NON-ATTORNEYS CONDUCT INQUIRIES

Compliance officers, managers, and other non-attorneys may often conduct the initial inquiry to determine whether there is "credible evidence." As non-attorneys, they are simply company representatives and form no attorney-client relationship or privilege, even for the company. Therefore, a less expansive warning could be given, as attorney professional responsibility rules are not applicable and the non-attorney is less likely to confuse the employee about whether he or she "represents" the employee. At a minimum, the following points should be conveyed:

- The investigator is there on behalf of the company to conduct a confidential inquiry;

- The interview is confidential and the employee is expected to keep it confidential; and

- The investigator will share the information provided with the company.

In addition, consideration should be given to conveying the following additional points, although a non-attorney would have no ethical obligation to do so:

- Although the employee is obligated to keep the information confidential, the company has a right to disclose the information to anyone.

- Depending on the information learned by the company during the interview or learned at some later point, the company may be required by law or its Government contract to disclose the information to the Government.

SECTION 12: PAST PERFORMANCE AND CONTRACTOR RESPONSIBILITY DETERMINATION REQUIREMENTS

I. INTRODUCTION

The regulations promulgated with the Mandatory Disclosure Rule made a significant revision to the FAR with respect to past performance evaluations. Specifically, the definition of "past performance information" at FAR 42.1501 was revised to include "the contractor's record of integrity and business ethics." Appendix B, 73 Fed. Reg. at 67,091.[87] This revision raises a number of important questions for the source selection process that are the subject of this Section. First, the revision raises a threshold practical question of how the Government will go about collecting information regarding a "contractor's record of integrity and business ethics." The Preamble to the Rule indicates that the FAR Councils declined to require agencies to "collect distinctive data and information on contractor responsibility." 73 Fed. Reg. at 67,086. Yet one possible conclusion from the revision is that the FAR Councils intended for agencies to collect and consider information that is not currently being collected; otherwise there would have been no point in expanding the scope of "past performance information."[88] As discussed below, implementing the Councils' directive to collect this new information, while at the same time

---

[87] As revised, FAR 42.1501 defines past performance information as follows:

> Past performance information is relevant information, for future source selection purposes, regarding a contractor's actions under previously awarded contracts. It includes, for example, the contractor's record of conforming to contract requirements and to standards of good workmanship; the contractor's record of forecasting and controlling costs; the contractor's adherence to contract schedules, including the administrative aspects of performance; the contractor's history of reasonable and cooperative behavior and commitment to customer satisfaction; the contractor's record of integrity and business ethics, and generally, the contractor's business-like concern for the interest of the customer.

[88] Another interpretation, however, is that the FAR Councils simply intended to make FAR 42.1501 consistent with existing agency practices of considering contractors' integrity and business ethics.

avoiding the collection of "distinctive data and information on contractor responsibility," presents a number of logistical choices and challenges.

Once these threshold challenges are overcome and the information is collected, the question then becomes, what must an agency do with this information? The Rule envisions that a contractor's record of integrity and business ethics may be relevant to an agency's source selection decision in two contexts: (1) the agency's past performance evaluation; and (2) the agency's determinations of present responsibility. In each context, agencies must navigate a number of legal and practical choices to determine the extent to which they will consider this new information and how it will be considered. The remainder of this Section addresses each of these questions in turn.

The Task Force is aware that, at the time this Guide was written, there were pending rulemakings that will have an effect on the matters discussed herein. *See* 74 Fed. Reg. 45,394 (Sept. 2, 2009) (proposing new FAR 42.1503(f)); 74 Fed. Reg. 45,579 (Sept. 3, 2009) (proposing amendments to FAR Part 9). Nonetheless, the Task Force believes there is value in discussing the ramifications of the regulations as they currently exist.

II. METHODS OF COLLECTING PAST PERFORMANCE INFORMATION

The FAR Councils declined to require agencies to collect "distinctive" information on contractor responsibility:

> The proposed rule has added a cross reference in Part 42 to promote the inclusion of business integrity in past performance. The request to collect distinctive data and information on contractor responsibility is outside the scope of this rule.

Appendix B, 73 Fed. Reg. at 67,086. Thus, while seeking to "promote" inclusion of integrity-related information in past performance considerations, the Councils essentially abstained from the development of any specific regulations.

Currently, past performance information is maintained in a disparate fashion by various agencies. The basic repository for such information is the Past Performance Information Retrieval System ("PPIRS"), which is maintained by DOD's Naval Sea Logistics Center. DOD alone maintains three separate databases that feed into PPIRS, including the Contractor Performance Assessment Reporting System ("CPARS"). NASA maintains information of this sort in its Past Performance Database ("PPDB"). DHS and DOE are transitioning to CPARS, while other civilian agencies use the Contractor Performance System ("CPS") maintained by NIH. *See* GAO, *Better Performance Information Needed to Support Agency Contract Award Decisions*, GAO-09-374 (April 23, 2009).[89]

Effective July 1, 2002, all of these systems were to feed into PPIRS, so that federal contracting officials would have access to all relevant information. However, the GAO has found that the information in PPIRS is incomplete. It includes information for only a small percentage of federal contracts, and even for the contracts that are covered, useful information (such as information about terminations for default and subcontract management) is not systematically maintained. *Id.* at 11-14. Moreover, many agency officials report that their lack of confidence in the objectivity of past performance information has led them to rely on factors other than past performance in award decisions. *Id.* at 8-10.

Further complicating matters, Section 872 of the Defense Authorization Act of 2009 (Pub. L. 110-417) requires the creation of a new database of information regarding integrity and performance of federal contracts, including convictions in criminal proceedings, most dispositions in civil and administrative proceedings related to federal contracting, default terminations, suspensions, debarments, and nonresponsibility determinations. The statute

---

[89] Available at http://www.gao.gov/new.items/d09374.pdf.

requires the "federal agency official responsible for awarding the contract or grant" to "review the database" and "consider all information in the database with regard to any offer or proposal." Pub. L. No. 110-147, § 872(e)(2)(A). The statute further requires the FAR to be amended to require contractors with contracts greater than $10 million to update the database. *Id.* § 872(f). The Section 872 requirement raises the question whether this information in the database will be considered the type of information to be considered under FAR Subpart 42.15, and whether this database will be linked to PPIRS and the agencies' past performance databases.[90] Moreover, there is a pending Rule proposing to amend FAR Part 9 to implement these statutory requirements. *See* 74 Fed. Reg. at 45,580.

The inclusion of ethics and integrity issues in past performance information raises several issues:

- First, will contractor disclosures under the Mandatory Disclosure Rule now be used as an additional source of past performance information? At present, the FAR contemplates information collected only by means of evaluations of contractor performance (such as CPARS data), or when specifically requested to support future award decisions. FAR 42.1502(a). If so, then the disclosures a contractor makes under the Rule may have a direct impact on that contractor's past performance evaluation for future awards. Similarly, would contractors continue to have the right under FAR 42.1503(b) to submit comments or additional information when the adverse past performance information at issue results from disclosures the contractor itself made?

- Are there appropriate sources of information regarding integrity and business ethics *other* than "traditional" sources? For example, are agency SDOs or OIGs appropriate sources of information not otherwise available in a past performance database or derived from a contractor disclosure? If such sources of information are appropriate, will the contractor be permitted to supplement the record or otherwise address any adverse

---

[90] Effective July 1, 2009, agencies are now required to submit an electronic record of contractor performance in PPIRS. 74 Fed. Reg. 31,557. On September 2, 2009, the FAR Councils proposed a new rule that would, *inter alia*, require contracting officers to provide information about defective pricing determinations, default terminations, and any subsequent conversion or withdrawal of these actions to the PPIRS within 10 days of the action. 74 Fed. Reg. 45,394.

information regarding this information? Does it make a difference, for example, if there is an ongoing investigation of the contractor? Does this kind of information increase the risk of "blacklisting"?

The Preamble to the Rule acknowledges a concern regarding potential blacklisting but concludes that the process for soliciting adverse information under FAR 15.306(b)(1) and (d)(3) and 42.1503(b), as well as the rules for assessing contractor responsibility under FAR Subpart 9.1, are sufficient to address this concern. Appendix B, 73 Fed. Reg. at 67,080. However, this response presumes that contractors will be permitted to comment on adverse information obtained through these "nontraditional" sources. At present, it is not known whether this assumption is correct.

III. EVALUATION OF PAST PERFORMANCE

A. The Rule Does Not Diminish Agencies' Discretion to Determine How Past Performance Will Be Evaluated

By revising the definition of "past performance information" to include "the contractor's record of integrity and business ethics," the Rule raises an important question whether agencies must now evaluate integrity and business ethics as part of their past performance evaluations in negotiated procurements. *See* Appendix B, 73 Fed. Reg. at 67,091. Although the Preamble states that the FAR Councils sought to "promote the inclusion of business integrity in past performance," Appendix B, 73 Fed. Reg. at 67,086, agencies likely retain the discretion they have historically enjoyed to decide what past performance information they will consider in their evaluations, and how that information will be evaluated.

Agencies are generally required to evaluate past performance in negotiated procurements in excess of the simplified acquisition threshold, unless they document why past performance is not an appropriate evaluation factor. FAR 15.304(c)(3). Nevertheless, agencies have long enjoyed broad discretion to determine "the approach for evaluating past performance" that will be employed in a given procurement.[91] The Rule did not amend FAR Part 15 or otherwise explain whether or how an agency must consider a "contractor's record of integrity and business ethics" as part of its evaluation of a contractor's past performance under FAR 15.305(c)(3). Instead, the past performance provisions of the Rule amend FAR Subpart 42.15, which merely provides policies and procedures for "recording and maintaining contractor performance information." FAR 42.1500. Although information compiled under that Subpart is "relevant information for future source selection purposes," FAR 42.1501, it is only one of several sources of relevant information, and there is no requirement that agencies must consult this information in the evaluation of proposals. *See Si-Nor, Inc.*, B-292748.2, 2004 CPD ¶ 10 n.2 (Jan. 7, 2004). Instead, agencies are free to base their past performance evaluations on other sources of information, such as questionnaire or survey responses from references identified by the offeror.

The absence of an express directive to consider this information as part of every past performance evaluation stands in contrast to the FAR's present responsibility regulations, which specifically require the CO to consider whether the contractor has "a satisfactory record of integrity and business ethics (*see, e.g.*, Subpart 42.15)." Appendix A, FAR 9.104-1(d). This contrast, and the absence of similarly explicit language in FAR Part 15, suggests that the FAR Councils did not intend to alter fundamentally the manner in which agencies evaluate past performance for source selection purposes.

Accordingly, agencies have discretion to determine the extent to which a contractor's record of integrity and business ethics will be considered in the evaluation of past performance in a negotiated procurement, as well as the types of information that will be considered. So long as

---

[91] *See* FAR 15.305(a)(2)(ii); *General Dynamics-Ordinance & Tactical Systems*, B-295987, 2005 CPD ¶ 114 (May 20, 2005) ("The evaluation of past performance, including the agency's determination of the relevance and scope of the offeror's performance history to be considered, is a matter of agency discretion. . . .").

the agency's approach to evaluating this information is clearly identified in the solicitation, and so long as the agency treats the offerors equally and in accordance with the solicitation, an agency's past performance evaluation will continue to be entitled to deference.

B.   Practical Considerations and Limits on Agency Discretion in the Evaluation of a Contractor's Record of Integrity and Business Ethics

There are several legal and practical considerations that should be taken into account when determining whether and how to evaluate a contractor's record of integrity and business ethics. First, agencies should clearly spell out in the solicitation how past performance will be evaluated, and what sources of information will be considered. *See, e.g.*, FAR 15.304(d) ("The general approach for evaluating past performance information shall be described"). As discussed above, the agency has discretion to determine whether it will consult past performance information compiled under FAR Subpart 42.15, or whether it will instead base its evaluation on other sources of information such as questionnaire/survey responses or any of the "nontraditional" sources identified above. The most efficient way to avoid a dispute regarding the scope of the evaluation is to place all offerors on notice of precisely what the agency intends to do.

Once an agency undertakes to evaluate offerors' records of integrity and business ethics, the agency's discretion is not unlimited. For example, GAO has held that "some information is simply too close at hand to ignore." *GTS Duratek, Inc.*, B-280511.2, 98-2 CPD ¶ 130 (Oct. 19, 1998) (sustaining protest where agency failed to consider information personally known to the evaluators); *accord Seattle Sec. Services, Inc. v. United States*, 45 Fed. Cl. 560, 568-69 (2000) (holding that information regarding protester's performance under the incumbent contract was "too relevant and close at hand to ignore"). Accordingly, where information regarding a contractor's record of integrity and business ethics is personally known to the evaluators and source selection officials, or where the information concerns a similar contract with the same agency (*e.g.*, the incumbent contract) an agency may abuse its discretion if it fails to consider that information as part of its past performance evaluation. *Morrison Knudsen Corp.*, B-280261, 98-2 CPD ¶ 63 (Sept. 9, 1998) ("Where we have charged an agency with responsibility for considering information close at hand in its past performance evaluation, that information has generally concerned contracts for the same services, with the same procuring activity, or at least information personally known to the evaluators."). In this regard, however, agencies must be careful to distinguish between known, verified information regarding a contractor's record of integrity and business ethics on the one hand, and publicly known information regarding *allegations* of improper conduct, such as those contained in media reports, on the other.

Agencies must also take care to avoid making *de facto* responsibility determinations in the course of evaluating past performance. FAR 15.503(a)(2)(i) emphasizes that the "comparative assessment of past performance information is separate from the responsibility determination required under Subpart 9.1." This concern is arguably heightened in the context of a contractor's record of integrity and business ethics, as the FAR now makes this information relevant to both past performance and responsibility considerations. Moreover, an adverse finding regarding a contractor's record of integrity and business ethics, if repeated in successive procurements, may constitute a *de facto* debarment that improperly avoids the procedural safeguards provided under FAR Subpart 9.4. *See generally JCI Envt'l Servs.*, B-250752, 93-1 CPD ¶ 29 (Apr. 7, 1993) (addressing protester's argument that past performance evaluation constituted a *de facto* debarment).

Other issues that agencies should consider when exercising their discretion include:

- **Lack of Relevant Past Performance Information.** Agencies should distinguish between offerors that have a negative record of integrity and business ethics and offerors that simply have no relevant information on this point. FAR 15.305(a)(2)(iv) provides that offerors in the latter category may not be penalized for their lack of relevant past performance. *See, e.g., The MIL Corp.*, B-294836, 2005 CPD ¶ 29 (Dec. 30, 2004) (sustaining protest where agency gave protester a "red" rating due to the offeror's lack of past performance).

- **Discussions.** FAR 15.306(d)(3) provides that, where discussions are held, agencies must discuss with each offeror in the competitive range "adverse past performance information to which the offeror has not yet had an opportunity to respond." In the wake of the Rule, these discussions should now include negative information regarding a contractor's record of integrity and business ethics. Moreover, even where discussions are not held, FAR 15.306(a)(2) provides that "offerors may be given the opportunity to clarify certain aspects of proposals (*e.g.*, the relevance of an offeror's past performance information and adverse past performance information to which the offeror has not previously had an opportunity to respond)." Although agencies have considerable discretion whether to seek clarification regarding negative past performance information, GAO has held that it is unreasonable not to allow an offeror to respond where "there clearly is a reason to question the validity of the past performance information, for example, where there are obvious inconsistencies between a reference's narrative comments and the actual ratings the reference gives the offeror." *General Dynamics - Ordinance & Tactical Systems*, B-295987, 2005 CPD ¶ 114 (May 20, 2005).

- **Predecessor Companies, Key Personnel, and Subcontractors.** FAR 15.305(a)(2)(iii) provides that agencies "should take into account past performance information regarding predecessor companies, key personnel who have relevant experience, or subcontractors that will perform major or critical aspects of the requirement when such information is relevant to the instant acquisition." Although agencies enjoy discretion to determine when information regarding these entities and individuals is "relevant," agencies may not evaluate past performance information concerning entities that will not be involved in performing the contract. *See, e.g., Universal Building Maint., Inc.*, B-282456, 99-2 CPD ¶ 32 (July 15, 1999) ("[I]n determining whether one company's performance should be attributed to another, an agency must consider the nature and extent of the relationship between the two companies — in particular, whether the workforce, management, facilities, or other resources of one may affect contract performance by the other.").

IV. PRESENT RESPONSIBILITY

Federal contracting officers are bound under Subpart 9.1 of the FAR to make an affirmative finding of a prospective contractor's responsibility prior to making an award.[92] The FAR requires that this determination include a finding that the contractor has "a satisfactory record of integrity and business ethics." Appendix A, FAR 9.104-1(d). The Rule adds a new cross-reference to the amended FAR 42.15. *Id.*

While Subpart 9.1 of the FAR generally identifies various areas to which a determination of responsibility must be directed, it does not specify a standard of evidence or minimal due process to be applied in rendering responsibility decisions. This is particularly important when handling potential disclosures under the new Mandatory Disclosure Rule that could result in a criminal investigation or prosecution since the contracting officer's responsibility determination must include a finding that the contractor has "a satisfactory record of integrity and business ethics." *See* Appendix A, FAR 9.104-1(d). Moreover, in many cases a disclosure of potential wrongdoing or overbilling, even if ultimately resolved in a manner favorable to the contractor making the disclosure, will result in a federal investigation at some level.

Unlike the rules governing a federal suspension or debarment official's decisionmaking under FAR Subpart 9.4 or the Non-procurement Common Rule at 2 CFR Part 180, responsibility determinations by contracting officers and assistance award officials do not address situations in which the federal Government has competing interests between its contract award and

---

[92] FAR 9.103(b). As a general matter, the contractor is primarily obligated to make the same affirmative responsibility finding with respect to its prospective subcontractors. However, the FAR authorizes the contracting officer in appropriate cases to make the determination of responsibility of the contractor's proposed subcontractor directly. *See* FAR 9.104-4. Failure by the contractor to exercise that obligation prior to award places the contractor in danger of having its own responsibility questioned by the department or agency conducting the procurement and could even result in the contractor's own debarment if its failure to comply with the obligation later results in, or contributes to, serious misconduct or poor performance by the subcontractor. *See* FAR 9.4.

administration interests and its investigation and prosecutorial interests. When such proceedings are to be conducted in a parallel fashion, relevant information in the matter is unlikely to be available to either the contractor or the contracting officer. Since the contracting officer must make a final decision with regard to the prospective contractor's responsibility under circumstances that precludes either party to the decision having access to the information, what standard of evidence or information is he or she to apply in making a decision? Furthermore, even if access to the information is obtained, there is no process under the FAR for the contracting officer to receive or protect that information from disclosure to the contractor while the Government conducts its investigation or initiates legal proceedings based on the same or similar facts.

Assuming that the contractor and the contracting officer are unable to gain access to information potentially relevant to a decision about the prospective contractor's responsibility during an investigation, the contractor may be unable to make an affirmative demonstration sufficient to satisfy the contracting officer. Because the regulation places the burden on the contractor to prove its responsibility once the contracting officer has a basis for questioning the contractor's record of integrity, a possible end result is a finding of non-responsibility. The contractor could also suffer the same outcome repeatedly by that department or agency on subsequent procurements until the investigation or legal proceedings are concluded. Such repeated findings of non-responsibility by contracting officers without resorting to the suspension or debarment process may constitute a *de facto* debarment. *See Leslie and Elliott Co., Inc. v. Garrett*, 732 F. Supp. 191 (D.D.C. 1990); *Hellenic Am. Neighborhood Action Comm. v. City of New York*, 933 F. Supp. 286 (S.D.N.Y. 1996).

FAR 9.104-5(2) instructs the contracting officer to refer a matter to the appropriate suspending or debarring official if an offeror's certification "indicates the existence of an indictment, charge, conviction, or civil judgment." It does not require the contracting officer to make a similar referral where the contractor makes a disclosure on the basis of "credible evidence" of misconduct or overbilling during the exercise of its due diligence and look-back obligations. Indeed, preventing this type of case-by-case decisionmaking by contracting and assistance award officials and the risk of *de facto* debarment was one of the reasons why the Government-wide suspension and debarment system of uniform rules and due process protections was instituted in the early 1980s. Since then, matters that involve the potential suitability of a contractor or grantee to receive federal funds on the basis of its ethics or integrity have been deemed more appropriately handled in the suspension and debarment process rather than the contracting officer's responsibility determination process. Even if the suspending official determines that suspension would be a prudent course of action, the contractor may convince the suspending official to exercise his or her discretion to impose conditions under an interim administrative agreement rather than issuing or continuing a suspension. With the new Rule, however, there may be a theoretical danger that contractors and their subcontractors will be subject to repeated denial of contract or assistance awards on the basis of their disclosures without the procedural safeguards that would be afforded them in the suspension and debarment process. There has been no indication to date, however, that this concern has materialized.

V. PRACTITIONER GUIDELINES

- Contractor reports of "credible evidence" of wrongdoing (especially submissions made out of an "abundance of caution") will often be incomplete in some respect. Offerors should be given an opportunity to rebut adverse information of this kind, just as would be the case with other adverse past performance information.

- For the same reason, unresolved allegations and investigations should not form the basis of adverse contracting officer present responsibility determinations.

- To minimize the risk of *de facto* debarment, contracting officers should consider deferring adverse responsibility determinations based on reports relating to unresolved matters of this kind to the cognizant SDO.

- Practitioners should be aware of the potential for *de facto* debarment as a result of contracting officer responsibility determinations and be prepared to seek injunctive or other relief in the event the contractor is denied award repeatedly on the basis of the contractor's disclosure under the Rule.

SECTION 13: STRUCTURING ETHICS AWARENESS PROGRAMS AND INTERNAL CONTROL SYSTEMS

I. **ETHICS AWARENESS PROGRAMS**

A. **Background**

Before December 12, 2008, the Government did not require that its contactors have a business ethics awareness program. DFARS Subpart 203.70, 48 C.F.R. § 203.70, applicable only to defense contractors, did express an expectation but not a requirement that such contractors have a business ethics and conduct program. FAR 9.406-1, which listed mitigating factors to be considered by debarring officials in reaching debarment decisions, named as one factor whether the contractor had effective standards of conduct and internal control systems in place at the time the cause for debarment arose. And, importantly, Chapter 8 of the U.S. Sentencing Commission Guidelines for Organizations, as amended effective November 1, 2005, emphasized a "compliance and ethics program" as an essential element of an effective program to prevent and detect wrongdoing in the organization.[93]

The preceding regulatory and policy encouragements for contractor business ethics awareness programs have now been made mandatory for covered contractors. Unlike the disclosure portion of the Mandatory Disclosure Rule, there is no specific commentary on this matter in the Preamble to the Rule. Accordingly, in developing guidance for structuring an effective business ethics awareness program, the Task Force has drawn on experience under the regulatory and policy provisions mentioned above. Additionally, this subsection I should be read

---

[93] Moreover, preceding the current Rule, effective December 24, 2007, the FAR was amended to require that companies with non-commercial contracts performed within the United States expected to exceed $5 million and with a performance period of 120 days or more must have a written code of business ethics and an internal control system. *See* Appendix F, 72 Fed. Reg. at 65,882.

in connection with the closely related guidance on Internal Control Systems in subsection II below.

B. Company Values

A company should identify its company values that will serve as the foundation of its ethics and business conduct program.

- Identify those ethical values to which the company leadership gives top and consistent priority. What does the company stand for? How does the company want to be perceived by its stakeholders, especially its Government customers?

- For a Government contractor, these values often include honesty, integrity, quality, accountability, trust, respect, creativity, and citizenship.

C. Code of Business Ethics

Building on the foundation of the company values, the Code should express the company business ethics and conduct expected of all personnel.

- The Code must be in writing, be issued under the personal endorsement of the CEO, and provided to all personnel.

- The Code should include the company rule on high risk compliance areas (see below).

- The Code should provide instructions on how to report suspected wrongdoing and how to ask questions about ethical dilemmas.

D. Inquiry and Reporting Mechanisms

It is important that the Code include a place for employees, suppliers, customers, and others who do business with the company to ask questions or raise areas of concern.

- The Code should designate specific individuals or positions that can answer questions regarding the Code or ethical obligations and concerns.

- The company should consider appointing a compliance officer who can oversee inquiries and reports that relate to the Code.

- Employees, suppliers, customers, and others doing business with the company should never be dissuaded against making a good faith inquiry or report.

E. Information and Awareness Program

In addition to publishing a code of conduct, it is necessary to continue to communicate the company's commitment to ethics and compliance to employees.

- Always as part of new employee orientation.

- Annual requirement for each employee to read the Code and acknowledge having done so.

- Unscheduled information and awareness briefings to keep affected employees informed of changes in law, policy and regulations that affect their responsibilities.

- Periodic reminders to report suspected wrongdoing within established company channels.

- An important best practice is to keep the message fresh and to use multiple means of communication and information.

F. Program Assessment and Evaluation

Part of maintaining an effective Ethics and Business Conduct Program is conducting regular program assessments and evaluations.

- Have a mechanism to receive and consider employee suggestions on what is and is not working with respect to the Program.

- The Program should be reviewed and revised as appropriate when the company undergoes changes, such as acquiring a new division or group.

- There should also be consistent, periodic reviews of the Program that focus on all aspects of the Program, particularly its effectiveness, and changes to the Program should be made as necessary.

G. Leadership Commitment

The visible commitment of a company's leadership at all levels is imperative to the success of the program.

- Responsibilities of leaders include being familiar with all aspects of the Program and abiding by them.

- Leaders should take swift and appropriate action with respect to any actual or potential violations that come to their attention.

- Leaders should strive to instill the importance of the Program in all employees under their supervision.

- Leaders should make themselves available to all company personnel to answer questions, provide guidance, or direct personnel to where they may be able to find appropriate guidance.

H. DII Guidance on Creating and Maintaining an Effective Ethics and Business Conduct Program

The Defense Industry Initiative on Business Ethics and Conduct has promulgated useful guidance entitled "Creating and Maintaining an Effective Ethics and Business Conduct Program," which is available at http://www.defenseethics.org/images/DII_Toolkit.pdf.

II. INTERNAL CONTROL SYSTEMS

A. Regulatory Requirements

FAR 52.203-13 (Contractor Code of Business Ethics and Conduct) was originally published on November 23, 2007, effective December 24, 2007. *See* Appendix F. The Rule applied to prime and subcontracts exceeding $5 million and over 120 days and required that:

- Within 30 days of award contractors must have a written code of ethics and conduct, provide a copy to each employee involved in the contract, and promote compliance with its code;

- Within 90 days of award contractors must have an ongoing awareness program promoting business ethics and proper conduct and an internal control system to facilitate timely identification and notification of improper conduct in connection with Government contracts; and

- Contractors provide proper training in ethics, compliance and technical/regulatory requirements to employees and principals.

In the Rule effective December 12, 2008, the scope of FAR 52.203-13 was expanded to:

- Require timely identification and reporting of credible evidence of certain criminal offenses and civil FCA violations by contractors;

- Require full cooperation with any Government agencies responsible for audit, investigation, or corrective action; and

- Sets minimum standards for an internal control system.

The new clause at FAR 52.203-13 (Appendix A) further provides that, at a minimum, these internal control systems shall include the following:

(A) Assignment of responsibility at a sufficiently high level and adequate resources to ensure effectiveness of the business ethics awareness and compliance program and internal control system.

(B) Reasonable efforts not to include an individual as a principal, whom due diligence would have exposed as having engaged in conduct that is in conflict with the Contractor's code of business ethics and conduct.

(C) Periodic reviews of company business practices, procedures, policies, and internal controls for compliance with the Contractor's code of business ethics and conduct and the special requirements of Government contracting, including —

   (1) Monitoring and auditing to detect criminal conduct;

   (2) Periodic evaluation of the effectiveness of the business ethics awareness and compliance program and internal control system, especially if criminal conduct has been detected; and

   (3) Periodic assessment of the risk of criminal conduct, with appropriate steps to design, implement, or modify the business ethics awareness and compliance program and the internal control system as necessary to reduce the risk of criminal conduct identified through this process.

(D) An internal reporting mechanism, such as a hotline, which allows for anonymity or confidentiality, by which employees may report suspected instances of improper conduct, and instructions that encourage employees to make such reports.

(E) Disciplinary action for improper conduct or for failing to take reasonable steps to prevent or detect improper conduct.

(F) Timely disclosure, in writing, to the agency OIG, with a copy to the Contracting Officer, whenever, in connection with the award, performance, or closeout of any Government contract performed by the Contractor or a subcontractor thereunder, the Contractor has credible evidence that a principal, employee, agent, or subcontractor of the Contractor has committed a violation of Federal criminal law involving fraud, conflict of interest, bribery, or gratuity violations found in Title 18 U.S.C. or a violation of the civil False Claims Act (31 U.S.C. 3729-3733).

(1) If a violation relates to more than one Government contract, the Contractor may make the disclosure to the agency OIG and Contracting Officer responsible for the largest dollar value contract impacted by the violation.

(2) If the violation relates to an order against a Government-wide acquisition contract, a multi-agency contract, a multiple-award schedule contract such as the Federal Supply Schedule, or any other procurement instrument intended for use by multiple agencies, the contractor shall notify the OIG of the ordering agency and the OIG of the agency responsible for the basic contract, and the respective agencies' contracting officers.

(3) The disclosure requirement for an individual contract continues until at least three years after final payment on the contract.

(4) The Government will safeguard such disclosures in accordance with paragraph (b)(3)(ii) of this clause.

(G) Full cooperation with any Government agencies responsible for audits, investigations, or corrective actions.

B.   Guidance for an Effective System

There are seven key areas in an effective system of internal control to assure an adequate compliance system is in place and functioning.

1.   Management Commitment to the Program

Management must set the "tone from the top" and demonstrate a genuine commitment to the ethics and compliance program. This commitment must be visible to all employees, from executive management down to work force.

2. Adequate Policies and Procedures

Not only is a firm record of the program and having detailed policies and procedures in place a wise decision, it is required by the regulation. The documentation of policies will provide a solid baseline for the design of compliance reviews and will minimize confusion between the Government and the contractor as to the interpretation of adequate ethics and business conduct controls as described by the new rules. The policies should be comprehensive and provide clear guidance on what is expected and what are the ramifications for failure to comply. Moreover, a final written policy will provide the foundation for training of new and existing employees.

3. Dedication of Qualified Internal Resources for Implementation and Practice

No effort can succeed unless supported by dedicated resources with the requisite skill and available time, and an effective ethics and compliance program is no different. Company management should ensure that responsibility for meeting the requirements of the Rule is held by an individual or office with the authority and manpower to do so. Some typical places within the company which manage the responsibility for compliance with the Code are the general counsel's office, head of compliance, or potentially an ethics officer. Smaller companies may give the CFO or other executive position the authority to enforce this Rule. The risk is that assigning responsibility to a layer of management that is already overburdened, or one that does not have a high enough level of authority, may result in inadequate implementation of controls or a system of periodic internal review with too narrow a focus.

4. Proper Training in Ethics and Compliance

Training is vital to disseminating information in a manner that demonstrates the company's attitude toward the subject matter and to ensure the program is effective. To begin with, training is required by the Rule. In the interests of time, possibly because the Rule requires that a business ethics awareness and conduct program be in place within 90 days of a covered contract award, contractors could be tempted to simply circulate the code of ethics document, along with any policies and procedures which have been developed to maintain compliance. However, this may not go far enough to ensure that every employee has received and understands the company's position on ethics and compliance, including potential recourse if the policies are not followed. Furthermore, the Rule requires that appropriate technical and regulatory training be conducted. A best practice is to require all employees to receive training when they begin employment, when changes are made to the policies or regulations, and as a remedial training course if they have been noncompliant with company policies.

5. Documentation of Compliance Policies and Procedures, Including Responsibility for Compliance Oversight

The system of periodic internal review required by the Rule demands reviews be conducted of business practices, procedures, policies, and internal controls environment for compliance with the Rule. Policies and procedures should be established to reflect the company's compliance attitude within the framework of the company's business. The internal review process should provide an on-going evaluation of the adequacy of those policies and procedures and a mechanism should exist to update them in the event that inadequacies are identified.

6. Self Reviews and Independent Reviews According to Policies and Procedures and Government Guidelines

A combination of internal review and independent review is a best practice to ensure that the periodic internal review process is operating effectively and objectively. Independent review can occur through use of internal resources if care is taken to ensure a minimum of organizational conflict of interest. External resources are the best way to achieve a fully independent evaluation of a company's internal controls, policies, and procedures and the review process.

7. Establishment of Processes to Address Audit Findings, Determine the Need for Disclosures, and Implement Corrective Actions

Finally, a process should be established to address all findings of the internal review process. Findings should be documented, along with the company's rationale as to whether or not disclosures should be made. An effective process with guidelines for document creation and retention will be a company's best defense against allegations that it failed to perform due diligence in accordance with the Code or that it failed to make a mandatory disclosure.

C. Action Items for Consideration

Contractors should consider the following action items to assure that their internal controls are in place and functioning effectively.

- Update training programs not only in the ethics area but also in other compliance areas such as estimating and pricing, purchasing, cost accounting, etc., to assure they are current and complete.

- Perform or update a "gap" analysis to identify areas needing improvement.

- Establish a formal documentation process for investigations and reviews that clearly establishes the procedures employed, the results of the investigation, and the basis for disclosure or nondisclosure.

- Assure adequately trained investigative resources are available.

- Revise, as necessary, standard subcontractor flowdown clauses.

- Update final payment process to assure there are no "significant" overpayments.

D. Potential Impact of the Rule on External Audits and Financial Reporting

Since the disclosure of a potential violation may have a significant impact on a company's financial statements, the company's external auditors will most likely perform additional analysis and require additional information. As part of the auditor's assessment in conformance with the Statement on Auditing Standards 99, *Consideration of Fraud* (SAS 99), the auditor will consider the potential impact that a covered issue may have on the financial statements, and will likely also consider the company's compliance program. In particular, the auditor will likely assess the program to determine if it complies with the minimum requirements of the Rule, if the program has been properly designed and implemented, and if the program is effective in reducing risk and ensuring disclosure of overpayments, violations of the False Claims Act, and relevant criminal violations. The auditor will likely use this assessment to understand the potential risks and develop an audit plan. The auditor may increase its audit testing and analysis if the planning assessment determines that the compliance program, as designed and implemented, may not be effective.

Auditors will also seek additional information and representations from management. Management should anticipate seeing the management representation letter expanded to include coverage of the Ethics and Compliance program, and in particular a requirement for a representation that all matters identified under the program have been disclosed as required by the Mandatory Disclosure Rule. In addition, the auditors will likely also ask that the legal letter include a discussion of any matters disclosed in accordance with the Mandatory Disclosure Rule. The auditors will also seek to obtain disclosures from management regarding any internal assessments of the company's ethics and compliance program, as well as a description of any significant changes to the program, including revisions to internal controls.

E. Disclosures and Accruals in Company Financial Statements Under Current FAS 5

All companies and especially SEC registrants will need to evaluate each instance or matter being investigated or disclosed to ascertain if it needs to be disclosed in accordance with Financial Accounting Standards ("FAS") 5, *Accounting for Contingencies*. FAS 5 requires measurement and disclosure if the contingency is either "probable," which is defined as "future event or events are likely to occur," or "reasonably probable," which is defined as "more than remote but less than likely." The disclosure should provide both a description of the contingency and the estimated loss, which may be provided as a range of exposure. Even in those instances where an estimate cannot be made, the disclosure of the matter is still required within the footnotes of the financial statements. Where the contingency is considered to be only "remote," no disclosure is required. A key consideration will be for management to determine if the "credible evidence" associated with a disclosure equates to a determination that the event is "probable" or "reasonably probable" to result in a loss contingency. Management will need to assess this question, and should also seek guidance from outside experts such as its auditors and lawyers to determine if matters disclosed under the Mandatory Disclosure Rule meet the requirements of FAS 5 with regard to disclosure within the financial statements.

F. Disclosures and Accruals in Company Financial Statements Under the Proposed Amendments to FAS 5

In 2008 the Financial Accounting Standards Board ("FASB") issued proposed revisions to FAS 5. The proposed revisions to FAS 5 maintain the same circumstances for disclosure of a loss contingency.[94] However, the proposed revisions require substantially more in the disclosures within the financial statements. The proposed amendments, by requiring substantially more qualitative information regarding the contingency, would likely result in each mandatory disclosure being disclosed separately, since each likely will have differing qualitative information. However, the separate disclosure requirement may be waived when separate disclosure of each matter may be prejudicial to the company's litigation position. In these instances, the company would be required to disclose the contingencies on a combined or

---

[94] Available at http://www.fasb.org/ed_contingencies.pdf.

aggregate basis in a matter that does not allow the information to be linked to a specific issue or matter. However, the company will need to provide an explanation as to why the information is aggregated.

In addition, the proposed FAS 5 revisions may even require disclosure of a potential matter that is considered remote if it may have a severe impact on the financial statements and will be resolved within the year. The proposed revisions will also remove the ability to disclose without an estimate. Instead, if there is no amount associated with a contingency, the company must include its "best estimate of the maximum exposure to loss" within its disclosure.[95] The proposed revisions require a company to disclose an estimate of loss or range of loss even if the company does not believe that the current claim amount represents the full loss exposure to the company. The proposed revisions also include specific disclosure requirements, such as:

- A description of the loss contingency, including "how it arose, its legal or contractual basis, its current status and the anticipated timing of its resolution";

- Significant assumptions used to determine the estimated loss or range of loss;

- An assessment of the most likely outcome of the contingency;

- A description of factors that are likely to impact the outcome, including the potential impact of each factor on the outcome;

- A description of insurance or indemnification arrangements that may result in recovery of all or part of the loss; and

- For each period in which a statement of income is provided, a reconciliation of the changes in the estimated loss.[96]

---

[95] *Id.* at ¶ 7(a)(2).

[96] *Id.* at ¶ 7(b)-(c).

At its August 2009 meeting, the FASB continued deliberations of the proposed changes to FAS 5, and while the final guidance has not been issued, it is clear that there will be requirements for increased disclosure in financial statements.

G. Factors the DCAA Will Likely Examine When Evaluating Internal Controls

Beginning in 2009, the DCAA began requesting that contractors provide information concerning their systems for compliance with the Mandatory Disclosure Rule. A sample redacted request is found at Appendix O. This request states that the DCAA is seeking information:

> verifying that [the contractor] . . . provides appropriate disclosure to the government of information needed to fulfill its responsibilities. *We define adequate disclosure as disclosure to DCAA and the ACO of all findings that significantly impact within 5-10 days of identification;* . . . and disclosure of adjustments to government contract costs and improvements to underlying business systems. Please provide a list of violations to the code of conduct/ethics which occurred in the past 12 months.

Appendix O at 2 (emphasis added). The DCAA audit request also asks for documentation of the contractor's mechanisms (hotline program, ombudsman program, etc.) for employees to use in identifying and reporting noncompliances and requests "a list of reported noncompliances during the past 12 months." *Id.* DCAA also asks for the contractor's policies and procedures "detailing the steps for timely reporting to appropriate Government officials of any suspected violation of law in connection with Government contracts." *Id.* at 3. Finally, the DCAA audit request seeks production of the contractor's policies and procedures related to "management intervention and/or overrides" of the compliance internal control system or disclosures of violations. *Id.*

Subsequently, the DCAA issued "Audit Guidance on Federal Acquisition Regulation (FAR) Revisions Related to Contractor Codes of Business Ethics and Conduct" (July 23, 2009), available at http://www.dcaa.mil/mmr/09-PAS-014.pdf. By this document, the DCAA amended its master audit program to include verification:

that the contractor's policies and procedures provide for timely disclosure . . . when there is credible evidence of a violation of Federal criminal law involving fraud, conflict of interest, bribery, gratuity, or a violation of the civil False Claims Act in connection with Government contracts. . . . Request a copy of any disclosures made and verify that the contractor complied with their policies and procedures.

Similarly, the DCAA Contract Audit Manual (DCAM) has been revised (effective June 30, 2009) to state that the contractor's internal controls and policies and procedures must ensure:

[t]imely disclosure in writing to the agency Office of Inspector General (OIG), with a copy to the contracting officer, when there is credible evidence of violation of Federal criminal law involving fraud, conflict of interest, bribery, or gratuity violations, or a violation of the civil False Claims Act in connection with Government contracts. Auditors should ensure that the contractor's policies and procedures include a reasonable definition of credible evidence, and a reasonable timeframe for disclosure once credible evidence is obtained.

DCAM Section 5.306(a)(6). However, the Rule provides no authority for the DCAA to determine the "reasonableness" of credible evidence definitions or disclosure timeframes.

When evaluating a contractor's ethics and internal control systems, it is reasonable to expect that the DCAA will generally be performing the following procedures:

- Verifying policies, procedures, training, and compliance with policies and procedures. This will include reviewing the written code of conduct, the ethics training program, and the contractor's monitoring program.

- Evaluating the contractor's self-governance program. The evaluation will include the following:

    - Verifying a system to report noncompliances is in place (*i.e.*, a hotline or ombudsman program);

    - Determining if the contractor participates in self-governance programs such as DII or Coordinated Audit Planning;

    - Establishing whether policies and procedures address timely reporting of issues to Government officials and call for cooperation with Government agencies; and

    - Verifying that DOD Hotline poster is properly displayed.

- Reviewing for management intervention and overrides. The evaluation will include the following:

    - Determining whether policies and procedures address the frequency of management intervention, require documentation and approval of intervention, and prohibit management overrides; and

    - Evaluating compliance with policies and procedures.

- Evaluating internal and external audit functions related to current accounting systems. The evaluation will generally consist of

    - Determining whether the system provides for internal and/or external audits;

    - Reviewing external audit reports on material weaknesses in internal controls and/or management letters; and

    - Reviewing the annual report or Form 10K for SEC registrants.

SECTION 14: NONPROCUREMENT TRANSACTIONS

I. INTRODUCTION

Nonprocurement transactions are non-contractual transactions with the federal Government. These include grants, cooperative agreements, scholarships, fellowships, contracts of assistance, federal loans, loan guarantees, subsidies, insurances, payments for specified uses, and donation agreements. 2 C.F.R. § 180.900. As many universities, hospitals, corporations, and non-profit organizations know, the award and administration of nonprocurement transactions are governed by a separate regulatory scheme from Government procurement contracts (which are subject to the FAR).[97] The Mandatory Disclosure Rule discussed in this Guide is completely FAR-based and specifically states that it does not apply to grants. Appendix B, 73 Fed. Reg. at 67,084 ("[T]his regulation applies only to contracts using appropriated funds, not to grants.")[98] This raises the question of why this Guide includes a chapter on nonprocurement transactions.

The answer is that the Government has begun to mandate disclosure requirements in connection with nonprocurement transactions similar to those included in the FAR Mandatory Disclosure Rule. For example, a similar but broader disclosure requirement must be included in

---

[97] FAR 2.101 defines "acquisition" as "acquiring by contract with appropriated funds of supplies or services (including construction) by and for the use of the Federal Government through purchase or lease, whether the supplies or services are already in existence or must be created, developed, demonstrated, and evaluated. Acquisition begins at the point when agency needs are established and includes the description of requirements to satisfy agency needs, solicitation and selection of sources, award of contracts, contract financing, contract performance, contract administration, and those technical and management functions directly related to the process of fulfilling agency needs by contract."

[98] *See also* Appendix B, 73 Fed. Reg. at 67,084-85 ("[T]his regulation applies only to contracts using appropriated funds, not to grants. . . . This rule is not imposing any requirements on grant recipients.") The Preamble states that the Mandatory Disclosure Rule "does not and is not intended to address contractor compliance programs and integrity reporting with respect to agency grant-making procedures. Given the legal differences between a grant and a contract that concern performance and termination for default, the creation of a single Government standard addressing contractor compliance programs and integrity reporting is not practical and is outside the scope of the rule." *Id.*

all American Recovery and Reimbursement Act ("Recovery Act")[99] grants and cooperative agreements. *See* Office of Management and Budget, Executive Office of the President, OMB Mem. No. M-09-15, Updated Implementing Guidance for the American Recovery and Reinvestment Act of 2009, §§ 5.9, 7.4 (Apr. 3, 2009), available at http://www.whitehouse.gov/omb/assets/memoranda_fy2009/m09-15.pdf [hereinafter "OMB Guidance"]. The Government has also begun to amend the suspension and debarment rule that applies to nonprocurement transactions (known as the "Common Rule"). At some point in the future, the Common Rule will include a similar, as yet undefined, disclosure requirement that provides a new ground for suspension or debarment. The Common Rule may also add a requirement for compliance programs. Exactly when, and to what extent, the Common Rule will be amended is "unknown."[100] These requirements indicate that the Government is moving towards requiring all recipients of federal funds to disclose information about certain types of violations or potential violations or risk being suspended or debarred from receiving federal funding or doing business with the Government.

This means that anyone who receives federal funds should be prepared to identify, investigate, and disclose information about certain violations and potential violations. Anyone receiving or considering receiving federal funding should be aware of the issues and risks that arise when the recipient must disclose information that is potentially damaging to the recipient. For this reason, the FAR Mandatory Disclosure Rule provides a point of reference for examining

---

[99] The Recovery Act is also sometimes referred to as the Stimulus Act.

[100] "It is unknown when the NSTC [National Science and Technology Council] initiative to develop compliance guidance for recipients of Federal research funding from all agencies across the Federal Government will be completed. The Councils do not agree to delay the FAR rule pending the outcome of this particular initiative. Often the regulations for grants use the FAR as a model." Appendix B, 73 Fed. Reg. at 67,085.

issues that arise under these other disclosure requirements, even if they are not identical to the FAR Rule. This means that to the extent the disclosure requirements include the same language, anyone receiving federal funding should consult the guidance provided to Government contractors under the FAR rule throughout this publication.

This Section examines the similarities and differences between the FAR Rule and the Recovery Act disclosure requirement, focusing on the implications where the two requirements diverge. This Section also examines some of the issues that may arise if the Common Rule is amended to include the same requirement as the FAR Rule. As explained below, the disclosure requirements under both the Recovery Act and Common Rule are broader (and more onerous) than those of the FAR Mandatory Disclosure Rule.

II. THE RECOVERY ACT DISCLOSURE REQUIREMENT

As part of the Government's effort to jumpstart the United States economy, the Government is spending some of the Recovery Act funding on Government programs. Some of these Government programs have traditionally been supported, at least in part, by federal grants and cooperative agreements. Recipients of Recovery Act funding used to support nonprocurement transactions (which will be referred to as "grantees" for the remainder of this Section) are subject to an unprecedented level of transparency and accountability. The Government has heightened transparency and accountability requirements for Recovery Act funds to let Americans know where their tax dollars are going and how they are being spent.

To meet the objective of providing transparency and accountability, the Office of Management and Budget ("OMB") has issued several installments of Government-wide guidance. This guidance provides federal agencies with requirements and guidelines for awarding and overseeing Recovery Act funds. Grantees receiving Recovery Act funding are addressed only in one installment of this guidance. OMB issued this installment on April 3,

2009. The OMB Guidance instructs agencies to include a mandatory disclosure requirement in all grants and cooperative agreements funded at least in part by the Recovery Act. The Recovery Act disclosure requirement is worded similarly to the FAR Mandatory Disclosure Rule, but it is not identical. The language of the Recovery Act disclosure requirement presents a number of issues that warrant examination.

A. The Recovery Act Disclosure Requirement

The OMB Guidance requires agencies to include a disclosure requirement in each grant, subgrant, loan, loan guarantee, and cooperative agreement. According to this disclosure requirement, grantees receiving Recovery Act funds to support nonprocurement transactions must:

> promptly refer to an appropriate inspector general[101] any credible evidence that a principal, employee, agent, contractor, sub-grantee, subcontractor, or other person has submitted a false claim under the False Claims Act or has committed a criminal or civil violation of laws pertaining to fraud, conflict of interest, bribery, gratuity, or similar misconduct involving those funds.

OMB Guidance, §§ 5.9, 7.4. Unfortunately, this is the extent of the discussion regarding this disclosure obligation. The OMB Guidance provides no additional information regarding how to interpret this obligation. Grantees[102] must remember that the language in the award document prevails over the language cited above. However, the following discussion explores issues that arise as a result of the language in the OMB Guidance because it provides the basis for what will likely appear in an award document. To the extent that disclosure issues overlap with those of the FAR Rule, recipients of Recovery Act funds should consult the rest of this Guide where

---

[101] The Inspector General for the agency from which the grantee received funding.

[102] This Section uses the term "grantee" to include subgrantees and recipients of loans, loan guarantees, and cooperative agreements, because the same requirements apply.

similar questions arise. Thus, the starting point is to examine where the Recovery Act disclosure requirement deviates from the FAR Rule.

B. Similarities and Differences Between the Recovery Act and FAR Mandatory Disclosure Rule Requirements

The OMB Guidance does not provide any interpretation of the disclosure requirement for recipients of Recovery Act funds. However, the Recovery Act disclosure requirement raises many of the same questions raised by the FAR Rule. For example:

- What is "credible evidence?"

- Who is a "principal?"

- What is a "false claim" under the 2009 amendments to the civil False Claims Act?

- What benefits can a compliance program offer?

- What information should be included in a disclosure?

- Does past conduct need to be reported?[103]

- Must reportable violations occur using particular funds?[104]

- How much time can pass before a report is untimely?[105]

Because these issues resemble those that arise under the FAR Rule, grantees should refer to the discussions relating to these issues in the other chapters of this Guide.

---

[103] Although the answer to this question is yes, the question remains of how long ago conduct could have occurred and still require reporting; see discussion below.

[104] The requirement to disclose violations "involving" funds made available under the Recovery Act is similar to the FAR Rule's requirement to disclose violations "in connection with" Government contracts and is not further discussed here.

[105] Although the FAR Rule requires "timely disclosure" of credible evidence of a violation, because "prompt" is not defined or described in any detail, these standards will likely be viewed similarly. As described in Section 6, the timing for disclosure includes permitting time to investigate a potential violation to determine whether "credible evidence" of a violation exists.

In addition, the Recovery Act disclosure requirement poses some unique issues that are discussed further below. These include:

- How does a grantee identify the "other persons" for whom it must disclose a violation?

- What types of violations must be disclosed?

- Is there any time limitation on disclosing past violations?

- Does this disclosure requirement apply to Recovery Act funding received from state grants?

Although the OMB Guidance does not address these issues, the FAR Rule and the Common Rule provide some insight. However, many of these issues arise from catch-all language that is not included in the FAR Rule. The fact that the FAR Rule and the Common Rule include different definitions for the same term also affects these issues. Although the differing definitions of the Common Rule have greater implications for language adopted from the FAR Rule (as discussed below), this Section will only include those that relate directly to the language in the OMB Guidance.

Recovery Act grantees are reminded that the exact Recovery Act disclosure requirement would depend on language incorporated into the award document itself. Grantees should consider seeking written clarification on the limits to their disclosure obligations from the agency based on the language in the award document before accepting funds. As another reminder, the Common Rule does not yet include any disclosure requirement, especially one that provides a new ground for suspension or debarment.

C. Identifying the "Other Persons" for Whom a Grantee Must Disclose Violations

The OMB Guidance provides that agencies must require each grantee who receives Recovery Act funding to disclose credible evidence of violations of "a principal, employee, agent, contractor, sub-grantee, subcontractor, *or other person.*" OMB Guidance, §§ 5.9, 7.4. The OMB Guidance does not define "person." Without further information, this requirement seemingly has no limits. The FAR Rule does not include a similar catch-all. However, the Common Rule does include a definition of "person." Unfortunately, this definition is quite broad, and does not seem to limit the persons for whom a grantee must disclose a violation. Eventually, when the Common Rule is amended, it may include some of the limits established in the FAR Rule.

As a starting point, the plain language in the OMB Guidance means that each agency would require a grantee who received Recovery Act funds to disclose credible evidence of *any* potential violation of which it learns. For example, under this broad interpretation, a grantee who is performing research and development activities on a defense project could be required to disclose credible evidence that a consultant had not undertaken proper testing on a product sold to the Government under a completely separate, and unrelated, contract on a project that used Recovery Act funds. Disclosure could be required here because the Government may see the nonconforming testing as a potential False Claims Act violation by an "other person" — the consultant.

Although the Common Rule provides some assistance by defining "person," the definition does not limit the requirement to disclose a violation of an "other person." The Common Rule defines "person" as "any individual, corporation, partnership, association, unit of government, or legal entity, however organized." 2 C.F.R. § 180.985. Using this definition, a grantee must disclose a violation by virtually anyone.

In comparison, the FAR Rule provides some limits on what violations must be disclosed. The FAR Rule requires contractors to report violations only when a "principal" has knowledge of credible evidence of a violation, and the violation is "in connection" with the contractor's contract or a related subcontract. Although what exactly this means may not be perfectly clear, it limits what type and when disclosures are required of contractors. This language may be adopted in the future Common Rule amendment. But, as described below, this would present different issues for the Common Rule because it defines "principal" more broadly than the FAR Rule. Hopefully, the Common Rule will not include the catch-all requirement to disclose a violation of "other persons" in light of these broad definitions.

D. Types of Violations to Be Disclosed

Grantees should be aware that the conduct that must be disclosed under the Recovery Act disclosure requirement is much broader than under the FAR Rule. According to the OMB Guidance, agencies must require each grantee who receives Recovery Act funding to disclose credible evidence of:

- a "false claim under the False Claims Act;" or
- a "criminal or civil violation of laws pertaining to fraud, conflict of interest, bribery, gratuity, or similar misconduct involving those funds."

OMB Guidance, §§ 5.9, 7.4. In contrast to the FAR Rule, neither of these categories distinguishes between federal and state law, or criminal and civil law. This means that a grantee would need to disclose credible evidence of a violation of criminal or civil law, whether federal or state law. For False Claims Act violations, grantees must apparently disclose any potential false claim, whether under federal or state false claims statutes, and whether a criminal or civil violation. This is also true for violations involving fraud, conflict of interest, bribery, or gratuity. However, this second category also adds the catch-all "or similar misconduct" language. As a result, grantees must disclose a wider array of violations than contractors.

1. **Violations of the False Claims Act**

According to the Recovery Act disclosure requirement, a grantee could be required to disclose a violation of the federal civil or criminal False Claims Acts, as well as any state's civil or criminal False Claims Acts. Reporting violations of the federal civil or criminal False Claims Act may not add a huge burden as much of the conduct that violates one may violate the other. In contrast, the requirement to disclose any violation of any of the 50 states' laws in addition to the federal laws poses an additional, potentially difficult burden on grantees.

The FAR Rule is more limited in scope because it does not require reporting violations of state law. The FAR Rule specifically requires disclosure of *only* violations of the federal civil False Claims Act and specified federal criminal statutes.

Grantees should be aware that they face increased exposure, even if they were only required to report violations of the federal civil False Claim Act. This is because the May 2009 amendments to the civil False Claims Act have increased grantee exposure to False Claims Act liability. (These amendments are described above in Section 2.) The 2009 False Claims Act amendments change definitions and expand the types of conduct that can violate the law. For example, grantees (at any tier) may now violate the False Claims Act by knowingly and improperly retaining a "significant overpayment." Although the OMB Guidance does not specifically require grantees to disclose "significant overpayments," retaining a significant overpayment may create False Claims Act liability under the 2009 amendments. Thus, a grantee would need to disclose any instance in which it received too much money.

2. Violations Involving Fraud, Conflict of Interest, Bribes, Gratuities, or Similar Misconduct

Grantees should note that unlike the FAR Rule, the Recovery Act disclosure requirement is not limited to violations of federal criminal laws under Title 18 of the United States Code.[106] This means that grantees must also disclose violations of state criminal laws and other federal civil laws involving fraud, conflict of interest, bribes, gratuities, or similar misconduct. The Recovery Act guidance also requires disclosure of "similar misconduct" involving Recovery Act funds. This catch-all language could be interpreted to require disclosure of misconduct not rising to the level of a criminal or civil violation, or misconduct that resembles fraud, conflict of interest, bribery, gratuity, or something else entirely. Although it is not clear, grantees may also be required to disclose violations of the Anti-Kickback Act or the Foreign Corrupt Practices Act, among other laws. Regardless, it appears that grantees may be required to disclose credible evidence of a much broader variety of legal violations.

E. Absence of Time Limitation on Disclosing Past Violations

The Recovery Act disclosure obligation includes no limit on how long after a violation occurs a grantee must make a disclosure. Without a time limit, a grantee could be required to disclose reportable events years after they occurred. Such a disclosure requirement may serve little purpose if a statute of limitations has run on the violation.

In contrast, the FAR Rule takes a slightly more manageable approach by limiting a contractor's disclosure requirement to three years after final payment. Appendix A, FAR 9.406-2(b)(1)(iv), 9.407-2(a)(8), 52.203-13(c)(2)(F). The OMB Guidance includes no similar limitation. This means that a grantee has an ongoing obligation to disclose credible evidence of

---

[106] DOJ had recommended clarifying that the Rule required disclosure of violations of Title 18 of the United States Code rather than leaving the requirement broader.

any violation — even more than three years after the completion of the project for which Recovery Act funds were used.

F. Application of Disclosure Requirement to Recovery Act Funding Received from State Grants

According to the OMB Guidance, agencies must include the disclosure requirement for each "grantee or sub-grantee awarded funds made available under the Recovery Act." OMB Guidance, § 5.9. This would include states as "grantees" and recipients of grants from states as "sub-grantees." Hence, the disclosure requirement applies to any recipient of a state grant (cooperative agreement, etc.) that includes any Recovery Act funding.

G. Enforcement of the Recovery Act's Disclosure Obligation

Unlike the FAR Rule, the OMB Guidance does not include a ground for suspension or debarment for failure to disclose credible evidence of the listed violations. Nor does the current version of the nonprocurement suspension and debarment provision include such a ground. *See* 2 C.F.R. § 180.804. However, federal debarment officials have taken the position that even without a specific ground for debarment, failure to make required disclosures would be actionable under the "catch-all" provisions of both the FAR and the Common Rule.

Thus, it appears that until the nonprocurement suspension and debarment clause is amended, which is in progress, the primary modes of enforcement will be through the "catch-all" provisions of the Common Rule and the award document itself. Because federal debarment officials may take action under the Common Rule's "catch-all" provisions, grantees should carefully review the grant award and ask questions of the agency regarding the mandatory disclosure obligations before accepting any grant funds. Recipients of Recovery Act funding would be well advised to enter an advance agreement with the agency regarding the entity's disclosure obligations. Such an agreement could clarify many of the questions raised in this

Section, such as for what other persons a grantee must disclose violations, what types of conduct must be disclosed, and when the disclosure obligation ends. In addition, grantees should monitor changes to the Common Rule for a new ground for suspension or debarment for failing to disclose violations similar to the ground in the FAR. This new change in the Common Rule poses separate issues, as described below. Grantees should understand what to look for in any future amendment to the Common Rule.

III. THE POTENTIAL COMMON RULE DISCLOSURE REQUIREMENT

The Government frequently tries to use the FAR as a model for drafting nonprocurement rules. Adopting the FAR Mandatory Disclosure Rule as a ground for suspension or debarment without any changes would raise the same issues for grantees as it raises for contractors. These issues are addressed at length in other Sections. However, adopting the language of the FAR Rule without considering the nature of nonprocurement transactions and the Common Rule's existing definitions poses additional, unique issues that will be addressed in this Section. First and most significantly, the Common Rule includes a different definition of "principal" than the FAR Rule. Hence any future amendment to the Common Rule should consider the implications of the different definition of "principal" or amend the definition in the Common Rule so that it is consistent with the definition in the FAR. Second, use of the FAR Rule's time limitation would impose a broader disclosure requirement on recipients of federal nonprocurement funding than on federal contractors.

A. Differing Definitions of "Principal"

If not addressed during drafting of the amended Common Rule, the differing definitions of "principal" would result in an onerous burden on recipients of federal nonprocurement funding. The FAR Rule defines "principal" as "an officer, director, owner, partner, or a person having primary management or supervisory responsibilities within a business entity (*e.g.*, general manager; plant manager; head of a subsidiary, division, or business segment; and similar positions)." FAR 2.101. Although the Preamble to the FAR Rule advises that the term "principal" "should be interpreted broadly, and could include compliance officers or directors of internal audit, as well as other positions of responsibility," Appendix B, 73 Fed. Reg. at 67,079, it is clear that contractors can be suspended or debarred only for failure to disclose credible evidence of violations known to supervisory personnel employed by the contractor.

In contrast, the Common Rule defines "principal" as:

1. An officer, director, owner, partner, principal investigator, or other person within a participant with management or supervisory responsibilities related to a covered transaction; or

2. A consultant or other person, whether or not employed by the participant or paid with Federal funds, who —

    a) Is in a position to handle Federal funds;

    b) Is in a position to influence or control the use of those funds; or,

    c) Occupies a technical or professional position capable of substantially influencing the development or outcome of an activity required to perform the covered transaction.

2 C.F.R. § 180.995. Although the first category of "principals" under the Common Rule appears to be consistent with the FAR Rule, the second category clearly imposes an additional burden on recipients of federal nonprocurement funding beyond anything contemplated by the FAR Councils.

This second category of "principals" would require recipients of federal nonprocurement funding to report information known beyond supervisory personnel within the organization. In addition, recipients of federal nonprocurement funding would be required to report information known by: (1) low level personnel who function at a much deeper level in an awardee's organization; and (2) consultants, whether or not they are employed by the organization or paid with federal funds. This could include requiring reporting by low-level accounting personnel, auditors, scientists, primary investigators, graduate students, and many others, including an organization's lawyers. Such a requirement would essentially require recipients of federal nonprocurement funding to implement much more robust compliance programs than those contemplated by the FAR for federal contractors.

The question is how broad the Government intends the new nonprocurement suspension and debarment rule to be. The Task Force's recommendation is that the nonprocurement rule should not be any broader than the rule for contractors. This recommendation is based in part on the fact that both the Common Rule and FAR suspension and debarment rules are intended for the same Inspectors General and suspension and debarment officers. These agency officials should be called upon to enforce one standard. Moreover, some entities perform both contracts and nonprocurement transactions for the Government. These entities should also be held to the same standard, regardless of the type of transaction. For this reason, the same definition of "principal" should be used for both the procurement and nonprocurement communities.

B. Time Limitations and Looking Back

Any time limitation that the Common Rule may include based on the FAR Rule should address the issue of when "final payment" occurs for nonprocurement transactions. The FAR Mandatory Disclosure Rule requires disclosure of violations that occur at any point up to three years after "final payment." Appendix A, FAR 9.407, 9.408. Nonprocurement transactions do not involve the same "final payment" mechanisms employed under procurement contracts. However, the closeout requirements for nonprocurement transactions are typically based on the funding period or the date of project completion specified in the terms and conditions of the award or in agency implementing instructions. Either of these events may provide a better trigger point for nonprocurement disclosure requirements. Or, perhaps another standard that could be used as a trigger is the submission of a final expenditure report (which currently serves as the trigger for document retention timing). Regardless of what event triggers the requirement to disclose violations, the Common Rule should include a time limitation at least equivalent to the FAR Rule so that recipients of federal nonprocurement funding are not required to disclose stale information about events that transpired years in the past.

IV. IDENTIFYING AREAS OF RISK AND MITIGATING DAMAGES

Even if the Recovery Act and the future amendment to the Common Rule do not specifically require implementation of a compliance program, all grantees and recipients of federal nonprocurement funding will benefit from implementing a compliance program and internal controls. Nonprocurement funding recipients are already required to have a code of conduct.[107] Section 13 above describes the FAR requirements for contractor compliance programs, which provides useful information for codes of conduct promulgated by grantees. Even if compliance programs are not specifically required, as explained in Section 13, a recipient of federal nonprocurement funding would need to implement a compliance program in order to detect reportable conduct and comply with the requirement to disclose known violations.

---

[107] The regulation at 2 C.F.R. § 215.42 applies to institutions of higher education, hospitals, and other non-profit organizations. It states, "The recipient shall maintain written standards of conduct governing the performance of its employees engaged in the award and administration of contracts. No employee, officer, or agent shall participate in the selection, award, or administration of a contract supported by Federal funds if a real or apparent conflict of interest would be involved. Such a conflict would arise when the employee, officer, or agent, any member of his or her immediate family, his or her partner, or an organization which employs or is about to employ any of the parties indicated herein, has a financial or other interest in the firm selected for an award. The officers, employees, and agents of the recipient shall neither solicit nor accept gratuities, favors, or anything of monetary value from contractors, or parties to subagreements. However, recipients may set standards for situations in which the financial interest is not substantial or the gift is an unsolicited item of nominal value. The standards of conduct shall provide for disciplinary actions to be applied for violations of such standards by officers, employees, or agents of the recipient."

V. MAKING A DISCLOSURE

Finally, if required to make a disclosure, grantees and other recipients of federal nonprocurement funding should consider including with the disclosure the kinds of disclaimers, limitations, or qualifications described in Section 7. Disclosures should be limited to stating the facts and neither admit nor deny that the conduct violated a law or regulation. This approach complies with the requirement to disclose and provides the Government with the information it seeks in order to conduct an investigation into whether a law or regulation was violated. At the same time, limiting a disclosure to the facts without any legal analysis or discussion of "credible evidence" should help protect entities facing lawsuits based on this information from being deemed to have made an admission of a violation.

APPENDICES

FAR 3.1003 Requirements.

(a) *Contractor requirements.*

(1) Although the policy at 3.1002 applies as guidance to all Government contractors, the contractual requirements set forth in the clauses at 52.203-13, Contractor Code of Business Ethics and Conduct, and 52.203-14, Display of Hotline Poster(s), are mandatory if the contracts meet the conditions specified in the clause prescriptions at 3.1004.

(2) Whether or not the clause at 52.203-13 is applicable, a contractor may be suspended and/or debarred for knowing failure by a principal to timely disclose to the Government, in connection with the award, performance, or closeout of a Government contract performed by the contractor or a subcontract awarded thereunder, credible evidence of a violation of Federal criminal law involving fraud, conflict of interest, bribery, or gratuity violations found in Title 18 of the United States Code or a violation of the civil False Claims Act. Knowing failure to timely disclose credible evidence of any of the above violations remains a cause for suspension and/or debarment until 3 years after final payment on a contract (see 9.406-2(b)(1)(vi) and 9.407-2(a)(8)).

(3) The Payment clauses at FAR 52.212-4(i)(5), 52.232-25(d), 52.232-26(c), and 52.232-27(l) require that, if the contractor becomes aware that the Government has overpaid on a contract financing or invoice payment, the contractor shall remit the overpayment amount to the Government. A contractor may be suspended and/or debarred for knowing failure by a principal to timely disclose credible evidence of a significant overpayment, other than overpayments resulting from contract financing payments as defined in 32.001 (see 9.406-2(b)(1)(vi) and 9.407-2(a)(8)).

(b) *Notification of possible contractor violation.* If the contracting officer is notified of possible contractor violation of Federal criminal law involving fraud, conflict of interest, bribery, or gratuity violations found in Title 18 U.S.C.; or a violation of the civil False Claims Act, the contracting officer shall—

(1) Coordinate the matter with the agency Office of the Inspector General; or

(2) Take action in accordance with agency procedures.

* * *

FAR 9.406-2 Causes for debarment.

The debarring official may debar—

. . . .

 (b)(1) A contractor, based upon a preponderance of the evidence, for any of the following—

 . . . .

  (vi) Knowing failure by a principal, until 3 years after final payment on any Government contract awarded to the contractor, to timely disclose to the Government, in connection with the award, performance, or closeout of the contract or a subcontract thereunder, credible evidence of—

   (A) Violation of Federal criminal law involving fraud, conflict of interest, bribery, or gratuity violations found in Title 18 of the United States Code;

   (B) Violation of the civil False Claims Act (31 U.S.C. 3729-3733); or

   (C) Significant overpayment(s) on the contract, other than overpayments resulting from contract financing payments as defined in 32.001.

FAR 9.407-2 Causes for suspension.

(a) The suspending official may suspend a contractor suspected, upon adequate evidence, of—

. . . .

(8) Knowing failure by a principal, until 3 years after final payment on any Government contract awarded to the contractor, to timely disclose to the Government, in connection with the award, performance, or closeout of the contract or a subcontract thereunder, credible evidence of—

(i) Violation of Federal criminal law involving fraud, conflict of interest, bribery, or gratuity violations found in Title 18 of the United States Code;

(ii) Violation of the civil False Claims Act (31 U.S.C. 3729-3733); or

(iii) Significant overpayment(s) on the contract, other than overpayments resulting from contract financing payments as defined in 32.001. . . .

FAR 52.203-13 Contractor Code of Business Ethics and Conduct.

As prescribed in 3.1004(a), insert the following clause: Contractor Code of Business Ethics and Conduct (Dec 2008)

(a) *Definitions.* As used in this clause—

"Agent" means any individual, including a director, an officer, an employee, or an independent Contractor, authorized to act on behalf of the organization.

"Full cooperation"— (1) Means disclosure to the Government of the information sufficient for law enforcement to identify the nature and extent of the offense and the individuals responsible for the conduct. It includes providing timely and complete response to Government auditors' and investigators' request for documents and access to employees with information; (2) Does not foreclose any Contractor rights arising in law, the FAR, or the terms of the contract. It does not require—
  (i) A Contractor to waive its attorney-client privilege or the protections afforded by the attorney work product doctrine; or
  (ii) Any officer, director, owner, or employee of the Contractor, including a sole proprietor, to waive his or her attorney client privilege or Fifth Amendment rights; and
(3) Does not restrict a Contractor from—
  (i) Conducting an internal investigation; or
  (ii) Defending a proceeding or dispute arising under the contract or related to a potential or disclosed violation.

"Principal" means an officer, director, owner, partner, or a person having primary management or supervisory responsibilities within a business entity (*e.g.*, general manager; plant manager; head of a subsidiary, division, or business segment; and similar positions).

"Subcontract" means any contract entered into by a subcontractor to furnish supplies or services for performance of a prime contract or a subcontract.

"Subcontractor" means any supplier, distributor, vendor, or firm that furnished supplies or services to or for a prime contractor or another subcontractor.

"United States," means the 50 States, the District of Columbia, and outlying areas.

(b) *Code of business ethics and conduct.*

(1) Within 30 days after contract award, unless the Contracting Officer establishes a longer time period, the Contractor shall—
- (i) Have a written code of business ethics and conduct; and
- (ii) Make a copy of the code available to each employee engaged in performance of the contract.

(2) The Contractor shall—
- (i) Exercise due diligence to prevent and detect criminal conduct; and
- (ii) Otherwise promote an organizational culture that encourages ethical conduct and a commitment to compliance with the law.

(3)(i) The Contractor shall timely disclose, in writing, to the agency Office of the Inspector General (OIG), with a copy to the Contracting Officer, whenever, in connection with the award, performance, or closeout of this contract or any subcontract thereunder, the Contractor has credible evidence that a principal, employee, agent, or subcontractor of the Contractor has committed—

    (A) A violation of Federal criminal law involving fraud, conflict of interest, bribery, or gratuity violations found in Title 18 of the United States Code; or

    (B) A violation of the civil False Claims Act (31 U.S.C. 3729-3733).

(ii) The Government, to the extent permitted by law and regulation, will safeguard and treat information obtained pursuant to the Contractor's disclosure as confidential where the information has been marked "confidential" or "proprietary" by the company. To the extent permitted by law and regulation, such information will not be released by the Government to the public pursuant to a Freedom of Information Act request, 5 U.S.C. Section 552, without prior notification to the Contractor. The Government may transfer documents provided by the Contractor to any department or agency within the Executive Branch if the information relates to matters within the organization's jurisdiction.

(iii) If the violation relates to an order against a Governmentwide acquisition contract, a multi-agency contract, a multiple-award schedule contract such as the Federal Supply Schedule, or any other procurement instrument intended for use by multiple agencies, the Contractor shall notify the OIG of the ordering agency and the IG of the agency responsible for the basic contract.

(c) *Business ethics awareness and compliance program and internal control system.* This paragraph (c) does not apply if the Contractor has represented itself as a small business concern pursuant to the award of this contract or if this contract is for the acquisition of a commercial item as defined at FAR 2.101. The Contractor shall establish the following within 90 days after contract award, unless the Contracting Officer establishes a longer time period:

(1) An ongoing business ethics awareness and compliance program.

(i) This program shall include reasonable steps to communicate periodically and in a practical manner the Contractor's standards and procedures and other aspects of the Contractor's business ethics awareness and compliance program and internal control system, by conducting effective training programs and otherwise disseminating information appropriate to an individual's respective roles and responsibilities.
(ii) The training conducted under this program shall be provided to the Contractor's principals and employees, and as appropriate, the Contractor's agents and subcontractors.

(2) An internal control system.

(i) The Contractor's internal control system shall—
(A) Establish standards and procedures to facilitate timely discovery of improper conduct in connection with Government contracts; and
(B) Ensure corrective measures are promptly instituted and carried out.
(ii) At a minimum, the Contractor's internal control system shall provide for the following:
(A) Assignment of responsibility at a sufficiently high level and adequate resources to ensure effectiveness of the business ethics awareness and compliance program and internal control system.
(B) Reasonable efforts not to include an individual as a principal, whom due diligence would have exposed as having engaged in conduct that is in conflict with the Contractor's code of business ethics and conduct.
(C) Periodic reviews of company business practices, procedures, policies, and internal controls for compliance with the Contractor's

A-6

code of business ethics and conduct and the special requirements of Government contracting, including—

> (1) Monitoring and auditing to detect criminal conduct;
> (2) Periodic evaluation of the effectiveness of the business ethics awareness and compliance program and internal control system, especially if criminal conduct has been detected; and
> (3) Periodic assessment of the risk of criminal conduct, with appropriate steps to design, implement, or modify the business ethics awareness and compliance program and the internal control system as necessary to reduce the risk of criminal conduct identified through this process.

(D) An internal reporting mechanism, such as a hotline, which allows for anonymity or confidentiality, by which employees may report suspected instances of improper conduct, and instructions that encourage employees to make such reports.

(E) Disciplinary action for improper conduct or for failing to take reasonable steps to prevent or detect improper conduct.

(F) Timely disclosure, in writing, to the agency OIG, with a copy to the Contracting Officer, whenever, in connection with the award, performance, or closeout of any Government contract performed by the Contractor or a subcontract thereunder, the Contractor has credible evidence that a principal, employee, agent, or subcontractor of the Contractor has committed a violation of Federal criminal law involving fraud, conflict of interest, bribery, or gratuity violations found in Title 18 U.S.C. or a violation of the civil False Claims Act (31 U.S.C. 3729-3733).

> (1) If a violation relates to more than one Government contract, the Contractor may make the disclosure to the agency OIG and Contracting Officer responsible for the largest dollar value contract impacted by the violation.
> (2) If the violation relates to an order against a Governmentwide acquisition contract, a multi-agency contract, a multiple-award schedule contract such as the Federal Supply Schedule, or any other procurement instrument intended for use by multiple agencies, the contractor shall notify the OIG of the ordering agency and the IG of the agency responsible for the basic contract, and the respective agencies' contracting officers.

(3) The disclosure requirement for an individual contract continues until at least 3 years after final payment on the contract.

(4) The Government will safeguard such disclosures in accordance with paragraph (b)(3)(ii) of this clause.

(G) Full cooperation with any Government agencies responsible for audits, investigations, or corrective actions.

(d) *Subcontracts.*

(1) The Contractor shall include the substance of this clause, including this paragraph (d), in subcontracts that have a value in excess of $5,000,000 and a performance period of more than 120 days.

(2) In altering this clause to identify the appropriate parties, all disclosures of violation of the civil False Claims Act or of Federal criminal law shall be directed to the agency Office of the Inspector General, with a copy to the Contracting Officer.

67064 Federal Register / Vol. 73, No. 219 / Wednesday, November 12, 2008 / Rules and Regulations

DEPARTMENT OF DEFENSE

GENERAL SERVICES ADMINISTRATION

NATIONAL AERONAUTICS AND SPACE ADMINISTRATION

48 CFR Chapter 1

[Docket FAR 2008–0003, Sequence 3]

Federal Acquisition Regulation; Federal Acquisition Circular 2005–28; Introduction

AGENCIES: Department of Defense (DoD), General Services Administration (GSA), and National Aeronautics and Space Administration (NASA).

ACTION: Summary presentation of final rule.

SUMMARY: This document summarizes the Federal Acquisition Regulation (FAR) rule agreed to by the Civilian Agency Acquisition Council and the Defense Acquisition Regulations Council in this Federal Acquisition Circular (FAC) 2005–28. A companion document, the Small Entity Compliance Guide (SECG), follows this FAC. The FAC, including the SECG, is available via the Internet at *http://www.regulations.gov.*

DATES: For effective date, *see* the document following this notice.

FOR FURTHER INFORMATION CONTACT: For clarification of content, contact the analyst whose name appears in the table below in relation to the FAR case. Please cite FAC 2005–28, FAR Case 2007–006. For information pertaining to status or publication schedules, contact the FAR Secretariat at (202) 501–4755.

Rule listed in FAC 2005–28.

Item	Subject	FAR case	Analyst
I	Contractor Business Ethics Compliance Program and Disclosure Requirements	2007–006	Woodson.

SUPPLEMENTARY INFORMATION: A summary of the FAR rule follows. For the actual revisions and/or amendments to this FAR case, refer to FAR Case 2007–006.

FAC 2005–28 amends the FAR as specified below: Item I—Contractor Business Ethics Compliance Program and Disclosure Requirements (FAR Case 2007–006).

This final rule amends the Federal Acquisition Regulation to amplify the requirements for a contractor code of business ethics and conduct, an internal control system, and disclosure to the Government of certain violations of criminal law, violations of the civil False Claims Act, or significant overpayments. The rule provides for the suspension or debarment of a contractor for knowing failure by a principal to timely disclose, in writing, to the agency Office of the Inspector General, with a copy to the contracting officer, certain violations of criminal law, violations of the civil False Claims Act, or significant overpayments. The final rule implements "The Close the Contractor Fraud Loophole Act," Public Law 110–252, Title VI, Chapter 1. The statute defines a covered contract to mean "any contract in an amount greater than $5,000,000 and more than 120 days in duration." The final rule also provides that the contractor's Internal Control System shall be established within 90 days after contract award, unless the Contracting Officer establishes a longer time period (*See* FAR 52.203–13(c)). The internal control system is not required for small businesses or commercial item contracts.

Dated: November 5, 2008.
Al Matera,
Director, Office of Acquisition Policy.
[FR Doc. E8–26810 Filed 11–10–08; 8:45 am]
BILLING CODE 6820–EP–P

DEPARTMENT OF DEFENSE

GENERAL SERVICES ADMINISTRATION

NATIONAL AERONAUTICS AND SPACE ADMINISTRATION

48 CFR Parts 2, 3, 9, 42 and 52

[FAC 2005–28; FAR Case 2007–006; Item I; Docket 2007–001; Sequence 11]

RIN 9000–AK80

Federal Acquisition Regulation; FAR Case 2007–006, Contractor Business Ethics Compliance Program and Disclosure Requirements

AGENCIES: Department of Defense (DoD), General Services Administration (GSA), and National Aeronautics and Space Administration (NASA).

ACTION: Final rule.

SUMMARY: The Civilian Agency Acquisition Council and the Defense Acquisition Regulations Council (Councils) have agreed on a final rule amending the Federal Acquisition Regulation (FAR) to amplify the requirements for a contractor code of business ethics and conduct, an internal control system, and disclosure to the Government of certain violations of criminal law, violations of the civil False Claims Act, or significant overpayments. This final rule implements Pub. L. 110–252, Title VI, Chapter 1.

DATES: *Effective Date:* December 12, 2008.

Applicability: The Contractor's Internal Control System shall be established within 90 days after contract award, unless the Contracting Officer establishes a longer time period (*See* FAR 52.203–13(c)). The Internal Control System is not required for small businesses or for commercial item contracts.

FOR FURTHER INFORMATION CONTACT: Mr. Ernest Woodson, Procurement Analyst, at (202) 501–3775 for clarification of content. For information pertaining to status or publication schedules, contact the FAR Secretariat at (202) 501–4755. Please cite FAC 2005–28, FAR case 2007–006.

SUPPLEMENTARY INFORMATION:

Table of Contents

A. Background
B. Discussion and Analysis
  1. Interrelationship of previous final rule, first proposed rule, second proposed rule, and new statute.
  2. Mandatory standards for internal control system.
  3. Mandatory disclosure to the OIG.
  4. Full Cooperation.
  5. Suspension/Debarment.
  6. Extend to violation of civil False Claims Act.
  7. Application to acquisition of commercial items.
  8. Application to contracts to be performed outside the United States.
  9. Other applicability issues.
  10. Additional recommendations.
  11. Regulatory Flexibility Act concerns.
  12. Paperwork Reduction Act (PRA).
  13. E.O. 12866.
C. Regulatory Flexibility Act
D. Paperwork Reduction Act

A. Background

This case is in response to a request to the Office of Federal Procurement Policy from the Department of Justice, dated May 23, 2007, and the Close the Contractor Fraud Loophole Act, Public Law 110–252, Title VI, Chapter 1. This final rule amends the Federal Acquisition Regulation to require Government contractors to—

• Establish and maintain specific internal controls to detect and prevent improper conduct in connection with the award or performance of *any* Government contract or subcontract; and

• Timely disclose to the agency Office of the Inspector General, with a copy to the contracting officer, whenever, in connection with the award, performance, or closeout of a Government contract performed by the contractor or a subcontract awarded thereunder, the contractor has credible evidence of a violation of Federal criminal law involving fraud, conflict of interest, bribery, or gratuity violations found in Title 18 of the United States Code; or a violation of the civil False Claims Act (31 U.S.C. 3729–3733).

• The rule also provides as cause for suspension or debarment, knowing failure by a principal, until 3 years after final payment on any Government contract awarded to the contractor, to timely disclose to the Government, in connection with the award, performance, or closeout of the contract or a subcontract thereunder, credible evidence of—

A. Violation of Federal criminal law involving fraud, conflict of interest, bribery, or gratuity violations found in Title 18 of the United States Code;

B. Violation of the civil False Claims Act; or

C. Significant overpayment(s) on the contract, other than overpayments resulting from contract financing payments as defined in FAR 32.001, Definitions.

DoD, GSA, and NASA published a proposed rule in the **Federal Register** at 72 FR 64019, November 14, 2007, entitled "Contractor Compliance Program and Integrity Reporting." The public comment period closed on January 14, 2008. (This was a follow-on case to the final rule under FAC 2005–22, FAR case 2006–007 that was published in the **Federal Register** at 72 FR 65868, November 23, 2007, effective December 24, 2007.) A second proposed rule was published in the **Federal Register** at 73 FR 28407, May 16, 2008, entitled "Contractor Compliance Program and Integrity Reporting." The public comment period on the second proposed rule closed on July 15, 2008.

On June 30, 2008, the Close the Contractor Fraud Loophole Act (Pub. L. 110–252, Title VI, Chapter 1) was enacted as part of the Supplemental Appropriations Act, 2008. This Act requires revision to the FAR within 180 days of enactment, pursuant to 2007–006, "or any follow-on FAR case to include provisions that require timely notification by Federal contractors of violations of Federal criminal law or overpayments in connection with the award or performance of covered contracts or subcontracts, including those performed outside the United States and those for commercial items." The statute also defines a covered contract to mean "any contract in an amount greater than $5,000,000 and more than 120 days in duration."

First proposed rule. The first proposed rule, published in the **Federal Register** on November 14, 2007, proposed the following:

1. *New causes for suspension/debarment.* A contractor may be suspended and/or debarred for knowing failure to timely disclose—

• An overpayment on a Government contract; or

• A violation of Federal criminal law in connection with the award or performance of any Government contract or subcontract.

2. *Changes to the requirement for a code of business ethics and conduct (52.203–XX).*

• Amplify the requirement to promote compliance with the code of business ethics.

• Require timely disclosure to the agency Office of the Inspector General (OIG), with a copy to the contracting officer, whenever the contractor has reasonable grounds to suspect a violation of criminal law in connection with the award or performance of the contract or any subcontract thereunder.

3. *Mandatory requirements for internal control system based on U.S. Sentencing Guidelines (USSG).*

• Provide more detail with regard to the ongoing business ethics awareness and compliance program (see 52.203–XX paragraph(c)(1)).

• Make all the stated elements of the internal control system mandatory, rather than examples (see 52.203–XX (c)(2)(ii)).

A. Add a new paragraph requiring assignment of responsibility within the organization for the ethics awareness and compliance program and internal control system.

B. Require reasonable efforts not to include as principals individuals who have engaged in illegal conduct or conduct otherwise in conflict with the contractor's code of business ethics and conduct.

C. Provide additional detail with regard to the requirement for periodic reviews.

D. Require that the internal reporting mechanism or hotline must allow for anonymity or confidentiality.

E. Provide that disciplinary action will be taken not only for improper conduct, but also for failing to take reasonable steps to prevent or detect improper conduct.

F. Require timely disclosure, in writing, to the agency OIG, with a copy to the contracting officer, whenever the contractor has reasonable grounds to believe that a violation of Federal criminal law has been committed in connection with the award or performance of any Government contract performed by the contractor or the award or performance of a subcontract thereunder.

G. Require full cooperation with any Government agencies responsible for audit, investigation, or corrective actions.

Second proposed rule. The second proposed rule, published in the **Federal Register** on May 16, 2008, proposed the following:

1. Require inclusion of the clause at FAR 52.203–13 in contracts and subcontracts that will be performed outside the United States.

2. Require inclusion of the clause at FAR 52.203–13 in contracts (and subcontracts) for all acquisitions of a commercial item. However, similar to small businesses, a formal business ethics awareness and compliance program and internal control system are not required in contracts and subcontracts for the acquisition of commercial items.

3. Add a new cause for suspension and/or debarment, *i.e.*, knowing failure to timely disclose the violation of the civil False Claims Act (civil FCA) in connection with the award or performance of any Government contract or subcontract.

The first two of these three proposed changes are now required by statute (Pub. L. 110–252, Title VI, Chapter 1). (As pointed out by one of the respondents, there was an error in the amendatory language in the **Federal Register**. At FAR 3.1004, the introductory text should have been deleted, rather than showing 5 asterisks, indicating that the introductory text is still present. However, the preamble made our intent very clear and this will be clarified in the final rule).

Rule on Contract Debts. DoD, GSA, and NASA published a proposed rule, FAR case 2005–018, in the **Federal**

Register at 71 FR 62230, October 24, 2006, regarding contract debts. The final rule was published in the **Federal Register** at 73 FR 53997, September 17, 2008, as part of Federal Acquisition Circular 2005–27. The intent of this rule is to evaluate existing controls and procedures for ensuring that contract debts are identified and recovered in a timely manner, properly accounted for in each agency's books and records, and properly coordinated with the appropriate Government officials.

One of the following payment clauses should be included in each Government solicitation and contract:

—52.212–4, Contract Terms and Conditions—Commercial Items, basic clause and Alternate I.
—52.232–25, Prompt Payment.
—52.232–26, Prompt Payment for Fixed-Price Architect-Engineer Contracts.
—52.232–27, Prompt Payment for Construction Contracts.

These Payment clauses for years have contained the requirement to immediately notify the contracting officer if the contractor becomes aware of any overpayment on a contract financing or invoice payment. Compliance with this requirement fulfills the statutory requirement of Pub. L. 110–252 for timely notification of overpayments.

In addition, under the Contract Debts rule, these Payment clauses were modified to require that if the contractor becomes aware of a duplicate contract financing or invoice payment or if the contractor becomes aware that the Government has otherwise overpaid on a contract financing or invoice payment, the contractor shall—

• Remit the overpayment amount to the payment office cited in the contract along with a description of the overpayment; and

• Provide a copy of the remittance and supporting documentation to the contracting officer.

Because issues of overpayment were addressed in FAR case 2005–018, the Councils did not include additional coverage on contract debt in the subject FAR Case, except for adding—

• Knowing failure to timely disclose significant overpayment as a cause for debarment/suspension as stated at Subpart 9.4 Debarment, Suspension, and Ineligibility; and

• A cross reference at 3.1003(a)(3) to this new cause of suspension/debarment at Subpart 9.4.

B. Discussion and Analysis

The FAR Secretariat received 43 responses to the first proposed rule. The FAR Secretariat received comments on the second proposed rule from 25 respondents of which 15 respondents had also submitted comments on the first proposed rule and 10 respondents were submitting comments for the first time. Overall, 18 of the 53 respondents were from Government agencies, including many responses from agency Offices of the Inspector General (OIG).

In the second proposed rule the Councils specifically requested comments on three issues:

• Elimination of the exemption from inclusion of the clause FAR 52.203–13 for contracts and subcontracts that will be performed entirely outside the United States.

• Elimination of the exemption from inclusion of the clause FAR 52.203–13 for contracts (and subcontracts) for all acquisitions of a commercial item under FAR Part 12.

• Requirement for mandatory disclosure of violations of the civil FCA (31 U.S.C. 3729–3733) (in the clause, in the internal control system required by the clause, and as a cause for suspension or debarment).

Comments on the second proposed rule that do not relate to these three issues, unless presenting a new and pertinent perspective, have not been separately addressed in this preamble.

1. Interrelationship of Previous Final Rule, First Proposed Rule, Second Proposed Rule, and New Statute

a. Previous Final Rule, FAR Case 2006–007

The first proposed rule under FAR case 2007–006 ("first proposed rule"), proposed increases to the requirements introduced by final rule, FAR case 2006–007 ("previous final rule"), in the ways enumerated in the Background section above. Thirteen respondents remarked on the relationship to the previous final rule, some suggesting changes to the previous final rule as well as the first proposed rule.

i. Like the previous final rule under 2006–007.

• No further change needed. One respondent expressed the belief that the previous final rule is adequate to protect the Government's interest. Several other respondents supported the previous final rule's voluntary disclosure. One respondent questioned the need for the first proposed rule in light of the recent implementation of "more expansive contractor compliance standards in the FAR."

• The first and second proposed rules enhance the previous rule. One Government agency explicitly supported the major provisions of both rules as sound business practices, highlighting their contribution to cost control as well as mission safety.

Response: No response necessary.

ii. Ethics code. With regard to the requirement for a code of conduct, one respondent considered that just having a code is meaningless. Several other respondents also objected to the requirement for a code of business ethics and conduct in the previous final rule under FAR case 2006–007, stating that existing contractor ethics standards work well and that these contractual requirements are redundant, add costs and other burdens, and are likely to generate additional uncertainties.

Several respondents objected to the outdated method of communicating the code, requiring a copy to each employee engaged in the contract. One respondent recommended that it may be more effective to refer employees to Web sites or provide tutorials in person, on-line, or through other means. This suggestion could minimize burdens through the use of information technology, as requested in the preamble to the proposed rule for this case.

Another respondent also objected that many institutions have more than a single code of conduct, each addressing different aspects of conduct that together cover all aspects of conduct that the FAR rule requires.

Response: The Councils do not agree that a code of conduct is meaningless. It can serve several related purposes. For a firm's business partners, including the Government, it provides a basis for evaluating the firm's responsibility, including special standards of responsibility when appropriate. It also provides a basis for internal policy development, for example human resources policies. And when something goes wrong, the code is meaningful for enforcement and for understanding and perhaps incorporating lessons learned.

While requiring establishment of a code will add costs and require effort on the part of entities that do not have them already, the Councils agree with several respondents that those resources are reasonable and justified to mitigate other and larger risks to the success and efficiency of Government projects. Because many entities already have made the investment, the rule will level the playing field in competitive environments.

The Councils agree that flexibility in the method of communicating the code to employees is appropriate, and the rule has been changed to require that it be made available to each employee engaged in performance of the contract. The Councils note that the rule does not preclude having multiple codes of conduct applicable to different segments of contractors' business lines.

iii. Training.

• Training requirement is too burdensome. One respondent was concerned that the requirements for training could take substantial time away from performing on their contracts to train staff on an unknown scope of Federal criminal law. The Government would incur costs from this activity through delays in the fulfillment of contracts and increased contractor expenses that will be passed along to customers.

Response: The Councils recognize that contract costs are reflected in prices, but do not consider schedules to be impacted by this requirement. By identifying the scope of violations of the Federal criminal law as those involving fraud, conflict of interest, bribery, or gratuity violations found in Title 18 of the United States Code, the Councils believe that the training requirements have been more clearly defined and the contractor's training requirement has been reduced.

• Require training on civil FCA. Several respondents proposed that Government contractors be required to educate their employees about the protections available under the civil FCA. The Department of Justice, Criminal Division (DoJ) suggested that contractors should also be required to include in their "business ethics awareness" obligation, reflected in the proposed rule at FAR 52.203–13(c)(2)(ii)(F), training on the civil FCA.

Response: The Councils do not agree that it is necessary under this case to dictate to contractors what they need to cover in business ethics training. If we highlight education on the civil FCA, or other specific areas, the contractors may place undue emphasis only on those areas mentioned in the regulations. The business ethics training courses may cover appropriate education on the civil FCA, as well as many other areas such as conflict of interest and procurement integrity and other areas determined to be appropriate by the contractor, considering the relevant risks and controls.

iv. Hotline posters. One respondent commented that the physical display of multiple hotline posters in common work areas is impractical and wasteful. Another respondent also objects to using hotline posters on the walls of the institution as being the most effective way of communication at every institution.

Response: The issue of multiple hotline posters was resolved under the final rule 2006–007. The requirement for hotline posters is outside the scope of this case.

b. Relationship of Second Proposed Rule to First Proposed Rule

One respondent questioned whether certain requirements of the first proposed rule that did not appear in the second proposed rule had been deleted.

Response: The preamble of the second proposed rule specified that it included only the sections of the rule affected by the three changes; it was only addressing three issues, not providing a completely revised proposed rule. Therefore, the fact that language in the first proposed rule that would not be affected by the 3 issues of concern was not repeated in the second proposed rule does not imply that that language was being deleted.

c. Relationship of Second Proposed Rule to New Statute

One respondent recommends that any disclosure requirement be limited to violations of the types specified in the "Closing the Contractor Fraud Loophole Act (Pub. L. 110–252, Title VI, Chapter 1)" (*i.e.*, exclude violations of the civil FCA). This respondent also states that the statute does not require the disclosure to the OIG and the penalties of debarment/suspension are not required by the new statute, so should be eliminated.

Another respondent also makes the point that since the new law does not address disclosure of violations of the civil FCA, that requirement should not be included in the final rule under this case.

One respondent notes particularly that the new law does not require the "reasonable grounds to believe" standard, reporting to the Inspector General, or failure to report as an independent basis for suspension or debarment.

Response: This rule was initiated as a matter of policy. Although the new statute reinforces and provides a statutory basis for some aspects of the rule, the fact that any part of the rule is not required by statute does not alter the rationale that provided the underpinning for those aspects of the rule. Each aspect of the rule not required by statute must be considered on its own merits.

2. Mandatory Standards for Internal Control System

a. Minimum Requirements for the Internal Control System

One respondent considered that the previously recommended, now mandatory, internal control practices will be inadequate if they are considered to be maximum as well as minimum requirements. Another respondent considered the establishment of an internal control system that satisfies a laundry list of mandates will be overly burdensome. Another respondent would prefer that contractors be left free to choose to implement the USSG "in the prudent exercise of their business discretion," rather than being required to do so. Likewise, another respondent stated that contractors may want to consider the USSG in designing compliance programs but, absent a statute or Executive order, they should not be made mandatory in the regulations.

Response: The rule does reflect minimum expectations. Competing firms are free to establish the highest ethical standards they consider to be appropriate to the business at hand. This case establishes a framework for institutional ethics management and disclosure and does not prescribe specific ethical requirements.

b. Relation of Rule to the USSG

i. Rule is consistent with the USSG. An agency OIG stated that the proposed rule should benefit Federal contractors. It provides guidance for contractors consistent with U.S. Sentencing Commission guidance on effective compliance and ethics programs for organizations. Compliance with the rule should assist contractors subject to the Sarbanes-Oxley Act of 2002 in fulfilling their responsibilities under the Act.

Response: None needed.

ii. USSG should be incorporated by reference. Several respondents commented that rather than using the ad hoc form of the USSG standards for compliance and ethics program, the actual USSG standards should simply be incorporated by reference. Conformity with the USSG will prevent contractors unknowingly failing to comply with all the USSG although complying with the FAR. Formal adoption of the USSG will create uniform criteria. A respondent recommended that all the descriptive paragraphs in (ii) be deleted, instead inserting: "The Contractor's internal control system shall provide for a compliance and ethics program that meets the standards of the Federal Organizational Sentencing Guidelines, as amended from time to time, United States Sentencing Commission Guidelines Manual: Sentencing of Organizations, section 8B2.1.

Response: These respondents would use the USSG Guidelines, in place of the FAR spelling out the required elements of internal control systems. However, the Councils prefer to spell out the elements. This lets the contractors know what is expected. The USSG are the source of the FAR text, but the FAR text is intentionally not adopting them verbatim. The procurement regulations are not the USSG; the contractor setting up an internal control system is in a different situation than a company accused of a crime. Some elements of the USSG are not appropriate for a procurement regulation. However, by making the minimum requirements generally consistent with the USSG, the Councils believe that a contractor should be in a better position if accused of a crime.

iii. Essential parts of the USSG are missing. One respondent commented that essential parts of the USSG are missing. One example is the reference to the use of an incentive system in compliance programs that encourages and rewards companies for implementing effective programs, following the model of the Organizational Sentencing Guidelines. The respondent recommends modifying 52.203–13(c)(1)(ii)(E) by inserting after "detect improper conduct" the words "and appropriate incentives to perform in accordance with the compliance and ethics program".

Another example the respondent uses is the standard for effectively responding to violations, and taking steps to prevent recurrence. Without these, a company's program would not be considered effective under the USSG.

Response: The Councils note that the respondent must have intended to cite FAR 52.203–13(c)(2)(ii)(E). The Councils do not want to require incentives for employees within contractors' internal control systems. This is within companies' discretion. The mitigating factors for debarment (9.406–1(a)) already include consideration of remedial action (*e.g.*, (6), (7), and (8)) taken by the contractor.

The FAR does cover responding to violations, and preventing recurrence, in FAR 52.203–13(c)(2)(i), and throughout (c)(2)(ii).

c. Principals

Several respondents asked for interpretation of the clause paragraph (c)(2)(ii)(B) requirement that the internal control system provide for reasonable efforts not to include within the organization principals whom due diligence would have exposed as having engaged in conduct that is illegal or otherwise in conflict with the Contractor's code of business ethics and conduct."

• Is the "organization" the entire contractor, instead of the organization responsible for the code?
• Is the code retroactive to catch criminal behavior in the past?
• Is it only Federal crimes, or state and local as well?
• What about non-criminal behavior that did not violate the Contractor's code at the time?
• What kind of due diligence is necessary—a simple pre-employment questionnaire, or instead a costly background check with interviews of friends and neighbors?

Response:
• The Councils have revised the draft final rule (paragraphs (c)(2)(ii)(A), (B), and (C) of the clause 52.203–13) to eliminate use of the term "organization". This term was a carryover from the USSG. This rule is addressed to the contractor—the entity that signed the contract, and subcontractors thereunder.
• The code of conduct is not itself retroactive. However, it is necessary to distinguish conduct of an employee during his/her employment, from past conduct uncovered during a background check of a prospective hire. That past conduct need not be disclosed to the Government, but should be part of the decision whether to hire the individual.
• Past criminal behavior of any type, even criminal behavior unrelated to contracting, calls into question whether the individual at the present time has integrity and is a proper role model for company staff. This is not a mandate to fire the individual, but to determine whether the individual is currently trustworthy to serve as a principal of the company.
• Behavior that was not criminal and did not violate a business's code as it existed at the time, is not the subject of this rule. In response to this comment, the Councils have revised paragraph (c)(2)(ii)(B) to delete the words "illegal or otherwise." The term "illegal" is too broad and could include even a traffic violation. The Contractor's code of business ethics and conduct should cover the types of behavior that this requirement is intended to address.
• The level of background check required depends on the circumstances. This is a business decision, requiring judgment by the contractor.

The source of the FAR clause paragraph (c)(2)(ii)(B) is the USSG Manual paragraph 8B2.1.(b)(3). The Commentary on this paragraph includes this statement: "With respect to the hiring or promotion of principals, an organization shall consider the relatedness of the individual's illegal activities and other misconduct (*i.e.*, other conduct inconsistent with an effective compliance and ethics program) to the specific responsibilities the individual is anticipated to be assigned and other factors such as: (i) the recency of the individual's illegal activities and other misconduct; and (ii) whether the individual has engaged in other such illegal activities and other such misconduct."

d. Periodic Review

One respondent asked for an interpretation of the clause paragraph (c)(2)(ii)(C) requirement for periodic review of business practices. For "monitoring and auditing", is standard business practice and generally acceptable accounting principals sufficient? What system for assessing the "risk of criminal conduct" would be sufficient? Is there a Government program that is an acceptable process?

Response: Standard business practice for "monitoring and auditing to detect criminal conduct" which conforms to generally accepted accounting principles should be sufficient. The "monitoring and auditing" is amplification of the current FAR requirement for periodic review and auditing, from the FAR case 2006–007 published in November 2007.

One respondent stated that annual audits of research processes may already review compliance with policies for ethical conduct of research funded under Federal contracts. The FAR can acknowledge, through an Alternate to the clause, that duplication of review is not required where reviews under other rules already cover the necessary subjects.

Response: The FAR is not requiring wasted duplication of effort. No change to the regulation is necessary.

3. Mandatory Disclosure to the OIG

Of the 43 respondents that commented on the first proposed rule, 36 commented specifically on subparagraph (b)(3) of the clause 52.203–13, Contractor Code of Business Ethics and Conduct, which requires mandatory disclosure, in writing, to the agency OIG, with a copy to the contracting officer, whenever the contractor has reasonable grounds to believe that a principal, employee, agent, or subcontractor of the contractor has committed a violation of Federal criminal law in connection with the award or performance of the contract or any subcontract thereunder.

Six agency OIGs, as well as several Government agencies all specifically concurred with the mandatory disclosure of violations by contractors.

Other respondents, including agency OIGs, while concurring with mandatory disclosure, suggested improvements in the way this requirement is implemented in the rule.

The other 17 respondents that commented specifically on the mandatory disclosure disagreed with this approach and recommended voluntary disclosure.

a. Need for Mandatory Disclosure

Note that the following comments in this section all preceded the enactment of the statute that requires mandatory disclosure, so that the issues are now primarily moot.

i. Major departure from long-standing policy. One respondent stated that this rule is a major departure from long-standing and proven Federal policies that encourage voluntary disclosures. Likewise, another respondent stated that mandatory disclosure runs counter to many established Government processes. One respondent considered the proposed regulation to be a "sea change" in the fundamental approach to compliance followed by the Government. Another respondent noted that in 1986 a proposal from DoD to make fraud disclosures mandatory foundered on "state action" grounds. In 1988, then Secretary of Defense Richard Cheney withdrew a proposed rule that would have governed such programs on the grounds that "to be meaningful, corporate codes of conduct must be adopted by contractors voluntarily, not mandated in procurement regulations (54 FR 30911)". Another respondent also cited a 1996 GAO report on the DoD Voluntary Disclosure Program (GAO/NSIAD–96–21) in which the GAO quotes the DoJ as praising the DoD Voluntary Disclosure Program.

Several respondents cited the DFARS regulations as being a model for voluntary disclosure. Several other respondents stated that many Federal agencies that have considered mandatory disclosure rules have declined to adopt them in favor of voluntary disclosure programs (*e.g.*, Department of Health and Human Services in 2000 (65 FR 40170) and in 2004 (69 FR 46866)).

Response: There is no doubt that mandatory disclosure is a "sea change" and "major departure" from voluntary disclosure, but DoJ and the OIGs point out that the policy of voluntary disclosure has been largely ignored by contractors for the past 10 years. In addition, in that same time period mandatory disclosure has been adopted for banks and public companies and stressed by the U.S. Sentencing Commission and DoJ, as further discussed in the following sections.

ii. Is voluntary disclosure working? Various respondents stated that the proposed rule fails to demonstrate that there is a need for change based on failure of voluntary disclosure. According to these respondents, neither DoJ nor the Councils have cited data supporting the claim that voluntary disclosure is not effective. One respondent stated that a purported paucity of participants in the DoD IG Voluntary Disclosure Program does not establish a decline in contractor disclosures to the Government sufficient to justify a mandatory disclosure requirement. Another respondent stated that DoJ is comparing the last few years to data from 20 years ago. One respondent cited disclosures for FY 2005–2007 that are relatively level. Another respondent cited the December 2006 issue of Corporate Counsel that voluntary disclosures are increasing rather than decreasing, citing Mr. Mark Mendelssohn of DoJ and a recent report by Sherman & Sterling. Even if there is a decline in disclosure under the DoD Voluntary Disclosure Program, another respondent found that the leap to mandatory disclosure "gives rise to a perverse implication that justification for mandating regulations can be asserted simply because no one has shown that the activity to be regulated is not happening."

One respondent stated that the assumptions about the reason for the decrease are misplaced. Another respondent firmly believed that there is need for analysis of the reasons for any decline in voluntary disclosures. Even if mandatory disclosures to the DoD IG Voluntary Disclosure Program are decreasing, several respondents suggested the following possible explanations:

• Less emphasis by DoD.
• Fewer reportable violations.
• More instances resolved as contract matters, with reports to contracting officers or heads of contracting activities or to audit agencies like DCAA and DCMA.
• Perception that the Government is slow in processing voluntary disclosures.
• Lack of restrictions on use of disclosure reports in criminal or civil actions or in administrative actions against individuals.

One respondent elaborated that there may be fewer voluntary disclosures because self-governance is working to prevent and detect contract formation and contract performance issues before they result in criminality or civil fraud. Reduction in the rate of voluntary disclosures would be an expected byproduct of improved internal processes, enhanced training, better internal controls, and an improved culture of ethics and compliance.

One respondent stated that a number of companies have commented that delays in processing disclosures to the OIG are a significant factor in their decision to report problems to the contracting officer instead of to the DoD Voluntary Disclosure Program.

One respondent suggested other avenues for disclosure that are more relevant to the kinds of illegal activity being found these days, such as—

• The DoJ Antitrust Division. Voluntary disclosures to DoJ have increased as disclosures to the DoD IG program have decreased (*see http:// www/usdoj.gov/atr/public/speeches/ 232716.htm#N_1_*);
• The Department of State Directorate of Defense Trade Controls. This program has been very successful at inducing voluntary disclosures (*see* GAO–05–234 (Feb 2005)); and
• Foreign Corrupt Practices Act. Enforcement actions for violations of the FCPA have also grown, again largely due to voluntary disclosures made by corporations (*see* "U.S. Targets Bribery Overseas Globalization; Reforms Give Rise to Spike in Prosecutions," The Washington Post (Dec 5, 2007)).

One respondent suggested that mandatory reporting should be replaced with a strong voluntary disclosure program modeled after the DoJ Antitrust Division's Corporate Leniency Programs.

Another respondent noted that it is DoJ, not DoD, that apparently believed that the mandatory disclosure provisions were necessary. This respondent interpreted this to mean that DoD is satisfied with the number and types of disclosures being made.

One respondent stated that DoJ should be required to demonstrate that there is an upward trend of criminal prosecutions of the top 100 Government contractors where it was established that contractor principals were aware of violations of the law and made a conscious decision not to disclose those violations to the Government. Similarly, another respondent suggested that DoJ should offer factual support for its thesis that crimes are occurring and being found and yet not being reported voluntarily. One respondent also wanted DoJ to explain why other less burdensome changes, such as improving the existing voluntary disclosure programs, cannot be used to achieve the desired result.

On the other hand, in the DoJ letter of May 23, 2007, DoJ stated that its experience suggests that few corporations have actually responded to the invitation of DoD that they report or voluntarily disclose suspected instances of fraud. An agency OIG stated that the vast majority of crimes involving contractors that it investigates are not reported by the contractor. Another agency OIG stated that Government contractors are coming forward significantly less frequently with voluntary disclosures. It considered that this mandatory requirement may be the most effective way for the Government to monitor its vendors.

Response: In the DoJ letter dated May 23, 2007, which requested the Administrator of the Office of Federal Procurement Policy, Mr. Paul Denett, to open this case, DoJ states that its experience suggests that few companies have actually responded to the invitation of DoD to report or voluntarily disclose suspected instance of fraud. The respondents do not dispute that relatively few contractors are using the DoD Voluntary Disclosure Program. The contractor groups, in their public comments on the rule, implicitly concede that the Voluntary Disclosure program is not being used and blame DoJ and the OIG. Some claim that informal disclosures are being made to the contracting officers but offer no specific evidence.

Even if it is true that there are comparatively fewer violations now than 20 years ago or that some situations are resolved administratively, there are still significant numbers of violations occurring and being prosecuted that have not been self-disclosed.

Importantly, the incentive to self-disclose Antitrust violations is not applicable. Antitrust deals with the Sherman Act and the Clayton Act, which prohibit conspiracy in restraint of interstate or foreign trade and regulate practices that may be potentially detrimental to competition (price discrimination, exclusive dealing contracts, etc.). Under the Antitrust Division's Corporate Leniency Program, the first company that reports the violation receives immunity from prosecution. That type of circumstance does not apply here.

iii. Existing legal requirements and regulations as models for the rule.

In the DoJ letter of May 23, 2007, DoJ stated that—

• Unlike healthcare providers or financial institutions, there is at present no general requirement that contractors alert the Government immediately as a matter of routine when fraud is discovered;

• DoJ has been careful not to ask contractors to do anything that is not already expected of their counterparts in other industries;

• Our Government's expectations of its contractors has not kept pace with the reforms in self-governance in industries such as banking, securities, and healthcare. Several respondents all considered that for far too long contractors have played by different rules than their counterparts in other industries, such as health care providers and research grant recipients. A Government agency commented that healthcare providers and banks have had such a requirement for many years. An agency OIG commented that in the past 15 years there have been significant reforms in industries such as banking, securities, and healthcare, yet we have not asked the same of Government contractors.

In the DoJ letter of May 23, 2007, DoJ stated that the requested changes are modeled on existing requirements found in other areas of corporate compliance such as the Sarbanes-Oxley Act of 2002 and expand slightly on the Contractor Standards of Conduct in DFARS 203.7000. DoJ also noted that the National Reconnaissance Office (NRO) has begun requiring its contractors to disclose contract fraud and other illegal activities.

a. More far-reaching. However, one respondent stated that the proposed rule imposes substantially more far-reaching and draconian disclosure obligations on Government contractors than those presently made applicable to financial institutions by submission of Suspicious Activity Reports (12 CFR 21.11). The financial institution has to report a crime if the financial institution is an actual or potential victim of the criminal activity. Where a contractor is a victim of a crime committed by an employee or another person, the employee's conduct is not imputed to the contractor. Therefore, the corporation does not incur the risk of criminal liability when it reports an employee violation and is not incriminating itself.

According to another respondent, the current laws and regulations are not sweeping and burdensome, but are specific and narrowly focused. The respondent pointed out that the Anti-Kickback Act and Foreign Corrupt Practices Act limit their mandatory disclosure to a very limited class of activity. The respondent also pointed out that Sarbanes-Oxley contemplates internal reporting mechanisms and review mechanisms at the highest levels before any reporting occurs. The other respondent also addressed the internal control certification required by the Sarbanes-Oxley Act of 2002. Sarbanes-Oxley applies to a contractor that is a public company. Section 302 of Sarbanes-Oxley does not require that a public company disclose to the Government conduct it believes may be a violation of criminal law.

Response: Many of the public comments reveal a basic misunderstanding of the existing mandatory disclosure requirements found in the healthcare, banking, and securities areas. Each requirement effectively mandates disclosure of fraud as broad as the particular regulatory issue being addressed can reach. Beyond that limitation, these other requirements are no more limited than the proposed rule, particularly with the further changes in the final rule with regard to the types of Federal crimes covered.

In particular, the Councils do not agree with the interpretation of 12 CFR 21.11. 12 CFR 21.11 requires financial institutions to report suspicious activities committed or attempted against the bank or involving a transaction or transactions conducted through the bank, where the bank was used to facilitate a criminal transaction.

Even though Section 302 of Sarbanes-Oxley does not require a public company to disclose to the Government conduct it believes may be a violation of criminal law, there are pre-existing securities laws and regulations that require disclosure to the SEC. Sarbanes-Oxley does not provide immunity from prosecution for wrong-doing but provides protection against third-party liability with regard to a lawsuit by the persons accused of wrongdoing.

b. Conforming the FAR? One respondent stated that if the FAR Council is relying on conforming the FAR to regulations applicable to other industries as a justification, the Council should state this explicitly and provide a detailed analysis of the regulations in other areas on which it is relying.

Response: The Councils did not rely on conforming the FAR to regulations applicable to other industries as a justification, but merely cited some parallels. The FAR regulations are designed to suit the particular circumstances of acquisition.

c. Particular public need/statutory basis? One respondent stated that current disclosure programs are not instructive. The respondent also stated that these programs are targeted towards a particular public need, and in most cases are the product of legislation that was enacted in response to a particular public scandal or important national need. In enacting statutory schemes, Congress saw a particular need and targeted legislation to address the particular need (Sarbanes-Oxley, the

Anti-Kickback Act, the Foreign Corrupt Practices Act, and banking laws).

Several respondents were concerned that the same justification does not exist for this proposed rule as the cited statutes and regulations. One respondent stated that the Council has not provided a rational basis to explain why such a significant change to the FAR is necessary. The respondent asserted that the proposed rule could be challenged under the Administrative Procedure Act (APA) because the FAR Council has not provided a "rational basis" to justify the mandatory disclosure requirement, nor is there statutory authority behind the FAR Council to issue a regulation providing for mandatory disclosure of criminal acts. The respondent therefore concluded that the FAR Council lacks the authority to issue the regulation (*See AFL/CIO v. Kahn, 472 F. Supp. 99 (D.D.C. 1979), rev'd, 618 F. 2d 784 (D.C.Cir. 1979)*). One respondent saw this as particularly important in light of DoJ's reliance upon the example of other statutorily-mandated disclosure programs (Sarbanes-Oxley, Foreign Corrupt Practices Act, etc.) as justification for this regulatory initiative. The respondent stated that the mandatory disclosure provisions in the proposed rule are neither the product of specific findings or legislation, nor any perceived critical national need, and thus are not appropriately compared to other existing mandatory disclosure programs.

Response: The DoJ proposed a mandatory disclosure program in order to emphasize the critical importance of integrity in contracting. The public demands honesty and integrity in corporations with which the Government does business. If there is concern that there is not a current public need warranting proceeding with this case, the Councils cite the public outcry over the overseas exemption in the first proposed rule and the recent enactment of the Close the Contractor Fraud Loophole Act (Pub. L. 110–252, Title VI, Chapter 1). The Act requires exactly what the first rule proposed, except that the overseas and commercial item exemptions have been eliminated. However, the rule did not require this legislation in order to have the authority to proceed in this case. The Councils issue rules under the authority of the Office of Federal Procurement Policy Act as well as 40 U.S.C. 121(c), 10 U.S.C. chapter 137, and 42 U.S.C. 2473(c). The Administrator for Federal Procurement Policy may prescribe Governmentwide procurement policies to be implemented in the FAR (41 U.S.C. 405). This case was opened at the request of OFPP. This case is making clear what was already expected. It is not unreasonable or "capricious" to require contractors doing business with the Government to disclose violations of the civil False Claims Act (civil FCA) or a violation of Federal criminal law involving fraud, conflict of interest, bribery, or gratuity violations found in Title 18 of the United States Code that have occurred in connection with the award, performance, or closeout of any Government contract performed by the contractor or a subcontract thereunder. Existing DoJ guidelines addressing corporate prosecution standards, while certainly not providing amnesty, suggest that if a company discloses such violations, the prosecution will be of the individuals responsible for the violation, not the entire organization.

d. *Empirical support that mandatory disclosure will achieve the Councils' objective.* One respondent stated that mandating disclosure without empirical support to show that it will achieve the Councils' objectives will be susceptible to challenge. The APA requires courts to strike down rules devoid of factual support. Another respondent also cited the APA, and that a rule may be set aside if it is arbitrary or capricious (5 U.S.C. 706).

Response: The Councils point to the testimony from DoJ and various OIGs that the experience with the NRO mandatory disclosure clause has been positive (see next paragraph). The Councils further cite the enactment of the Close the Contractor Fraud Loophole Act (see prior section), which now mandates many of these revisions to the FAR.

e. *The NRO requirement.* An agency OIG noted that similar contractually imposed disclosure requirements have been successfully implemented by the NRO. According to DoJ, the NRO reports that this requirement has improved its relationships with its contractors and enhanced its ability to prevent and detect procurement fraud. Another agency OIG stated that adoption of the NRO clause resulted in increased and earlier disclosure of wrongdoing and better working relationships built upon greater sharing of information and trust. It also led to the conclusion that it is more effective for a contractor to mandatorily disclose information pursuant to a requirement, than it is for a contractor to be in a position of offering up information that it could be criticized, or even sued, for providing.

One respondent, however, stated that the NRO requirement is not an appropriate model for all Government contractors because it requires disclosure of potential illegal activity related to the conduct of intelligence operations in the interest of national security and thus is not instructive. In fact, according to another respondent, the unique nature of the NRO and its responsibilities are major reasons cited as justification for its disclosure program. Similarly, the other respondent stated that, while the NRO's mandatory disclosure program was not the product of legislation, it was the direct product of an obvious and public awareness that we live in a different world after September 11, 2001.

Furthermore, several respondents cited problems with the NRO disclosure program. One respondent stated that "it is far from clear at this point whether the NRO mandatory disclosure program is or will be productive", citing anecdotal reports from the contractor community suggesting that the program is not as effective as the NRO claims. One respondent cited problems experienced by contractors subject to the NRO OIG reporting clause, claiming that the NRO OIG has inserted itself in the administration of contracts by using the clause as the basis to become involved in all aspects of the contractor ethics functions and corporate investigations. For example, the respondent stated that the OIG has used this clause to investigate, as a Federal offense, matters as mundane as employees who have been disciplined for leaving work early while reporting they were present. The respondent does not believe that OIG agents should be routinely involved in company internal ethics functions and contract administration. The respondent quoted Mr. Paul Denett, Administrator of the Office of Federal Procurement Policy: "The IG serves a purpose, but it needs to be limited to core areas."

However, the response from the National Procurement Fraud Task Force (NPFTF), signed by the IG of the NRO, stated that the requirement for mandatory reporting has worked very well at NRO: The reporting of wrongdoing has increased, comes earlier, and has led to a good working relationship. NPFTF considers that this model can have a similar impact across the Federal Government, and that the situation at NRO is not unique.

Response: Almost all the agency OIGs submitting public comments cite the success of the clause initiated by the NRO OIG as a reason for supporting this rule for their agency procurements.

As to limiting the role of the OIG to its core area, the core area of the OIG is to investigate fraud, conflict of interest, bribery, and gratuity violations. OIG agents will not be routinely involved in company internal ethics functions and contract administration unless violations are disclosed. The final rule has been revised to more closely focus the situations that must be disclosed by limiting violations of criminal law to violations involving fraud, conflict of interest, bribery, or gratuity violations found in Title 18 of the United States Code (see B.3.b.iii.).

iv. Will mandatory disclosure make reporting easier or better? In the DoJ letter of May 23, 2007, DoJ stated that if the FAR were more explicit in requiring such notification, it would serve to emphasize the critical importance of integrity in contracting. An agency OIG stated that the requirement will simplify the contractors' decision on whether to disclose suspected violations. Likewise, another agency OIG stated that the contractor is in a stronger position when reporting for the purpose of complying with a mandatory requirement than if voluntarily disclosing information, for which it could be criticized, or even sued. Another agency OIG commented that making self-reporting a requirement gives the honest contractor employees necessary leverage over those who may seek to shield the employer when wrongdoing is noticed or suspected.

On the other hand, some other respondents believed that if employees know that everything they report will be passed on to the Government, this may result in less reporting up the chain of the company rather than more. One respondent saw substantial potential to decrease rather than enhance cooperation with company compliance efforts.

The respondent was concerned that the likelihood of severe consequences will necessarily change the relationship of the company and its employees. Every interview will have the potential of resulting in employees being reported. It may be that investigative targets may not only be entitled to counsel, but to Miranda warnings, if the company is deemed to be acting on behalf of the Government. Further, another respondent was concerned that mandatory reporting may violate existing contracts with a labor union and may be an unfair labor practice if imposed without bargaining, citing *American Elec. Power Co.*, 302 NLRB 161(1991). Resistance by the employees can undercut the entire compliance program. A respondent also believed that employees may be reluctant to come forward if they are aware that the contractor will be required to report their co-workers, or report the company itself, to the OIG. This respondent cited studies by the framers of the USSG who undertook significant research addressing these issues.

Response: The Councils believe that by mandating disclosure, contractor executives and their counsel will be more inclined to make the required disclosure to the OIG, as opposed to either not disclosing or informally alerting the contracting officer, who is not in a position to evaluate the criminal behavior of individual employees. By mandating disclosure to the OIG, the rule will add weight to the arguments inside a corporation that good business practices in the long run favor compliance and disclosure. Nothing in the proposed rule requires administration of "Miranda" warnings. The rule does not place contractors in the role of law enforcement officers. With regard to the concerns about labor agreements, contractors can find ways to disclose without violating labor union provisions that protect individual privacy of workers.

v. Cooperative atmosphere more effective. According to one respondent, voluntary disclosure fosters a cooperative environment and rewards contractors that adopt effective internal controls. Another respondent considered that it is a key principle to promote self-governance as the preferred model to ensure compliance. This respondent quoted the Packard Commission findings in June 1986 that self-governance is the most promising mechanism to foster improved contract compliance. Self-governance makes the difference between responsibility for compliance and a mere facade of compliance. This respondent concluded that, based on 20 years of experience, both scholars and industry leaders believe that the current system of voluntary disclosure encourages companies to develop a stronger culture while still affording the Government broad remedies to protect the Government's interests. Under mandatory disclosure, contractors may focus on the ambiguities of the letter of the rule rather than the spirit of mutual commitment. One respondent expressed long standing support for and experience with voluntary self-reporting. It is concerned that mandatory self-reporting could discourage partnerships with the Government. One respondent cited the "fundamental principle" that contractor compliance programs resulting from internal company commitments to ethical behavior are more likely to be effective in preventing illegal behavior than programs imposed by "overbearing regulations."

Response: The Councils disagree. See "Is voluntary disclosure working?" at paragraph B.3.a.ii.

vi. Incentives. Several respondents contended that existing Government programs and contractor initiatives offer ample incentives for contractors to voluntarily report procurement violations.

• Several respondents pointed out that contractors may receive favorable consideration in debarment proceedings if they have voluntarily disclosed the conduct in question.

• Several respondents cited the civil FCA, which provides contractors with an incentive to report potentially fraudulent behavior. Organizations will voluntarily disclose to avoid lengthy and costly whistleblower litigation (*qui tam* actions). According to several respondents, voluntary disclosure can undermine a court's jurisdiction to entertain future *qui tam* cases and can mean the difference between maximum and reduced penalties.

• Several respondents also addressed the reduced penalties under the guidelines of the USSG, adopted in 1991, which are predicated on a model of rewarding voluntary reports. Two respondents stated that the proposed rule is inconsistent with the favorable treatment of voluntary disclosures under the USSG.

• Respondents cited the Deputy Attorney General's January 20, 2003, memorandum, "Principles of Federal Prosecution of Business Organizations," which provides to Federal prosecutors guidance governing charging decisions with respect to corporations and sentencing. Several respondents also cited Deputy Attorney General Paul J. McNulty's memorandum of December 12, 2006, which demonstrated that the DoJ considers an organization's voluntary disclosure and cooperation in determining whether to bring charges.

Various respondents were concerned that the proposed rule may eliminate the ability of a contractor to claim the benefit of "timely and voluntary disclosure" to the Government. One respondent recommended that, if the rule is finalized, a contractor should not be precluded from seeking and receiving leniency because a disclosure is made in compliance with the rule. One respondent stated that the proposed rule is not more consistent with the USSG, but actually contradicts them.

One respondent stated that the Councils must consider these concerns and evaluate the extent to which eliminating incentives to voluntary disclosure will affect a contractor's decision to disclose underlying behavior. The respondent believed that eliminating incentives could cause contractors to adopt a protective posture in the face of evidence of potential criminal behavior.

Another respondent suggested that, instead of mandating compliance and ethics programs, the Councils should open a new FAR case to develop an incentive-based approach. This respondent was concerned that the logic of penalizing contractors for failure to disclose a crime, rather than offering incentives, will not work. The disclosure obligation applies only if a crime has already occurred. If there is already a crime, then the company is already subject to punishment. Failure to disclose will only be an aggravating factor. So, if a company fails to disclose, it may escape punishment, but if it discloses, it will likely still be subject to punishment for the crime committed. Therefore, punishment for failure to disclose may not be sufficient incentive to disclose.

Response: There is nothing in this rule that removes any of the existing incentives. The incentives in the FAR (FAR 9.406–1(a)) and the USSG are not limited to "voluntary" disclosures but to "disclosures." Even if disclosure is "mandatory," incentives will still be offered to promote compliance.

b. Vagueness of Rule

i. "Reasonable grounds to believe." Numerous respondents were concerned that the rule does not specify what constitutes "reasonable grounds." One respondent stated that "reasonable grounds" is subject to varying interpretations, and may be viewed as an even lower standard than "probable cause." Should the contractor report based on mere suspicion or based on evidence that criminal activity has occurred? Because of this lack of clarity, several respondents were concerned that companies may tie up Government resources with a mountain of meaningless legal trivia. Numerous respondents stated that there will be substantial over-reporting because contractors may report even remotely possible criminal conduct out of an abundance of caution. One respondent considered that this will raise company costs through the investigation of baseless claims and incidents. Several other respondents stated that there will be an enormous amount of time spent sorting out the true criminal activity and truly significant problems.

One respondent suggested that the proposed rule will potentially subject an employer to civil actions brought by an employee when the reports forwarded by the employer to the Federal Government (because conceivably "reasonable grounds" existed) ultimately are determined to lack merit.

Response: The Councils have replaced "reasonable grounds to believe" with "credible evidence." DoJ Criminal Division recommended use of this standard after discussions with industry representatives. This term indicates a higher standard, implying that the contractor will have the opportunity to take some time for preliminary examination of the evidence to determine its credibility before deciding to disclose to the Government. See also the following discussion of "timely disclosure."

ii. Timely disclosure.

There are 3 aspects of timely disclosure that are of concern to the respondents:

• To which violations/contracts does timely disclosure apply?
• How much time does a contractor have to disclose a possible violation after first hearing something about it?
• How do we transition into this rule? How is timeliness measured for violations that the contractor may already know about and did not disclose prior to becoming subject to this rule?

Further, in analyzing these issues, there are 3 separate requirements for timely disclosure in this rule which may affect the response to the above questions:

• The contract clause requirement to disclose (paragraph (b)(3)).
• The contract clause requirement for an internal control system (paragraph (c)(2)(ii)(F)).
• Failure to timely disclose as a cause for suspension/debarment regardless of requirement for contract clause or internal control system (Subpart 9.4).

a. To which violations/contracts does timely disclosure apply?

Various respondents were concerned about whether the rule can apply to violations that occurred before the effective date of the rule, the date of the bid, or the date the clause is incorporated into the contract.

• Effective date of the rule. Numerous respondents recommended that the rule be made applicable only to conduct occurring on or after the date the rule is effective. The respondents argued that there is presently no requirement in the FAR for a contractor to disclose to the Government criminal violations committed by its employees. The respondents cited case law to support the argument that application of the rule to conduct occurring before the rule effective date would be impermissible. One respondent stated that the reporting requirement should be "prospective only". Otherwise this requirement may impose an unreasonable burden.

• Date the clause is incorporated. Another respondent questions whether the rule is meant to cover past acts, or only acts going forward from the date the clause is incorporated into a contract. According to one respondent, to punish entities for past acts would violate constitutional ex post facto prohibitions.

• Date of the bid. One respondent suggested that the violation would have to occur after the date of the bid.

Several respondents also looked at the end of the period during which violations that occur must be reported. One respondent suggested that completion of performance would be appropriate.

DoJ suggested limiting the mandatory disclosure of overpayments or criminal violations to matters discovered by the contractor within three years after contract completion.

Response: The first significant point to remember is that in all cases the reportable violations are linked to the performance of Government contracts. In the case of the contract clause direct requirement for contractor disclosure, the reportable violations are limited to the contract containing the clause. So the questions raised by the respondents about occurrence of violations are not an issue with regard to the contract clause disclosure requirement, because violations would necessarily occur during award or performance of the contract, through contract closeout, which would necessarily be after the effective date of the rule and after incorporation of the clause. (**Note:** The clause will be included in solicitations and resultant contracts after the effective date of the rule, in accordance with FAR 1.108(d)).

However, in the case of internal control systems and suspension/debarment, the proposed rule states that reportable violations could occur in connection with "any Government contract." This could be overly broad in two regards—

• Does it apply to violations on the contracts of other contractors?
• Does it apply to contracts closed out 20 years ago?

The Councils have made clear in the final rule that this disclosure requirement is limited to contracts awarded to the contractor (or subcontracts thereunder). It was not the intent of the proposed rule to require contractors to report on violations of other contractors under contracts unrelated to their own contracts.

The Councils do not agree with the respondents who think that disclosure under the internal control system or as a potential cause for suspension/

debarment should only apply to conduct occurring after the date the rule is effective or the clause is included in the contract, or the internal control system is established. The laws against these violations were already in place before the rule became effective or any of these other occurrences. This rule is not establishing a new rule against theft or embezzlement and making it retroactive. The only thing that was not in place was the requirement to disclose the violation. If violations relating to an ongoing contract occurred prior to the effective date of the rule, then the contractor must disclose such violations, whether or not the clause is in the contract and whether or not an internal control system is in place, because of the cause for suspension and debarment in Subpart 9.4.

However, the Councils agree that this requirement should not stretch back indefinitely into the past (*e.g.*, contracts that were closed 20 years ago). At that point, relevance with regard to present responsibility has diminished, there is less availability of evidence to support an investigation, there is more difficulty locating the responsible parties (who is the contracting officer?), and there should be some reasonable limitation on a contractor's liability after contract closeout.

The Councils considered using contract closeout as the end point for the requirement to disclose fraud, but according to the DoJ, often contract fraud occurs at the time of closeout, and cutting off the obligation to disclose at that point would exempt many of these violations from the obligation to disclose. Three years after final payment is consistent with most of the contractor record retention requirements (*see* Audit and Records clauses at FAR 52.214–26 and 52.215–2). Therefore, the Councils concur with the DoJ recommendation that the mandatory disclosure of violations should be limited to a period of three years after contract completion, using final payment as the event to mark contract completion.

Therefore, the Councils have added the phrase "Until 3 years after final payment on any Government contract awarded to the contractor" at 9.406–2(b)(1)(vi) and 9.407–2(a)(8), and has added in the clause at paragraph (c)(2)(ii)(F) the statement that "The disclosure requirement for an individual contract continues until at least 3 years after final payment on the contract." To make the applicability during the close-out phase of a contract clearer, the Councils have revised the draft final rule in all applicable places to refer to "award, performance, or closeout."

b. Does "timely" allow sufficient time between first learning of the allegation and the disclosure?

One respondent objected that "timely" is very broad in scope which could permit contracting officers to have inconsistent interpretations of what is timely. One respondent questioned whether "timely" means upon first learning of an allegation or only upon conducting an adequate internal investigation. The respondent recommended that the regulations should include a set period of time (*i.e.*, 90 days) for any reporting requirement. Another respondent recommended that the regulations might allow 60 days to determine if there are reasonable grounds to conclude that the contractor committed a crime. The 60 day period would start when a principal of the company suspects that a crime might have been committed, but lacks reasonable grounds for concluding that a crime has been committed. An agency OIG suggested "timely" should be replaced with "within 30 calendar days."

Another respondent was concerned that when "timely" disclosure must occur is ambiguous because the timing of a violation is troublesome. Contractors often settle cases without any admission of fault or liability. The rise in deferred and non-prosecution agreements in criminal cases brought by the Government against contractors creates confusion regarding disclosure of criminal violations.

According to many respondents, the proposed rule may require premature reporting. One respondent questioned the requirement to notify without delay, whenever the contractor becomes "aware" of violations of Federal criminal law. According to this respondent, the rule does not clarify what constitutes "awareness." Several other respondents were concerned that the proposed amendment does not appear to allow a contractor to complete an internal investigation before notifying the OIG and contracting officer. Several respondents considered that an internal investigation could be compromised by premature reporting. One respondent recommended that the rule should allow the contractor the opportunity to comply with its ethics and compliance program and conduct an internal investigation prior to disclosure to the Government. Contractors should be required to report only actual violations of law, not those incidents that have not been confirmed as actual violations.

One respondent pointed out that existing voluntary disclosure protocols allow for internal investigation by the reporting parties before a disclosure is made. Another respondent stated that under the DoD Voluntary Disclosure Program, if the preliminary investigation reveals evidence to suggest that disclosure is warranted, contractors may disclose information sufficient for preliminary acceptance into the DoD Voluntary Disclosure Program, and then have 60 days to complete a fuller investigation. This rule provides no guidance on preliminary steps afforded to a contractor.

One respondent also recommended that the contractor be explicitly provided with a reasonable period of time to internally investigate a potential violation.

DoJ suggested that the preamble to the final rule should make clear that nothing in the rule is intended to preclude a contractor from continuing to investigate after making its initial disclosure to the Government. DoJ would expect that the OIG or the contracting officer will encourage the contractor to complete its internal investigation and make full report of its findings.

In their comment on the second proposed rule, one respondent recommends that the preamble should explain that a contractor, with the contracting officer's approval, may tailor the "timely reporting" provision of its internal control system in order to make meaningful reports to the contracting officer.

Response: First, the Councils note that the new statute uses the term "timely" in setting forth disclosure requirements. The Councils considered, and rejected, adding a set period of time, *e.g.*, 30 days, to the disclosure requirement. It was decided that doing so would be arbitrary and would cause more problems than it would resolve, *e.g.*, how to determine when the 30 days begins.

Further, the Councils believe that using the standard of "credible evidence" rather than "reasonable grounds to believe" will help clarify "timely" because it implies that the contractor will have the opportunity to take some time for preliminary examination of the evidence to determine its credibility before deciding to disclose to the Government. Until the contractor has determined the evidence to be credible, there can be no "knowing failure to timely disclose." This does not impose upon the contractor an obligation to carry out a complex investigation, but only to take reasonable steps that the contractor considers sufficient to determine that the evidence is credible.

The Councils note that there is no rigidness to our proposed requirement to establish an internal control system. The rule just sets forth minimum requirements. The contractor can use its own judgment in the details of setting up a system that meets the minimum requirements. The clause does not require contracting officer approval of this system.

c. *Transitioning into the rule. Meaning of "timely" when the knowledge of credible evidence pre-dates the requirements of this rule.* One respondent stated that the reporting requirement should be "prospective only". Otherwise this requirement may impose an unreasonable burden.

Response: As just discussed, the disclosure requirement is prospective only. Although violations on the current contract might have occurred during the pre-award phase and violations on other contracts may have already occurred prior to establishment of the internal control system or prior to the effective date of the rule, timely disclosure of the violation can only be measured from the time when the requirement to disclose the violation came into effect, even if credible evidence of the violation was previously known to the contractor.

With regard to the contractual disclosure requirement, the timely disclosure would be measured from the date of determination of credible evidence or the date of contract award, whichever event occurs later.

With regard to the disclosure requirement of the internal control system, it can only become effective upon establishment of the internal control system. The violation can have occurred with regard to any Government contract which is still open or for which final payment was made within the last 3 years, so may predate establishment of the internal control system. Therefore, timely disclosure of credible evidence as required by the internal control system would be measured from the date of determination by the contractor that the evidence is credible, or the date of establishment of the internal control system, whichever event occurs later.

With regard to the knowing failure by a principal to timely disclose credible evidence of a violation or significant overpayments as a cause for suspension or debarment, the violation can have occurred with regard to any Government contract, which is still open or for which final payment was made within the last 3 years, so may predate the effective date of the rule. Therefore, timely disclosure of credible evidence as required by the rule as a cause for suspension or debarment would be measured from the date of determination by the contractor that the evidence is credible, or from the effective date of the rule, whichever event occurs later.

To some extent, the effective date of the rule actually trumps the other events, because the failure to timely disclose as a cause for suspension/debarment is independent of the inclusion of the contract clause in the contract or the establishment of an internal control system. At least in those instances where disclosure was not timely in regard to effective date of the rule, but was reported as soon as the clause was in the contract, or as soon as the control system was in place, then it would not be a violation of the contract or a mark against the control system. It could still be a cause for suspension or debarment, although the Councils consider that suspension or debarment would be unlikely, if the contractor came forward as soon as the clause or the internal control system was in place (before that, the contractor might have been unaware of the requirement to disclose).

iii. "Criminal violation in connection with contract award or performance." Numerous respondents stated that the rule fails to specify what constitutes a "criminal violation" "in connection with contract award or performance". Some of these respondents made the following comments:

• The broad nature of the phrase "violation of Federal criminal law in connection with contract award or performance" places a heavy burden. The Government is in the best position to provide specific guidance to contractors as to the violations that would be considered covered by this new requirement. Otherwise, each contractor will have to develop its own list and explanations to its employees as to what constitutes criminal violations.

• If the FAR Council proceeds with the rule, it should provide a specific list of the criminal violations that the contractor is required to disclose.

• The self-reporting requirements should be revised to provide the specific circumstances under which self-reporting is required.

• The provision is vague in regard to the type of "criminal violation" covered, leaving open application of the rule to non-procurement related offenses. If an employee commits a criminal violation while driving on Federal lands in the course of performing a contract, must the traffic violation be reported to the agency OIG? Also, the agency OIGs may receive reports about violations of Federal tax law or Occupational Safety and Health laws that occur in connection with the performance of the contract, over which the OIGs do not have jurisdiction. This can result in unnecessary or inappropriate reports.

• The proposed rule does not elaborate on the nexus between the perceived criminal conduct and the Federal contract so as to trigger the reporting requirement. A contractor's silence could be alleged to be a false statement where the employer had "reason to believe" that one of its employees, agents, or subcontractors had violated criminal law in connection with a contract.

• The rule should define more clearly what is reportable and when the obligation to report is triggered.

One Government agency suggested adding "potential" to "violation."

DoJ also suggested tightening the standard for disclosure by adding the phrase "involving fraud, conflict of interest, bribery, or gratuity violations found in Title 18 of the United States Code."

Response: The Councils have adopted the more specific description of criminal law suggested by DoJ as responsive to many of the concerns expressed by the respondents.

As to nexus with the contract, the clause stipulates in paragraph 52.203–13(b)(3)(i) that the violation should have occurred "in connection with the award, performance, or closeout of this contract, or any subcontract thereunder." With regard to the internal control system disclosure required in paragraph 52.203–13(c)(2)(ii)(F) and the cause for debarment or suspension in Subpart 9.4, the violation must be in connection with the award, performance, or closeout, of any Government contract performed by the contractor, or a subcontract thereunder, and the obligation to disclose information lasts until 3 years after final payment. If there is no connection to a Government contract performed by the contractor, or a subcontract thereunder, then it need not be disclosed.

The Councils do not consider it necessary to add "potential" to "violation" because that preceding language already is in terms of "credible evidence." That does not necessarily mean that a violation has occurred, but the principals are looking for "credible evidence" that a violation has occurred. "Potential violation" would open it even wider and could result in too many unnecessary disclosures.

iv. *Level of employee with knowledge.* Several respondents wanted the rule to identify the level of contractor employee whose knowledge will be imputed to the contractor, such that the contractor has the requisite knowledge. Absent such identification, consistent with the doctrine of *respondeat superior* applied in Federal criminal law, a contractor may be deemed to have requisite knowledge warranting disclosure if any employee at any level is aware of conduct which may constitute a Federal criminal offense. This could cause a contractor to be accused of violating the mandatory disclosure provision before the contractor's management becomes aware of the offense and before the appropriate steps for disclosure may be undertaken. One respondent stated that it is unreasonable to expect all knowledge to be passed up the chain. Several respondents recommended revision of the proposed rule to require that a contractor principal must have the requisite knowledge of a Federal criminal law violation before that knowledge will be imputed to a contractor.

Response: The Councils concur that for debarment and suspension, a principal must have the requisite knowledge in order for mandatory disclosure to be applicable. See response under the heading "Suspension/Debarment", "Who has knowledge?" at paragraph B.5.e.

c. Disclosure to OIG. One respondent considered that the proposed rule would essentially require contractors and subcontractors to become fraud detection and reporting entities. Must contractors become experts in forensic accounting and private investigation? This respondent considered that the proposed rule essentially would "deputize" contractors and subcontractors as agents of the OIG. One respondent also considered that the company is now acting as an agent of the Government.

Is "the agency OIG" the OIG for the agency which awarded the contract under which the action in question took place? One respondent was concerned when contractor is required to disclose to different inspectors general because the proposed rule is silent on what actions and procedural safeguards are to be implemented in the various offices of the Inspectors General. A contractor that deals with a variety of different Federal agencies will unreasonably be faced with significantly increased risk and uncertainty.

Several respondents considered that a likely outcome of the mandatory reporting to the agency OIG will be to remove from a contracting officer or agency the authority or the ability to settle and compromise the issues by a disclosure. One industry association indicated that member companies report that in their experience, the vast majority of potential violations disclosed to a contracting officer or other agency official are quickly resolved as an administrative matter. Once a matter is referred to the DoD OIG as a potential criminal or civil fraud matter, under the Contract Disputes Act the contracting officer loses his or her ability to compromise or settle the issue. One respondent was also concerned about the impact of the proposed rule on the influence and authority of the contracting officer. The respondent considered that disclosure to the OIG passes the leadership role on any subsequent investigation and review to the OIG's office and undercuts the authority and ability of the contracting officer to manage contracts.

One respondent noted that under the DFARS rule, the OIG only needs to be notified when appropriate. One respondent considered that mandatory notification to the OIG defeats the concept of internal audits and correction of possible irregularities. The respondent is concerned that, once the OIG is brought into the process, both the contracting officer and the contractor/subcontractor lose control of the process.

One respondent was concerned with the ability of the OIG to handle an increased level of reports. One respondent stated that their experience with the capability of the OIG's offices to deal with complicated, sophisticated and/or fact-intensive issues is very mixed at best. Current demands have placed substantial strain in the ability of the OIG's offices to support investigations, and delays are commonplace. "According to the respondent, 'competing demands for resources to support overseas investigations and Homeland Security defense have drained whatever experienced resources existed" at the agency OIGs.

An agency OIG suggested replacing "agency Office of the Inspector General" with "A President-selected and Senate-approved Inspector General or designated Federal entity Inspector General." The agency OIG stated that this better describes the correct agency to which the contractor should report potential violations.

Response: There is nothing in the proposed rule that "deputizes" contractors. The Councils have concluded that it is appropriate for contractors to send the reports directly to the OIG, with a copy to the contracting officer, because it is the OIG that is responsible for investigating the disclosure.

The disclosure would be to the OIG of the agency that awarded the subject contract. The Councils have added clarification that if a violation relates to more than one Government contract, the Contractor may make the disclosure to the agency OIG and Contracting Officer responsible for the largest dollar value contract impacted by the violation. If the violation relates to an order against a Governmentwide acquisition contract, a multi-agency contract, a multiple-award schedule contract such as the Federal Supply Schedule, or any other procurement instrument intended for use by multiple agencies, the contractor shall notify the OIG of the ordering agency and the IG of the agency responsible for the basic contract.

Whether OIGs can handle an increase in the level of reporting depends on the expected level of increase. The Councils do not anticipate that companies are going to flood the OIG with trivialities, as some respondents fear. The Council also notes that the agency OIGs were all strongly in favor of this rule.

The Councils do not agree with the suggestion of one agency IG that the rule should specify "A President-selected and Senate-approved Inspector General or designated Federal entity Inspector General." Although this is probably accurate, the Councils consider it too complicated for some contractors to determine. It is the opinion of the Councils that, if a contractor submits a report to the wrong OIG, that OIG will forward it to the appropriate OIG.

Throughout the rule, the Councils have used the words "disclose" and "disclosure" for consistency, rather than in some places using the word "notify" or "report".

4. Full Cooperation

The proposed rule states at paragraph (c)(2)(ii)(G) of FAR 52.203–XX (now 52.203–13) that a contractor Code of Business Ethics and Conduct shall, at a minimum, have an internal control system that provides "full cooperation with any Government agencies responsible for audit, investigation, or corrective actions."

a. Waiver of Privileges/Protections/Rights

Many respondents expressed concern that compliance with the rules requiring disclosure and full cooperation would be interpreted to—

• Require contractors waive an otherwise valid claim of attorney-client privilege or protections afforded by the attorney work product doctrine, both protecting attorney-client communications; or

• Interfere with an employee's right under the Fifth Amendment of the U.S. Constitution covering the right of an individual not to be compelled to incriminate itself.

One respondent recommended addition of strong language to preserve privilege protections.

DoJ and an agency OIG indicated awareness of these concerns in their comments and recommended clarification in the final rule. DoJ proposed that the final rule state explicitly:

"Nothing in this rule is intended to require that a contractor waive its attorney-client privilege, or that any officer, director, owner, or employee of the contractor, including a sole proprietor, waive his or her attorney-client privilege or Fifth Amendment rights."

Response: It is doubtful any regulation or contract clause could legally compel a contractor or its employees to forfeit these rights. However, the Councils have revised the final rule to provide such assurance. To address concern that cooperation might be interpreted to require disclosure of materials covered by the work product doctrine, the Councils have added a definition of "full cooperation" at 52.203–13(a) to make clear that the rule does not mandate disclosure of materials covered by the attorney work product doctrine.

For comparison purposes, it is instructive to refer to the flexible approach adopted in the USSG:

> Waiver of attorney-client privilege and of work product protections is not a prerequisite to a reduction * * * unless such waiver is necessary in order to provide timely and thorough disclosure of all pertinent information known to the organization.

It also is worth pointing out the DoD Voluntary Disclosure Program never required waiver as a condition of participation. Contractors in that program routinely found ways to report wrongdoing without waiving the attorney-client privilege or providing their attorney memoranda reflecting their interviews that normally are covered by the work product doctrine.

Any limitation in this rule should not be used as an excuse by a contractor to avoid disclosing facts required by this rule. Facts are never protected by the attorney-client privilege or work product doctrine. Moreover, the Fifth Amendment has no application to corporations, so the only sensitive area is mandatory disclosure or cooperation by individuals or sole proprietors, which is addressed in the clarification.

b. Indemnification of Employees

Several respondents expressed concern that full cooperation will be interpreted as prohibiting a contractor from indemnifying its employees or their individual counsel to the extent permitted or required by state law or the contractor's charter or bylaws. Several respondents expressed concern that the Government may view indemnification of contractor employees as not cooperating. One respondent asked if there was a difference between "cooperation" and "full cooperation" and, more seriously, whether full cooperation restricted a contractor's ability to make counsel available to its employees. Several respondents pointed to the district court opinion in *U.S.* v. *Stein,* 435 F.Supp. 2d 330 (SDNY 2006), and 440 F.Supp. 2d 315 (SDNY 2006) that suggests the Government viewed KPMG's practice of paying for employees' legal costs pursuant to indemnification rules was not "cooperation" favored by the prosecutors in that case.

Response: With regard to indemnification of employees for legal costs, State law—not Federal—controls. Just as full cooperation cannot mean a company forfeits its attorney-client privilege, there is no reason to think it means employees forfeit their right to indemnification from their employers. On December 12, 2006, DOJ addressed this issue in a memorandum sent to all DoJ attorneys by Deputy Attorney General Paul McNulty ("McNulty Memorandum"), stating:

> Prosecutors generally should not take into account whether a corporation is advancing attorneys' fees to employees or agents under investigation and indictment. Many state indemnification statutes grant corporations the power to advance the legal fees of officers under investigation prior to a formal determination of guilt. As a consequence, many corporations enter into contractual obligations to advance attorneys' fees through provisions contained in their corporate charters, bylaws or employment agreements. Therefore, a corporation's compliance with governing state law and its contractual obligations cannot be considered a failure to cooperate.

c. Requirement to Fire an Employee

One respondent asked that the rule clarify that cooperation does not mean a contractor must fire an employee.

Response: It is inappropriate for the Government to direct a contractor to fire an employee, although the Government may require that an employee be removed from performance of the Government contract. However, most corporate compliance programs assert that violation of law or company policy is grounds for dismissal. Also note the internal control system requirements for principals at paragraph (c)(2)(ii)(B) of the clause.

d. Ability To Conduct a Thorough and Effective Internal Investigation

Several respondents expressed concern that cooperation or disclosure will be interpreted to interfere with a contractor's ability to conduct a thorough and effective internal investigation. Some respondents were concerned that a contractor continuing to investigate a matter after reporting would be deemed not cooperating. One respondent recommended that the rule state explicitly that: "A contractor has a reasonable time to investigate a potential investigation * * * and that nothing in the rule prohibits or restricts a contractor from conducting an internal investigation."

Response: Any interpretation of full cooperation that would suggest a limit on contractors conducting internal investigations would be clearly at odds with the intent of the rule, which encourages compliance program investigations, reporting, and cooperation.

e. Defending a Proceeding or Dispute Arising From or Related to Disclosure

Various respondents expressed concern that full cooperation will be interpreted to preclude a contractor from defending itself in a proceeding or dispute arising from or related to the disclosure. One respondent raised concerns that a rule mandating full cooperation could be interpreted as prohibiting a contractor from "vigorously defending its actions." Another respondent observed that full cooperation might require a contractor to waive its right to appeal the results of an audit.

Response: Nothing in the rule would foreclose a contractor from advancing a defense or an "explanation" for the alleged fraud or corruption arising in a Government contract. This includes being free to use any administrative or legal rights available to resolve any dispute between the Government and the contractor. The rule is intended simply to require the contractor to be forthcoming with its customer, the Government, with regard to credible evidence relating to alleged fraud or corruption in its Government contracts.

f. Expansion of Audit Rights and Access to Records

Various respondents asked to what extent full cooperation overrode the limits on Government audit rights and access to records limitations, giving the Government "unfettered access" to individuals to conduct interviews, even though the current audit access clauses are limited to documents. Expanding on that, one respondent also asked if the rule requires contractors to give the Government "full access to their financial and proprietary information, beyond that required by existing contract clauses." Another respondent also observed that the Government may invoke the requirement in connection with disputes before the Board of Contract Appeals or U.S. Court of Federal Claims. One respondent requested clarification that the cooperation requirement applies only to agencies affected by the conduct and not the entire Government.

Response: The proposed rule was not intended to have any application or impact on the Government's exercise of its audit and access to records rights in the routine contract administration context except as the issue arises when a contractor discloses fraud or corruption or the Government independently has evidence sufficient to open an investigation of fraud and solicit the contractor's cooperation. The issue of contractor cooperation in this rule arises primarily in the context of Government investigation of contract fraud and corruption and any application of this rule in any other context by the Government would be clearly overreaching.

g. Inadvertent Failure as Non-Cooperation

One respondent feared that an "inadvertent" failure to provide documents in a routine DCAA audit would be deemed non-cooperative.

Response: The rule has no application to routine DCAA audits.

h. Need for Definition

Many respondents asked for an expanded definition of "full cooperation" in order to reduce the potential for misinterpretation of the rule, resulting in the concerns addressed in the preceding paragraphs.

Response: Contractors are not expected to block Government auditors and investigators' access to information found in documents or through its employees in furtherance of a contract fraud or corruption investigation.

Generally speaking, it is also reasonable for investigators and prosecutors to expect that compliant contractors will encourage employees both to make themselves available and to cooperate with the Government investigation.

That also applies to responding to reasonable Government requests for documents. Ignoring or offering little attention to detail in responding to auditor or investigator requests or subpoenas for documents or information may, in some circumstances, be obstruction of justice and, if established, certainly would not be deemed full cooperation.

According to the USSG, cooperation must be both timely and thorough:

• To be timely, the cooperation must begin essentially at the same time as the organization is officially notified of a criminal investigation.

• To be thorough, the cooperation should include the disclosure of all pertinent information known by the organization.

—A prime test of whether the organization has disclosed all pertinent information is whether the information is sufficient for law enforcement personnel to identify—

—The nature and extent of the offense; and

—The individual(s) responsible for the criminal conduct.

—However, the cooperation to be measured is the cooperation of the organization itself, not the cooperation of individuals within the organization. If, because of the lack of cooperation of particular individual(s), neither the organization nor law enforcement personnel are able to identify the culpable individual(s) within the organization despite the organization's efforts to cooperate fully, the organization may still be given credit for full cooperation.

The DoD Voluntary Disclosure Program described expected cooperation in some detail in its standard agreement (the "XYZ Agreement"), and it may be a useful reference in this circumstance where the contractor discloses credible evidence of fraud or corruption under this rule. However, the detail found there goes significantly beyond the scope of this rule and is best addressed on a case-by-case basis.

The final rule includes a definition that incorporates some of the concepts in the USSG and the general principle that cooperation must be both timely and thorough. It is intended to make clear that cooperation should include all information requested as well as all pertinent information known by the contractor necessary to complete the investigation, whether the information helps or hurts the contractor. Contractors are expected to make their employees available for Government investigators and auditors investigating contract fraud and corruption and respond in a timely and complete manner to Government requests for documents and other information required to conduct an investigation of contract fraud and corruption.

Responding to concerns expressed by the respondents, the Councils have incorporated the following definition into the final rule at 52.203–13(a):

"Full cooperation"—

(1) Means disclosure to the Government of the information sufficient for law enforcement to identify the nature and extent of the offense and the individuals responsible for the conduct. It includes providing timely and complete response to Government auditors' and investigators' requests for documents and access to employees with information;

(2) Does not foreclose any contractor rights arising in law, the FAR, or the terms of the contract. It does not require—

(i) A contractor to waive its attorney-client privilege or the protections afforded by the attorney work product doctrine; or

(ii) Any officer, director, owner, or employee of the contractor, including a sole proprietor, to waive his or her attorney client privilege or Fifth Amendment rights; and

(3) Does not restrict a contractor from—

(i) Conducting an internal investigation; or

(ii) Defending a proceeding or dispute arising under the contract or related to a potential or disclosed violation.

5. *Suspension/Debarment*

a. New Cause for Suspension or Debarment

Various respondents expressed concern that the proposed rule establishes failure to timely disclose a violation as a new cause for suspension or debarment, rather than suspension or debarment just for the underlying violation.

Response: The requirement for timely disclosure could in some circumstances be considered a new cause for suspension or debarment. However, the question of timely disclosure will not come up unless the Government independently discovers that there has been a significant overpayment, a violation of the civil FCA, or a violation of Federal criminal law to be disclosed, that the Contractor knew about and elected to ignore. It is unlikely that any contractor would be suspended or debarred absent the determination that a violation had actually occurred. Present responsibility is the ultimate basis of suspension or debarment.

b. Unnecessary and Not Good Policy

Many respondents criticized the additional suspension and debarment coverage in the proposed rule as

unnecessary and redundant to existing regulations that—
• Provide strong incentives for contractors to voluntarily disclose criminal behavior;
• Require a prospective contractor to demonstrate a satisfactory record of integrity and business ethics; and
• Provide a "panoply of methods for prosecuting and eliminating those companies that fail to abide by the highest ethical and legal standards."

One respondent stated that the proposed suspension and debarment for "violation of Federal criminal law" simply repeats much of what is contained in FAR 9.406–2 and 9.407–2. Another respondent considered the suspension and debarment regulations punitive.

Response: As addressed in the preceding paragraph, the added causes for suspension/debarment add the requirement to timely disclose the violation and are not duplicative of the violation itself as a cause for suspension/debarment.

The suspension and debarment policies and standards are not punitive. The purpose of suspension and debarment is to ensure that the Government does business only with responsible contractors, not to punish. This final rule continues to embrace the responsibility standard.

c. Mitigating Factors

Several respondents were concerned whether the proposed rule maintains the current scheme of ten mitigating factors at FAR 9.406–1(a) or renders it meaningless by establishing failure to disclose itself as a cause for debarment (thus preventing "voluntary" disclosure).

Response: The mitigating factors currently at FAR 9.406–1(a) will continue to be used, and a contractor's timely disclosure to the Government will continue to be a mitigating factor. As stated in the response in paragraph B.3.a.vi. "Incentives", above, the incentives in the FAR and the USSG are not limited to "voluntary" disclosures but to "disclosures."

Even if disclosure is "mandatory," incentives will still be offered to promote compliance. The Councils do not recommend any revision as a result of these comments.

d. Undefined Terms

Many respondents expressed concern that terms such as "knowing," "timely" "reasonable grounds to believe," and "overpayment" are undefined and will thus put contractors at risk. One Government respondent suggested adding "knew, should have known, or" to "had reasonable grounds to believe."

Response: See responses under paragraph B.3.b."Vagueness of rule." for discussions of "timely," and "reasonable grounds to believe."

With regard to the term "knowing failure to disclose" the "knowing" refers to the failure to disclose. "Knowing failure to disclose" was added in the proposed rule to the causes for debarment at FAR 9.406–2(b)(1)(vi) and the causes for suspension at FAR 9.407–2(a)(8). Requiring a "knowledge" element to the cause for action actually provides more protection for contractors. The Councils do not agree with adding "or should have known." The principals are only required to disclose what they know. Further, using the standard of "credible evidence" rather than "reasonable grounds to believe" will help clarify "knowing" (See response at "Vagueness of rule" at paragraph B.3.b.i., "Reasonable grounds to believe").

The term "overpayment" is described in a number of FAR clauses and provisions and does not require a definition with respect to suspension and debarment. For further discussion of overpayments, see response at "Suspension and Debarment", paragraph B.5.f. "Limit or abandon suspension/debarment for failure to disclose overpayment".

e. Who has knowledge?

One respondent stated that a contractor should be suspended or debarred for failing to disclose violations of Federal criminal law only if a "principal" of the company (as defined in the proposed contract clause) has knowledge of the crime. Failure to disclose crime should not be a basis for suspension or debarment if lower-level employees, who are not managers or supervisors, commit a crime and conceal the crime from the contractor's supervisory-level personnel.

Response: Paragraph (a)(2) of the clause at FAR 52.209–5 defines "principals" to mean "officers; directors; owners; partners; and, persons having primary management or supervisory responsibilities within a business entity (*e.g.*, general manager; plant manager; head of a subsidiary, division, or business segment, and similar positions)". The Councils agree with the respondent and have revised 3.1003(a)(2), 9.406–2(b)(1)(vi), and 9.407–2(a)(8) to make disclosure mandatory when a principal of the company has knowledge. The Councils have also added the definition of a principal at FAR 2.101 because it now applies to more than a single FAR part, and revised both definitions to be singular rather than plural.

The Councils note that this definition should be interpreted broadly, and could include compliance officers or directors of internal audit, as well as other positions of responsibility.

f. Limit or Abandon Suspension/Debarment for Failure To Disclose Overpayment

One respondent stated that the proposed ability to suspend or debar for failure to disclose an "overpayment" on a Government contract may create operational difficulties because contracts are subject to reconciliation processes with payments audited and adjusted over time. Likewise, another respondent stated that singling out routine contract payment issues, which are daily events, with errors on both sides, is simply unworkable. The respondent cites a situation where a defense contractor did disclose an overpayment to the payment office, only to be told that it was wrong, yet was later made the subject of a *qui tam* action. Another respondent likewise objected to making reporting of overpayments grounds for suspension or debarment rather than a matter of contract administration. The respondent stated that the proposed rule does not connect overpayments to the criminal law violations upon which the rest of the proposed rule is focused.

One respondent recommended that the FAR Council should abandon the proposed changes that would make failure to disclose an "overpayment" a new cause for suspension or debarment because a number of current FAR clauses already require the contractor to disclose specific types of overpayments, *e.g.*, 52.232–25, 52.232–26, 52.232–27, and 52.212–4(i)(5). These clauses treat such overpayments as a matter of contract administration and do not treat them as a matter of possible fraud and a basis for suspension or debarment. In addition, the Part 9 provisions should state explicitly that the cause for suspension or debarment is for violation of the requirements in FAR 52.232–25, 52.232–26, 52.232–27, and 52.212–4(i)(5). The respondent noted that the proposed rule did not demonstrate that the present FAR provisions requiring the disclosure of overpayments are ineffective.

On the other hand, another respondent stated that contractors currently have no obligation to report overpayment.

One respondent was more specifically concerned that overpayments can result from indirect rate variances or similar credits that can occur years after contract performance and that can put the contractor in an over-billed situation. The severe sanctions that could inure to contractors so situated seem patently unfair. The respondent suggested either excluding rate variances or applying the section only to payments made during or immediately following contract performance.

Another respondent was concerned that this ethics rule creates potential inconsistency in the treatment of overpayments with the existing regulatory provisions of the FAR, and recommends deletion of the issue of "overpayment" as a basis for suspension and debarment.

DoJ suggested some answers to these concerns. DoJ considers that a duty to disclose an overpayment is just as important as the disclosure of criminal violations, and the requirement to disclose both will save the contractor from having to decide whether a criminal violation has in fact occurred in the case of an overpayment. However, DoJ concedes that a materiality requirement is appropriate to limit the scope of the requirement to disclose overpayments.

Response: The Councils dispute the allegation that "contractors currently have no obligation to report overpayments" and refers the respondent to the payment clauses at FAR 52.232–25, 52.232–26, 52.232–27, and 52.212–4(i)(5). Although other clauses already require reporting of overpayment, this inclusion of the requirement in Subpart 9.4 to disclose significant overpayments is necessary to make it clear that, if a contractor does not meet this condition of the contract, it can be subject to suspension or debarment.

The Councils agree with the suggestion by the DoJ that it is appropriate to limit the application of suspension or debarment to cases in which the unreported overpayment is significant. This will resolve some of the respondents' concerns over routine contract payment issues. The Councils have revised the final rule to address only significant overpayments, which implies more than just dollar value and depends on the circumstances of the overpayment as well as the amount. Since contractors are required by the Payment clauses to report and return overpayments of any amount, it is within the discretion of the suspension and debarment official to determine whether an overpayment is significant and whether suspension or debarment would be the appropriate outcome for failure to report such overpayment.

Rate variances do not need to be specifically excluded by the case because this issue is already taken care of in Part 32 and the Payment clauses. Rate variances are not considered overpayments until the rates are determined. The suggestion to apply the section only to payments made during or immediately following contract performance would not necessarily exempt rate variances, depending on when the rates are determined.

Further, the Councils decided to exclude knowing failure to report overpayments that result from contract financing payments, as defined in FAR 32.001, as grounds for suspension or debarment. Even though such overpayments must be reported and returned under the Payment clauses, these ongoing payments that are not the final payment on a contract are often based on estimates, and are subject to correction as the contract progresses. This rule is aimed at the type of overpayment that the contractor knows will result in unjust enrichment, and yet fails to disclose it.

The Councils have ensured that there is no overlap or inconsistency between this final rule and the current FAR requirements relating to overpayment, as well as the Contract Debt case published as part of Federal Acquisition Circular 2005–27 on September 17, 2008 (73 FR 53997).

g. Blacklisting

One respondent had a different concern, that the proposed changes in Part 42 with regard to past performance would allow "blacklisting" of contractors through consideration of "integrity and business ethics" in the past performance evaluation without due process protections. The respondent stated that the suspension and debarment procedures are the proper means to address responsibility issues.

Response: A contractor's satisfactory record of integrity and business ethics has long been one of the required elements for determining that a prospective contractor is responsible (see FAR 9.104–1(d)). The rules for assessing responsibility at FAR Subpart 9.1 provide for sufficient standards to ensure that offerors are treated fairly. FAR 15.306(b)(1) and (d)(3), and 42.1503(b) give the contractor the opportunity to comment on adverse past performance. The Councils do not recommend any change as a result of this comment.

h. Amendment of the Civil FCA

One respondent believed that the proposed cause for suspension/debarment language effectively amends the civil FCA. The respondent objected to changing contractors' obligations regarding overpayments without using the legislative procedure.

Response: The Councils disagree that the rule intended to, or did, amend the civil FCA outside the legislative process. The civil FCA provides a legal tool to counteract fraudulent billings turned in to the Federal Government by encouraging "whistleblowers" who are not affiliated with the Government to file actions against Federal contractors, claiming fraud against the Government. It also provides incentives to contractors to self-disclose. This does not preclude the Government from imposing an obligation on Federal contractors to themselves disclose to the Government if instances of overpayment are known to the company principals, and to hold them liable for knowing failure to disclose such an overpayment. This rule provides another tool to determine present responsibility of Government contractors.

FAR Subpart 9.4 provides debarment/suspension as a possible consequence for conviction of or civil judgment for commission of fraud or a variety of criminal offenses, although those statutes may already provide criminal or civil penalties for violation thereof. For example, the Sherman Act (15 U.S.C. 1–7) provides statutory penalties, including fines and imprisonment, for violation of the antitrust provisions of the statute. It is not inconsistent with the statute, nor does it require legislative amendment to include in the FAR that violation of the Federal statutes in submission of an offer is cause for debarment or suspension.

i. Technical Corrections

The Councils moved FAR 3.1002(c) to 3.1003(a)(2), because it presents a requirement rather than just policy guidance. In addition, the term "Mandatory" was removed from the phrase "Mandatory requirements" at 3.1003, because it is redundant. The title of paragraph (a)(1) of FAR 3.1003 has been amplified to indicate that this paragraph is describing contractor requirements.

6. *Extend to Violation of Civil False Claims Act*

a. Support Application to Disclosure of Violations of the Civil FCA

The Department of Justice, Civil Division, which is responsible for the enforcement of the civil FCA, fully supports the extension of the proposed rule to require that contractors report violations of the civil FCA, 31 U.S.C. 3729 *et seq.*, and to provide that the knowing failure to timely disclose such violations may be grounds for

suspension or debarment. Various respondents, including agency OIGs, express support for these provisions.
Response: Concur.

b. Same Issues as Raised With Regard to Other Mandatory Disclosures

Numerous respondents suggested that certain of their objections to the original proposal to require disclosure of criminal violations and to make a knowing failure to timely disclose such violations grounds for suspension or debarment, also apply to an expanded requirement that contractors disclose civil FCA violations. For example, some commented that disclosure should not be required because the conduct constituting violation of federal criminal law or the civil FCA is potentially broad and subject to varying interpretations by the Government, contractors and courts (and by relators in civil *qui tam* suits); that the requirement that violations be "timely" disclosed upon "reasonable grounds to believe" a violation has occurred are subject to varying interpretations as to when and under what circumstances a violation must be disclosed; that there is no rational basis for the proposed rule; that the rule would impose an unreasonable burden on contractors; and, that knowing failure to timely disclose should not be cause for suspension or debarment.

Response: These areas of concern common to both criminal and civil violations are addressed in other sections of this report. As discussed more fully elsewhere, the Councils have replaced the "reasonable grounds to believe" standard of the proposed rule with a "credible evidence" standard in the final rule, and to specify that the violation must have a nexus to contract award, performance or close-out, and to clarify that it is the knowledge of the principal that triggers the suspension and debarment cause. See responses under "Vagueness of rule" at paragraph B.3.b.i. (Reasonable grounds to believe); B.3.b.ii.(Timely disclosure); B.3.b.iii. (Criminal violation in connection with contract award or performance); and B.3.b.iv. (Level of employee with knowledge).

c. Issues Particular to the Civil FCA

i. Difficult to determine if violation has occurred. Several respondents urged that contractors should not be required to disclose violations of the civil FCA or be subject to suspension or debarment for a knowing failure to do so on a timely basis because, they suggest, the potential misconduct covered by the Act is broad, and the application of the statute raises many difficult factual and legal issues that the Government, contractors, relators and courts interpret in various ways. For example, one respondent argues that the contractor and the Government are not always aligned on whether a violation of the civil FCA has occurred, and suggests that it is impractical to assume that an average contractor employee will know definitively when a violation of the civil FCA has occurred. Several respondents observe that that there are many difficult legal and factual issues that arise in civil FCA matters, such as whether a submission constitutes a "claim", whether a statement is "false," and whether the person making the statement or submitting the claim acted with the requisite knowledge. Another respondent argues the courts are in conflict over what conduct constitutes a violation of the civil FCA. Another respondent considers it unfair to require contractors to make civil FCA liability determinations given conflicting judicial interpretations of the civil FCA and the contractor's inability to access relevant facts. This respondent argues that certain Federal appellate courts and the United States Supreme Court have read a materiality requirement into the civil FCA even though that element is not stated explicitly in the text. One respondent cites a split in the circuits regarding whether an entity that is subject to complex regulatory requirements can be held liable under the civil FCA when the entity bases its conduct on a reasonable interpretation of an ambiguous statute or regulation. Another respondent states that whereas federal crimes are fairly well-defined, novel and aggressive interpretations of the civil FCA have created an environment in which many claims of breach of a contract might be construed as civil FCA violations.

Based on the premise that violations of the civil FCA are difficult to define, several respondents concluded that contractors will be subject to suspension and debarment if the contractor misinterprets the circumstances and does not report a violation, even if there exists an honest disagreement about whether a violation of the civil FCA has occurred.

Response: The Councils do not agree that the requirements of the civil FCA cannot be reasonably ascertained and understood by contractors, and expects that contractors doing business with the Government are taking appropriate steps to ensure their compliance with that statute and all other applicable laws. The most recent amendments to the statute were made in 1986, and a significant body of case law interpreting the statute, and the 1986 amendments in particular, has developed in that time period. These cases interpret the various elements of a civil FCA violation, including the definition of a claim, falsity, knowledge, and damages.

Although the Councils recognize that some issues concerning the proper application of the civil FCA remain unsettled and subject to further judicial interpretation, this is not unique to the civil FCA.

Moreover, the disclosure requirement applies only where the contractor has "credible evidence" that a violation of the civil FCA has occurred. The contractor is subject to suspension and debarment for failure to timely disclose the violation only where the contractor does so knowingly. Genuine disputes over the proper application of the civil FCA may be considered in evaluating whether the contractor knowingly failed to disclose a violation of the civil FCA.

In this regard, the Councils note that the mere filing of a *qui tam* action under the civil FCA is not sufficient to establish a violation under the statute, nor does it represent, standing alone, credible evidence of a violation. Similarly, the decision by the Government to decline intervention in a *qui tam* action is not dispositive of whether the civil FCA has been violated, nor conclusive of whether the contractor has credible evidence of a violation of the civil FCA.

ii. Broad scope of civil FCA. Several respondents suggested that requiring contractors to disclose violations of the civil FCA significantly expands the situations in which disclosure must be considered, and notes that the civil FCA can be violated even in situations where the Government suffers no financial loss. One respondent states that the civil FCA encompasses an "almost limitless universe of activities."

Response: The Councils do not agree that requiring disclosure of civil FCA violations will significantly broaden the situations where disclosure must be considered. Concerning the suggested breadth of the civil FCA, please see response to "Issues particular to the civil FCA", at paragraph B.6.c.i. "Difficult to determine if violation has occurred". The first proposed rule required contractors to disclose significant overpayments and violations of criminal law in connection with a Government contract or subcontract awarded thereunder, and the addition of the civil FCA is a natural extension of the rule. When a claim or payment comes under review, it often is not known at the outset of the investigation whether the matter is an overpayment, or a civil or criminal violation. In many cases, the same investigation must be done to determine the nature of the conduct at issue. The same fraud may be actionable under the civil FCA or its criminal analogs, and require proof of the same general elements. *See, e.g.*, 18 U.S.C. 287 (criminal False Claims Act); 18 U.S.C. 1001 (false statements).

Moreover, the fact that a course of conduct can violate the civil FCA even if the Government does not suffer a financial loss does not mean that disclosure is not relevant to the contractor's present responsibility. For example, the Government may avoid a financial loss because a contracting officer alertly catches and declines to pay a false or fraudulent claim, or perhaps because the false claim is disclosed by the contractor.

iii. Mitigation in civil FCA for voluntary disclosure. One respondent argues that there is no need to make failure to timely disclose a civil violation of the civil FCA a basis for suspension and debarment because the civil FCA already provides that damages may be reduced from trebles to doubles where the contractor discloses a violation to the United States. Another respondent suggests that the proposed FAR rule would convert these otherwise voluntary disclosures into mandatory disclosures, thereby preventing contractors from benefiting from the damages reduction provision of the civil FCA. One respondent requests that the final rule clarify that any mandatory reporting obligation is not intended to and does not prevent a contractor from seeking, and the Government from providing, reduced damages as a result of a disclosure made in compliance with the new contract provision.

Response: The Councils do not agree that the reduced damages available to contractors who disclose violations of the civil FCA in accordance with that Act obviates the need for the proposed amendment to make a failure to timely disclose a violation the basis for suspension or debarment. These provisions address two separate Governmental interests. The damages provisions of the civil FCA address the Government's ability to recoup its loss as a result of a violation, and recognize that timely disclosure is an important means for mitigating that loss. Suspension and debarment is concerned with the contractor's present responsibility. Timely disclosure of violations of the civil FCA is an important indicator of the contractor's present responsibility.

The mitigating provisions of the civil FCA apply to any disclosure that meets the requirements set forth in 31 U.S.C. 3729(a)(A). There is nothing in the FAR rule that would preclude a contractor from meeting the actual requirements of the reduced damages provision of the civil FCA. (See response at paragraphs B.3.a.vi. and B.5.c. discussing the mitigating factors in the USSG and in the FAR.) In its comments to the proposed rule, the Civil Division of DOJ, which enforces the civil FCA for the United States, noted that a contractor that meets both the disclosure requirements of the FAR and the civil FCA "would receive the dual benefit of qualifying to seek reduced damages under the civil FCA and avoiding the potential for suspension and debarment under the FAR."

iv. Proposed amendments to the civil FCA. Several respondents suggest that a contractor making a mandatory disclosure of a violation of the federal civil FCA risks prompting a potential relator to file a *qui tam* suit based on the disclosure, and note that the public disclosure bar under existing law likely would not bar such a suit. These respondents further suggest that this risk is increased if proposed amendments to the civil FCA (S.2041 and H.4854) are enacted because they would eliminate the public disclosure bar as a jurisdictional defense to a *qui tam* suit.

Response: The Councils recognize that mandatory disclosure of a violation of the civil FCA presents a risk that a *qui tam* action will follow. This risk is not unique for disclosures of civil FCA violations; the same risk arises from disclosures of overpayments and violations of criminal law. Furthermore, the underlying violation itself presents a risk of a *qui tam* action. Timely disclosure of a knowing violation offers the contractor an opportunity to demonstrate its present responsibility to avoid suspension or debarment, and to obtain a reduction in damages under the civil FCA.

v. Healthcare and banking. Several respondents disagreed with the view expressed by DOJ that the civil FCA reporting requirement imposes on Government contractors the same disclosure standards as those required of the healthcare and banking industries, and that no law requires disclosure of a civil FCA violation.

Response: See response, in paragraph B.3.a.iii.*a.* under "Mandatory disclosure to the OIG", "More far-reaching".

vi. Inherently governmental. One respondent objects that requiring contractors to disclose violations of the civil FCA to the Government would force contractors to interpret and enforce Federal law, which epitomizes an inherently governmental function.

Response: The Councils disagree that the mandatory disclosure provisions result in a transfer of an inherently governmental function to contractors. As noted in response B.6.c.i. above, individuals and entities contracting with the Government are subject to the civil FCA, and the Government expects that its contractors will take appropriate steps to ensure their compliance with all applicable laws. Compliance necessarily requires that contractors interpret the law as it may apply to their own circumstances and conduct, and this obligation is no different whether the law is civil or criminal. The Government will continue to exercise its independent judgment as to the proper interpretation of the civil FCA, to enforce the civil FCA consistent with applicable law, and to pursue violations of that law where appropriate, irrespective of whether those violations are brought to its attention by a contractor's disclosure or otherwise.

vii. Technical correction. One respondent is concerned that with addition of disclosure of violations of the False Claims Act, it is not entirely clear whether the limiting clause "in connection with the award or performance of this contract or any subcontract thereunder" applies to reporting both violations of Federal criminal law and violations of the civil FCA.

Response: Concur. The Councils have modified the rule accordingly.

7. Application to Acquisition of Commercial Items

a. Support Application to Acquisition of Commercial Items

An agency OIG, in commenting on the first proposed rule, believed that the responsibility of the contractor to report potential violations of criminal law or safety issues related to Government contracts or subcontracts should not be based on contract type and should not exclude commercial contracts from the reporting requirement.

In response to the question on the expansion of the second proposed rule to apply to commercial items, various respondents, including many agency OIGs, support application to contracts for the acquisition of commercial items.

Response: Concur.

b. Do Not Support Application to Acquisition of Commercial Items

Several respondents state that the proposed rule is inconsistent with Public Law 103–355 and FAR Part 12.

Another respondent is concerned that application of the proposed rule to commercial acquisitions will be difficult for educational institutions to implement.

Another respondent states that DoJ fails to show any deference to OFPP with respect to commercial item policy, asserting without any rationale or elaboration that there would be no reason to exclude so-called commercial item contracts. This respondent states that the rule cannot be applied to commercial items without specific authorization by Executive Order or statute.

One respondent believes that applying Government-unique clauses to commercial suppliers will drive them away from the Government marketplace. Since this respondent recognizes that this is now required by statute, they will continue to seek a repeal of the statute.

Another respondent recommends against requiring commercial item contractors to develop new, Government-only ethics standards that result in a company having two standards of conduct, one for Government business and one for everything else.

Response: The disclosure requirements of the new statute specifically apply to commercial items. Furthermore, the statute includes the words "pursuant to FAR Case 2007–006 or any follow-on FAR case" which the Councils interpret as covering the inclusion of the civil FCA as addressed in the second proposed rule.

c. Application to Commercial Subcontracts

One respondent questions whether application of the proposed rule to the business practices of a commercial vendor that has no direct contractual relationship with the Federal Government has any relevance to assuring proper stewardship of Federal funds.

One respondent is concerned that without a more distinct definition of "subcontractor," the flowdown obligation may be applied more broadly than necessary. The respondent requests additional guidance in order to distinguish actual subcontractors from entities that may be contracted to provide collateral services to the commercial contractor (*e.g.*, service vendors, licensors, corporate subsidiaries).

Further, another respondent states that revision to FAR Subpart 44.4 or FAR clauses 52.212–4 or 52.212–5 and clause 52.244–6 would be necessary before this requirement can be flowed down to commercial item subcontractors, but because the proposed rule has neglected to specify changes, there is no proposed authorization to revise those clauses in the final rule.

Response: "Subcontract" and "subcontractor" are defined at FAR 44.101. To clarify the meaning in this context, the Councils have borrowed from those definitions for use in the text at 3.1001 and in the clause at FAR 52.203–13.

The Councils are authorized to make any revisions to Subpart 44.4, Part 12 and Part 44, necessary to conform changes in the final rule, as long as changes in the final rule are reasonably foreseeable from either the proposed rule text or the discussions in the preamble. This constitutes adequate notice to the public. Both the text and preamble of the May 16, 2008, proposed rule were specific that the rule would apply to subcontracts. The Councils have made appropriate conforming changes to 52.212–5 and 52.244–6.

d. Other Concerns

One respondent questions whether the phrase "if 52.212–4 appears in this contract" (52.203–13(c)) is another way of saying it is a commercial item contract.

Response: Yes, inclusion of clause 52.212–4 in the prime contract would indicate that it is a contract for the acquisition of commercial items. However, now that the final rule requires flow down to commercial subcontracts, this phrase is inadequate for indicating a subcontract for commercial items, and has been revised accordingly.

e. Comments on the First Proposed Rule That Are No Longer Applicable

One respondent was concerned that the opportunity for substantial confusion exists with the rule and recommends additional guidance on how the rule impacts companies selling commercial items under FAR Part 8 acquisitions.

Another respondent was concerned that the proposed language at 3.1004 "awarded under FAR Part 12" is likely to be misunderstood as applying only when the policies of FAR Part 12 are used exclusively and the procedures in Parts 13, 14, and 15 are not used.

Another respondent was concerned that the proposed rule does not properly address the exemption for commercial item vendors.

One respondent was concerned that the proposed rule does not justify imposing the new cause for suspension or debarment based on failure to disclose a "violation", and that will also place restrictions on commercial contractors that are not required by law and not consistent with the commercial market place.

Response: These comments are no longer applicable because the statute now requires application of most of this rule to commercial item contracts.

8. Application to Contracts To Be Performed Outside the United States

a. Support Application Outside the United States

Four respondents to the first proposed rule questioned the exceptions for overseas contacts.

• DoJ disagreed with excluding contracts performed entirely outside the United States from the requirements of the rule. The respondent indicates that the United States is still party to such contracts and potentially a victim when overpayments are made or when fraud occurs in connection with the contacts.

• One respondent was concerned that the rule exempts contracts performed overseas without providing an explanation as to why a basic policy of a code of ethics and business conduct should not apply overseas.

• An agency OIG believed that the responsibility of the contractor to report potential violations of criminal law or safety issues related to Government contracts or subcontracts should not be based on contract type and should not exclude contracts performed outside the United States from the reporting requirements.

• Another agency OIG believed that it is counterproductive to exclude contracts performed entirely outside the United States because the United States is still party to such contracts and may be victimized when overpayments are made or fraud occurs in connection with those contracts. The respondent also argues the contracts require greater vigilance because they are performed overseas where U.S. resources and remedies are more limited; and that the inclusion would reduce the vulnerabilities that often plague overseas programs and increase the effectiveness of those programs.

In response to the proposed expansion overseas in the second proposed rule, various respondents, including several agency OIGs, support making the requirements of this rule applicable to contracts and subcontracts performed outside the United States.

Response: Concur.

b. Do Not Support Application Outside the United States

One respondent raised the concern that if any part of the work is performed outside the United States, labor and privacy laws in Europe would prohibit mandatory reporting by employees.

Another respondent is concerned that extension of the requirements to contracts and subcontracts performed outside the U.S. will likely have a significant and negative effect on academic institutions' ability to engage international partners. It is inappropriate and impractical to expect our international partners to do business in the same way as U.S. organizations. Many foreign academic institutions are instrumentalities of foreign governments and are subject to their own laws and regulations. Without flexibility, it will be impossible to pursue the international research and education

One respondent also believes that it is unreasonable and impractical to expect foreign firms to understand and be able to comply with the unique procedural requirements the U.S. imposes on its contractors. This respondent recognizes that this is now required by statute and it will seek a repeal of the statute.

Response: The disclosure requirements of the new statute specifically apply to acquisitions to be performed outside the United States. Furthermore, the statute includes the words "pursuant to FAR Case 2007–006 * * * or any follow-on FAR case" which the Councils interpret as covering the inclusion of the civil FCA as addressed in the second proposed rule.

9. *Other Applicability Issues*

a. Educational Institutions

i. Exempt educational and research institutions. One respondent requested that educational and research institutions be granted the same exemption afforded small business by making the requirement for a formal training and/or awareness program and internal control systems inapplicable to such institutions.

Response: By passing the "Close the Contractor Fraud Loophole Act," Congress made clear its preference for fewer, rather than more exemptions. The requirements at 3.1002(b) are that the ethics and compliance training program be suitable to the size of the entity and extent of its involvement in Government contracting. Further, this regulation applies only to contracts using appropriated funds, not to grants.

ii. Imposition of procurement requirements on grant recipients. One respondent stated that OMB regulation 2 CFR 215.40 forbids agencies to impose procurement requirements on grant recipients unless required by statute or Executive order or approved by OMB.

Response: This rule is not imposing any requirements on grant recipients. The FAR does not apply to contracts awarded using grant money. Federal Government grant recipients who are also Federal Government contractors must comply with both the grant regulations and the FAR, as applicable.

b. Subcontractors

Various responses were received on the obligations imposed by this rule between contractors and subcontractors and the flow down of this rule to subcontractors.

Response: The Councils note that the same rationale that supports the application of the rule to prime contractors supports the application to subcontractors. The same reasonable efforts the contractor may take to exclude from its organizational structure principals whom due diligence would have exposed as engaging in illegal acts are the same reasonable efforts the contractor should take in selecting its subcontractors. Subcontractors should also use those same reasonable efforts in employment and subcontracting efforts.

i. Obligation to report violations by subcontractors. According to several respondents, prime contractors should not be responsible for oversight of their subcontractors and should not be subject to debarment for failure of a subcontractor to meet the requirement of the rule. The respondents were concerned that the rule renders prime contractors police for their subcontractors which respondents consider unreasonable and burdensome. One respondent was also concerned that rule creates a contractual obligation on the part of the contractor to ensure that its subcontractors perform as required by the rule. Another respondent stated that the rule fails to define the obligation of the contractor to police its subcontractors with regard to the required compliance program and integrity reporting. It is unclear what degree of due diligence the Government expects of the contractor.

Response: There is no requirement for the contractor to review or approve its subcontractors' ethics codes or internal control systems. Verification of the existence of such code and program can be part of the standard oversight that a contractor exercises over its subcontractors. The prime contractor is subject to debarment only if it fails to disclose known violations by the subcontractor. Therefore, a change to the rule is not necessary.

ii. Disclosure through the prime contractor. One respondent was concerned that the rule mandates that the disclosures go directly to the Government and not through the prime contractor. DoJ was concerned that some subcontractors may not be comfortable making disclosure through the prime contractor and suggested that a mechanism through which a subcontractor makes a disclosure be addressed in the final rule.

Response: The clause flow down in paragraph (d)(2) states that in altering the clause to identify the appropriate parties, all disclosures of violations of the civil FCA or of Federal criminal law shall be directed to the agency OIG, with a copy to the contracting officer. The clause does not require disclosure through the prime contractor.

iii. Liability for erroneous disclosure. One respondent was concerned that the rule creates a potential significant liability for the contractor if disclosures concerning subcontractors turn out to be in error. The respondent requested the Councils to consider whether damages assessed against contractors for erroneous reports would be allowable costs. Also, the respondent was concerned that the rule is unclear about the disclosure of criminal violations by subcontractors, and suggests that the Councils revise the rule to make the disclosure requirements for the contractor and the subcontractor parallel.

Response: The Councils revised the rule to require the contractor to disclose credible evidence of a violation of Federal criminal law in connection with the contract or any subcontract under the contract. This revision provides to the contractor sufficient opportunity to take reasonable steps to determine the credibility of any possible disclosure prior to disclosing it to the agency Inspector General and contracting officer. The potential for erroneous disclosure is minimized by requiring the contractor to disclose only credible evidence of violations, thereby reducing the contractor's potential liability for damages associated with erroneously disclosing alleged violations which are not substantiated.

c. Small Businesses (See Also Paragraph 11. "Regulatory Flexibility Act Concerns", for Comments on Initial Regulatory Flexibility Analysis)

i. Support level of applicability to small businesses. An agency OIG supported the application of the basic requirements of the rule to small business because the rule avoids imposing unnecessary burdens on small businesses by creating expensive paperwork requirements. Likewise, another agency OIG considered the exemption for small business contractors (from the requirements for a formal internal control system) reasonable. Another agency OIG also indicated that undesirable results for small business which could have resulted from initial drafts of the rule have been mediated by this rule.

Response: Concur.

ii. Overly burdensome on small business: One respondent believed that the rule is an overly burdensome and unrealistic policing requirement that imposes significant new cost requirements and is particularly burdensome for small businesses; effectively precluding such businesses from competing for prime contract work or as a high-tier subcontractor.

• *Response:* Although the rule may have a significant economic impact on a substantial number of small entities with respect to the disclosure requirement, the rule is structured to minimize its impact on small business concerns by making the requirement for formal training programs and internal control systems inapplicable to small businesses, and limiting the disclosure requirement of violations of Federal criminal law to those violations involving fraud, conflict of interest, bribery, or gratuity violations found in Title 18 of the United States Code, although the rule did add the reporting of violations of the False Claims Act. The Councils do not believe that a change to the rule is necessary.

d. Dollar Threshold or Minimum 120 Day Performance Period

i. Recommend no threshold and no minimum performance period. One agency OIG commented on the rule's threshold of $5 million and 120-day performance period. The agency OIG believed that the application of the rule should not be determined on the basis of the dollar value or the period of performance of the contract. The respondent was concerned that, at times, contracting officers have awarded smaller dollar value contracts or modifications instead of one large dollar contract to circumvent various thresholds that trigger requirements. The respondent believed that the public and members of Congress have similar expectations of all contractors no matter the contract value or type.

Response: The Close the Contractor Fraud Loophole Act (Pub. L. 110–252, Section 6103) now defines a covered contract for application of this regulation as any contract in an amount greater than $5 million and more than 120 days in duration. The Councils also note that, regardless of whether the clause is included in the contract, the suspension and debarment provisions in Subpart 9.4 apply to all contractors, regardless of contract value or duration.

ii. Applicability of thresholds to Federal Supply Schedule (FSS) contracts and Blanket Purchase Agreements (BPA). One respondent requests explanation of the applicability of the thresholds to FSS contracts. The respondent does not believe that FAR 1.108(c) adequately clarifies the issue. Are the thresholds based on each individual order?

Response: According to FAR 1.108(c), unless otherwise specified, if the action establishes a maximum quantity of supplies or services to be acquired, the final anticipated dollar value must be the highest final priced alternative to the Government, including the dollar value of all options. That is, if it is anticipated that the dollar value of orders on an FSS contract will exceed $5 million, then this clause is included in the basic contract against which orders are placed.

e. Single Government Standard Also Applicable to Grants

One respondent was concerned that multiple Federal agencies already have compliance guidelines and regulations in place, or in development, and believes the rule may be inconsistent with other Federal agency requirements. The respondent requested that a single Federal Government-wide standard be created to foster integrity and honesty that applies to both Government contracts and Federal grants.

Response: The Councils acknowledge the respondent's concern. However, this rule establishes a Government-wide standard for contractor compliance programs and integrity reporting with respect to Government contract awards. Under the rule, all Federal agencies will be required to implement the same requirements in the same manner consistent with the award of Federal contracts. However, the rule does not and is not intended to address contractor compliance programs and integrity reporting with respect to agency grant-making procedures. Given the legal differences between a grant and a contract that concern performance and termination for default, the creation of a single Government standard addressing contractor compliance programs and integrity reporting is not practical and is outside the scope of the rule.

10. *Additional Recommendations*

a. Defer Final Rule Until

i. More experience with 2006–007. One respondent suggested that the FAR Council evaluate experience with the final rule, before proposing changes. The FAR Council should withdraw the proposed rule in favor of allowing covered contractors to implement the November 23, 2007, final rule.

ii. Completion of the National Science and Technology Council initiative. Several respondents urged the FAR Council to defer further action on proposed FAR Case 2007–006 pending completion of the National Science and Technology Council (NSTC) initiative to develop compliance guidance for recipients of Federal research funding from all agencies across the Federal Government.

iii. Further action on related legislation that would expand the scope of the civil FCA. One respondent requests postponement until after enactment of pending legislation on the civil FCA.

iv. Public hearings. One respondent alternatively suggests additional public comment in light of the pertinent intervening legislation and public hearings.

Response: The intervening legislation requires implementation of this rule in the FAR within 180 days of enactment of Pub. L. 110–252 (by December 26, 2008). Therefore, the Councils will proceed with this rule without delay.

At the time of publishing the final rule (2006–007), the proposed rule (2007–006) under this case had already been published. The preamble of the final rule under 2006–007 stated the intent to address mandatory disclosure and full cooperation under the follow-on rule.

It is unknown when the NSTC initiative to develop compliance guidance for recipients of Federal research funding from all agencies across the Federal Government will be completed. The Councils do not agree to delay the FAR rule pending the outcome of this particular initiative. Often the regulations for grants use the FAR as a model.

b. Expand Policy and Clause to Cover Overpayments

DoJ and an agency IG commented that the drafters of the proposed rule neglected to incorporate "knowing failure to timely disclose an overpayment" in the first reference at 3.1002(c).

Several respondents proposed that the language in the proposed FAR clause be expanded to also include instances of overpayment. More inclusive language removes any ambiguity (and loopholes) about what should be revealed to the Government. By expanding the scope to include overpayments, contractors are no longer asked to label (or mislabel) their activity as "criminal". In the opinion of the respondents, the proposed rule does not match the stated objective of encouraging Government notification of fraud and overpayments.

Response: The mandatory reporting of overpayments is addressed in the

Payments clauses. However, to aid in clarity, we have added a cross reference at FAR 3.1003 to the Payment clauses and the knowing failure to timely disclose significant overpayments as a cause for suspension/debarment in FAR Subpart 9.4.

c. Create a Contractor Integrity and Business Ethics Information Section in FAR Part 42

One respondent urged the FAR Councils to create a contractor integrity and business ethics section in FAR Part 42 that would require Government officials to record and maintain integrity and business ethics information that can be shared with Government officials. Although contractor performance and responsibility are part of FAR Subpart 9.1, the respondent requests that distinctive data and information be collected on each.

Another respondent, on the other hand, is very satisfied that the rule only proposed one change to the contractor past performance information in FAR 42.1501, and properly reinforces the existing emphasis on contractor cooperation across a broad range of contract administration matters, including cooperation with investigations.

Response: The proposed rule has added a cross reference in Part 42 to promote the inclusion of business integrity in past performance. The request to collect distinctive data and information on contractor responsibility is outside the scope of this rule. The past performance databases are controlled by the agencies. (See also response to "Suspension/Debarment", paragraph B.5.g. "Blacklisting")

d. Add Safety Issues

An agency IG suggested that safety issues should be included in the mandatory disclosure requirement.

Response: Adding explicit coverage of safety issues is outside the scope of this case.

e. Protection of Contractor Disclosures

The proposed rule states at 3.1002 (Policy) that contractors should have an internal control system that facilitates timely discovery of improper conduct in connection with Government contracts. A contractor may be suspended or debarred for knowing failure to timely disclose a violation of Federal criminal law in connection with the award or performance of any Government contract performed by the contractor.

DoJ suggested that, in order to encourage contractors to submit information, the Councils may wish to recommend to agencies that the submitted information be maintained confidentially to the extent permitted by law and that any disclosure of the information under FOIA should only be made after full consideration of institutional, commercial, and personal privacy interests that could be implicated by such a disclosure. In particular, agencies should be mindful that the Trade Secrets Act operates as a prohibition on the discretionary disclosure of any information covered by Exemption 4 of the FOIA, unless disclosure is otherwise authorized by law.

Response: The Councils have added the following provision to the final rule, similar to the provision employed by the DoD Voluntary Disclosure Program (DoD Directive 5106.01, April 23, 2006) in "XYZ" agreements with contractors pursuant to DoD Voluntary Disclosure Program Guidance (IGD 5505.50, CIPO, April 1990) (see *http://www.dodig.mil/Inspections/vdprogram.htm*): "The Government, to the extent permitted by law and regulation, will safeguard and treat information obtained pursuant to the contractor's disclosure as confidential where the information has been marked "confidential" or "proprietary" by the company. To the extent permitted by law and regulation, such information will not be released by the Government to the public pursuant to a Freedom of Information Act request, 5 U.S.C. section 552, *et. seq.*, without prior notification to the contractor. The Government may transfer documents provided by the contractor to any department or agency within the Executive Branch if the information relates to matters within the organization's jurisdiction."

The addition of the above provision will provide appropriate assurance to contractors about the Government's protection afforded to disclosures.

11. Regulatory Flexibility Act concerns

a. IRFA Does Not Identify a Rational Basis for the Rule

Several respondents criticized the Initial Regulatory Flexibility Analysis (IRFA) as deficient because they believe that it does not identify a rational basis for the rule. They claim that there is no empirical or anecdotal evidence to explain why the mandatory disclosure requirement is required for the proper functioning of the procurement system.

Response: See response to "Mandatory disclosure to the OIG", "Empirical support that mandatory disclosure will achieve the Councils' objective", at paragraph B.3.a.iii.*d.*

b. The IRFA Underestimates the Number of Small Businesses Affected and the Associated Costs

Several respondents also considered that the IRFA underestimates the number of small businesses affected, as it only describes the estimated 28 small businesses which conclude that disclosure is required, rather than the larger number which will have to conduct internal investigations before concluding that disclosure is not required. One respondent pointed out the costs to run a compliance program. Another respondent pointed out that the IRFA does not ascertain the costs when a company chooses to retain outside counsel to investigate, which could range from $1 million to $20 million. The rule will cost small businesses over $1 billion a year (calculation—for each report there would be 5 internal investigations at a cost of $5 million per contractor and $2.5 million per subcontractor.)

Response: First, the IRFA estimated an impact on 45 small businesses, not just the 28 covered by the clause.

Second, an ethical company that learns that an employee may have committed a violation of Federal criminal law would not ignore this information. A company would normally investigate allegations of wrongdoing within the company as a sound business practice. If there was clearly no violation, the investigation would be short. Although the rule allows contractors time to take reasonable steps to determine that evidence of wrongdoing is credible, it does not direct contractors to carry out any particular level of internal investigation. The IRFA focused on the effort which results from this rule—disclosure to the Government—although there are other incentives outside this rule which could cause a contractor to voluntarily disclose violations to the Government, such as the U.S. Sentencing Guidelines. Although the IRFA does not include the cost of the investigation in its calculations, the FAR does not require or envision a small business paying millions of dollars for an investigation. The respondent's calculated cost estimates are not supported or credible.

The FAR did give relief for the costs of running a compliance program by leaving it to the discretion of the small business and paragraph (c) of the clause is not mandatory for small businesses.

c. Imposition of Suspension and Debarment Will Disproportionately Damage Small Businesses

One respondent stated that small businesses do not have the resources that large businesses do. They do not have the resources to institute compliance programs. They are more likely to be caught in the suspension and debarment process. They lack the leverage to negotiate agreements in lieu of debarment. Therefore, the rule's reliance on suspension and debarment as an enforcement mechanism will disproportionately damage small businesses.

Response: The Councils agree that small businesses often have fewer resources than other than small business. Nonetheless, the Councils cannot give further flexibility here. The Councils have already eliminated the requirement for the internal control system for small businesses. The Councils cannot establish a different suspension or debarment standard for small businesses.

d. Estimate of Small Businesses That Would Disclose if No Mandatory Requirement

One respondent quoted the IRFA as estimating that, in the absence of the proposed disclosure requirement, 1 percent of small business contractors that are aware of a violation would voluntarily report it. This suggests, according to the respondent, that the FAR Council believes that mandatory disclosure would lead to a 100-fold increase in the number of reported violations. The respondent states that there is no support for this estimate and no rational basis to support a claim that this disclosure requirement is needed for the effective functioning of the procurement system.

Response: The respondent has drawn an unwarranted conclusion about the estimated impact of mandatory disclosure. The estimated 1% disclosure rate in the IRFA is for small businesses that do not have the clause in their contract (*i.e.*, small dollar value or short performance period). There was no estimate in the IRFA about what percentage of this population would disclose if the clause were included. Further, any estimates about this segment of the population cannot be extrapolated to a conclusion about the effect of mandatory disclosure requirements on higher dollar value, noncommercial contracts or contracts with large businesses.

e. Recordkeeping Requirements

One respondent objected that the IRFA did not provide a full discussion of the projected recordkeeping and compliance requirements. Good business sense will require a contractor to develop and keep more records for the purpose of documenting its investigation.

Response: The Councils agree that recordkeeping would be wise, but the rule does not require recordkeeping beyond the recordkeeping that would be part of the contractor's normal business practices. Under 5 U.S.C. 601, the term "recordkeeping requirement" is defined as a requirement imposed by an agency on persons to maintain specified records.

f. Duplication, Overlap, or Conflict

Several respondents criticized the statement in the IRFA that the rule does not duplicate, overlap, or conflict with any other Federal rules. The respondents state that the IRFA—

• Ignored the obvious interrelationship with the civil Federal civil FCA and its *qui tam* provisions;

• Did not address the inconsistency between the proposed rule and the Federal Sentencing Guidelines; and

• Did not address that the rule is inconsistent with a voluntary disclosure being a mitigation consideration in the FAR debarment and suspension proceedings and under the civil FCA because disclosure would be mandatory rather than voluntary.

Response: Under 5 U.S.C. 601, "rule" is defined as meaning "any rule for which the agency publishes a general notice of proposed rulemaking pursuant to section 553(b) of this title or any other law * * *". Codified laws are not a rule. The Sentencing Guidelines are, strictly speaking, also not a rule. However, the Councils disagree that this rule is duplicative of the civil FCA. Any inadvertent inconsistency with the Guidelines has been considered in formulating this final rule.

Regarding mitigation and voluntary disclosure, see "Mandatory disclosure to the OIG", "Incentives" at paragraph B.3.a.vi.

12. Paperwork Reduction Act (PRA)

a. Burden Underestimated

One respondent stated that the Councils' Paperwork Reduction Act analysis is inadequate. The estimates are so conservative as to be unrealistic. If it only takes 20 hours to conduct pre-disclosure review and draft a corresponding report, why does it take the Government a year to decide whether to intervene in a traditional *qui tam* case? The respondent points out that "burden" includes all aspects of the reporting process, including the separation of reportable events from non-reportable events.

Another respondent also considers the estimated burden of 3 hours per report woefully inadequate, considering the time needed by respondents to investigate and determine whether a civil FCA violation or criminal violation occurred.

Response: Burden includes estimated hours only for those actions which a company would not undertake in the normal course of business. The Government does not direct companies to investigate. In the normal course of business, a company that is concerned about ethical behavior will take reasonable steps to determine the credibility of allegations of misconduct within the firm. It is left to the discretion of the company what these reasonable steps may entail. The Government has added the requirement to disclose to the Government when credible evidence of misconduct is obtained, which would not necessarily otherwise occur. The estimated hours in the regulatory flexibility analysis and the paperwork burden act analysis are to cover the hours required for preparing and reviewing the disclosure to the Government when credible evidence has been obtained. The estimated hours must also be viewed as an average between the hours that a simple disclosure by a very small business might require and the much higher numbers that might be required for a very complex disclosure by a major corporation. However, upon further discussion with subject matter experts, the Councils have revised the estimated hours to 60 hours per response, considering particularly the hours that would be required for review within the company, prior to release to the Government.

b. Recordkeeping and Other Compliance Requirements

One respondent stated that the projected recordkeeping and compliance requirements are far more burdensome than reflected in the IRFA. The contractor must keep and maintain extensive records any time it investigates allegations or suspicions of violations. Even if a company determines that disclosure is not required, the contractor must keep records of its decision-making process in order to defend against possible future accusations of failure to disclose.

Another respondent states that time is required for 1400 covered contractors to establish systems for complying with this regulation.

Response: See the response in previous section on Regulatory Flexibility Analysis (B.11.).

c. Data and Methodology Should Be Made Part of the Rulemaking Record

Response: The public can request copies of the supporting statements.

13. Executive Order 12866

a. Significant Rule

A number of respondents are concerned that this rule is a significant rule in accordance with E.O. 12866 section 3.(f). One respondent is concerned that, by extending the rule to cover commercial acquisitions and overseas contracts, a review requirement as a "major rule" or a significant rule under section 3.(f)(1) may have been unintentionally triggered. Another respondent believes that the rule should have a cost-benefit analysis.

One respondent states that the addition of violations of the civil FCA as a ground for mandatory disclosure is sufficient standing alone to trigger review under Section 6(b) of E.O. 12866.

Another respondent submits that this is a significant regulatory action because it will, among other things, adversely affect in a material way a sector of the economy (Government contractors).

Several respondents also state that the second proposed rule raises important legal and policy issues, another grounds for the Office of Information and Regulatory Affairs (OIRA) to declare a rule significant under E.O. 12866, under section 3.(f)(4).

One respondent suggests that it was a Freudian slip when the FR notice for the first proposed rule stated that the first proposed rule *was* a significant regulatory action and therefore *was not* subject to review.

Response: The first proposed rule was declared to be a significant rule by OIRA. The typographical error was in the second half of the sentence, not the first. The rule was subject to review under the Executive order and was so reviewed. OIRA did not declare the second proposed rule to be a significant rule.

All rules are sent through the Office of Information and Regulatory Affairs for determination as to whether the rule is significant. OMB's Office of Information and Regulatory Affairs has determined this is a significant rule, and not a major rule.

b. Violates E.O. 12866

One respondent states that the proposed rule violates the E.O. 12866 requirement that rules be "consistent, sensible, and understandable" and that agencies promulgate only such regulations as are required by law, are necessary to interpret the law, or are made necessary by compelling public need. This respondent submits that just because DoJ wants to make its job easier is not sufficient grounds for rulemaking.

Response: This rule is required by law and by compelling public need. The Councils have made every effort to make the draft final rule consistent, sensible, and understandable.

This is a significant regulatory action and, therefore, was subject to review under Section 6(b) of Executive Order 12866, Regulatory Planning and Review, dated September 30, 1993. This rule is not a major rule under 5 U.S.C. 804.

C. Regulatory Flexibility Act

The Regulatory Flexibility Act, 5 U.S.C. 601, *et seq.,* applies to this final rule. The Councils prepared a Final Regulatory Flexibility Analysis (FRFA), and it is summarized as follows:

1. Statement of the need for, and objectives of, the rule.

This rule amends the Federal Acquisition Regulation to require Government contractors to—

• Establish and maintain specific internal controls to detect and prevent improper conduct in connection with the award or performance of any Government contract or subcontract; and

• Notify without delay the agency Office of the Inspector General, with a copy to the contracting officer, whenever, in connection with the award, performance, or closeout of a Government contract awarded to the contractor or a subcontract awarded thereunder, the contractor has credible evidence of a violation of Federal criminal law involving fraud, conflict of interest, bribery, or gratuity violations found in 18 U.S.C. or a violation of the civil False Claims Act.

This case is in response to a request to the Office of Federal Procurement Policy from the Department of Justice and Public Law 110–252. Based on the requirements of Pub. L. 110–252, the rule was expanded to include the clause 52.203–13 in contracts performed overseas and contracts for the acquisition of commercial items.

The objective of the rule is to emphasize the critical importance of integrity in contracting and reduce the occurrence of improper or criminal conduct in connection with the award and performance of Federal contracts and subcontracts.

2. Summary of the significant issues raised by the public comments in response to the initial regulatory flexibility analysis, a summary of the assessment of the agency of such issues, and a statement of any changes made in the proposed rule as a result of such comments.

a. IRFA does not identify a rational basis for the rule. Several respondents criticized the Initial Regulatory Flexibility Analysis (IRFA) as deficient because they believe that it does not identify a rational basis for the rule. They claim that there is no empirical or anecdotal evidence to explain why the mandatory disclosure requirement is required for the proper functioning of the procurement system.

Response: DoJ and various OIGs provided testimony that the experience with the National Reconnaissance Organization mandatory disclosure clause has been positive. Further, enactment of the Close the Contractor Fraud Loophole Act (Pub. L. 110–252, Sec VI, Chapter 1) now mandates many of these revisions to the FAR.

b. The IRFA underestimates the number of small businesses affected and the associated costs. Some respondents considered that the IRFA underestimates the number of small businesses affected, as it only describes the estimated 28 small businesses which conclude that disclosure is required, rather than the larger number which will have to conduct internal investigations before concluding that disclosure is not required. Respondents pointed out the costs to run a compliance program and that the IRFA does not ascertain the costs when a company chooses to retain outside counsel to investigate, which could range from $1 million to $20 million. The rule will cost small businesses over $1 billion a year (calculation—for each report there would be 5 internal investigations at a cost of $5 million per contractor and $2.5 million per subcontractor).

Response: First, the IRFA estimated an impact on 45 small businesses, not just the 28 covered by the clause. Further, an *ethical* company *that* finds out an employee may have committed a violation of Federal criminal law would not ignore this. A company would normally follow up allegations of wrongdoing within the company as a sound business practice. If there was clearly no violation, the investigation would be short. Although the rule allows contractors time to take reasonable steps to determine that evidence of wrongdoing is credible, it does not direct contractors to carry out any particular level of internal investigation. The IRFA focused on the effort which results from this rule—reporting to the Government. Although there are other incentives outside this rule which could cause a contractor to voluntarily disclose violations to the Government, such as the U.S. Sentencing Guidelines. Although the IRFA does not include the cost of the investigation in its calculations, the FAR does not require or envision a small business paying millions of dollars for an investigation. The respondent's calculated cost estimates are not supported or credible.

The FAR did give relief for the costs of running a compliance program by leaving it to the discretion of the small business; paragraph (c) of the clause is not mandatory for small businesses.

c. Imposition of suspension and debarment will disproportionately damage small businesses. A respondent stated that small businesses don't have the resources that large businesses do. They do not have the resources to institute compliance programs. They are more likely to be caught in the suspension and debarment process. They lack the leverage to negotiate agreements in lieu of debarment. Therefore, the rule's reliance on suspension and debarment as an enforcement mechanism will disproportionately damage small businesses.

Response: The Councils agree that small businesses have fewer resources than other than small businesses. Nonetheless, the Councils cannot give further flexibility here. The Councils have already eliminated the requirement for the internal control system for small businesses. The Councils cannot establish a different suspension or debarment standard for small businesses.

d. Estimate of small businesses that would report if no mandatory requirement. One respondent quoted the IRFA as estimating that, in the absence of the proposed disclosure requirement, 1% of small business contractors that are aware of a violation would voluntarily report it. This suggests, according to the respondent, that the FAR Council believes that mandatory disclosure would lead to a 100 fold increase in the number of reported violations. The respondent states that there is no support for this estimate.

Response: The respondent has drawn an unwarranted conclusion about the estimated impact of mandatory disclosure. The estimated 1% disclosure rate in the IRFA is for small businesses that do not have the clause in their contract (i.e., small dollar value or short performance period). There was no estimate in the IRFA about what percentage of this population would report if the clause were included. Further, any estimates about this segment of the population cannot be extrapolated to a conclusion about the effect of mandatory disclosure requirements on higher dollar value contracts of duration more that 120 days or contracts with large businesses. The number of small businesses affected cannot be known exactly because there is no data at this time on disclosures that will result from this rule, but the numbers represent the best estimate of subject matter experts in the Government.

e. Recordkeeping requirements. One respondent objected that the IRFA did not provide a full discussion of the projected recordkeeping and compliance requirements. Good business sense will require a contractor to develop and keep more records for the purpose of documenting its investigation.

Response: Although recordkeeping would be wise, the rule does not require it. Under 5 U.S.C. 601, the term "recordkeeping requirement" is defined as a requirement imposed by an agency on persons to maintain specified records.

f. Duplication, overlap, or conflict. Several respondents criticized the statement in the IRFA that the rule does not duplicate, overlap, or conflict with any other Federal rules. The respondents state that the IRFA ignores the obvious interrelationship with the Federal False Claims Act and its *qui tam* provisions and it did not address the inconsistency between the proposed rule and the Federal Sentencing Guidelines. The rule is inconsistent with a voluntary disclosure being a mitigation consideration in the FAR debarment and suspension proceedings and under the False Claims Act because disclosure would be mandatory rather than voluntary.

Response: Under 5 U.S.C. 601, "rule" is defined as meaning any rule for which the agency publishes a general notice of proposed rulemaking pursuant to section 553(b) of this title. Codified laws are not a rule. The Sentencing Guidelines are, strictly speaking, also not a rule. However, the Councils disagree that this rule is duplicative of the False Claims Act and any inadvertent inconsistency with the Guidelines has been considered in formulating this final rule. The FAR, the U.S. Sentencing Guidelines, and the civil False Claims Act consider any self-disclosure to constitute a mitigating circumstance, whether voluntary or mandatory.

3. Description and estimate of the number of small entities to which the rule will apply.

The rule imposes a clause in contracts that exceed $5 million and a performance period greater than 120 days. Based on FY 2006 data collected from the Federal Procurement Data System, the Councils estimate that this clause will apply to 2700 prime contractors per year, of which 1050 companies are small business concerns.

The clause also flows down to subcontracts that exceed $5 million, and we estimate that approximately 1050 additional small business concerns will meet these conditions. We calculate the number of small business concerns that will be required by the clause to report violations of Federal criminal law with regard to a Government contract or subcontracts as follows:

1050 prime contractors + 1050 subcontractors = 2100 × 4% = 84.

In addition, although there is no clause required, all contractors will be on notice that they may be suspended or debarred for failure to report known violations of Federal criminal law with regard to a Government contract or subcontract. In FY 2006 there were 144,854 small business concerns listed in FPDS–NG with unique DUNS numbers. We estimate that of the listed small business concerns, approximately 116,000 (80%) will receive contracts in a given fiscal year. Government small business experts guess that at least twice that number of small businesses (232,000) will receive subcontracts. However, the only small business concerns impacted by this cause for suspension or debarment are those that are aware of violation of Federal criminal law with regard to their Government contracts or subcontracts. Subtracting out those contracts and subcontracts covered by the clause (1050 each), we estimate this number as follows: (114,950 + 230,950 = 345,900 × 1% = 3,459). We estimate a lower percentage than used for contracts and subcontracts that contain the clause, because these are lower dollar contracts and subcontracts, including commercial contracts, and there may be less visibility into violations of Federal criminal law. Because there is no contract clause, we estimate that only 1% of those contractors/subcontractors that are aware of a violation of Federal criminal law in regard to the contract or subcontract will voluntarily report such violation to the contracting officer (3459 × 1% = 34). The estimated number of small businesses in the FRFA (119) has increased from the IRFA (45) because of the applicability of the clause to commercial contracts and contracts to be performed outside the United States and because the disclosure requirement now applies to violations of the civil False Claims Act as well as violations of Federal criminal law.

4. Description of projected reporting, recordkeeping, and other compliance requirements of the rule, including an estimate of the classes of small entities which will be subject to the requirement and the type of professional skills necessary for preparation of the report or record.

The rule requires contractors to report to the agency office of the inspector general, with a copy to the contracting officer, violations of Federal criminal law in connection with the award or performance of any Government contract or subcontract for contracts that exceed $5 million with a contract performance period greater than 120 days, and the same criteria for flow down to subcontracts. Such a report would probably be prepared by company management, and would probably involve legal assistance to prepare and careful review at several levels. There are no recordkeeping requirements in the rule.

5. Description of the steps the agency has taken to minimize the significant economic impact on small entities consistent with the state objectives of applicable statute, including a statement of the factual, policy, and legal reasons for selecting the alternative adopted in the final rule and why each one of the other significant alternatives to the rule considered by the agency which affect the impact on small entities was rejected.

The Councils adopted the following alternatives in order to minimize the impact on small business concerns:

• The final rule requires small businesses to "make a copy of the code available" to each employee (rather than "provide a copy"). The Councils rejected the addition of a requirement that small businesses must specifically make each employee aware of the duties and obligations under the code.

• The requirement for formal training programs and internal control systems is inapplicable to small business concerns. Large businesses are still required to have an ongoing business ethics and conduct awareness and compliance program

• *Disclosure* of violations of criminal law is limited to violations of Federal criminal law involving fraud, conflict of interest, bribery, or gratuity violations found in 18 U.S.C., rather than any violation of criminal law.

• The violations that must be *disclosed* do not include violations under the contracts of other contractors.

• The period of occurrence of violations that must be *disclosed* is limited to 3 years after contract closeout, rather than extending indefinitely.

The Councils could not exclude small businesses that provide commercial items, because Pub. L. 110–252 requires application to contracts for the acquisition of commercial items.

The Councils decided to require disclosure of violations of civil False Claims Act (from both large and small businesses), *as requested by the Department of Justice,* because to achieve the objectives of this rule, it is crucial to deal with responsible contractors, whether large or small. It is not necessarily evident at the beginning of an investigation whether an incident is simply an overpayment, a civil false claim, or a criminal violation. There is no rational reason to exclude civil false claims from the mandatory disclosure requirement.

Interested parties may obtain a copy of the FRFA from the FAR Secretariat. The FAR Secretariat has submitted a copy of the FRFA to the Chief Counsel for Advocacy of the Small Business Administration.

D. Paperwork Reduction Act

The Paperwork Reduction Act (44 U.S.C. Chapter 35) applies because the final rule contains an information collection requirement (ICR). The clause at 52.203–13 requires the Contractor to disclose "credible evidence of a violation" of Federal criminal law or a violation of the False Claims Act, involving fraud, conflict of interest, bribery, or gratuity violations found in Title 18 of the United States Code. We received one comment from the public on this disclosure requirement. Based on the comment that the Government's estimated burden of 3 hours per response was inadequate, the Councils have revised the estimated burden hours to 60 hours per response. This change particularly considers the hours that would be required for review of the collection within a company, prior to release to the Government. Based on the revised estimated burden of 60 hours per response, the annual reporting burden is revised as follows:

Respondents:		284
Responses per respondent:	×	1
Total annual responses:		284
Preparation hours per response:	×	60
Total response burden hours:		17,040
Averages wages ($75 + 32.85% OH):	×	$100
Estimated cost to the Public:		$1,704,000

Accordingly, the FAR Secretariat has forwarded a request for approval of a new information collection requirement concerning 9000–00XX to the Office of Management and Budget under 44 U.S.C. 3501, *et seq.*

List of Subjects in 48 CFR Parts 2, 3, 9, 42 and 52

Government procurement.

Al Matera,

Director, Office of Acquisition Policy.

■ Therefore, DoD, GSA, and NASA amend 48 CFR parts 2, 3, 9, 42 and 52 as set forth below:

■ 1. The authority citation for 48 CFR parts 2, 3, 9, 42 and 52 continues to read as follows:

Authority: 40 U.S.C. 121(c); 10 U.S.C. chapter 137; and 42 U.S.C. 2473(c).

PART 2—DEFINITIONS OF WORDS AND TERMS

■ 2. Amend section 2.101 in paragraph (b)(2) by adding, in alphabetical order, the definition "Principal" to read as follows:

2.101 Definitions.

* * * * *

(b) * * *

(2) * * *

Principal means an officer, director, owner, partner, or a person having primary management or supervisory responsibilities within a business entity (*e.g.*, general manager; plant manager; head of a subsidiary, division, or business segment; and similar positions).

* * * * *

PART 3—IMPROPER BUSINESS PRACTICES AND PERSONAL CONFLICTS OF INTEREST

■ 3. Revise section 3.1001 to read as follows:

3.1001 Definitions.

As used in this subpart—

Subcontract means any contract entered into by a subcontractor to furnish supplies or services for performance of a prime contract or a subcontract.

Subcontractor means any supplier, distributor, vendor, or firm that furnished supplies or services to or for a prime contractor or another subcontractor.

United States means the 50 States, the District of Columbia, and outlying areas.

■ 4. Amend section 3.1003 by revising the section heading and paragraph (a); redesignating paragraph (b) as paragraph (c), and adding a new paragraph (b) to read as follows:

3.1003 Requirements.

(a) *Contractor requirements.* (1) Although the policy at 3.1002 applies as guidance to all Government contractors, the contractual requirements set forth in the clauses at 52.203–13, Contractor Code of Business Ethics and Conduct, and 52.203–14, Display of Hotline Poster(s), are mandatory if the contracts meet the conditions specified in the clause prescriptions at 3.1004.

(2) Whether or not the clause at 52.203–13 is applicable, a contractor may be suspended and/or debarred for knowing failure by a principal to timely disclose to the Government, in connection with the award, performance, or closeout of a Government contract performed by the contractor or a subcontract awarded thereunder, credible evidence of a violation of Federal criminal law involving fraud, conflict of interest, bribery, or gratuity violations found in Title 18 of the United States Code or a violation of the civil False Claims Act. Knowing failure to timely disclose credible evidence of any of the above violations remains a cause for suspension and/or debarment until 3 years after final payment on a contract (see 9.406–2(b)(1)(vi) and 9.407–2(a)(8)).

(3) The Payment clauses at FAR 52.212–4(i)(5), 52.232–25(d), 52.232–26(c), and 52.232–27(l) require that, if the contractor becomes aware that the Government has overpaid on a contract financing or invoice payment, the contractor shall remit the overpayment amount to the Government. A contractor may be suspended and/or debarred for knowing failure by a principal to timely disclose credible evidence of a significant overpayment, other than overpayments resulting from contract financing payments as defined in 32.001 (see 9.406–2(b)(1)(vi) and 9.407–2(a)(8)).

(b) *Notification of possible contractor violation.* If the contracting officer is notified of possible contractor violation of Federal criminal law involving fraud, conflict of interest, bribery, or gratuity violations found in Title 18 U.S.C.; or a violation of the civil False Claims Act, the contracting officer shall—

(1) Coordinate the matter with the agency Office of the Inspector General; or

(2) Take action in accordance with agency procedures.

* * * * *

■ 5. Amend section 3.1004 by removing the introductory text and revising the introductory text of paragraph (b)(1) to read as follows:

3.1004 Contract clauses.

* * * * *

(b)(1) Unless the contract is for the acquisition of a commercial item or will be performed entirely outside the United States, insert the clause at FAR

PART 9—CONTRACTOR QUALIFICATIONS

■ 6. Amend section 9.104–1 by revising paragraph (d) to read as follows:

9.104–1 General standards.

* * * * *

(d) Have a satisfactory record of integrity and business ethics (for example, see Subpart 42.15).

* * * * *

■ 7. Amend section 9.406–2 by revising the introductory text of paragraph (b)(1) and adding paragraph (b)(1)(vi) to read as follows:

9.406–2 Causes for debarment.

(b)(1) A contractor, based upon a preponderance of the evidence, for any of the following—

* * * * *

(vi) Knowing failure by a principal, until 3 years after final payment on any Government contract awarded to the contractor, to timely disclose to the Government, in connection with the award, performance, or closeout of the contract or a subcontract thereunder, credible evidence of—

(A) Violation of Federal criminal law involving fraud, conflict of interest, bribery, or gratuity violations found in Title 18 of the United States Code;

(B) Violation of the civil False Claims Act (31 U.S.C. 3729–3733); or

(C) Significant overpayment(s) on the contract, other than overpayments resulting from contract financing payments as defined in 32.001.

* * * * *

■ 8. Revise section 9.407–2 by redesignating paragraph (a)(8) as paragraph (a)(9) and adding a new paragraph (a)(8); to read as follows:

9.407–2 Causes for suspension.

(a) * * *

(8) Knowing failure by a principal, until 3 years after final payment on any Government contract awarded to the contractor, to timely disclose to the Government, in connection with the award, performance, or closeout of the contract or a subcontract thereunder, credible evidence of—

(i) Violation of Federal criminal law involving fraud, conflict of interest, bribery, or gratuity violations found in Title 18 of the United States Code;

(ii) Violation of the civil False Claims Act (31 U.S.C. 3729–3733); or

(iii) Significant overpayment(s) on the contract, other than overpayments resulting from contract financing payments as defined in 32.001; or

* * * * *

PART 42—CONTRACT ADMINISTRATION AND AUDIT SERVICES

■ 9. Amend section 42.1501 by revising the last sentence to read as follows:

42.1501 General.

* * * It includes, for example, the contractor's record of conforming to contract requirements and to standards of good workmanship; the contractor's record of forecasting and controlling costs; the contractor's adherence to contract schedules, including the administrative aspects of performance; the contractor's history of reasonable and cooperative behavior and commitment to customer satisfaction; the contractor's record of integrity and business ethics, and generally, the contractor's business-like concern for the interest of the customer.

PART 52—SOLICITATION PROVISIONS AND CONTRACT CLAUSES

■ 10. Amend section 52.203–13 by—
■ a. Revising the date of clause;
■ b. Revising paragraph (a);
■ c. Revising paragraphs (b)(1)(i), (b)(1)(ii), (b)(2) and adding paragraph (b)(3); and
■ d. Revising paragraphs (c) and (d).
The revised text reads as follows:

52.203–13 Contractor Code of Business Ethics and Conduct.

* * * * *

Contractor Code of Business Ethics and Conduct

(Dec 2008)

(a) *Definitions.* As used in this clause—

Agent means any individual, including a director, an officer, an employee, or an independent Contractor, authorized to act on behalf of the organization.

Full cooperation—(1) Means disclosure to the Government of the information sufficient for law enforcement to identify the nature and extent of the offense and the individuals responsible for the conduct. It includes providing timely and complete response to Government auditors' and investigators' request for documents and access to employees with information;

(2) Does not foreclose any Contractor rights arising in law, the FAR, or the terms of the contract. It does not require—

(i) A Contractor to waive its attorney-client privilege or the protections afforded by the attorney work product doctrine; or

(ii) Any officer, director, owner, or employee of the Contractor, including a sole proprietor, to waive his or her attorney client privilege or Fifth Amendment rights; and

(3) Does not restrict a Contractor from—

(i) Conducting an internal investigation; or

(ii) Defending a proceeding or dispute arising under the contract or related to a potential or disclosed violation.

Principal means an officer, director, owner, partner, or a person having primary management or supervisory responsibilities within a business entity (*e.g.*, general manager; plant manager; head of a subsidiary, division, or business segment; and similar positions).

Subcontract means any contract entered into by a subcontractor to furnish supplies or services for performance of a prime contract or a subcontract.

Subcontractor means any supplier, distributor, vendor, or firm that furnished supplies or services to or for a prime contractor or another subcontractor.

United States means the 50 States, the District of Columbia, and outlying areas.

(b) * * *
(1) * * *
(i) Have a written code of business ethics and conduct;
(ii) Make a copy of the code available to each employee engaged in performance of the contract.
(2) The Contractor shall—
(i) Exercise due diligence to prevent and detect criminal conduct; and
(ii) Otherwise promote an organizational culture that encourages ethical conduct and a commitment to compliance with the law.
(3)(i) The Contractor shall timely disclose, in writing, to the agency Office of the Inspector General (OIG), with a copy to the Contracting Officer, whenever, in connection with the award, performance, or closeout of this contract or any subcontract thereunder, the Contractor has credible evidence that a principal, employee, agent, or subcontractor of the Contractor has committed—

(A) A violation of Federal criminal law involving fraud, conflict of interest, bribery, or gratuity violations found in Title 18 of the United States Code; or

(B) A violation of the civil False Claims Act (31 U.S.C. 3729–3733).

(ii) The Government, to the extent permitted by law and regulation, will safeguard and treat information obtained pursuant to the Contractor's disclosure as confidential where the information has been marked "confidential" or "proprietary" by the company. To the extent permitted by law and regulation, such information will not be released by the Government to the public pursuant to a Freedom of Information Act request, 5 U.S.C. Section 552, without prior notification to the Contractor. The Government may transfer documents provided by the Contractor to any department or agency within the Executive Branch if the information relates to matters within the organization's jurisdiction.

(iii) If the violation relates to an order against a Governmentwide acquisition contract, a multi-agency contract, a multiple-award schedule contract such as the Federal Supply Schedule, or any other procurement instrument intended for use by multiple agencies, the Contractor shall notify the OIG of the ordering agency and the IG of the agency responsible for the basic contract.

(c) Business ethics awareness and compliance program and internal control system. This paragraph (c) does not apply if the Contractor has represented itself as a small business concern pursuant to the award of this contract or if this contract is for the acquisition of a commercial item as defined at FAR 2.101. The Contractor shall establish the following within 90 days after contract award, unless the Contracting Officer establishes a longer time period:

(1) An ongoing business ethics awareness and compliance program.

(i) This program shall include reasonable steps to communicate periodically and in a practical manner the Contractor's standards and procedures and other aspects of the Contractor's business ethics awareness and compliance program and internal control system, by conducting effective training programs and otherwise disseminating information appropriate to an individual's respective roles and responsibilities.

(ii) The training conducted under this program shall be provided to the Contractor's principals and employees, and as appropriate, the Contractor's agents and subcontractors.

(2) An internal control system.

(i) The Contractor's internal control system shall—

(A) Establish standards and procedures to facilitate timely discovery of improper conduct in connection with Government contracts; and

(B) Ensure corrective measures are promptly instituted and carried out.

(ii) At a minimum, the Contractor's internal control system shall provide for the following:

(A) Assignment of responsibility at a sufficiently high level and adequate resources to ensure effectiveness of the business ethics awareness and compliance program and internal control system.

(B) Reasonable efforts not to include an individual as a principal, whom due diligence would have exposed as having engaged in conduct that is in conflict with the Contractor's code of business ethics and conduct.

(C) Periodic reviews of company business practices, procedures, policies, and internal controls for compliance with the Contractor's code of business ethics and conduct and the special requirements of Government contracting, including—

(1) Monitoring and auditing to detect criminal conduct;

(2) Periodic evaluation of the effectiveness of the business ethics awareness and compliance program and internal control system, especially if criminal conduct has been detected; and

(3) Periodic assessment of the risk of criminal conduct, with appropriate steps to design, implement, or modify the business ethics awareness and compliance program and the internal control system as necessary to reduce the risk of criminal conduct identified through this process.

(D) An internal reporting mechanism, such as a hotline, which allows for anonymity or confidentiality, by which employees may report suspected instances of improper conduct, and instructions that encourage employees to make such reports.

(E) Disciplinary action for improper conduct or for failing to take reasonable steps to prevent or detect improper conduct.

(F) Timely disclosure, in writing, to the agency OIG, with a copy to the Contracting Officer, whenever, in connection with the award, performance, or closeout of any Government contract performed by the Contractor or a subcontractor thereunder, the Contractor has credible evidence that a principal, employee, agent, or subcontractor of the Contractor has committed a violation of Federal criminal law involving fraud, conflict of interest, bribery, or gratuity violations found in Title 18 U.S.C. or a violation of the civil False Claims Act (31 U.S.C. 3729–3733).

(1) If a violation relates to more than one Government contract, the Contractor may make the disclosure to the agency OIG and Contracting Officer responsible for the largest dollar value contract impacted by the violation.

(2) If the violation relates to an order against a Governmentwide acquisition contract, a multi-agency contract, a multiple-award schedule contract such as the Federal Supply Schedule, or any other procurement instrument intended for use by multiple agencies, the contractor shall notify the OIG of the ordering agency and the IG of the agency responsible for the basic contract, and the respective agencies' contracting officers.

(3) The disclosure requirement for an individual contract continues until at least 3 years after final payment on the contract.

(4) The Government will safeguard such disclosures in accordance with paragraph (b)(3)(ii) of this clause.

(G) Full cooperation with any Government agencies responsible for audits, investigations, or corrective actions.

(d) *Subcontracts.* (1) The Contractor shall include the substance of this clause, including this paragraph (d), in subcontracts that have a value in excess of $5,000,000 and a performance period of more than 120 days.

(2) In altering this clause to identify the appropriate parties, all disclosures of violation of the civil False Claims Act or of Federal criminal law shall be directed to the agency Office of the Inspector General, with a copy to the Contracting Officer.

(End of clause)

■ 11. Amend section 52.209–5 by revising the date of clause; and paragraph (a)(2) to read as follows:

52.209–5 Certification Regarding Responsibility Matters.

* * * * *

Certification Regarding Responsibility Matters

(Dec 2008)

* * * * *

(a) * * *

(2) *Principal,* for the purposes of this certification, means an officer, director, owner, partner, or a person having primary management or supervisory responsibilities within a business entity (*e.g.,* general manager; plant manager; head of a subsidiary, division, or business segment; and similar positions).

* * * * *

■ 12. Amend section 52.212–5 by—
■ a. Revising the date of the clause;
■ b. Redesignating paragraphs (b)(2) through (b)(40) as (b)(3) through (b)(41), respectively, and adding a new paragraph (b)(2);
■ c. Removing from paragraph (e)(1) "paragraphs (i) through (vii)" and adding "paragraphs (e)(1)(i) through (xi)" in its place; and.
■ d. Redesignating paragraphs (e)(1)(i) through (e)(1)(x) as paragraphs (e)(1)(ii) through (e)(1)(xi), respectively, and adding a new paragraph (e)(1)(i).

The added and revised text reads as follows:

52.212–5 Contract Terms and Conditions Required To Implement Statutes or Executive Orders—Commercial Items.

* * * * *

Contract Terms and Conditions Required To Implement Statutes or Executive Orders—Commercial Items

(Dec 2008)

* * * * *

(b) * * *

(2) 52.203–13, Contractor Code of Business Ethics and Conduct (DEC 2008)(Pub. L. 110–252, Title VI, Chapter 1 (41 U.S.C. 251 note)).

* * * * *

(e) * * *
(1) * * *

(i) 52.203–13, Contractor Code of Business Ethics and Conduct (DEC 2008) (Pub. L. 110–252, Title VI, Chapter 1 (41 U.S.C. 251 note)).

* * * * *

52.213–4 [Amended]

■ 13. Amend section 52.213–4 by—
■ a. Revising the date of the clause to read (DEC 2008); and
■ b. Removing from paragraph (a)(2)(vi) "(MAR 2007)" and adding "(DEC 2008)" in its place.

■ 14. Amend section 52.244–6 by—
■ a. Revising the date of the clause;
■ b. Redesignating paragraphs (c)(1)(i) through (c)(1)(vi) as paragraphs (c)(1)(ii) through (c)(1)(vii), respectively, and adding a new paragraph (c)(1)(i).

The added and revised text reads as follows:

52.244–6 Subcontracts for Commercial Items.

* * * * *

Subcontracts for Commercial Items

(Dec 2008)

* * * * *

(c)(1) * * *

Federal Register / Vol. 73, No. 219 / Wednesday, November 12, 2008 / Rules and Regulations

(i) 52.203–13, Contractor Code of Business Ethics and Conduct (DEC 2008) (Pub. L. 110–252, Title VI, Chapter 1 (41 U.S.C. 251 note).

* * * * *

[FR Doc. E8–26953 Filed 11–10–08; 8:45 am]
BILLING CODE 6820–EP–P

DEPARTMENT OF DEFENSE

GENERAL SERVICES ADMINISTRATION

NATIONAL AERONAUTICS AND SPACE ADMINISTRATION

48 CFR Chapter 1

[Docket FAR 2008–0003, Sequence 3]

Federal Acquisition Regulation; Federal Acquisition Circular 2005–28; Small Entity Compliance Guide

AGENCIES: Department of Defense (DoD), General Services Administration (GSA), and National Aeronautics and Space Administration (NASA).

ACTION: Small Entity Compliance Guide.

SUMMARY: This document is issued under the joint authority of the Secretary of Defense, the Administrator of General Services and the Administrator of the National Aeronautics and Space Administration. This Small Entity Compliance Guide has been prepared in accordance with Section 212 of the Small Business Regulatory Enforcement Fairness Act of 1996. It consists of a summary of the rule appearing in Federal Acquisition Circular (FAC) 2005–28 which amends the FAR. An asterisk (*) next to a rule indicates that a regulatory flexibility analysis has been prepared. Interested parties may obtain further information regarding this rule by referring to FAC 2005–28 which precedes this document. These documents are also available via the Internet at *http://www.regulations.gov.*

FOR FURTHER INFORMATION CONTACT: Laurieann Duarte, Regulatory Secretariat, (202) 501–4225. For clarification of content, contact the analyst whose name appears in the table below.

RULE LISTED IN FAC 2005–28

Item	Subject	FAR case	Analyst
*I	Contractor Business Ethics Compliance Program and Disclosure Requirements	2007–006	Woodson.

SUPPLEMENTARY INFORMATION: A summary of the FAR rule follows. For the actual revisions and/or amendments to this FAR case, refer to FAR Case 2007–006.

FAC 2005–28 amends the FAR as specified below: Item I—Contractor Business Ethics Compliance Program and Disclosure Requirements (FAR Case 2007–006)

This final rule amends the Federal Acquisition Regulation to amplify the requirements for a contractor code of business ethics and conduct, an internal control system, and disclosure to the Government of certain violations of criminal law, violations of the civil False Claims Act, or significant overpayments. The rule provides for the suspension or debarment of a contractor for knowing failure by a principal to timely disclose, in writing, to the agency Office of the Inspector General, with a copy to the contracting officer, certain violations of criminal law, violations of the civil False Claims Act, or significant overpayments. The final rule implements "The Close the Contractor Fraud Loophole Act," Public Law 110–252, Title VI, Chapter 1. The statute defines a covered contract to mean "any contract in an amount greater than $5,000,000 and more than 120 days in duration." The final rule also provides that the contractor's Internal Control System shall be established within 90 days after contract award, unless the Contracting Officer establishes a longer time period (*See* FAR 52.203–13(c)). The internal control system is not required for small businesses or commercial item contracts.

Dated: November 5, 2008.

Al Matera,
Director, Office of Acquisition Policy.
[FR Doc. E8–26809 Filed 11–10–08; 8:45 am]
BILLING CODE 6820–EP–P

applicable law in accordance with 601.1.7. Adult chickens, turkeys, guinea fowl, doves, pigeons, pheasants, partridges, and quail as well as ducks, geese, and swans are mailable as follows:

a. The mailer must send adult fowl by Express Mail in secure containers approved by the manager of Mailing Standards (see 608.8.0 for address).

b. The number of birds per parcel must follow the container manufacturer limits and each bird must weigh more than 6 ounces.

c. Indemnity may be paid only for loss, damage, or rifling, and not for death of the birds in transit if there is no visible damage to the mailing container.

[Delete 9.3.5, Adult Chickens, and renumber 9.3.6 through 9.3.13 as new 9.3.5 through 9.3.12.]

* * * * *

We will publish an appropriate amendment to 39 CFR Part 111 to reflect these changes if our proposal is adopted.

Neva R. Watson,
Attorney, Legislative.
[FR Doc. E7–2817 Filed 2–15–07; 8:45 am]
BILLING CODE 7710-12-P

DEPARTMENT OF DEFENSE

GENERAL SERVICES ADMINISTRATION

NATIONAL AERONAUTICS AND SPACE ADMINISTRATION

48 CFR Parts 2, 3, and 52

[FAR Case 2006–007; Docket 2007–0001; Sequence 1]

RIN 9000–AK67

Federal Acquisition Regulation; FAR Case 2006–007, Contractor Code of Ethics and Business Conduct

AGENCIES: Department of Defense (DoD), General Services Administration (GSA), and National Aeronautics and Space Administration (NASA).

ACTION: Proposed rule with request for comments.

SUMMARY: The Civilian Agency Acquisition Council and the Defense Acquisition Regulations Council (Councils) are proposing to amend the Federal Acquisition Regulation (FAR) to address Contractor Code of Ethics and Business Conduct and the display of Federal agency Office of the Inspector General (OIG) Fraud Hotline Poster.

DATES: Interested parties should submit written comments to the FAR Secretariat on or before April 17, 2007 to be considered in the formulation of a final rule.

ADDRESSES: Submit comments identified by FAR case 2006–007 by any of the following methods:

• Federal eRulemaking Portal: *http://www.regulations.gov*.Search for any document by first selecting the proper document types and selecting "Federal Acquisition Regulation" as the agency of choice. At the "Keyword" prompt, type in the FAR case number (for example, FAR Case 2006–007) and click on the "Submit" button. Please include any personal and/or business information inside the document.You may also search for any document by clicking on the "Advanced search/document search" tab at the top of the screen, selecting from the agency field "Federal Acquisition Regulation", and typing the FAR case number in the keyword field. Select the "Submit" button.

• Fax: 202–501–4067.

• Mail: General Services Administration, Regulatory Secretariat (VIR), 1800 F Street, NW, Room 4035, ATTN: Laurieann Duarte, Washington, DC 20405.

Instructions: Please submit comments only and cite FAR case 2006–007 in all correspondence related to this case. All comments received will be posted without change to *http://www.regulations.gov*, including any personal and/or business confidential information provided.

FOR FURTHER INFORMATION CONTACT: Mr. Ernest Woodson, Procurement Analyst, at (202) 501–3775 for clarification of content. For information pertaining to status or publication schedules, contact the FAR Secretariat at (202) 501–4755. Please cite FAR case 2006–007.

SUPPLEMENTARY INFORMATION:

A. Background

FAR Part 3 provides guidance on improper business practices and personal conflicts of interest, but it does not discuss the contractor's responsibilities with regard to code of ethics and business conduct and the avoidance of improper business practices. Currently, three agencies (the Departments of Defense, Veterans Affairs, and the Environmental Protection Agency) maintain policy for contractor code of ethics and business conduct and the contractor's responsibility to avoid improper business practices. With few exceptions, the agencies' clauses and prescriptions are very similar to one another, in that they– establish agency policy and recommend contents of a contractor's system of management and internal controls in connection with Government contracts; establish contract dollar thresholds for display of the agency Inspector General poster; provide instructions for obtaining the hotline posters; and provide exemptions to displaying posters. However, the agencies' policies differ on the contract dollar thresholds and the address and phone number of the Office of the Inspector General (OIG) to obtain a fraud hotline poster.

In view of the significant sums of Federal dollars spent by agencies to acquire goods and services, this rule establishes a clear and consistent policy regarding contractor code of ethics and business conduct, responsibility to avoid improper business practices, and procedures for displaying an agency OIG Fraud Hotline poster to facilitate the reporting of wrongdoing in Federal contracting. This rule also recognizes the need for agencies to cooperate with the Department of Homeland Security to ensure that contracts funded with disaster assistance funds require display of any event-specific fraud hotline posters announcing ad hoc or other special hotline reporting information applicable to the specific contract. This rule proposes amending the FAR to add FAR Subpart 3.10, Contractor Code of Ethics and Business Conduct, that will—

1. Define the "*United States*" to mean the 50 States, the District of Columbia and outlying areas as used in FAR 25.003, and exclude contracts performed outside the United States from the requirements of the rule.

2. Include policy stating that contractors "*should*" have a code of ethics and business conduct.

3. Exclude commercial item contracts awardedpursuant to FAR Part 12 from the requirements of the rule, because the rule will not implement statute or executive order, and because ethics programs and hotline posters are not standard commercial practices as stipulated by the Federal Acquisition Streamlining Act.

4. Provide that contractors receiving awards inexcess of $5,000,000 that have performance periods of 120 days or more, shall have a written code of ethics and business conduct within 30 days after contract award. Furthermore, the contractor shall promote compliance by establishing, within 90 days after contract award, an employee ethics and compliance training program and an internal control system proportionate to the size of the company and extent of its business with the Federal Government.

5. Provide that contractors receiving awards inexcess of $5,000,000 shall

display the agency OIG fraud hotline poster and, when appropriate, any special disaster relief poster from Department of Homeland Security, at work locations in the United States and at the company website if the contractor has established a company website for the purposes of providing information to employees.

6. Provide alternates to the basic clause to accommodate those agencies that do not have posters and to accommodate agencies that choose to require the display of a fraud hotline poster at contract award thresholds at or below $5,000,000.

7. Include a flowdown provision that applies tosubcontracts at the same dollar level as the prime contract.

8. Provide for remedies if the contractor fails to comply with the clause.

This is not a significant regulatory action and, therefore, was not subject to review under Section 6(b) of Executive Order 12866, Regulatory Planning and Review, dated September 30, 1993. This rule is not a major rule under 5 U.S.C. 804.

B. Regulatory Flexibility Act

The Councils do not expect this proposed rule to have a significant economic impact on a substantial number of small entities within the meaning of the Regulatory Flexibility Act, 5 U.S.C. 601, *et seq.*, because the rule does not require contractors to have a written code of ethics and business conduct, employee ethics and compliance training program, or internal control system for contracts valued at $5 million or less; and provides that when such programs are required, they shall be suitable to the size of the company and the extent of the company's business with the Federal Government. Under the rule, contractors have the ability to determine the simplicity or complexity and cost of their programs.

An Initial Regulatory Flexibility Analysis has, therefore, not been performed. We invite comments from small businesses and other interested parties. The Councils will consider comments from small entities concerning the affected FAR Parts 2, 3, and 52 in accordance with 5 U.S.C. 610. Interested parties must submit such comments separately and should cite 5 U.S.C. 601, *et seq.* (FAR case 2006–007), in correspondence.

C. Paperwork Reduction Act

The Paperwork Reduction Act does not apply because the proposed changes to the FAR do not impose information collection requirements that require the approval of the Office of Management and Budget under 44 U.S.C. 3501, *et seq.*

List of Subjects in 48 CFR Parts 2, 3, and 52

Government procurement.

Dated:February 7, 2007.

Ralph De Stefano,

Director, Contract Policy Division.

Therefore, DoD, GSA, and NASA propose amending 48 CFR parts 2, 3, and 52 as set forth below:

1. The authority citation for 48 CFR parts 2, 3, and 52 continues to read as follows:

Authority: 40 U.S.C. 121(c); 10 U.S.C. chapter 137; and 42 U.S.C. 2473(c).

PART 2 — DEFINITIONS OF WORDS AND TERMS

2. Amend section 2.101 in paragraph (b), in the definition "United States," by redesignating paragraphs (1) through (6) as paragraphs(2) through)(7), respectively, and adding a new paragraph (1) to read as follows:

2.101 Definitions.

* * * * *

(b)* * *

"United States," when used in a geographic sense, means the 50 States and the District of Columbia, except as follows:

(1) For use in Subpart 3.10, see the definition at 3.1001.

* * * * *

PART 3—IMPROPER BUSINESS PRACTICES AND PERSONAL CONFLICTS OF INTEREST

3. Add Subpart 3.10 to read as follows:
Sec.
3.1000 Scope of subpart.
3.1001 Definitions.
3.1002 Policy.
3.1003 Procedures.
3.1004 Contract clause.

Subpart 3.10—Contractor Code of Ethics and Business Conduct

3.1000 Scope of subpart.

This subpart prescribes policies and procedures for the establishment of contractor code of ethics and business conduct, and display of agency Office of Inspector General (OIG) fraud hotline posters.

3.1001 Definitions.

"United States,"as used in this subpart, means the 50 States, the District of Columbia, and outlying areas.

3.1002 Policy.

Government contractors must conduct themselves with the highest degree of integrity and honesty. Contractors should have a written code of ethics and business conduct. To promote compliance with such code of ethics and business conduct, contractors should have an employee ethics and compliance training program and an internal control system that–

(a) Are suitable to the size of the company and extent of its involvement in Government contracting;

(b) Facilitate timely discovery and disclosure of improper conduct in connection with Government contracts; and

(c) Ensure corrective measures are promptly instituted and carried out.

3.1003 Procedures.

Contracting officers shall ensure that the requirements of this subpart are implemented using the following procedures:

(a) *Exceptions.* Commercial item contracts performed under Part 12 or performed outside the United States do not apply to this subpart and are not required to —

(1) Have an employee ethics and compliance training program and internal control systems; or

(2) Have the contractor display the fraud poster.

(b) *Contracts exceeding $5,000,000.*

(1) Contracts exceeding $5,000,000 shall require the contractor to—

(i) Display the agency OIG fraud hotline poster, unless the agency does not have a fraud hotline poster; and

(ii) Display the Department of Homeland Security (DHS) disaster assistance poster in accordance with paragraph (d)(2) of this section.

(2) In addition to the requirements of paragraph(b)(1) of this section, contracts exceeding $5,000,000 with performance periods of 120 days or more shall require the contractor to—

(i) Have a written code of ethics and business conduct; and

(ii) Establish an employee ethics and compliance training program and internal control systems commensurate with the size of the company and its involvement in Government contracting.

(c) *Contracts valued at $5,000,000 or less.* Agencies may establish policy and procedures for display of the agency OIG fraud hotline poster, without imposing the requirements of paragraph (b)(2) of this section, in contracts valued at $5,000,000 or less.

(d) *Fraud Hotline Poster.* (1) Agencies are responsible for determining the need for, and content of, their respective agency OIG fraud hotline poster(s).

(2) When requested by the Department of Homeland Security (DHS), agencies shall ensure that contracts funded with disaster assistance funds require display of any event-specific fraud hotline poster applicable to the specific contract. As established by the agency, such posters may be displayed in lieu of, or in addition to, the agency's standard poster.

3.1004 Contract clause.

(a)(1) Insert the clause at FAR 52.203–XX, Contractor Code of Ethics and Business Conduct, in solicitations and contracts expected to exceed $5,000,000 and the performance period is 120 days or more, except when the contract –

(i) Will be awarded pursuant to the procedures inFAR Part 12; or to address Contractor Code of Ethics and Business Conduct and the display of Federal agency Office of the Inspector General (OIG) Fraud Hotline Poster.

(ii) Will be performed outside the United States. (2) The contracting officer shall insert the website link(s) or other contact information for obtaining the agency and/or DHS poster.

(b) Insert the clause with its Alternate I–

(1) When the agency does not have a fraud hotline poster; and

(2) When the requirements of 3.1003(d)(2) do not apply.

(c) Insert the clause with its Alternate II–

(1) When the contract performance period is less than 120 days; or

(2) If the agency has established policies and procedures for display of the OIG fraud hotline poster at a lesser amount. The contracting officer shall insert the agency authorized lesser amount in paragraph (d) of this section.

PART 52—SOLICITATION PROVISIONS AND CONTRACT CLAUSES

4. Add section 52.203–XX to read as follows:

52.203–XX Contractor Code of Ethics and Business Conduct.

As prescribed in 3.1004(a), insert the following clause:
CONTRACTOR CODE OF ETHICS AND BUSINESS CONDUCT (DATE)

(a) *Definition.*
"United States," as used in this clause, means the 50 States, the District of Columbia, and outlying areas.

(b) *Code of ethics and business conduct.* (1) Within 30 days after contract award, the Contractor shall have a written code of ethics and business conduct.

(2) (i) The Contractor shall promote compliance with its code of ethics and business conduct. Within 90 days after contract award, the Contractor shall establish—

(A) An employee ethics and compliance training program; and

(B) An internal control system.

(ii) Such program and system shall be suitable to the size of the company and its involvement in Government contracting.

(c) *Internal control system.*(1) The Contractor's internal control system shall—

(i) Facilitate timely discovery and disclosure of improper conduct in connection with Government contracts; and

(ii) Ensure corrective measures are promptly instituted and carried out.

(2) For example, the Contractor's internal control system should provide for—

(i) Periodic reviews of company business practices, procedures, policies, and internal controls for compliance with the Contractor's code of ethics and business conduct and the special requirements of Government contracting;

(ii) An internal reporting mechanism, such as a hotline, by which employees may report suspected instances of improper conduct, and instructions that encourage employees to make such reports;

(iii) Internal and/or external audits, as appropriate;

(iv) Disciplinary action for improper conduct;

(v) Timely reporting to appropriate Government officials of any suspected violations of law in connection with Government contracts or any other irregularities in connection with such contracts; and

(vi) Full cooperation with any Government agencies responsible for either investigation or corrective actions.

(d) Display of fraud hotline poster(s). (1) During contract performance, the Contractor shall prominently display the _____ (*Contracting Officer shall insert (i) appropriate agency name(s) and/or (ii) title of applicable DHS event-specific fraud hotline poster*) fraud hotline poster(s) in common work areas within business segments performing work under this contract and at contract work sites. The Contractor is not required to display the poster(s) in common work areas and contract sites outside the United States.

(2) Additionally, if the Contractor maintains a company website as a method of providing information to employees, the Contractor shall display an electronic version of the poster(s) at the website.

(3) The _____ poster(s) may be obtained from _____. (*Contracting Officer shall insert the website(s) or other contact information for obtaining the poster(s).*)

(e) *Remedies.* In addition to the other remedies available to the Government, the Contractor's failure to comply with the requirements of this clause may render the Contractor subject to—

(1) Withholding of contract payments; or

(2) Loss of award fee, consistent with the award fee plan, for the performance period in which the Government determined Contractor non-compliance.

(f) *Subcontracts.* (1) The Contractor shall include the substance of this clause, including this paragraph (f), in all subcontracts that exceed $5,000,000, except when the subcontract—

(i) Is for the acquisition of a commercial item; or

(ii) Is performed outside the United States.

(2) The Contractor is not required to include the requirements of paragraphs (b) and (c) of this clause in subcontracts that have performance periods of less than 120 days.

(End of clause)

Alternate I (DATE). As prescribed in 3.1004(b), delete paragraph (d), and redesignate paragraphs (e) and (f) as paragraphs (d) and (e).

Alternate II (DATE). As prescribed in 3.1004(c), delete paragraphs (b), (c) and (f) from the basic clause, redesignate paragraphs (d) and (e) as paragraphs (b) and (c) and insert the following paragraph (d):

(d) *Subcontracts.* The Contractor shall include the substance of this clause, including this paragraph (d), in all subcontracts that exceed $ _____ (*Contracting Officer shall insert $5,000,000 or the amount authorized by agency procedures*), except when the subcontract—

(1) Is for the acquisition of a commercial item; or

(2) Is performed outside the United States.

[FR Doc. 07–698 Filed 2–15–07; 8:45 am]

BILLING CODE 6820–EP–S

U.S. Department of Justice

Criminal Division

Assistant Attorney General   Washington, D.C. 20530

May 23, 2007

Honorable Paul A. Denett
Administrator
Office of Federal Procurement Policy, OMB
Eisenhower Executive Office Building
1650 Pennsylvania Avenue NW, Room 263
Washington, DC 20503

         Re: Proposed Changes to the Federal Acquisition Regulation

Dear Mr. Denett:

       I am writing to propose some additions and modifications to the Federal Acquisition Regulation (FAR) that the Department of Justice believes are consistent with the purpose of the FAR System "to deliver on a timely basis the best value product or service to the customer, while maintaining the public's trust and fulfilling public policy objectives." To better fulfill this purpose, we propose that the FAR be modified to require that contractors establish and maintain internal controls to detect and prevent fraud in their contracts, and that they notify contracting officers without delay whenever they become aware of a contract overpayment or fraud, rather than wait for its discovery by the government.

       Our proposal is modeled on existing requirements found in other areas of corporate compliance such as the Sarbanes-Oxley Act of 2002, and it expands slightly on the Contractor Standards of Conduct set out by the Department of Defense at DFARS 203.7000. We have been careful not to ask contractors to do anything that is not already expected of their counterparts in other industries, and we have avoided imposing any unnecessary burdens on small businesses or creating any expensive paper work requirements. We note also that the National Reconnaissance Office (NRO) through a contract clause recently has begun requiring its contractors to disclose contract fraud and other illegal activities. The NRO reports that this requirement has improved its relationships with its contractors and enhanced its ability to prevent and detect procurement fraud.

       While we recognize that many government contractors have taken steps to establish corporate compliance programs, our experience suggests that few have actually responded to the invitation of the Department of Defense (DOD) that they report or voluntarily disclose suspected instances of fraud. Moreover, unlike healthcare providers or financial institutions, there is at present no general requirement that contractors alert the government immediately as a matter of routine when overpayments or fraud are discovered. We believe that if the FAR were more explicit in requiring such notification, it would serve to emphasize the critical importance of integrity in contracting. In deference to the expertise of the Office of Federal Procurement Policy ("OFPP"), the attached outline prepared by our prosecutors merely suggests the recommended language and possible locations in the FAR for these proposed changes.

In October, the Deputy Attorney General and I announced the formation of the National Procurement Fraud Initiative. To fulfill the goals set by that initiative, we have committed ourselves to working for the consideration of any policy and regulatory change that would effectively reduce the exposure of federal contracts to fraud and corruption. I greatly appreciate the participation of your Deputy, Rob Burton, in this effort.

As you know, the 1980's witnessed significant innovations in the federal procurement system. Many of those reforms, including corporate compliance programs and corporate self-governance, were adopted with industry cooperation, and were later incorporated into evolving regulatory schemes in other business sectors and industries. In fact, the United States Sentencing Guidelines' treatment of corporations, adopted in 1991, borrowed heavily from reforms that were first instituted for government contractors in 1986. However, since that time, our government's expectations of its contractors has not kept pace with reforms in self-governance in industries such as banking, securities and healthcare.

Consistent with OFPP's existing procedures, I ask that you take the necessary steps to open a FAR case and expedite the review of these proposed changes. Note the proposal excludes small businesses from the administrative demands associated with establishing a compliance program, but we believe all contractors, regardless of size, should be expected to report fraud when they become aware of it. I have asked Steve Linick, the Director of our National Procurement Fraud Initiative, to work with you and your staff as this matter proceeds. Steve can be reached at 202-353-1630, or at steve.linick@usdoj.gov.

Finally, I have been advised that the review and approval process in the defense and civilian agencies can sometimes be lengthy, so I am hopeful that you will pursue all means at your disposal to fast track the consideration of this proposal. I believe reforms of this sort present a sufficiently "urgent and compelling circumstance" to support a determination that any rule issuance resulting from this process be considered as an "interim" rule.

Thank you very much for your consideration.

Alice S. Fisher
Assistant Attorney General
Criminal Division, Department of Justice

cc: Paul J. McNulty, Deputy Attorney General
    Rachel Brand, Assistant Attorney General
    Robert Burton, Deputy Administrator, OMB
    Steve A. Linick, Director, NPFTF
    National Procurement Fraud Initiative Members

OUTLINE OF DOJ's PROPOSED FAR CHANGES

As part of its National Procurement Fraud Initiative, the Department of Justice is proposing several changes to the Federal Acquisition Regulation (FAR):

1. Modify FAR Part 3 or 9 to provide that as part of a contractor's obligation to maintain "a satisfactory record of integrity and business ethics," all contractors with more than $5 million in federal contracts in the prior two consecutive calendar years are required to have a compliance program or other internal controls to detect and prevent fraud and other criminal violations as described in the <u>United States Sentencing Guidelines</u>, Section 8B2.1 Effective Compliance and Ethics Program, Attachment A. We intend to propose similar language in our written comments to FAR case 2006-007, which currently is pending at OMB.

2. Expand on FAR Part 3 or Part 9 with a new section "Contractor Integrity Reporting" requiring that all responsible contractors:

   a) notify the contracting officer in writing whenever the contractor becomes aware of an event affecting its initial or continuing right to receive any payment(s) under the contract. *{modeled on existing requirements for healthcare providers found at 42 U.S.C. 1320a-7b(3), Attachment B. Essentially, this provision would require a contractor to disclose any overpayments without waiting for government discovery. To limit the scope of this provision, it may be necessary to include a materiality requirement. Currently, it appears that the FAR only requires notification of overpayments for acquisition of commercial items, see FAR 52.212-4(i)(5)}.*

   b) notify the contracting officer in writing whenever the contractor has reasonable grounds to believe an officer, director, employee, agent, or subcontractor of the contractor may have committed a violation of federal criminal law in connection with the award or performance of any government contract or subcontract. *{modeled on Suspicious Activity Reports required by the Office of the Comptroller of the Currency found at 12 CFR 21.11, Attachment C, the Anti-kickback disclosures currently required by FAR 3.502-2(g) and Sarbanes-Oxley reporting requirements, Section 302(a)(5), Attachment D. To limit the scope of this provision, it may be necessary to include guidance that defines terms such as "reasonable grounds"}.*

3. Modify FAR 9.406-2, Causes for Debarment and 9.407-2 Causes for Suspension to include "knowing failure to timely disclose an overpayment or violation of federal criminal law as described above."

4. The contracting officer shall insert a clause at FAR 52.203 reflecting these requirements in all its solicitations and contracts.

5. The above language requiring notification of overpayments and fraud should be included

in all subcontracts valued over $1 million.

6. Note that the requirement for a compliance program is limited in paragraph 1 above to contractors with over $5 million in contracts for two consecutive years in order to exclude small contractors from any unnecessary administrative burden. The proposal does not relieve such contractors from the duty to report fraud as described in paragraph 2 above. OFPP may elect to increase or decrease that threshold amount based on their experience in addressing small business needs in other contractual requirements. There may also be a request to exclude so-called commercial contracts from the compliance program requirement, but there would be no reason to exclude those contractors from the reporting requirement.

Federal Register / Vol. 72, No. 219 / Wednesday, November 14, 2007 / Proposed Rules   **64019**

DEPARTMENT OF DEFENSE

GENERAL SERVICES ADMINISTRATION

NATIONAL AERONAUTICS AND SPACE ADMINISTRATION

48 CFR Parts 3, 9, 42, and 52

[FAR Case 2007–006; Docket 2007–0001; Sequence 11]

RIN: 9000–AK80

Federal Acquisition Regulation; FAR Case 2007–006, Contractor Compliance Program and Integrity Reporting

AGENCIES: Department of Defense (DoD), General Services Administration (GSA), and National Aeronautics and Space Administration (NASA).

ACTION: Proposed rule.

SUMMARY: The Civilian Agency Acquisition Council and the Defense Acquisition Regulations Council (Councils) are proposing to amend the Federal Acquisition Regulation (FAR), at the request of the Department of Justice (DoJ), in order to require contractors to have a code of ethics and business conduct, establish and maintain specific internal controls to detect and prevent improper conduct in connection with the award or performance of Government contracts or subcontracts, and to notify contracting officers without delay whenever they become aware of violations of Federal criminal law with regard to such contracts or subcontracts.

DATES: Interested parties should submit written comments to the FAR Secretariat on or before January 14, 2008 to be considered in the formulation of a final rule.

ADDRESSES: Submit comments identified by FAR case 2007–006 by any of the following methods:

• Federal eRulemaking Portal: *http://www.regulations.gov*. To search for any document, first select under "Step 1," "Documents with an Open Comment Period" and select under "Optional Step 2," "Federal Acquisition Regulation" as the agency of choice. Under "Optional Step 3," select "Proposed Rules". Under "Optional Step 4," from the drop down list, select "Document Title" and type the FAR case number "2007–006". Click the "Submit" button. Please include your name and company name (if any) inside the document. You may also search for any document by clicking on the "Search for Documents" tab at the top of the screen. Select from the agency field "Federal Acquisition Regulation", and type "2007–006" in the "Document Title" field. Select the "Submit" button.

• Fax: 202–501–4067.

• Mail: General Services Administration, Regulatory Secretariat (VIR), 1800 F Street, NW, Room 4035, ATTN: Laurieann Duarte, Washington, DC 20405.

Instructions: Please submit comments only and cite FAR case 2007–006 in all correspondence related to this case. All comments received will be posted without change to *http://www.regulations.gov*, including any personal and/or business confidential information provided.

FOR FURTHER INFORMATION CONTACT: Mr. Ernest Woodson, Procurement Analyst, at (202) 501–3775 for clarification of content. For information pertaining to status or publication schedules, contact the FAR Secretariat at (202) 501–4755. Please cite FAR case 2007–006.

SUPPLEMENTARY INFORMATION:

A. Background

On May 23, 2007, the Office of Federal Procurement Policy received a request from the Department of Justice to open a FAR case to require contractors to have a code of ethics and business conduct, establish and maintain specific internal controls to detect and prevent improper conduct in connection with the award or performance of Government contracts or subcontracts, and to notify contracting officers without delay whenever they become aware of violations of Federal criminal law with regard to Government contracts or subcontracts.

The Councils published a proposed rule under FAR Case 2006–007, Contractor Code of Ethics and Business Conduct, 72 FR 7588, February 16, 2007. That rule proposed creation of a new Subpart 3.10 to address the requirements for a contractor code of ethics and business conduct, and an associated clause at FAR 52.203–XX. The comment period on that proposed rule closed on April 17, 2007, and 27 responses were received. It is still the intent of the Councils to issue a final rule under that case, based on analysis of the public comments received, except that the final rule will not address mandatory disclosure to the Government.

That proposed rule covers some of the same areas requested by DoJ. However, several aspects of the DoJ request go beyond that proposed rule. The Councils therefore have decided to issue a new proposed rule under this FAR case 2007–006 to cover these new proposals.

Public comments are requested on the new changes not included in prior FAR Case 2006–007. Comments are also requested on mandatory disclosure, and full cooperation, which were in FAR case 2006–007 as examples in the clause of an internal control system. Also note that some paragraphs in that rule, which were not necessary for this rule, were not repeated and will be part of that case's final rule (hotline posters).

The new changes in this rule include:

Compliance program as part of contractor's obligation to have "a satisfactory record of integrity and business ethics"

As requested by DoJ, the Councils propose to amend the general standards of responsibility at FAR 9.104–1 to add a cross reference to Subpart 42.15, and to add at FAR 42.1501 "the contractor's record of integrity and business ethics" as relevant information to be included in past performance information. FAR 42.1501 already includes the requirement to report the contractor's record of conforming to contract requirements, which will include any information that the contractor has not complied with the clause at FAR 52.203–XX. For contractors that have had prior contracts subject to these new requirements, compliance as reflected in past performance rating will be an element for consideration in assessing whether a contractor meets the standard of having a satisfactory record of integrity and business ethics.

Applicability to small business concerns

The Councils propose that clause at FAR 52.203–XX be included in any contract that exceeds $5 million, but that the formal ethics awareness program and internal control system are not required if the contractor is a small business concern. This directly reduces the burden on small business concerns.

U.S. Sentencing Guidelines

The Councils propose to modify the clause at FAR 52.203–XX, Contractor Code of Ethics and Business Conduct, which was proposed under FAR Case 2006–007, to more closely match the U.S. Sentencing Commission Guidelines Manual, Section 8B2.1 (available at *http://www.ussc.gov/*). Not only DoJ requests this, but also a number of respondents to the proposed FAR rule 2006–007. The U.S. Sentencing Guidelines provide guidance on what the U.S. Sentencing Commission expects in the way of an effective compliance and ethics program from organizations convicted of a felony or Class A misdemeanor. DoJ and other respondents to the FAR Case 2006–007 proposed rule considered that that proposed rule left out important elements that are covered in the U.S. Sentencing Guidelines and that this can create confusion. Businesses (especially small businesses) may believe they have met all the compliance requirements of the U.S. Government by following the FAR; this will create a false sense of security. Therefore, this rule proposes the following changes to the clause at FAR 52.203–XX:

• Add definitions of "agent," and "principals." The definition of "principals," is the same as the definition used at FAR 52.209–5. This definition has the advantage that it is already included in the FAR, and includes all the personnel covered in the U.S. Sentencing Guidelines definitions of "governing authority" "high-level personnel," and "substantial authority personnel."

• Amplify the paragraph FAR 52.203–XX(b)(2) requirement to promote compliance with the code of business ethics.

• Provide more detail in paragraph FAR 52.203–XX(c)(1) with regard to the ongoing ethics and business conduct awareness and compliance program.

• In paragraph FAR 52.203–XX(c)(2), make all the stated elements of the internal control system mandatory, rather than guidance.

• Add a new paragraph FAR 52.203–XX(c)(2)(ii)(A) requiring assignment of responsibility at a sufficiently high level of the organization and adequate resources to ensure effectiveness of the business ethics awareness and compliance program and internal control system.

• Provide additional detail in paragraph FAR 52.203–XX(c)(2)(ii)(C) with regard to the requirement for periodic reviews.

• Provide that disciplinary action shall be taken not only for improper conduct, but also for failing to take reasonable steps to prevent or detect improper conduct by others.

Contractor Integrity Reporting

The Councils propose to address the reporting of violations of Federal criminal law in connection with the award or performance of a Government contract or subcontract conduct as follows:

• Add at FAR 3.1002 a cross-reference to FAR 9.406–2(b)(1)(v) and 9.407–2(a)(7), that contractors may be suspended and debarred for knowing failure to timely disclose a violation of Federal criminal law in connection with the award or performance of any Government contract performed by the contractor or a subcontract awarded thereunder.

• Modify the clause at FAR 52.203–XX(b)(3), which applies to both large and small business concerns, to require notification to the agency Office of the Inspector General, with a copy to the contracting officer, whenever the contractor has reasonable grounds to believe that a violation of criminal law has been committed in connection with the award or performance of the contract or any subcontract thereunder.

• Modify the clause at FAR 52.203–XX(c), which does not apply to small business concerns, to mandate that the internal control system of the contractor shall also include this requirement to report violations of Federal criminal law in connection with the award or performance of any Government contract performed by the contractor or a subcontract awarded thereunder.

According to DoJ, the requirement for mandatory disclosure is necessary because few companies have actually responded to the invitation of DoD that they report or voluntarily disclose suspected instance of violations of Federal criminal law relating to the contract or subcontract.

The Councils invite comment as to whether there should be any appropriate limitation on the reporting requirement that accomplishes the objectives of this rule, such as the time period during which the violations to be reported occurred (look back).

Use of clause in contracts for the acquisition of commercial items awarded under FAR Part 12

The Councils do not recommend application of the clause to contracts for the acquisition of commercial items. Requiring commercial contractors to comply with the rule would not be consistent with Public Law 103–355 that requires the acquisition of commercial items to resemble customarily commercial marketplace practices to the maximum extent practicable. Commercial practice encourages, but does not require, contractor codes of business ethics conduct. In particular, the intent of FAR Part 12 is to minimize the number of Government-unique provisions and clauses. The policy at FAR 3.1002 of the proposed rule does apply to commercial contracts. All Government contractors must conduct themselves with the highest degree of integrity and honesty. However, consistent with the intent of Pub. L. 103–355 and FAR Part 12, the clause mandating specific requirements contractor compliance program and integrity reporting is not required in commercial contracts.

Causes for debarment or suspension

As requested by DoJ, the Councils propose modification of FAR 9.406–2 and 9.407–2 to include new cause for debarment or suspension: a knowing failure to timely disclose an overpayment on a Government contract or violation of Federal criminal law in connection with the award or performance of any Government contract performed by the contractor or any subcontract thereunder.

Clause at FAR 52.203

Consistent with the proposed rule under FAR case 2006–007, the Councils propose use of the clause FAR 52.203–XX in solicitations and contracts expected to exceed $5 million if the performance period is 120 days or more, except for acquisitions under FAR Part 12 or contracts to be performed outside the United States.

Flowdown

The Councils propose flowdown of the clause FAR 52.203–XX to subcontracts valued at over $5 million, consistent with the proposed rule under FAR case 2006–007. The Councils decided that the same rationale that supports a threshold of $5 million for prime contracts, is applicable to subcontracts as well. The other conditions of the proposed rule under FAR case 2006–007 are also still applicable, *i.e.*, performance period of 120 days or more, and the subcontract is not for acquisition of commercial items or to be performed outside the United States.

Full cooperation

In addition, the Councils have included in the proposed rule the requirements that an internal control system must require full cooperation with any Government agencies responsible for audit, investigation, or corrective actions. This requirement was originally derived from the Defense Federal Acquisition Regulation Supplement (DFARS) guidance at DFARS 203.7001(a)(7), with the addition of the word "audit" in response to a public comment under FAR case 2006–007.

The Councils are not including this requirement in the final rule to be issued under FAR case 2006–007, in order to allow further public comment and analysis of the relationship to waiver of the attorney-client privilege.

This is a significant regulatory action and, therefore, was not subject to review under Section 6(b) of Executive Order 12866, Regulatory Planning and Review, dated September 30, 1993. This rule is not a major rule under 5 U.S.C. 804.

B. Regulatory Flexibility Act

The changes may have a significant economic impact on a substantial number of small entities within the meaning of the Regulatory Flexibility Act, 5 U.S.C. 601, *et seq.*, because it requires the contractor (including small business concerns) to notify the agency inspector general and the contracting officer in writing whenever the contractor has reasonable grounds to believe that a principal, employee, agent, or subcontractor of the contractor has committed a violation of Federal criminal law in connection with the award of performance of any Government contract or subcontract. Although the Councils do not expect this to be a significant burden on small businesses, because it only impacts those small businesses that need to report violations of Federal criminal law in connection with the award or performance of a Government contract, the Councils have prepared an Initial Regulatory Flexibility Analysis (IRFA) for public comment, that is summarized as follows:

This Initial Regulatory Flexibility Analysis (IRFA) has been prepared consistent with 5 U.S.C. 603.

The objective of the rule is to emphasize the critical importance of integrity in contracting and reduce the occurrence of improper or criminal conduct in connection with the award and performance of Federal contracts and subcontracts.

The rule imposes a clause that is applicable to contracts and subcontracts that exceed $5 million and with a performance period that exceeds 120 days. The clause does not apply to—

• Acquisition of commercial items, either at the prime or subcontract levels.

• Contracts or subcontracts performed outside the United States.

Although the clause requires all contractors to implement a code of business ethics, the clause requirements for a formal awareness/training program and internal control system will not apply to small business concerns.

The clause imposes a mandatory requirement to notify the agency Office of the Inspector General, with a copy to the contracting officer, whenever the contractor has reasonable grounds to believe that a principal, employee, agent, or subcontractor of the contractor has committed a violation of Federal criminal law in connection with the award or performance of the contract or any subcontract thereunder. All contractors and subcontractors subject to the clause are required to report such violations. In addition, regardless of inclusion of the clause, a new cause for debarment and suspension has been added, for failure to timely report any such known violation of Federal criminal law.

Based on Fiscal Year 2006 data collected from the Federal Procurement Data System, the Councils estimate that this clause will apply to 1800 prime contractors per year, of which 700 companies are small business concerns. The clause also flows down to subcontracts that exceed $5 million, and we estimate that approximately 700 additional small business concerns will meet these conditions. We calculate the number of small business concerns that will be required to submit the report of violation of Federal criminal law with regard to a Government contract or subcontracts as follows:

700 contractors + 700 subcontractors = 1,400×2% = 28.

In addition, although there is no clause required, all contractors will be on notice that they may be suspended or debarred for failure to report known violations of Federal criminal law with regard to a Government contract or subcontract. In Fiscal Year 2006 there were 144,854 small business concern listed in FPDS-NG with unique DUNS numbers. We estimate that of the listed small business concerns, approximately 116,000 (80 percent) will receive contracts in a given fiscal year. Government small business experts guess that at least twice that number of small businesses (232,000) will receive subcontracts. However, the only small business concerns impacted by this cause for suspension or debarment are those small business concerns that are aware of violation of Federal criminal law with regard to their Government contracts or subcontracts. Subtracting out those contracts and subcontracts covered by the clause (700), we estimate this number as follows: (115,300 + 231,300 = 346,600 x .5% = 1,733). We estimate a lower percentage than used for contracts and subcontracts that contain the clause, because these are lower dollar contracts and subcontracts, including commercial contracts, and there may be less visibility into violations of Federal criminal law. Because there is no contract clause, we estimate that only 1 percent of those contractors/ subcontractors that are aware of a violation of Federal criminal law in regard to the contractor or subcontract will voluntarily report such violation to the contracting officer.

The rule requires contractors to report to the agency inspector general and the contracting officer of violations of Federal criminal law in connection with the award or performance of any Government contract or subcontract for contracts and subcontracts that exceed $5 million, excluding contracts/ subcontracts to be performed outside the United States or awarded under FAR Part 12. Such a report would probably be prepared by company management, and would probably involve legal assistance to prepare.

The rule does not duplicate, overlap, or conflict with any other Federal rules.

The Councils adopted the following alternatives in order to minimize the impact on small business concerns:

•The requirement for formal training programs and internal control systems are inapplicable to small business concerns, rather than tying the requirement to a dollar threshold based on contract value, which might make the requirements applicable to some small business concerns.

• The requirement for mandatory reporting is limited to violations of Federal criminal law in connection with performance or award of a Government contract or subcontract, rather than requiring report of any improper conduct, even that which is not a violation of Federal criminal law.

The FAR Secretariat has submitted a copy of the IRFA to the Chief Counsel for Advocacy of the Small Business Administration. A copy of the IRFA may be obtained from the FAR Secretariat. The Councils will consider comments from small entities concerning the affected FAR Parts 3, 9, 42, and 52 in accordance with 5 U.S.C. 610. Comments must be submitted separately and should cite 5 U.S.C 601, et seq. (FAR case 2007–006), in correspondence.

C. Paperwork Reduction Act

The Paperwork Reduction Act (Pub. L. 104–13) applies because the proposed rule contains information collection requirements. Accordingly, the FAR Secretariat will submit a request for approval of a new information collection requirement concerning OMB Number 9000–00XX, Contractor Compliance Program and Integrity Reporting, to the Office of Management and Budget under 44 U.S.C. 3501, et seq.

There will be an estimated 20 burden hours for the required reporting to the contracting officer of violations of Federal criminal law in connection with the award or performance of any Government contract or subcontract.

Annual Reporting Burden:

Public reporting burden for this collection of information is estimated based on review of Fiscal Year 2006 contract awards as entered in the Federal Procurement Data System, the Councils estimate that 1400 contractors per year will be subject to the new clause FAR 52.203–XX (contracts greater than $5 million, not including contracts awarded under FAR Part 12). The Councils further estimate that of those 1400 contractors, 28 (2 percent) will report violations of Federal criminal law with regard to performance or award of a Government contract or subcontract. In addition, the Councils estimate that 17 contractors that do not have the clause at FAR 52.203–XX in the contract will also report such violations.

The annual reporting burden is estimated as follows:

Respondents: 45
Responses per respondent: 1
Total annual responses: 45
Preparation hours per response: 3
Total response burden hours: 135

D. Request for Comments Regarding Paperwork Burden

Submit comments, including suggestions for reducing this burden, not later than January 14, 2008 to: FAR Desk Officer, OMB, Room 10102, NEOB, Washington, DC 20503, and a copy to the General Services Administration, FAR Secretariat (VIR), 1800 F Street, NW, Room 4035, Washington, DC 20405. Please cite OMB Control Number 9000–00XX, Contractor Compliance

Program and Integrity Reporting, in all correspondence.

Public comments are particularly invited on: whether this collection of information is necessary for the proper performance of functions of the FAR, and will have practical utility; whether our estimate of the public burden of this collection of information is accurate, and based on valid assumptions and methodology; ways to enhance the quality, utility, and clarity of the information to be collected; and ways in which we can minimize the burden of the collection of information on those who are to respond, through the use of appropriate technological collection techniques or other forms of information technology.

Requester may obtain a copy of the justification from the General Services Administration, FAR Secretariat (VIR), Room 4035, Washington, DC 20405, telephone (202) 501–4755. Please cite OMB Control Number 9000–00XX, Contractor Compliance Program and Integrity Reporting, in all correspondence.

List of Subjects in 48 CFR Parts 3, 9, 42, and 52

Government procurement.

Dated: November 7, 2007

Al Matera,

Director, Office of Acquisition Policy.

Therefore, DoD, GSA, and NASA propose amending 48 CFR parts 3, 9, 42, and 52 as set forth below:

1. The authority citation for 48 CFR parts 3, 9, 42, and 52 continues to read as follows:

Authority: 40 U.S.C. 121(c); 10 U.S.C. chapter 137; and 42 U.S.C. 2473(c).

PART 3—IMPROPER BUSINESS PRACTICES AND PERSONAL CONFLICTS OF INTEREST

2. Add Subpart 3.10 to read as follows:

Subpart 3.10—Contractor Code of Business Ethics and Conduct

Sec.
3.1000 Scope of subpart.
3.1001 [Reserved]
3.1002 Policy.
3.1003 Mandatory requirements.
3.1004 Contract clauses.

3.1000 Scope of subpart.

This subpart prescribes policies and procedures for the establishment of contractor codes of business ethics and conduct.

3.1001 [Reserved]

3.1002 Policy.

(a) Government contractors must conduct themselves with the highest degree of integrity and honesty.

(b) Contractors should have a written code of business ethics and conduct. To promote compliance with such a code of business ethics and conduct, contractors should have an employee business ethics and compliance training program and an internal control system that—

(1) Are suitable to the size of the company and extent of its involvement in Government contracting;

(2) Facilitate timely discovery of improper conduct in connection with Government contracts; and

(3) Ensure corrective measures are promptly instituted and carried out.

(c) A contractor may be suspended and/or debarred for knowing failure to timely disclose a violation of Federal criminal law in connection with the award or performance of any Government contract performed by the contractor or a subcontract awarded thereunder (see 9.406–2(b)(1)(v) and 9.407–2(a)(7)).

3.1003 Mandatory requirements.

Although the policy in section 3.1002 applies as guidance to all Government contractors, the contractual requirements set forth in the clauses at 52.203–XX, Contractor Code of Business Ethics and Conduct are mandatory if the contracts meet the conditions specified in the clause prescriptions at 3.1004.

3.1004 Contract clauses.

Insert the clause at FAR 52.203–XX, Contractor Code of Business Ethics and Conduct, in solicitations and contracts if the value of the contract is expected to exceed $5,000,000 and the performance period is 120 days or more, except when the contract—

(a) Will be for the acquisition of a commercial item awarded under FAR Part 12; or

(b) Will be performed entirely outside the United States.

PART 9—CONTRACTOR QUALIFICATIONS

3. Amend section 9.104–1 by revising paragraph (d) to read as follows:

9.104–1 General standards.

* * * * *

(d) Have a satisfactory record of integrity and business ethics (for example, see Subpart 42.15);

* * * * *

4. Amend section 9.406–2 by revising paragraph (b)(1) introductory text and adding paragraph (b)(1)(v) to read as follows:

9.406–2 Causes for debarment.

* * * * *

(b)(1) A contractor, based upon a preponderance of the evidence, for any of the following—

* * * * *

(v) Knowing failure to timely disclose—

(A) An overpayment on a Government contract; or

(B) Violation of Federal criminal law in connection with the award or performance of any Government contract or subcontract.

* * * * *

5. Amend section 9.407–2 by redesignating paragraph (a)(7) as (a)(8) and adding a new paragraph (a)(7) to read as follows:

9.407–2 Causes for suspension.

(a) * * *

(7) Knowing failure to timely disclose—

(i) An overpayment on a Government contract; or

(ii) Violation of Federal criminal law in connection with the award or performance of any Government contract or subcontract; or

* * * * *

PART 42—CONTRACT ADMINISTRATION AND AUDIT SERVICES

6. Amend section 42.1501 by revising the last sentence to read as follows:

42.1501 General.

* * * It includes, for example, the contractor's record of conforming to contract requirements and to standards of good workmanship; the contractor's record of forecasting and controlling costs; the contractor's adherence to contract schedules, including the administrative aspects of performance; the contractor's history of reasonable and cooperative behavior and commitment to customer satisfaction; the contractor's record of integrity and business ethics, and generally, the contractor's business-like concern for the interest of the customer.

PART 52—SOLICITATION PROVISIONS AND CONTRACT CLAUSES

7. Add section 52.203–XX to read as follows:

52.203–XX Contractor Code of Business Ethics and Conduct.

As prescribed in 3.1004, insert the following clause:

CONTRACTOR CODE OF BUSINESS ETHICS AND CONDUCT (DATE)

(a) *Definitions.* As used in this clause—

Agent means any individual, including a director, an officer, an employee, or an independent contractor, authorized to act on behalf of the organization.

Principals means officers, directors, owners, partners, and, persons having primary management or supervisory responsibilities within a business entity (*e.g.*, general manager; plant manager; head of a subsidiary, division, or business segment, and similar positions).

United States means the 50 States, the District of Columbia, and outlying areas.

(b) *Code of business ethics and conduct.* (1) Within 30 days after contract award, unless the contracting officer establishes a longer time period, the Contractor shall—

(i) Have a written code of business ethics and conduct; and

(ii) Provide a copy of the code to each employee engaged in performance of the contract.

(2) The Contractor shall—

(i) Exercise due diligence to prevent and detect criminal conduct; and

(ii) Otherwise promote an organizational culture that encourages ethical conduct and a commitment to compliance with the law.

(3) The Contractor shall notify, in writing, the agency Office of the Inspector General, with a copy to the Contracting Officer, whenever the Contractor has reasonable grounds to believe that a principal, employee, agent, or subcontractor of the Contractor has committed a violation of Federal criminal law in connection with the award or performance of this contract or any subcontract thereunder.

(c) *Business ethics awareness and compliance program and internal control system for other than small businesses.* This paragraph (c) does not apply if the Contractor has represented itself as a small business concern pursuant to the award of this contract. The Contractor shall establish the following within 90 days after contract award, unless the contracting officer establishes a longer time period—

(1) *An ongoing business ethics and conduct awareness and compliance program.*
(i) This program shall include reasonable steps to communicate periodically and in a practical manner the Contractor's standards and procedures and other aspects of the Contractor's business ethics awareness and compliance program and internal control system, by conducting effective training programs and otherwise disseminating information appropriate to an individual's respective roles and responsibilities.

(ii) The training conducted under this program shall be provided to the Contractor's principals and employees, and as appropriate, the Contractor's agents and subcontractors.

(2) An internal control system.

(i) The Contractor's internal control system shall—

(A) Establish standards and procedures to facilitate timely discovery of improper conduct in connection with Government contracts; and

(B) Ensure corrective measures are promptly instituted and carried out.

(ii) At a minimum, the Contractor's internal control system shall provide for the following:

(A) Assignment of responsibility at a sufficiently high level of the organization and adequate resources to ensure effectiveness of the business ethics awareness and compliance program and internal control system.

(B) Reasonable efforts not to include within the organization principals whom due diligence would have exposed as having engaged in conduct that is illegal or otherwise in conflict with the Contractor's code of business ethics and conduct.

(C) Periodic reviews of company business practices, procedures, policies, and internal controls for compliance with the Contractor's code of business ethics and conduct and the special requirements of Government contracting, including—

(*1*) Monitoring and auditing to detect criminal conduct;

(*2*) Periodic evaluation of the effectiveness of the organization's business ethics awareness and compliance program and internal control system, especially if criminal conduct has been detected; and

(*3*) Periodic assessment of the risk of criminal conduct, with appropriate steps to design, implement, or modify the business ethics awareness and compliance program and the internal control system as necessary to reduce the risk of criminal conduct identified through this process.

(D) An internal reporting mechanism, such as a hotline, which allows for anonymity or confidentiality, by which employees may report suspected instances of improper conduct, and instructions that encourage employees to make such reports.

(E) Disciplinary action for improper conduct or for failing to take reasonable steps to prevent or detect improper conduct.

(F) Timely reporting, in writing, to the agency Office of the Inspector General, with a copy to the Contracting Officer, whenever the Contractor has reasonable grounds to believe that a principal, employee, agent, or subcontractor of the Contractor has committed a violation of Federal criminal law in connection with the award or performance of any Government contract performed by the Contractor or a subcontract thereunder; and

(G) Full cooperation with any Government agencies responsible for audit, investigation, or corrective actions.

(d) *Subcontracts.* (1) The Contractor shall include the substance of this clause, including this paragraph (d), in subcontracts that have a value in excess of $5,000,000 and a performance period of more than 120 days, except when the subcontract—

(i) Is for the acquisition of a commercial item; or

(ii) Is performed outside the United States.

(2) In altering this clause to identify the appropriate parties, all reports of violation of Federal criminal law shall be directed to the agency Office of the Inspector General, with a copy to the Contracting Officer.

(End of clause)

[FR Doc. 07–5670 Filed 11–9–07; 11:21 am]

BILLING CODE 6820–EP–S

DEPARTMENT OF COMMERCE

National Oceanic and Atmospheric Administration

50 CFR Part 648

[Docket No. 071030625–7626–01]

RIN 0648–XC84

Fisheries of the Northeastern United States; Summer Flounder, Scup, and Black Sea Bass Fisheries; 2008 Summer Flounder, Scup, and Black Sea Bass Specifications; 2008 Research Set-Aside Projects

AGENCY: National Marine Fisheries Service (NMFS), National Oceanic and Atmospheric Administration (NOAA), Commerce.

ACTION: Proposed specifications; request for comments.

SUMMARY: NMFS proposes specifications for the 2008 summer flounder, scup, and black sea bass fisheries and provides notice of three conditionally approved projects that will be requesting Exempted Fishing Permits (EFPs) as part of the Mid-Atlantic Fishery Management Council's (Council) Research Set-Aside (RSA) program. The implementing regulations for the Summer Flounder, Scup, and Black Sea Bass Fishery Management Plan (FMP) require NMFS to publish specifications for the upcoming fishing year for each of these species and to provide an opportunity for public comment. Furthermore, regulations under the Magnuson-Stevens Fishery Conservation and Management Act (Magnuson-Stevens Act) require a notice to be published to provide interested parties the opportunity to comment on applications for EFPs. The intent of this action is to establish harvest levels that assure the target fishing mortality rates (F) or exploitation rates specified for these species in the FMP are not exceeded and to allow for rebuilding of the stocks as well as to provide notice of EFP requests, all in accordance with the Magnuson-Stevens Act.

DATES: Comments must be received on or before December 3, 2007.

ADDRESSES: You may submit comments, identified by RIN 0648–XC84, by any one of the following methods:

• Electronic Submissions: Submit all electronic public comments via the Federal eRulemaking Portal *http://www.regulations.gov.*

• Mail and hand delivery: Patricia A. Kurkul, Regional Administrator, NMFS, Northeast Regional Office, One Blackburn Drive, Gloucester, MA 01930. Mark the outside of the envelope:

(2) Facility design solicitations and contracts that include the specification of energy-consuming products must comply with the requirements at subpart 23.2.

* * * * *

PART 52—SOLICITATION PROVISIONS AND CONTRACT CLAUSES

■ 10. Amend section 52.212–5 by revising the clause date to read ''(DEC 2007)''; redesignating paragraphs (b)(26) through (b)(38) as paragraphs (b)(27) through (b)(39); and adding a new paragraph (b)(26) to read as follows:

52.212–5 Contract Terms and Conditions Required to Implement Statutes or Executive Orders—Commercial Items.

* * * * *

(b) * * *

(26) FAR 52.223–15, Energy Efficiency in Energy-Consuming Products (DEC 2007) (42 U.S.C. 8259b).

* * * * *

■ 11. Amend section 52.213–4 by revising the clause date to read ''(DEC 2007)''; redesignating paragraphs (b)(1)(viii) through (b)(1)(xi) as paragraphs (b)(1)(ix) through (b)(1)(xii); and adding a new paragraph (b)(1)(viii) to read as follows:

52.213–4 Terms and Conditions—Simplified Acquisitions (Other Than Commercial Items).

* * * * *

(b) * * *
(1) * * *
(viii) 52.223–15, Energy Efficiency in Energy-Consuming Products (DEC 2007) (42 U.S.C. 8259b) (Unless exempt pursuant to 23.204, applies to contracts when energy-consuming products listed in the ENERGY STAR® Program or Federal Energy Management Program (FEMP) will be—
(A) Delivered;
(B) Acquired by the Contractor for use in performing services at a Federally-controlled facility;
(C) Furnished by the Contractor for use by the Government; or
(D) Specified in the design of a building or work, or incorporated during its construction, renovation, or maintenance.)

* * * * *

■ 12. Section 52.223–15 is added to read as follows:

52.223–15 Energy Efficiency in Energy-Consuming Products.

As prescribed in 23.206, insert the following clause:

ENERGY EFFICIENCY IN ENERGY-CONSUMING PRODUCTS (DEC 2007)
(a) *Definition.* As used in this clause—
Energy-efficient product— (1) Means a product that—
(i) Meets Department of Energy and Environmental Protection Agency criteria for use of the Energy Star trademark label; or

(ii) Is in the upper 25 percent of efficiency for all similar products as designated by the Department of Energy's Federal Energy Management Program.
(2) The term ''product'' does not include any energy-consuming product or system designed or procured for combat or combat-related missions (42 U.S.C. 8259b).
(b) The Contractor shall ensure that energy-consuming products are energy efficient products (*i.e.*, ENERGY STAR® products or FEMP-designated products) at the time of contract award, for products that are—
(1) Delivered;
(2) Acquired by the Contractor for use in performing services at a Federally-controlled facility;
(3) Furnished by the Contractor for use by the Government; or
(4) Specified in the design of a building or work, or incorporated during its construction, renovation, or maintenance.
(c) The requirements of paragraph (b) apply to the Contractor (including any subcontractor) unless—
(1) The energy-consuming product is not listed in the ENERGY STAR® Program or FEMP; or
(2) Otherwise approved in writing by the Contracting Officer.
(d) Information about these products is available for—
(1) ENERGY STAR® at *http://www.energystar.gov/products*; and
(2) FEMP at *http://www1.eere.energy.gov/femp/procurement/eep_requirements.html.*

(End of clause)

[FR Doc. 07–5799 Filed 11–21–07; 8:45 am]
BILLING CODE 6820–EP–S

DEPARTMENT OF DEFENSE

GENERAL SERVICES ADMINISTRATION

NATIONAL AERONAUTICS AND SPACE ADMINISTRATION

48 CFR Parts 2, 3, and 52

[FAC 2005–22; FAR Case 2006–007; Item II; Docket 2007–0001; Sequence 1]

RIN 9000–AK67

Federal Acquisition Regulation; FAR Case 2006–007, Contractor Code of Business Ethics and Conduct

AGENCIES: Department of Defense (DoD), General Services Administration (GSA), and National Aeronautics and Space Administration (NASA).
ACTION: Final rule.

SUMMARY: The Civilian Agency Acquisition Council and the Defense Acquisition Regulations Council (Councils) have agreed on a final rule amending the Federal Acquisition Regulation (FAR) to address the requirements for a contractor code of business ethics and conduct and the display of Federal agency Office of the Inspector General (OIG) Fraud Hotline Posters.

DATES: *Effective Date*: December 24, 2007
FOR FURTHER INFORMATION CONTACT: Mr. Ernest Woodson, Procurement Analyst, at (202) 501–3775 for clarification of content. For information pertaining to status or publication schedules, contact the FAR Secretariat at (202) 501–4755. Please cite FAC 2005–22, FAR case 2006–007.
SUPPLEMENTARY INFORMATION:

A. Background

DoD, GSA, and NASA published a proposed rule in the **Federal Register** at 72 FR 7588, February 16, 2007, to address the requirements for a contractor code of business ethics and conduct and the display of Federal agency Office of the Inspector General (OIG) Fraud Hotline Posters. The original comment period closed on April 17, 2007, but on April 23, 2007, the comment period was reopened and extended to May 23, 2007. We received comments from 42 respondents plus an additional late comment from one of the initial respondents. However, 15 of the respondents were only requesting extension of the comment period. The remaining 27 public comments are addressed in the following analysis.

The most significant changes, which will be addressed, are—
• The clause requirement for a formal training program and internal control system has been made inapplicable to small businesses (see paragraph 5.c.v. and 11. of this section);
• The contracting officer has been given authority to increase the 30 day time period for preparation of a code of business ethics and conduct and the 90 day time period for establishment of an ethics awareness and compliance program and internal control system, upon request of the contractor (see paragraph 6.c. of this section);
• The requirements in the internal control system relating to ''disclosure'' and ''full cooperation'' have been deleted, and moved to FAR Case 2007–006 for further consideration (see paragraphs 2.e. and 6.d. of this section);
• The clause 52.203–XX with 3 alternates has been separated into 2 clauses, one to address the contractor code of business ethics and conduct, and one to address the requirements for hotline posters (see paragraphs 3.h. and 10.b. of this section); and
• A contractor does not need to display Government fraud hotline posters if it has established a mechanism by which employees may

report suspected instances of improper conduct, and instructions that encourage employees to make such reports (see paragraph 7.a. of this section).

1. **General support for the rule.**

Comments: The majority of respondents expressed general support for the rule. These included consultants, industry associations, a non-profit contractor, a construction contractor, inspectors general and interagency IG working groups, other Government agencies, and individuals. Many respondents were laudatory of the rule in general. For example, one respondent considered the proposed rule to be a "good attempt" and another considered it to be "an outstanding, well thought-out and needed policy change." Others identified particular benefits of the proposed rule, such as—
- Reduce contract fraud;
- Reduce waste, fraud, abuse and mismanagement of taxpayers' resources;
- Enhance integrity in the procurement system by strengthening the requirements for corporate compliance systems; and
- Promote clarity and Government-wide consistency in agency requirements.

Response: None required.

2. **General disagreement with the rule as a whole.**

Although all respondents agree that contractors should conduct themselves with the highest degree of integrity and honesty, not all agree that the proposed rule is taking the right approach to achieve that goal.

a. **Ineffective.**

Comment: One respondent considers that this rule will not effectively correct the ethics and business conduct improprieties. Other respondents note that a written code of ethics does not ensure a commitment to compliance with its provisions.

Response: There is no law, regulation, or ethics code that ensures compliance. Laws, regulations, and ethics codes provide a standard against which to measure actions, and identify consequences upon violation of the law, regulation, or ethics code.

b. **Unnecessary or duplicative, potentially conflicting.**

Comment: One respondent views the rule as unnecessary, because it adds "a further level of compliance and enforcement obligations where contractors already are or may be contractually or statutorily obliged to comply." Another respondent comments that the rule is duplicative of other similar requirements. Furthermore, meeting multiple requirements for the same purpose can cause conflicts.

Response: This rule is not duplicative of existing requirements known to the Councils. The rule requires basic codes of ethics and training for companies doing business with the Government. Although many companies have voluntarily adopted codes of business ethics, there is no current Government-wide regulatory requirement for such a code. For DoD contracts, the Defense Federal Acquisition Regulation Supplement (DFARS) recommends such a code, but does not make it mandatory. Legislation such as the Sarbanes-Oxley Act of 2002 (Pub. L. 107–204), cited by some of the respondents, applies only to accounting firms and publicly traded companies. Sarbanes-Oxley focuses on auditor independence, corporate governance, internal control assessment, and enhanced financial disclosure. Sarbanes-Oxley provides broad definition of a "code of ethics" but does not specify every detail that should be addressed. It only requires publicly-traded companies to either adopt a code of ethics or disclose why they have not done so.

The respondents did not identify any specific points of conflict between this rule and other existing requirements. Since this requirement is broad and flexible, capturing the common essence of good ethics and standards of conduct, the Councils consider that it should reinforce or enhance any existing requirements rather than conflict with them.

c. **Negative effect on current compliance efforts.**

Comment: According to one respondent, the rule may have a "chilling effect" on current compliance efforts and may create a fragmented approach to standards of conduct.

Response: As stated in the prior response, this rule should enhance current compliance efforts.

d. Vague and too broad.

Comment: Several respondents consider the rule too vague and broad, so that it is open to different interpretations.

Response: The rule is intended to allow broad discretion. The specific requirements of the rule will be further addressed under paragraph 6. of this section.

e. **Change in role of Government.**

Comment: One respondent fears that the rule will "fundamentally change the Government's role in the design and implementation of contractor codes and programs" because it moves from "the well-established principles of self-governance and voluntary disclosure" to "contractual prescriptions and potentially mandatory disclosure." This respondent states that the proposed rule is not just a minor modification of existing policy. Rather, it "would change far more than the FAR Councils have acknowledged."

Response: This rule does constitute a change. The Councils are requiring that contractors establish minimum standards of conduct for themselves. However, the rule still allows for flexibility and, where appropriate, contractor discretion. The Councils have deleted any clause requirement relating to mandatory disclosure but it will be considered as part of the new FAR Case 2007–006 (72 FR 64019, November 14, 2007).

f. **Unduly burdensome and expensive for contractors.**

Comment: One respondent thinks that this rule imposes significant new requirements on contractors. Other respondents consider the requirement unduly burdensome for the contractors. They think the rule will be a disincentive to doing business with the Government.

Response: Most companies already have some type of ethics code. The mandatory aspects of this rule do not apply to commercial items, either at the prime or subcontract level. The rule has been changed to lessen the impact on small businesses (see paragraph 11. of this section).

g. **Impact on small business.**

Comment: Several respondents note the impact on small businesses.

Response: See detailed discussion of impact on small business at paragraph 11. of this section and changes to the rule to lessen that impact.

h. **Difficult to administer for Government.**

Comment: Several respondents consider the rule expensive and impractical to administer for the Government. One respondent comments on the further paperwork burdens on contracting officials, and that it cannot be effectively administered.

Response: There are no particularly burdensome requirements imposed on the Government by this rule. Review of contractors' compliance would be incorporated into normal contract administration. The Government will not be reviewing plans unless a problem arises.

i. **Rule should be withdrawn or issue 2nd proposed rule.**

Comment: One respondent requests that the rule be withdrawn. Several respondents recommend significant redrafting of the proposed rule and an opportunity to comment on a second proposed rule that makes important revisions.

Response: Although the Councils have made significant revisions to the proposed rule to address the concerns of the public, the revisions do not go beyond what could be anticipated from the text of the proposed rule and the preamble to the proposed rule. The changes are in response to the public comments. They do not rise to the level of needing republication under 41 U.S.C. 418b. However, the Councils published a new proposed rule on mandatory disclosure under FAR case 2007–006.

3. **Broad recommendations.**

a. **Should not cover ethics.**

Comment: One respondent recommends not using the term "ethics" throughout the rule. Contractors can and should develop and train employees on appropriate standards of business conduct and compliance for its officers, employees and others doing (or seeking to do) business with the Federal Government. However, contractors typically do not teach "ethics" to their employees.

Response: The term "ethics" is a term currently used throughout the FAR (reference FAR 3.104 and 9.104–1(d)) and is not considered to be an unfamiliar term to the professional business world. However, the Councils have modified the term to "business ethics," consistent with usage in other FAR parts.

b. **2005 Federal Sentencing Guidelines.**

Comments: Several respondents comment that the requirements of an internal control system should be like the United States Sentencing Commission 2005 Federal Sentencing Guidelines (Ch. 8 section 8B2.1), either by direct incorporation into the FAR or by reference. The proposed rule already included 8B2.1(b)(2) and (b)(3). One respondent is concerned that if they are not identical, businesses (especially small businesses) will believe they have met the compliance requirements of the U.S. Government by following the FAR; this will create a false sense of security. This respondent believes that the FAR requirements fall short when compared to the corporate sentencing guidelines. The respondent also points out that there are no clauses applying to smaller contracts, or to commercial item contracts, although companies with these contracts are still subject to the sentencing guidelines. Key requirements of the guidelines are omitted from the rule, such as knowledgeable leadership, exclusion of risky personnel, and individuals with day-to-day responsibility for implementing compliance systems.

Several respondents ask for a specific reference to be made in the rule to the U.S. Sentencing Guidelines.

• First, in this area of corporate compliance, it could be confusing if it appeared that the FAR was setting a different standard than the Sentencing Commission and the Federal courts, which implement the Guidelines.

• Second, the Sentencing Guidelines are subject to routine reexamination and revision by both the Sentencing Commission after substantial study and public comment, and the Federal courts in specific cases, allowing for adjustments to this proposed rule without having to open a new FAR case.

Therefore, the respondent believes that the Guidelines should serve as the baseline standard for a contractor's code of ethics and business conduct. By referencing the Guidelines, we would be able to ensure that the Federal Government speaks with one voice on corporate compliance.

Response: The initiators of the case asked that the FAR mirror the DFARS. The DFARS provisions are very similar to the Sentencing Guidelines and are adequate for this final rule. It would require public comment to include additional requirements from the Sentencing Guidelines as requirements in the FAR. The request to more closely mirror the Sentencing Guidelines is being considered as part of a separate case, FAR 2007–006.

c. **Make pre-award requirement.**

Comments: One respondent suggests making the rule a pre-award requirement, to ensure that only contracts are awarded to firms electing to conduct business in an ethical manner, consistent with FAR Part 9. The respondent believes that once contractors choose to implement the program with employees acknowledging the consequences of violations, it becomes a self-perpetuating program, requiring no additional actions by the contractor other than certification for new awards.

Response: FAR Part 9 (9.104–1(d)) already provides that a prospective contractor must have a satisfactory record in integrity and business ethics as a standard for determining a prospective contractor responsible as a pre-award requirement. The Councils believe that the respondent's suggestion would encumber or circumvent new contract awards which the Government wishes to encourage. Therefore, no change to the rule has been made.

d. **Hire certified management consultants (CMCs).**

Comments: One respondent recommends that the rule be amended to encourage Government agencies that are hiring consultants to hire Certified Management Consultants or those who ascribe or commit to a code of ethics from an acceptable professional organization such as the Institute of Management Consultants for all Government contracts, including consulting and/or advisory services.

Response: It is the contractors' responsibility to comply with the rule and establish a code of business ethics. The Government cannot endorse any particular business or organization as an appropriate contractor. Therefore, the Councils have not changed the rule in response to this comment.

e. **Use quality assurance systems.**

Comments: One respondent states that the rule does not lead to future improvements in compliance methods. The respondent recommends that, where possible, corporate compliance systems might be bolstered by drawing on and meshing compliance with existing quality assurance systems. Traditional quality assurance systems, used to capture errors, may be applied to corporate compliance systems to catch and root out ethical and legal failures.

Response: The cost of additional controls may or may not balance with the benefit received and should be carefully considered prior to implementation. While a contractor may elect to draw on existing systems as an additional internal control, the Councils have left the rule unchanged in this regard and do not specifically require use of existing quality assurance systems.

f. **Establish rewards rather than punishments.**

Comments: One respondent states that the regulation offers an opportunity to establish a regulation that rewards contractors who behave appropriately, contradicting the Federal Government's ". . . mindset to penalize the wrong doer rather than rewarding the desired behavior."

Response: The Councils do not agree that this regulation should include a special "reward" for contractors who behave ethically. The Government "rewards" contractors who perform satisfactorily through payment of profit on the contract, favorable past performance evaluations, and the potential award of additional contracts.

g. **Should not be mandatory - be more like the DFARS.**

Comments: Several respondents expressed the view that the FAR rule should be modeled on the DFARS rule at Subpart 203.70, which is discretionary rather than mandatory. It states that contractors should have standards of conduct and internal control systems. One of these respondents believes that the proposal to impose contractual mandates is misguided.

Response: The discretionary rule in the DFARS is no longer strong enough in view of the trend (U.S. Sentencing Guidelines and the Sarbanes-Oxley Act) to increase contractor compliance with ethical rules of conduct. According to the Army Suspension and Debarment Official, the majority of small businesses that he encounters in review of Army contractor misconduct, have not implemented contractor compliance programs, despite the discretionary DFARS rule.

However, with regard to the requirement for posters when the contractor has established an adequate internal reporting mechanism, see paragraph 7. of this section.

h. **More logical sequence for procedures and clause, and delete opening paragraph of procedures.**

Comment: One respondent recommends that the proposed changes at 3.1003 be rewritten in a logical sequence. This respondent also recommended that the clause paragraphs should be rewritten in logical sequence with the alternate versions sequentially deleting the last paragraphs instead of creating the delete and renumber provisions.

Another respondent recommends deletion of the opening paragraph at 3.1003 because following the procedures does not ensure that the policies are implemented.

Response: The procedures section has been completely rewritten to reduce redundancy and inconsistencies. The Councils have separated the clause into two clauses, which makes the second point about logical order in the clause moot. The opening paragraph at 3.1003 has been deleted.

4. **Policy.**

a. "Should" vs. "shall."

Comment: At least four respondents comment on an inconsistency between "should" in the policy and "shall" elsewhere. Section 3.1002, Policy, states that contractors "should" have a written code of ethics, etc, while the Section 3.1003, Procedures, and the contract clause at 52.203–13 makes the programs mandatory unless the contract meets one of several exceptions.

Response: The inconsistency was deliberate. The policy applies to all contractors but the specific mandatory requirements of the clause apply only if the contract exceeds $5 million and meets certain other criteria. Section 3.1003 has been rewritten as "Mandatory requirements" to clearly distinguish it from the policy, which applies to all Government contractors.

b. **"Suitable to" vs. "commensurate with."**

Comment: One respondent comments that the policy uses the phrase "suitable to" the size of the business whereas the clause uses the term "Commensurate with."

Response: The phrase "commensurate with" has been deleted from the clause.

5. **Exceptions—general.**

Comments: Two respondents commented on the exceptions to the rule in general.

• The rule be revised to list exceptions separately.

• The key exceptions to the rule in subpart 3.1003(a) and 3.1004(a)(1) are not consistent. 3.1003(a) exempts contracts awarded under FAR Part 12 from the required employee ethics and compliance-training program and internal control system, or displaying the fraud poster, but it does not list the exemption from having a written code of business ethics. 3.1004(a)(1) clearly exempts contracts awarded under FAR Part 12 from all of the clause requirements.

Response: The Councils partially concur with the respondents' recommendations. The Councils have revised the final rule to—

• Move the exceptions into the clause prescription; and

• Delete the conflicting wording in the proposed rule at 3.1003(a).

a. **Commercial items.**

i. **Concur with exception for commercial items.**

Comment: Two respondents agree that the rule should exclude contracts awarded under FAR Part 12. One respondent agrees with the intent of the rule concerning consistent standards of ethics and business conduct for Federal contracts, and the exclusion FAR 12. Another respondent agrees that all contractors should have written codes of conduct as a good business practice code of, but believes the FAR Part 12 exemption should be from the full coverage of the rule, including the written code of conduct requirement.

Response: The Councils note that the FAR Part 12 exemption does include exemption from the requirement for a written code of conduct (see introductory paragraph at beginning of this Section 5.)

ii. **Disagree with exception for commercial items.**

Comments: Three respondents comment that the rule should apply to commercial contracts. They note that although other Federal agencies currently maintain polices similar to the rule, none of the agencies exclude contracts for commercial services. One respondent recommends that the rule apply to commercial item contracts or require that such contractors should have compliance systems in place, especially since such firms fall under the Sentencing Commission's general expectation that corporations will put appropriate compliance systems in place. Another respondent is concerned that the "errant behavior of contractors" will not stop at contracts awarded under FAR Part 12 and by carving out a major segment of acquisitions to which the rule will not apply, the rule sub-optimizes its intended effect of reducing unethical behavior.

Response: The Councils do not agree the clause should be included in contracts awarded under Part 12. Requiring commercial item contractors to comply with the mandatory aspects of the rule would not be consistent with Public Law 103–355 that requires the acquisition of commercial items to resemble customarily commercial marketplace practices to the maximum extent practicable. Commercial practice encourages, but does not require, contractor codes of business ethics and conduct. In particular, the intent of FAR Part 12 is to minimize the number of Government-unique provisions and clauses. The policy at 3.1002 of the rule does apply to commercial contracts. All Government contractors must conduct themselves with the highest degree of integrity and honesty. However, consistent with the intent of Pub. L. 103–355 and FAR Part 12, the clause mandating specific requirements is not required to be included in commercial contracts.

iii. **Disagree with exception for commercial items if contract is for advisory and assistance services.**

Comment: One respondent believes that the rule should apply to all advisory and assistance services, some of which are commercial items.

Response: The Councils have not agreed to make further distinctions between the types of contracts to which the rule should apply. For the same reasons stated in answer to the prior comment, the Councils do not agree to application of this rule to advisory and assistance services that are commercial items.

b. **Outside U.S.**

Comment: Two respondents comment on the exception for contracts to be performed outside the United States, mostly from a definitional perspective.

i. **Supporting office in the U.S.**

Comment: One respondent suggests that the meaning of "work currently performed outside the United States" needs to be better defined. The proposed rule is unclear whether offices in the United States supporting the foreign project would be required to comply.

Response: The term "performed outside the United States" is used throughout the FAR several dozen times. There is never any explanation regarding possible application to offices in the United States supporting the foreign project. If part of a contract is performed in the United States and part of it is performed outside the United States, then the part performed in the United States is subject to whatever conditions apply to work performed in the United States.

ii. **Outlying areas.**

Comments: One respondent specifically endorses the exception for contracts performed outside the United States. However, the respondent requests clarification of the term "outlying areas."

Response: This term is defined in FAR 2.101.

c. **Dollar threshold.**

Eight respondents commented on the rule's $5 million threshold.

i. **Should not allow agencies to require posters below $5 million.**

Comments: One respondent does not support the requirement at the 3.1003(c) that authorizes agencies to establish policies and procedures for the display of the agency fraud hotline poster for contracts below $5 million.

Response: Federal agency budgets and missions vary and are distinct. Some agencies already require display of the hotline posters below the $5 million threshold. For this reason, agencies that desire to have contractors display the hotline poster should be allowed to implement the program in a way that meets their needs. Therefore, the Councils have not made any change to the rule in response to this comment.

ii. **There should be no threshold.**

Comment: Three respondents suggest removing the $5 million threshold and requiring all contractors to comply with the rule.

In addition, the late supplemental comment received from the U.S. Government Office of Ethics expressed concern that a specific instance of conflict of interest problems occurred with two contracts that would not meet the $5 million threshold.

Response: The Councils do not agree with removal of the threshold. Removing the $5 million dollar threshold and requiring all contractors to comply with the rule is not practical. At lower dollar thresholds, the costs may outweigh the benefits of enforcing a mandatory program. Nevertheless, the policy at 3.1002 applies to all contractors.

The Councils note with regard to the OIG audit report ED-OIG/A03F0022 of March 2007, that the contractor in question did not include the required conflict of interest clauses in its subcontracts and consulting agreements. This is the essence of the problem rather than the lack of a contractor code of ethics and compliance and internal control systems in contracts less than $5 million.

iii. **How is application of the threshold determined?**

Comment: One respondent is concerned that the rule fails to state how the $5 million threshold for the application of the clause is to be determined and questions if the threshold should apply to contracts with multi-years as the option years for such contracts may not be awarded, thereby impacting the total value of the contract award. The respondent recommends that the threshold apply to contracts with one term and only to the base year in contracts with options.

Response: FAR 1.108(c) provides uniform guidance for application of thresholds throughout the FAR.

iv. **$5 million threshold is too low.**

Comments: One respondent is concerned that many companies have not implemented programs that would adequately meet the rule and that the $5 million threshold is too low. It will therefore serve as a disincentive for many small and medium—sized companies who may not be willing or able to comply with the requirement to implement training and control systems.

Response: The $5 million threshold is consistent with the threshold established by the U.S. Department of Defense (DoD) for contractor ethics. DoD contracts with the largest number of Federal contractors. Therefore, the Councils have not made any change to the threshold for application of the clause. For revisions made to lessen the impact on small business see paragraph 11. of this section.

v. **Alternate standards.**

Comment: One respondent recommends that the rule focus on the size of the firm and its volume of Federal work over a more significant period of time, and that SBA size standards and some proportion of the work the contractor performs be used as determining factors.

Response: The Councils have revised the final rule to limit the requirement for formal awareness programs and internal control systems to large businesses, while retaining the $5 million threshold for application of the clause. The clause needs to be included, because it might flow down from a small business to a large business, from whom full compliance would be required. Although the proposed rule allowed contractors to determine the simplicity or complexity and cost of their programs "suitable to the size of the company and extent of its involvement in Government contracting," this left many respondents unsure as to what would be acceptable (see also paragraph 11. of this section).

Comment: One respondent is concerned that the rule does not adequately identify which contractors should be covered by the requirements and suggests that the kind of work and responsibilities of the contractor is a better indicator of the need for ethics rules than the size of the contract award.

Response: As a practical matter, all contractors doing business with the Government should have a satisfactory of integrity and business ethics, irrespective of the work the contractor is performing or the dollar amount of the contract. However, given the volume and complexities of work contractors perform for the Government, it is not practical to apply the rule on the basis of a contractor's work or responsibilities. It is more realistic for the Government to establish monetary thresholds and/or size standards to ensure its widest impact and viability.

d. **Performance period.**

Comments: Five respondents commented on the 120-day performance period, considering that 120 days is too short, because it takes longer than that to implement a compliance program, including an internal control system. Even if the compliance programs can be implemented in the required timeframe, that leaves as little as 30 days between implementation of the program and completion of the contract. The 120-day performance period operates as a disincentive to small and medium size companies. Some respondents recommend using a minimum of one year for the period of performance.

Response: The Councils do not concur that 120 days is too short. Although on an initial contract it may take some time to get the program established, on follow-on contracts the program will already be in operation. Many contracts responding to emergency situations are of short duration, and are the very type of contract that needs to be covered. The contracting officer is given leeway in the final rule to expand the 90-day period (See paragraph 6.c. of this section).

e. **Other exceptions.**

Comment: Two respondents submitted comments suggesting an expansion to the list of exceptions.

One respondent recommends two additional exceptions to the language at 3.1003, to make it clear that the new subpart is only applicable for new, open market, contract awards or agreements. Additional exceptions would include "delivery or task orders placed against GSA Federal Supply Contracts, using Part 8 procedures," and "orders placed against task order and delivery order contracts entered into pursuant to Subpart 16.5, Indefinite Delivery Contracts."

Another respondent recommends that research and development contracts issued to universities and other nonprofit organizations be exempt from the rule. Research institutions uniformly have business codes of conduct and internal controls to enable the reporting of improper conduct as well as disciplinary mechanisms (reference OMB Circular A–110). In addition, the National Science and Technology Council's Committee on Science is currently developing voluntary compliance guidelines for recipients of Federal research funding from all agencies across the Federal Government, to help recipients address the prudent management and stewardship of research funds and promote common policies and procedures among the agencies.

Response: The rule is not applicable to existing contracts. Therefore, an exception for delivery or task orders placed against GSA Federal Supply Contracts or issued under existing Indefinite Delivery Contracts is not necessary.

While universities and other nonprofit organizations may have existing guidelines, policies and procedures for business codes of conduct, there are many benefits of including a clause in new solicitations and contracts. The rule will strengthen the requirements for corporate compliance systems and will promote a policy that is consistent throughout the Government. Therefore, the Councils have not made any changes to the rule in this regard, although the burden on small businesses has been reduced (see 52.203–13(c)).

6. **Contractor program requirement.**
a. **Lack of specific guidelines.**
Comments: Various respondents express the view that the rule should be more specific about the required programs.
• Some provided examples of what should be included.
• One was concerned that contractors have increased risk of False Claims Act because when seeking payments under fixed-price construction contracts, they would have to certify that they sought compensation "only for performance in accordance with the specifications, terms, and conditions of the contract", including the new and highly subjective requirements in the proposed rule.
• One recommended that the FAR rule should be held until GAO finishes its study of contractor ethics at DoD.
• Another recommended that the Councils should establish a Government-industry panel to develop a minimum suggested code of ethics and business conduct based upon the best practices many contractors already employ.

Response: This rule gives businesses flexibility to design programs. Many sample codes of business ethics are available on-line. The specific issues that should be addressed may vary depending on the type of business. To provide more specific requirements would require public comment. The new FAR Case 2007–006 will propose the imposition of a set of mandatory standards for an internal control system. The Councils will welcome suggestions for further FAR revisions when the GAO finishes its study.

b. **Compliance.**
Comment: Several respondents questions how the contracting officer would verify compliance with the requirements. There is no requirement for submission to the Government. The internal control system states what should be included. Are these mandatory requirements or is it the judgment of the contracting officer?

Response: The contracting officer is not required to verify compliance, but may inquire at his or her discretion as part of contract administrative duties. Review of contractors' compliance would be incorporated into normal contract administration. The Government will not be routinely reviewing plans unless a problem arises. The Government does not need the code of ethics as a deliverable. What is important is that the Contractor develops the code and promotes compliance of its employees.

"Should" provides guidance and examples, rather than a mandatory requirement. The contracting officer does not judge the internal control system, but only verifies its existence.

c. **Time limits.**
Various suggestions were made about the time allotted to develop a code of ethics.
• One respondent recommends 180 days for the code.
• Another recommended an extension to 60 days after contract award.
• One respondent states that it takes significantly longer than 30 days to put a written code of conduct in place. In order to be successful, the process should include an analysis of what should be in the code, drafting the code, stakeholder input, publication, and communication of the resulting code. This is difficult to accomplish in less than 6 months and usually requires at least a year to do well.

The same respondents also commented about whether 90 days is sufficient to develop a training program and internal control systems. For example, one respondent comments that compliance training programs must be well designed and relevant to be effective. Establishing an internal-control system also takes significantly more than 90 days. According to the respondent, the rule would yield "cookie-cutter" compliance, devoid of any real commitment to ethics and compliance.

Response: Although the Councils consider that the specified time periods are generally adequate, the Councils have revised the clause so that companies needing more time can request an extension from the contracting officer. The Councils also note that an initial code and program can be subject to further development over time, as experience with it suggests areas for improvement.

d. **Internal Control Systems— mandatory disclosure and full cooperation.**
Comments: Six respondents consider the requirements for the internal control system regarding disclosure to the Government and full cooperation with the Government to be problematic. Reporting suspected violations of law is troubling and requested more information on the trigger to the requirement. One respondent expresses concern with possible violations of constitutional rights associated with the disclosures.

Other respondents are concerned that "full cooperation" can force companies to relinquish or waive the attorney-client privilege. One respondent requests that the preamble state that full cooperation does not waive attorney-client privilege or attorney work product immunity.

Another respondent recommends expansion of the full cooperation requirement to cover audits. Information received by the OIG may precipitate an audit, rather than a criminal investigation.

Response: The Councils note that the most controversial paragraphs (paragraphs (c)(2)(v) and (vi) in the proposed rule) were not mandatory, but were listed as examples of what a contractor internal control system should include. The mandatory disclosure requirement in paragraph (c)(1)(i) of the proposed rule was not clear about disclosure to whom. The Councils have removed the disclosure requirement at paragraph (c)(1)(i) of the proposed clause and the examples at (c)(2)(v) and (vi) from this final rule. These issues were included for further consideration in the proposed rule issued for public comment under FAR Case 2007–006.

7. **Display of posters.**
a. **Agency posters.**
i. **Government posters are unnecessary, if the contractor has internal reporting mechanisms.**
Comments: Several respondents do not agree that Government hotline posters should need to be displayed if the contractor has its own code of ethics and business conduct policy and processes already in place to conform to the DFARS rule.

One respondent cites DFARS 203.7001(b), which recognizes and permits companies to post their own internal hotline poster, in lieu of an agency Inspector General (IG) hotline poster, for employees to have an outlet to raise any issues of concern. The respondent believes this coverage is adequate and there is no need to impose an additional requirement to display agency IG hotline posters.

Another respondent states that the rule that requires all Federal contractors to post agency hotlines would deny such contractors the opportunity to funnel problems through their internal control systems and frustrate at least much of the purpose of establishing such systems. One respondent states that companies want an opportunity to learn about internal matters first and to be in the best position to take corrective action.

Another states that while the agencies currently all mandate that their contractors display a fraud hotline, none mandate that their contractors display a Government hotline. DoD, Veterans Administration, and Environmental Protection Agency currently require their contractors to post their agency hotlines unless they have "established a mechanism, such as a hotline, by which employees may report suspected instances of improper conduct, and instruction that encourage employees to make such reports." Several other respondents recommend that the FAR Councils take the same approach.

Response: Although the proposed rule did not prevent contractors from posting their own hotline posters, the Councils have determined that it will fulfill the objective of the case to mirror DFARS 252.203–7002, Display of DoD Hotline Poster, *i.e.*, display of the Government posters is not required if the contractor has established an internal reporting mechanism by which employees may report suspected instances of improper conduct along with instructions that encourage employees to make such reports.

ii. **Too many posters are unnecessary and potentially confusing.**
Comments: Several respondents believe that requiring all contractors to display the hotlines for all Federal agencies for which they are working—without regard to the number of such agencies, or the contractors' own efforts to encourage their employees to report any evidence of improper conduct—would have several negative and unintended consequences. Rather than facilitate reporting, multiple postings could confuse employees. To which agency should they report a particular problem? Adding agency-specific requirements to existing compliance programs dilutes the impact and message of the existing program and will likely lead to confusion among professionals. A bulletin board with myriad compliance references will be confusing at best.

Response: Each agency's IG may require specific requirements and information for posters. There is no central telephone number or website that serves as the hotline for all agency IGs. However, under the final rule, if the company has its own internal reporting mechanism by which employees may report suspected instances of improper conduct along with instructions that encourage employees to make such reports, there is no need to hang multiple agency posters.

iii. **Responsibility for determining the need for displaying an agency IG Fraud Hotline Poster?**
Comment: Several respondents note that the Inspector General Act of 1978 gives the agency's IG (not the agency) the responsibility for determining the need for, and the contents of, the fraud hotline poster.

Response: The Councils agree that it is not the agency that decides the need for the poster, but the agency IG. The Councils have made the requested change at FAR 3.1003(b).

b. **Department of Homeland Security (DHS) Posters.**
i. **Only when requested by DHS?**
Comment: One respondent states that in the **Federal Register** background and in the proposed language at 3.1003(d)(2) the guidance seems to imply that the display of the DHS poster is required for contracts funded with disaster assistance funds, when and only when so requested by DHS.

Response: This interpretation is correct. The final rule clarifies that it is the DHS Inspector General that requests use of the posters.

ii. **Different poster for each event is not best approach.**
Comment: One respondent believes that the contractor's own hotline, if one exists, is better suited to providing a mechanism for employees to report concerns than a different poster for each event.

Response: DHS Inspector General must determine whether to use event-specific or broad posters to cover multiple events. However, the Councils have revised the final rule to permit use of the Contractor's own hotline poster if the contractor has an adequate internal control system.

8. **Remedies.**
Comments: Four comments concerning proposed remedies were received. In general, two of the respondents questioned consistency in application, consistency, and due process, and two were generally opposed to the remedies.

• One respondent asks whether there "should be remedies for non-compliance when the contractor is not required to affirm or otherwise prove compliance, and when there is no adequate guidance for the CO regarding a determination of compliance?" Without guidance, contracting officers in different agencies may make different assessments of the same contractor.

• One respondent "cannot find any rational relationship between the proposed "remedies" and any damages or other losses that the Government might suffer from any breach of the new contractual requirements ethics codes and compliance programs." This respondent strongly recommends that the contractual remedies be limited to such equitable measures as may be necessary to bring the contractor into compliance with its contract obligations to implement certain procedures, and omit any monetary penalties.

• One respondent expressed a similar concern that the remedies "are improper, excessive and unwarranted."

• One respondent requests provision of due process with a proposal to include the following text; "Prior to taking action as described in this clause, the Contracting Officer will notify the Contractor and offer an opportunity to respond."

Response: The Councils have decided that remedies should not be specified in the clause. The FAR already provides sufficient remedies for breach of contract requirements.

9. **Flowdown.**

a. **Objections to rule also apply to flowdown.**

Naturally, those respondents that oppose the rule in general or in particular, will also oppose its flowdown in general or in particular. For example,

• *Comment*: One respondent recommends exempting this requirement for subcontracts less than one year in length, rather than 120 days.

Response: See discussion in paragraph 5.d. of this section.

• *Comment*: Another respondent states that this requirement will negatively impact universities, especially given the flow-down requirements for prime contracts. This respondent recommends that research and development contracts issued to universities and other nonprofit organizations should be exempt from this proposed rule.

Response: See discussion at paragraph 5.e. of this section.

• *Comment*: Another respondent states that the rule has not estimated the number of small business subcontractors that will be adversely impacted by this requirement.

Response: See discussion at paragraph 11. of this section.

b. **Rationale for the flowdown.**

Comment: One respondent states that there is no rationale provided for this troubling and perplexing flowdown requirement and would like it to be deleted from the rule. None of the agencies currently require any flowdown to subcontractors.

Response: The same rationale that supports application of the rule to prime contractors, supports application to subcontractors. Meeting minimum ethical standards is a requirement of doing business with the Government, whether dealing directly or indirectly with the Government. The rule does not apply to contracts/subcontracts less than $5 million, exempts all commercial contracts/subcontracts, and the final rule reduces the burden on small business, whether prime or subcontractor.

c. **Implementation.**

Comment: One respondent has questions about the implementation of the flowdown. What is a subcontract—does it include purchase orders? The Government and the construction industry have a different concept of "subcontract." They are concerned that the meaning of "subcontract" is therefore far from clear to general construction contractors and their subcontractors. Are prime contractors expected to distinguish subcontracts for commercial items from subcontracts for other goods and services?

Response: This issue is not specific to this case. Sometimes construction firms think that "subcontract" does not include purchase orders. The FAR does not make this distinction. The intent is that the flowdown applies to all subcontracts, including purchase orders. Prime contractors are expected to distinguish subcontracts for commercial items from subcontractors for other goods and services, not only for this rule but for many other FAR requirements (see FAR clause 52.244–6, Subcontracts for Commercial Items, which is included in all solicitation and contracts other than those for commercial items).

d. **Enforcement.**

Comment: Several respondents are concerned with how the flowdown requirement will be enforced. One respondent is concerned that prime contractors should not be responsible for subcontractors' compliance with this requirement. Monitoring of subcontracts would impose a significant new cost on prime contractors. Another respondent requests that the rule be revised to clarify that primes are not responsible for monitoring subcontractor compliance. This respondent is particularly concerned about the impracticality of a small or medium-sized business supervising the compliance of major subcontractors.

Response: The contractor is not required to judge or monitor the ethics awareness program and internal control systems of the subcontractors—just check for existence. The difficulty of a small business concern monitoring a large business subcontractor is true with regard to many contract requirements, not just this one. The Councils plan to further address the issue of disclosure by the subcontractor under the new FAR Case 2007–006.

10. **Clause prescriptions.**

a. **Extraneous phrase.**

Comment: Several respondents note that something is wrong with the following phrase in 3.1004(a)(1)(i): " ...or to address Contractor Code of Ethics and Business Conduct and the display of Federal agency Office of the Inspector General (OIG) Fraud Hotline Poster".

Response: The extraneous phrase has been removed from the final rule.

b. **Alternates.**

Comment: One respondent says that what "triggers the insertion of Alternate I or II clause language is ambiguous in the text of the Policy and Procedures sections of the rule and the confusion is compounded when read with the language used in the clause."

One respondent comments that if the contract period of performance is less than 120 days and the agency has not established a requirement for posting at a lower dollar level, there is no requirement to include the clause; in this case Alternate II is never invoked. Another respondent recommends at 3.1004(c)(2) changing "at a lesser amount" to "for contracts valued at $5 million or less".

Response: The Councils have decided to use two separate clauses, rather than one clause with alternates. The conditions for use of the alternates were so diverse, that it was impossible to comply with the FAR drafting conventions that the prescription for the clause should include both the requirements for the basic clause and any alternates. Although the Councils do not agree with the respondent (because the conditions are connected by "or" rather than "and"), any ambiguity in the prescription for Alternate II has been eliminated by the use of two clauses. The language at 3.1004(c)(2)(now 3.1004(b)(3)(ii)) has been clarified.

11. **Regulatory Flexibility Analysis.**

a. **Impact on small business requires regulatory flexibility analysis.**

Comment: Several respondents note that the rule will have a substantial impact on small business. The SBA Chief Counsel for Advocacy commented that the Councils should therefore publish an Initial Regulatory Flexibility Analysis. The SBA Chief Counsel for Advocacy points out that the minimal set-up cost for the ethics program and internal control system would be $10,000, according to one established professional organization; there would be further costs for maintaining the system, periodic training, and other compliance costs.

Another respondent asks how the finding that "ethics programs and hotline posters are not standard commercial practice" squares with the claim that the proposed rule "will not have a significant impact on a substantial number of small entities". The respondent notes the absence of any cost estimate, or impact on competition for contracts and subcontracts. Mid-sized and small construction contractors would find the cost and complexity of restructuring their internal systems, and continuously providing the necessary training to employees scattered across multiple sites, to be very substantial, and might well exceed benefits of pursuing Federal work. (Another respondent echoes this.) The respondent recommends the Councils undertake a fresh data-driven analysis of how severely such mandates are likely to impact small businesses, including the level of small business participation in Federal work.

Another respondent comments that the rule may have an unduly burdensome impact on Government contractors, particularly smaller contractors. It may deter small and minority owned businesses from entering the Federal marketplace and from competing for certain contracts.

b. **Alternatives.** Several alternatives were presented for small business compliance with the regulation.

• Since small business size standards for the construction industry are well over $5 million in annual revenue, the exclusion of contracts under $5 million is not likely to insulate small business from the cost of compliance. Federal construction contracts typically exceed $5 million, and small construction contractors regularly perform them. Instead of $5 million, the requirements should be linked to the size standards the SBA established, and some proportion of the work that the contractor performs for the Federal Government. The construction industry size standard for general contractors is $31 million in average annual revenue. The requirements should be imposed on only the firms that both exceed the standard and derive a large proportion of their revenue from Federal contracts.

• Delay the flow down requirement to small business subcontractors, pending review of data on impact on small business subcontractors (SBA Chief Counsel for Advocacy).

• Provide additional guidance for small businesses on a code of ethics commensurate with their size.

Response:

Exclusion of commercial items. The original Regulatory Flexibility Act statement as published did not identify the rule's exclusion for commercial items. The burdens of the clauses will not be imposed on Part 12 acquisitions of commercial items. This is of great benefit to small businesses.

Reduced burden for small businesses. The Councils acknowledge the difficulty and great expense for a small business to have a formal training program, and formal internal controls. The Councils also acknowledge that the public was confused about the proposed rule's flexible language for small business: "Such program shall be suitable to the size of the company."

The Councils have maintained the clause requirement for small businesses to have a business code of ethics and provide copies of this code to each employee. There are many available sources to obtain sample codes of ethics. However, the Councils have made the clause requirements for a formal training program and internal control system inapplicable to small businesses (see also paragraph 5.c.v. of this section).

Because the clause 52.203–13 is still included in the contract with small businesses, the requirements for formal training program and internal control systems will flow down to large business subcontractors, but not apply to small businesses.

The Councils note that if a small business subsequently finds itself in trouble ethically, the need for a training program and internal controls will likely be addressed by the Federal Government at that time, during a criminal or civil lawsuit or debarment or suspension.

This is not a significant regulatory action and, therefore, was not subject to review under Section 6(b) of Executive Order 12866, Regulatory Planning and Review, dated September 30, 1993. This rule is not a major rule under 5 U.S.C. 804.

B. Regulatory Flexibility Act

The Department of Defense, the General Services Administration, and the National Aeronautics and Space Administration certify that this final rule will not have a significant economic impact on a substantial number of small entities within the meaning of the Regulatory Flexibility Act, 5 U.S.C. 601, *et seq.*, because the rule does not require use of the clause requiring contractors to have a written code of business ethics and conduct if the contract is—

• Valued at $5 million or less;

• Has a performance period less than 120 days;

• Was awarded under Part 12; or

• Will be performed outside the United States.

Furthermore, after discussions with the Small Business Administration (SBA) Office of Advocacy, the Councils have made inapplicable to small businesses the clause requirement for a formal compliance awareness program and internal control system.

C. Paperwork Reduction Act

The Paperwork Reduction Act does not apply because the changes to the FAR do not impose information collection requirements that require the approval of the Office of Management and Budget under 44 U.S.C. 3501, *et seq.*

List of Subjects in 48 CFR Parts 2, 3, and 52

Government procurement.

Dated: November 16, 2007.

Al Matera,

Director, Office of Acquisition Policy.

■ Therefore, DoD, GSA, and NASA amend 48 CFR parts 2, 3, and 52 as set forth below:

■ 1. The authority citation for 48 CFR parts 2, 3, and 52 continues to read as follows:

Authority: 40 U.S.C. 121(c); 10 U.S.C. chapter 137; and 42 U.S.C. 2473(c).

PART 2—DEFINITIONS OF WORDS AND TERMS

■ 2. Amend section 2.101 in paragraph (b), in the definition "United States" by redesignating paragraphs (1) through (7) as paragraphs (2) through (8), respectively, and adding a new paragraph (1) to read as follows:

2.101 Definitions.

(b) * * *

United States * * *

(1) For use in Subpart 3.10, see the definition at 3.1001.

* * * * *

PART 3—IMPROPER BUSINESS PRACTICES AND PERSONAL CONFLICTS OF INTEREST

■ 3. Add Subpart 3.10 to read as follows:

Subpart 3.10—Contractor Code of Business Ethics and Conduct

Sec.
3.1000 Scope of subpart.
3.1001 Definitions.
3.1002 Policy.
3.1003 Mandatory requirements.
3.1004 Contract clauses.

Subpart 3.10—Contractor Code of Business Ethics and Conduct

3.1000 Scope of subpart.

This subpart prescribes policies and procedures for the establishment of contractor codes of business ethics and conduct, and display of agency Office of Inspector General (OIG) fraud hotline posters.

3.1001 Definitions.

United States, as used in this subpart, means the 50 States, the District of Columbia, and outlying areas.

3.1002 Policy.

(a) Government contractors must conduct themselves with the highest degree of integrity and honesty.

(b) Contractors should have a written code of business ethics and conduct. To promote compliance with such code of business ethics and conduct, contractors should have an employee business ethics and compliance training program and an internal control system that—

(1) Are suitable to the size of the company and extent of its involvement in Government contracting;

(2) Facilitate timely discovery and disclosure of improper conduct in connection with Government contracts; and

(3) Ensure corrective measures are promptly instituted and carried out.

3.1003 Mandatory requirements.

(a) *Requirements.* Although the policy in section 3.1002 applies as guidance to all Government contractors, the contractual requirements set forth in the clauses at 52.203–13, Code of Business Ethics and Conduct, and 52.203–14, Display of Hotline Poster(s), are mandatory if the contracts meet the conditions specified in the clause prescriptions at 3.1004.

(b) *Fraud Hotline Poster.* (1) Agency OIGs are responsible for determining the need for, and content of, their respective agency OIG fraud hotline poster(s).

(2) When requested by the Department of Homeland Security, agencies shall ensure that contracts funded with disaster assistance funds require display of any fraud hotline poster applicable to the specific contract. As established by the agency OIG, such posters may be displayed in lieu of, or in addition to, the agency's standard poster.

3.1004 Contract clauses.

Unless the contract is for the acquisition of a commercial item under part 12 or will be performed entirely outside the United States—

(a) Insert the clause at FAR 52.203–13, Contractor Code of Business Ethics and Conduct, in solicitations and contracts if the value of the contract is expected to exceed $5,000,000 and the performance period is 120 days or more.

(b)(1) Insert the clause at FAR 52.203–14, Display of Hotline Poster(s), if—

(i) The contract exceeds $5,000,000 or a lesser amount established by the agency; and

(ii)(A) The agency has a fraud hotline poster; or

(B) The contract is funded with disaster assistance funds.

(2) In paragraph (b)(3) of the clause, the contracting officer shall—

(i) Identify the applicable posters; and

(ii) Insert the website link(s) or other contact information for obtaining the agency and/or Department of Homeland Security poster.

(3) In paragraph (d) of the clause, if the agency has established policies and procedures for display of the OIG fraud hotline poster at a lesser amount, the contracting officer shall replace "$5,000,000" with the lesser amount that the agency has established.

PART 52—SOLICITATION PROVISIONS AND CONTRACT CLAUSES

■ 4. Add sections 52.203–13 and 52.203–14 to read as follows:

52.203–13 Contractor Code of Business Ethics and Conduct.

As prescribed in 3.1004(a), insert the following clause:

CONTRACTOR CODE OF BUSINESS ETHICS AND CONDUCT (DEC 2007)

(a) *Definition.*

United States, as used in this clause, means the 50 States, the District of Columbia, and outlying areas.

(b) *Code of business ethics and conduct.* (1) Within 30 days after contract award, unless the Contracting Officer establishes a longer time period, the Contractor shall—

(i) Have a written code of business ethics and conduct; and

(ii) Provide a copy of the code to each employee engaged in performance of the contract.

(2) The Contractor shall promote compliance with its code of business ethics and conduct.

(c) *Awareness program and internal control system for other than small businesses.* This paragraph (c) does not apply if the Contractor has represented itself as a small business concern pursuant to the award of this contract. The Contractor shall establish within 90 days after contract award, unless the Contracting Officer establishes a longer time period—

(1) An ongoing business ethics and business conduct awareness program; and

(2) An internal control system.

(i) The Contractor's internal control system shall—

(A) Facilitate timely discovery of improper conduct in connection with Government contracts; and

(B) Ensure corrective measures are promptly instituted and carried out.

(ii) For example, the Contractor's internal control system should provide for—

(A) Periodic reviews of company business practices, procedures, policies, and internal controls for compliance with the Contractor's code of business ethics and conduct and the special requirements of Government contracting;

(B) An internal reporting mechanism, such as a hotline, by which employees may report suspected instances of improper conduct, and instructions that encourage employees to make such reports;

(C) Internal and/or external audits, as appropriate; and

(D) Disciplinary action for improper conduct.

(d) *Subcontracts.* The Contractor shall include the substance of this clause, including this paragraph (d), in subcontracts that have a value in excess of $5,000,000 and a performance period of more than 120 days, except when the subcontract—

(1) Is for the acquisition of a commercial item; or

(2) Is performed entirely outside the United States.

(End of clause)

52.203–14 Display of Hotline Poster(s).

As prescribed in 3.1004(b), insert the following clause:

DISPLAY OF HOTLINE POSTER(S) (DEC 2007)

(a) *Definition.*

United States, as used in this clause, means the 50 States, the District of Columbia, and outlying areas.

(b) *Display of fraud hotline poster(s).* Except as provided in paragraph (c)—

(1) During contract performance in the United States, the Contractor shall prominently display in common work areas within business segments performing work under this contract and at contract work sites—

(i) Any agency fraud hotline poster or Department of Homeland Security (DHS) fraud hotline poster identified in paragraph (b)(3) of this clause; and

(ii) Any DHS fraud hotline poster subsequently identified by the Contracting Officer.

(2) Additionally, if the Contractor maintains a company website as a method of providing information to employees, the Contractor shall display an electronic version of the poster(s) at the website.

(3) Any required posters may be obtained as follows:

Poster(s)	Obtain from
_____	_____

(*Contracting Officer shall insert*— (i) Appropriate agency name(s) and/or title of applicable Department of Homeland Security fraud hotline poster); and

(ii) The website(s) or other contact information for obtaining the poster(s).)

(c) If the Contractor has implemented a business ethics and conduct awareness program, including a reporting mechanism, such as a hotline poster, then the Contractor need not display any agency fraud hotline posters as required in paragraph (b) of this clause, other than any required DHS posters.

(d) *Subcontracts.* The Contractor shall include the substance of this clause, including this paragraph (d), in all subcontracts that exceed $5,000,000, except when the subcontract—

(1) Is for the acquisition of a commercial item; or

(2) Is performed entirely outside the United States.

(End of clause)

[FR Doc. 07–5800 Filed 11–21–07; 8:45 am]

BILLING CODE 6820–EP–S

U.S. Department of Justice

Criminal Division

2007-006-31

Assistant Attorney General

Washington, D.C. 20530

General Services Administration
Regulatory Secretariat (VIR)
1800 F Street NW
Room 4035
Washington D.C. 20405
Attn: Laurieann Duarte

January 14, 2008

Re: Comments on FAR Case 2007-006

Dear Ms. Duarte:

On May 23, 2007, in a letter to the Office of Federal Procurement Policy, the Justice Department (on behalf of the National Procurement Fraud Task Force), proposed some modifications to the Federal Acquisition Regulation (FAR), which would require, among other things, that contractors notify the government whenever they become aware of a material overpayment or fraud relating to the award or performance of a contract or subcontract, rather than wait for the contract overpayment or fraud to be discovered by the government. Shortly thereafter, the Civilian Agency Acquisition Council and the Defense Acquisition Regulations Council began their review process and on November 14, 2007, published a proposed rule substantially incorporating the Department of Justice's requested changes to the FAR. We appreciate the fine work performed by the defense and civilian agencies in expeditiously evaluating and publishing our proposed FAR changes.

During the past several months, we have continued to consider ways to improve the proposed rule. The Justice Department continues to believe that mandatory disclosure of material overpayments and fraud is necessary and appropriate, and that government contractors should be held to the same disclosure standards as those in the healthcare and banking industries. We recognize that many government contractors have taken steps and are now required to establish corporate compliance programs, but our experience suggests that few have actually responded to the invitation of the Department of Defense (DOD) that they report or voluntarily disclose suspected instances of fraud.

I have attached some proposed modifications to FAR case 2007-006 addressing how some concerns might be meaningfully addressed in any Final Rule. (Attachment A). Among other things, these proposed modifications address the standard for disclosure of overpayments and criminal violations, cooperation and attorney-client privilege, the obligation to disclose potential violations of the False Claims Act, the grounds for suspension and debarment, the time limit for disclosures, and internal investigations by contractors.

Thank you for the opportunity to comment. If you have any questions, please feel free to call me directly or Steve Linick, the Director of the National Procurement Fraud Task Force, at 202-353-1630.

Sincerely,

Alice S. Fisher
Assistant Attorney General
Criminal Division, Department of Justice

Cc: Robert Burton, Deputy Administrator, OFPP
     National Procurement Fraud Task Force Members

006-31

ATTACHMENT A

DOJ's Proposed Modifications to FAR Case 2007-006

Based upon our discussions with the acquisition community, as well as contractors and their counsel, we recommend the following modifications to the proposed rule:

- <u>Contracts Performed Overseas.</u> Proposed FAR 3.1004: while the Justice Department agrees with the proposed exclusion of the contract clause for Part 12 commercial items, we do not agree with also excluding contracts "performed entirely outside the United States." Although these contracts may be performed outside of the United States, the United States still is a party to these contracts and potentially a victim when overpayments are made or when fraud occurs in connection with the contracts. Under these circumstances, the government still maintains jurisdiction to prosecute the perpetrators of the fraud. Moreover, these types of contracts, which in many cases support our efforts to fight the global war on terror, need greater contractor vigilance because they are performed overseas where U.S. government resources and remedies are more limited.

- <u>Overpayments</u>.

    - Proposed FAR 3.1002(c): it appears that the drafters neglected to incorporate "knowing failure to timely disclose an <u>overpayment</u>" reflected in proposed FAR 9.406-2(v)(A). In our view, the duty to disclose overpayments is just as important as the disclosure of a criminal violation and also relieves the contractor from having to decide whether there is an actual criminal violation before deciding to disclose. In addition, to limit the scope of the requirement to disclose overpayments, a materiality requirement is appropriate.

    - For some reason, the proposed rule does not also require disclosure of material overpayments in each of the instances in which it calls for disclosure of violations of federal criminal law. While the duty is captured in proposed FAR 9.406-2 and 9.407-2, it is not found at proposed FAR 3.1002 Policy section or the contractor Code found at proposed FAR 52.203-XX (c)(2)(ii)(F). The concept of a duty to disclose material overpayments is critical here, since it both requires and allows a contractor to make a disclosure without having to find evidence of fraud. The proposed rule should also explain that disclosures of overpayments need be made only to the contracting officer, and not the Inspector General.

    - The FAR Councils may want to consider defining "overpayments." What we originally intended to address were situations where the contractor, as a result of compliance efforts or just by accident, realized it had been overpaid under the contract without regard to fault. As an example only, a situation in which the contractor is overpaid as a result of a contractor computer error would be a circumstance where the Government would reasonably expect to be alerted to that fact when it is discovered. On the actual language, we would defer to the Councils.

- Standard for Disclosure of Overpayments and Criminal Violations. Proposed FAR 3.1002, 9.406-2 and 9.407-2: in order to avoid contractor concern that the proposal would require disclosure of every allegation of a criminal violation or overpayment without regard to merit, we suggest inserting either "reasonable grounds to believe," found elsewhere in the proposed rule or "credible information of . . . ." found at DFARS 252.246-7003 governing reports of Potential Safety Issues.

- Scope of Criminal Violations. Contractors may reasonably complain that requiring disclosure of any "violation of Federal criminal law" is too broad, even when limited by the phrase "in connection with the award or performance of any Government contract or subcontract." We would not object to including the following additional limiting language: "involving fraud, conflict of interest, bribery, or gratuity violations found in Title 18, United States Code."

- Obligation to Disclose Potential Violations of the Civil False Claims Act. We recommend that the grounds for suspension and debarment also include the knowing failure to disclose potential violations of the False Claims Act which would be added as a new section 9.406-2(b)(v)(C) and 9.407-2(a)(7)(iii). Since the proposed regulation already includes the knowing failure to disclose an overpayment as well as violations of federal criminal law as a basis for suspension and debarment, it would be an obvious omission to not include the FCA. Given the importance of the civil False Claims Act to the federal contract fraud enforcement effort, contractors should also be required to include in their "business ethics awareness" obligation reflected in the proposed Rule at 52.203-XX(c)(2)(ii)(F), "training on the False Claims Act" as is currently required of healthcare providers in § 6033 of the Deficit Reduction Act. A similar reference to the False Claims Act should be included in FAR 3.1002(c).

- Cooperation and Attorney-Client Privilege. In our earlier comments on proposed FAR 52.203 Code of Business Ethics and Conduct, we suggested these codes and compliance programs incorporate by reference Chapter 8 of the United States Sentencing Guidelines (USSG) for Organizations which is regularly reviewed and improved. In the absence of that, we recommend that proposed FAR 52.203 F and G incorporate USSG §8C2.5, Application Note 12, which explains what "cooperation" means, and include a statement that "nothing in the Rule is intended to require that a contractor waive its attorney-client privilege, or that any officer, director, owner, or employee of the contractor, including a sole proprietor, waive his or her attorney-client privilege or Fifth Amendment rights." That distinction is necessary because it has long been held that corporations are not covered by the Fifth Amendment to the United States Constitution. To add as a point of reference, it has been clearly stated in DOD's Voluntary Disclosure Program that contractors were not required to waive their attorney-client privilege, and there is no good reason to think that reservation will not work equally well in the mandated disclosures in the proposed rule.

- Time Limit for Disclosures. To avoid imposing a duty to disclose matters occurring many years ago, we suggest limiting the mandatory disclosure of overpayments or criminal violations to matters discovered by the contractor within three years of the contract completion.

- Grounds for Suspension and Debarment. In response to the concern that suspension or debarment is too severe a remedy for merely failing to disclose an overpayment or federal criminal violation, we would add to the proposed rule on grounds for suspension or debarment "for the purpose of defrauding the United States." See 42 U.S.C. §1320a-7b(a)(3). In the preamble, the Councils may want to be clear that the intent standard found described here, namely, "for the purpose of defrauding the United States," has no application to the False Claims Act.

- FOIA Exemption. For a variety of reasons, not the least of which is to encourage contractors to submit information pertaining to overpayments or violations of federal law even if such occurrences have not yet been confirmed, the Councils may wish to recommend to agencies that the submitted information be maintained confidentially to the extent permitted by law. The Councils may further wish to remind agencies that any decision by agencies to make a discretionary disclosure of information protected under the FOIA should be made only after full and deliberate consideration of the institutional, commercial, and personal privacy interests that could be implicated by such a disclosure. In particular, agencies should be mindful that the Trade Secrets Act operates as a prohibition on the discretionary disclosure of any information covered by Exemption 4 of the FOIA, unless such disclosure is otherwise authorized by law.

- Subcontractors. While we believe it is important to flow the disclosure obligation down to subcontractors, some subcontractors may not be comfortable making the disclosure to the government through the prime contractor. Accordingly, the mechanism through which a subcontractor makes a disclosure to the government may need to be addressed in any final rule.

- Contractor Internal Investigation. The final rule preamble should make clear that nothing in the rule is intended to preclude a contractor from continuing to investigate after making its initial disclosure to the government. In fact, much like the DOD Voluntary Disclosure Program, in most cases, we would expect that the Inspector General or the Contracting Officer will encourage the contractor to complete its internal investigation and make a full report of its findings.

ABA
**Defending Liberty
Pursuing Justice**

AMERICAN BAR ASSOCIATION

**Section of Public Contract Law
Writer's Address and Telephone**

2007-2008
CHAIR
Patricia A. Meagher
582 Market St, Ste 301
San Francisco, CA 94104
(415) 362-6517

CHAIR-ELECT
Michael W. Mutek
1200 S Jupiter Rd
Garland, TX 75042
(972) 205-5177

VICE-CHAIR
Karen L. Manos
1050 Connecticut Ave, NW, 2nd Flr
Washington, DC 20036
(202) 955-8536

SECRETARY
Donald G. Featherstun
560 Mission St, Ste 3100
San Francisco, CA 94105
(415) 397-2823

BUDGET AND FINANCE OFFICER
Carol N. Park-Conroy
7404 Rippon Rd
Alexandria, VA 22307
(703) 681-8507

SECTION DELEGATES
John S. Pachter
8000 Towers Crescent Dr, Ste 900
Vienna, VA 22182
(703) 847-6260

Mary Ellen Coster Williams
717 Madison Pl, NW, Ste 612
Washington, DC 20005
(202) 357-6660

IMMEDIATE PAST CHAIR
Michael A. Hordell
600 14th St, NW, 5th Flr
Washington, DC 20005
(202) 220-1232

PREVIOUS PAST CHAIR
Robert L. Schaefer
1049 Camino Dos Rios
Thousand Oaks, CA 91360
(805) 373-4608

COUNCIL MEMBERS
Daniel F. Doogan
Detroit, MI

Mark E. Hanson
Vienna, VA

Annejanette Kloeb Heckman
Herndon, VA

E. Sanderson Hoe
Washington, DC

James A. Hughes, Jr.
Arlington, VA

David F. Innis
San Francisco, CA

Sharon L. Larkin
Washington, DC

Rocco J. Maffei, Jr.
Akron, OH

Linda T. Maramba
McLean, VA

Stuart B. Nibley
Washington, DC

Scott E. Pickens
Washington, DC

Jeri K. Somers
Washington, DC

Holly Emrick Svetz
Tysons Corner, VA

**EDITOR, PUBLIC CONTRACT
LAW JOURNAL**
Karen L. Manos
Washington, DC

ITOR, THE PROCUREMENT LAWYER
John A. Burkholder
Los Angeles, CA

BOARD OF GOVERNORS LIAISON
Charles A. Weiss
St. Louis, MO

SECTION DIRECTOR
Marilyn Neforas
321 N Clark St, M/S 19.1
Chicago, IL 60610
(312) 988-5596

Suite 301
582 Market Street
San Francisco, CA 94104
Phone: (415) 362-6517
Fax: (415) 362-6519
pmeagher@rossimeagher.com

January 18, 2008

VIA FACSIMILE AND U.S. MAIL

General Services Administration
Regulatory Secretariat (VIR)
Attn: Ms. Laurieann Duarte
1800 F Street, N.W.
Room 4035
Washington, D.C. 20405

    Re: **FAR Case 2007-006, Contractor Compliance Program
And Integrity Reporting, 72 Fed. Reg. 64019 (Nov. 14,
2007).**

Dear Ms. Duarte:

    On behalf of the Section of Public Contract Law of the American Bar Association ("the Section"), I am submitting comments on the above-referenced proposed rule ("the Proposed Rule"). The Section consists of attorneys and associated professionals in private practice, industry, and Government service. The Section's governing Council and substantive committees contain members representing these three segments to ensure that all points of view are considered. By presenting their consensus view, the Section seeks to improve the process of public contracting for needed supplies, services, and public works.[1]

    The Section is authorized to submit comments on acquisition regulations under special authority granted by the Association's Board of Governors. The views expressed herein have not been approved by the House of Delegates or the

---

[1] Mary Ellen Coster Williams, the Section of Public Contract Law's representative to the ABA House of Delegates, and Jeri K. Somers, a member of the Section's Council, did not participate in the consideration of these comments and abstained from voting to approve and send this letter.

General Services Administration
January 18, 2008
Page 2

Board of Governors of the American Bar Association and, therefore, should not be construed as representing the policy of the American Bar Association.[2]

Introduction

The Section applauds the FAR Council and Department of Justice (DoJ) for their efforts to promote honesty, integrity, and fair dealing in government contracting, goals shared in the Section's principles as expressed in, for example, the Model Procurement Code. In furtherance of these goals, the Section generally believes that any contractor doing business with the Government would benefit from a code of ethics and business conduct and compliance procedures. The Section's comments relate not to the foregoing basic goals, but rather with the means of carrying them out.

The Proposed Rule includes a number of provisions that would significantly alter existing FAR rules regarding contractor compliance and ethics programs, including provisions that would (i) require contractors to establish and maintain a mandatory code of ethics and business conduct and internal controls (building upon the recent finalization of FAR Case 2006-007 and its compliance program requirements); (ii) require contractors to notify the Inspector General and Contracting Officer whenever they have "reasonable grounds" to believe that a violation of federal criminal law has occurred in connection with the award or performance of a government contract or subcontract; and (iii) subject contractors to suspension or debarment for any failure to "timely disclose" an "overpayment" or "[v]iolation of Federal criminal law in connection with the award or performance of any Government contract or subcontract." *See* 72 Fed. Reg. at 64022-23.

At the outset, the Section notes that there is no statutory authority for the FAR Council to issue a regulation providing for mandatory disclosure of criminal acts. The FAR Council therefore lacks the authority to issue the regulation. *See Am. Fed. of Labor & Congress of Indus. Orgs. v. Alfred E. Kahn*, 472 F. Supp. 99 (D.D.C. 1979), *rev'd*, 618 F. 2d 784 (D.C. Cir. 1979). This is particularly important in light of the DoJ's reliance upon the example of other statutorily-mandated disclosure programs (Sarbanes-Oxley, Foreign Corrupt Practices Act, etc.) as justification for this regulatory initiative.[3]

In addition, the Section finds little factual analysis of the need for the Proposed Rule. The Section suggests that the Council set forth additional analysis

---

[2] This letter is available in pdf format at http://www.abanet.org/contract/regscomm/home.html under the topic "Ethics."

[3] This rationale is cited in its May 23, 2007 letter to the Office of Federal Procurement Policy proposing the subject Proposed Rule.

General Services Administration
January 18, 2008
Page 3

and explanation. As discussed in more detail below, the Section finds provisions of the Proposed Rule that are vague or ambiguous, and that appear more likely to cause compliance issues than to resolve them. The Section also questions the need for the additional disclosure and other requirements specified in this Proposed Rule, particularly given the recent implementation of more expansive contractor compliance standards in the FAR (see 72 Fed. Reg. 65873 (Nov. 23, 2007)) and the existence of other voluntary disclosure programs and incentives such as those in the Federal Sentencing Guidelines and the existing suspension/debarment regime. If the FAR Council nonetheless elects to proceed with rulemaking based upon this proposal, it is the view of the Section that substantial revisions in both the substance and rationale in support of the Proposed Rule are necessary to make the Proposed Rules both reasonable and enforceable.

A. The Proposed Rule Does Not Provide The Requisite Explanation Of Need For Additional Disclosure Obligations

The Section maintains that the Proposed Rule is unsupported because the rationale for the mandatory disclosure requirement is unexplained. The DoJ states that the mandatory disclosure provision is required "because few companies have actually responded to the invitation of DoD that they report or voluntarily disclose suspected instance of violations of Federal criminal law relating to the contract or subcontract." 72 Fed. Reg. at 64020. We presume this statement refers to participation in the DoD Inspector General's ("DoD IG") Voluntary Disclosure Program. But this statement concerning the level of activity in the DoD IG Voluntary Disclosure Program does not establish that there is a need for a mandatory disclosure program. No supporting data is cited in support of this assertion and, indeed, the available data suggests the contrary is true – that voluntary disclosures remain a viable and regularly-used tool to address violations of law discovered by government contractors.

The number of contractor disclosures to the DoD IG voluntary disclosure program has been fairly level over the past several years, according to DoD IG reports. Further, to the extent that DoJ's claim is based upon a comparison of the level of disclosures over the past several years to the larger numbers reported when the program was initiated 20 years ago, its assumptions about the reason for that decrease are misplaced. By assuming that the level of illegality continues to be the same after 20 years and is simply not reported, the DoJ appears not to have given consideration to whether this may better be explained by the discussions below regarding other positive influences on the contractor community and the use of other approaches to address findings of noncompliance with law.

H-3

General Services Administration
January 18, 2008
Page 4

The Section believes a more careful analysis of the status of compliance programs will reveal that there has not been an overall decrease in contractor disclosures of violations of law. Although electing not to seek admission to the DoD IG Voluntary Disclosure Program, consistent with the program's voluntary nature, contractor disclosures continue to be made by other means – directly to contracting officers or heads of contracting activities, or to audit agencies like DCAA and DCMA, or to other disclosure programs that are more relevant to the kinds of illegality being found these days, such as those maintained by the DoJ Antitrust division and by the Department of State Directorate of Defense Trade Controls ("DDTC"). These disclosures are consistent with the voluntary disclosure policies many contractors have adopted as part of their ethics and compliance programs and do not reflect decreased vigilance or willingness to report illegality when appropriate. Indeed, the Section understands that in recent years voluntary disclosures to the DDTC regarding export control violations are very common and have increased as disclosures to the DoD IG program have decreased (*see* GAO-05-234 (Feb. 2005)), and that the DoJ Antitrust division's Corporate Leniency Program likewise has been very successful at inducing voluntary disclosures. *See* http://www.usdoj.gov/atr/public/speeches/227740.htm. Enforcement actions for violations of the Foreign Corrupt Practices Act also have grown, again largely due to voluntary disclosures made by corporations. *See* "U.S. Targets Bribery Overseas Globalization, Reforms Give Rise to Spike in Prosecutions," *The Washington Post* (Dec. 5, 2007).

Further, in recent years the DoJ program has not been very effective in achieving timely resolution of disclosures, and a further concern that the program often results in DoJ pursuit of the full consequences of all matters disclosed through criminal, civil or administrative actions, resulting in limited net benefit from the voluntary disclosure.

Thus, the growth in disclosures elsewhere, without similar growth in the DoD IG Voluntary Disclosure Program, suggests the Program's uncertain consequences may be persuading contractors to pursue other disclosure alternatives. Indeed, it appears more likely that the trend of the Program to trigger aggressive enforcement reactions rather than keeping open the possibility of cooperative resolutions and reduced penalties (such as more reliance on administrative remedies or no trebling of penalties in appropriate cases, as occurred more often in the early years of the Program) has put it in disfavor. The Section suggests that a better alternative would be to reassess and revise the Voluntary Disclosure Program rather than impose a new program as envisioned in the Proposed Rule.

General Services Administration
January 18, 2008
Page 5

The Section believes that the increased emphasis on compliance over the past decades also has resulted in a decrease in the number of reportable issues – matters are addressed and resolved before they can become major fraud matters. Thus more issues are being resolved quickly and administratively under particular contracts rather than growing over time into major compliance issues. Thus, decreasing use of the Voluntary Disclosure Program reflects the greatly enhanced contractor compliance programs implemented since the Voluntary Disclosure Program began. Common sense would suggest that, at some point, there would be a natural, and indeed desired, decline in Voluntary Disclosure reports as contractors put in place effectively-operated compliance and training programs, which were virtually non-existent in 1986 but are generally quite robust now (and have been so for over a decade). Indeed if voluntary disclosures stayed at the levels of the late 1980s and early 1990s, it would be an indication that the preventative effects of sound contractor training and compliance programs were not being realized. Section members who have been involved with training and compliance programs at the company level have witnessed the seriousness with which these programs are regarded and can attest to the impact these programs have in preventing the need for disclosures. These programs are working and have generally been working for quite some time.

Thus even if DoJ were correct regarding a claimed decrease in contractor participation in the DoD IG Voluntary Disclosure Program, it has not demonstrated a need for the proposed mandatory disclosure rule. Before such a major rule is adopted, the Section recommends that DoJ should offer factual support for its thesis that crimes are occurring and being found and yet not being reported voluntarily, and further should explain why other less burdensome changes – such as improving the existing voluntary disclosure programs – cannot be used to achieve the desired results.

B. The Proposed Rule Does Not Address Overlap and Inconsistency With Existing Disclosure Regimes

The existing regulatory and statutory schemes in place to encourage government contractors and other corporations to voluntarily disclose criminal behavior provide ample incentive to contractors and suggest that the mandatory disclosure requirement of the Proposed Rule would contribute little, if any, overall improvement in the number of disclosures made to the Government. The present regulatory system encourages government contractors to self-report wrongdoing by providing mitigating credit in suspension/debarment and criminal proceedings for such disclosures. Indeed, the Proposed Rule's mandatory disclosure scheme is sufficiently inconsistent with the present voluntary disclosure incentives that it could be viewed as making government contractors incapable of making

General Services Administration
January 18, 2008
Page 6

"voluntary" disclosures that other regulatory and statutory schemes seek to encourage. This would be an unfortunate consequence of the Proposed Rule.

1. **Existing Suspension And Debarment Regulations Provide Strong Incentives For Contractors To Voluntarily Disclose Criminal Behavior**

Pursuant to the FAR requirements that a prospective contractor be presently responsible, a contractor must demonstrate, *inter alia*, "a satisfactory record of integrity and business ethics." FAR 9.104-1(d). Under the FAR suspension and debarment provisions, the Government may assess a *de facto* blanket determination of non-responsibility when a contractor commits fraud or a criminal violation in connection with a federal contract. *See* FAR 9.406-2(a)(1) (Debarment); 9.407-2(a)(1) (Suspension).

As noted in the FAR, however, suspension and debarment are "serious" steps that are not to be imposed for "purposes of punishment," but "only in the public interest for the Government's protection." FAR 9.402(b). Suspension and debarment are therefore not intended as automatic responses but, instead, are protective measures that should be taken only after deliberative consideration of a host of designated mitigating factors and the exercise of due discretion. Mitigating factors may enable a contractor to demonstrate that, notwithstanding its underlying wrongdoing, the contractor is presently responsible. Suspension and debarment are inherently discretionary acts of the agency officials based on their judgment as to the pertinent circumstances. *See* FAR 9.406-1(a) (Debarment); FAR 9.407-1(b)(2) (Suspension).

Among the most important mitigating factors that the Government must consider in a debarment proceeding, and may consider in a suspension proceeding, is whether the contractor has voluntarily disclosed the grounds for suspension or debarment:

> The existence of a cause for debarment, however, does not necessarily require the contractor to be debarred; the seriousness of the contractor's acts or omissions and any remedial measures or mitigating factors should be considered . . . such as . . .
>
> > (2) Whether the contractor brought the activity cited as a cause for debarment to the attention of the appropriate Government agency in a timely manner [and]

H-6

General Services Administration
January 18, 2008
Page 7

> (3) Whether the contractor has fully investigated the circumstances surrounding the cause for debarment and, if so, made the result of the investigation available to the debarring official.

FAR 9.406-1(a) (Debarment); FAR 9.407-1(b)(2) (Suspension).

Given the prominence of disclosure as a mitigating factor for both debarment and suspension, contractors already have a substantial incentive to voluntarily disclose the same violations of federal criminal law that the Proposed Rule's mandatory disclosure requirement is geared toward.

The Proposed Rule's mandatory disclosure requirement would supersede a contractor's ability to voluntarily disclose the same wrongdoing and could be viewed as effectively eliminating the above-quoted two mitigating factors available for the Government's consideration in any suspension/debarment proceeding. Thus, not only would the mandatory disclosure requirement impose an unnecessary burden on contractors, it could also contradict the existing suspension/debarment scheme. The Section believes that the Proposed Rule inappropriately seeks to elevate suspension and debarment from its protective role to that of a penalty. In the absence of an authorizing statute, such a result well may be invalid. In any event, the claim of need for mandatory disclosure does not establish a statutory basis for it.

2. The Federal Sentencing Guidelines Provide Strong Incentives For Contractors To Voluntarily Disclose Criminal Behavior

Contractors also have a strong incentive to voluntarily disclose violations of federal criminal law because they can achieve dramatically-reduced penalties under the Federal Sentencing Guidelines for doing so. *See* U.S. Guidelines Manual, § 8C2.5(g). Because this incentive applies only if the corporate disclosure is rendered "prior to an imminent threat of disclosure or government investigation," timely voluntary disclosure by the contractor is critical to establish eligibility for this relief. *Id.*

The Proposed Rule could make it more difficult for a government contractor to be deemed to have made any "voluntary disclosure" under the Federal Sentencing Guidelines. A disclosure made in accordance with the Proposed Rule would arguably not be a "voluntary" disclosure. The Proposed Rule may therefore cast doubt on government contractors' ability to fully participate in the sentencing regimen established by Congress and implemented by the U.S. Sentencing Commission, and further, may contradict Congressional intent in enacting these policies regarding voluntary disclosures.

General Services Administration
January 18, 2008
Page 8

Further, because the Proposed Rule could effectively write out of the Sentencing Guidelines the benefits of voluntary disclosure, it is not 'more' consistent with the Sentencing Guidelines than the current compliance regime, as suggested in the supporting discussion for the Proposed Rule, but actually contradicts them. *See* 72 Fed. Reg. 64019.

3. The False Claims Act Provides Strong Incentives For Contractors To Voluntarily Disclose Fraudulent Behavior

The FCA also provides contractors with an incentive to report potentially fraudulent behavior. The FCA authorizes private individuals to file *qui tam* actions on behalf of the Government in those instances where the private relator has non-public information regarding contractor fraudulent billing or claims. Even in cases in which the Government does not elect to intervene and prosecute a FCA claim itself, *qui tam* actions can be costly and damaging to contractors.

Where a contractor knows of potential false claims exposure, it is often in the contractor's best interest to voluntarily disclose such wrongdoing to the Government because, *inter alia,* such disclosures can trigger the "public disclosure" bar to *qui tam* suits. While *qui tam* suits are frequently litigated in costly public litigation, a contractor's early disclosure to the Government can foster mutually-agreeable settlement among all the interested parties with little to no damaging public exposure.

Furthermore, voluntary disclosure under the FCA can dramatically reduce the potential liability of a contractor in the event the Government ultimately pursues a FCA claim. Rather than facing a per-event penalty of $5,500 to $11,000 and treble damages, a contractor that makes a voluntary disclosure pursuant to 31 U.S.C. § 3729(a) can reduce its potential liability to double damages. The benefits of voluntary disclosure can be substantial, and provide a strong incentive for contractors to make a voluntary disclosure of fraudulent behavior.

Finally, as with the Federal Sentencing Guidelines, the mandatory nature of the Proposed Rule again may call into question whether any disclosure would qualify as "voluntary" under the FCA, and therefore may reduce contractors' incentive to make such disclosures.

4. The Proposed Rule May Eliminate Important Incentives To Voluntarily Disclose Wrongdoing

As suggested above, the Proposed Rule may eliminate any mitigation that contractors might obtain in suspension/debarment, criminal, or FCA proceedings

General Services Administration
January 18, 2008
Page 9

by virtue of voluntarily disclosing wrongdoing. As a consequence, especially in cases involving serious fraud or criminal behavior, the Proposed Rule might actually create a perverse incentive for contractors to *refrain* from disclosing wrongdoing, notwithstanding the mandatory reporting mechanism. This is so because in those cases where suspension or debarment is the likely result of the contractor's underlying behavior requiring disclosure, the penalty for failing to disclose the underlying behavior may be no different: the risk of non-disclosure (*i.e.*, potential suspension/debarment) is no different from the risk of waiting to see if the Government detects the underlying wrongdoing on its own. Thus, without the incentive of some sort of consideration for a voluntary disclosure – through which the contractor might be able to avoid or reduce the impact of suspension or debarment through proactive voluntary steps – contractors may be inclined not to report wrongdoing. The Section believes such a result, albeit unintended, is not good public policy.

By eliminating these incentives, the Proposed Rule could cause contractors to adopt a protective posture in the face of evidence of potential criminal behavior, rather than pursuing disclosure. The Proposed Rule does not reflect consideration of these concerns or evaluation of the extent to which eliminating incentives to voluntary disclosure will affect a contractor's decision to disclose underlying behavior—mandatory or not.

5. Current Mandatory Disclosure Programs Are Not Instructive

DoJ cites to a number of existing statutory mandatory disclosure programs as support for the promulgation of the Proposed Rule, and also points to the National Reconnaissance Office's (NRO) claims regarding its own contractual disclosure program. However, in the Section's view this reliance is misplaced, as those programs are targeted towards a particular public need, and in most cases are the product of legislation that was enacted in response to a specific scandal or important national need. The Proposed Rule lacks both a targeted particular public need or statutory authority.

First, most of the mandatory programs which DoJ cites to support the need to promulgate the sweeping, government-wide mandatory disclosure program of the Proposed Rule were the product of legislation – Sarbanes Oxley, the Anti-Kickback Act, and the Foreign Corrupt Practices Act, and banking laws. In enacting these statutory schemes, Congress saw a particular need and targeted legislation to address that particular need. The result was not a sweeping and burdensome program but a specific and narrow requirement. The Anti-Kickback Act and Foreign Corrupt Practices Act, for example, limit their mandatory disclosure provisions to a very limited class of activity and present therefore a

General Services Administration
January 18, 2008
Page 10

limited burden on covered companies. These DoJ examples further contemplate at least some careful review and investigation by reporting entities before reports are made — Sarbanes Oxley, for example, contemplates internal reporting mechanisms and review mechanisms involving management at the highest levels before any reporting occurs, without a pre-emptive trigger of "whenever there is reasonable basis to believe" as in the Proposed Rule.

Second, in general, these mandatory disclosure programs were enacted by Congress in response to one or more specific scandals or series of scandals. The broadest of these legislative fixes, Sarbanes Oxley, came in response to perhaps the greatest series of corporate scandals and omissions the post-Depression era has ever seen. Untold numbers of innocent people were demonstrably and permanently damaged by the corporate scandals; Congress had to act, and it did, in a way that was targeted to prevent the specific problems that surfaced during the scandals.

Similarly, while the NRO's mandatory disclosure program was not the product of legislation, it was the direct product of an obvious and public awareness that we live in a different world after 9/11, and after some of the limited number of lapses that have occurred in the classified world in recent years. In fact, the unique nature of the NRO and its responsibilities are major reasons cited as justification for its disclosure program.

Further, it is far from clear at this point whether the NRO mandatory disclosure program is or will be productive.[4] However, it is quite evident that the NRO program is implemented in the world of classified contracts and anti-terrorism, again, an area in which both Congress and the Administration have made specific findings and are attempting to employ every possible tool to enhance national security, circumstances which are not present when promulgating a procurement rule of general applicability such as the Proposed Rule. The Section further notes that the NRO clause was not subject to notice and comment.

Similar justifications have not been proffered for the Proposed Rule. The mandatory disclosure provisions in the Proposed Rule are neither the product of specific Congressional findings or legislation nor any perceived critical national need and thus are not appropriately compared to other existing mandatory disclosure programs.

---

[4] The Section understands that at least some affected government contractors believe that the NRO's mandatory disclosure program suffers from the same defects that attend the sweeping mandatory disclosure program that is advanced in the Proposed Rule. Anecdotal reports from the contractor community suggest the program is not as effective as the NRO may claim and is extremely burdensome.

General Services Administration
January 18, 2008
Page 11

6. **Overpayments Are A Matter Of Contract Administration And Should Not Be Grounds For Suspension Or Debarment**

In a July 1999 report, GAO raised a concern that at the time there was "no requirement for contractors who have been overpaid to notify the government of overpayments or to return overpayments prior to the government issuing a demand letter." GAO/NSIAD-99-131 at 1 (July 1999). In 2002, the FAR Council responded by adding the requirement in FAR Clause 52.232-25(d) that contractors report overpayments:

> Overpayments. If the Contractor becomes aware of a duplicate contract financing or invoice payment or that the Government has otherwise overpaid on a contract financing or invoice payment, the Contractor shall immediately notify the Contracting Officer and request instructions for disposition of the overpayment.

See also 66 Fed. Reg. 65353 (Dec. 18, 2001). A year later, the FAR Council extended this requirement to commercial item contracts. *See* FAR Clause 52.212-4(i)(5); 68 Fed. Reg. 56682 (Oct. 1, 2003). Within this scheme, overpayments have, until now, been a matter of contract administration. *See* FAR 12.215 and FAR 32.008 (requiring Contracting Officer to oversee disposition of overpayment); FAR 52.216-7(g) (authorizing the Contracting Officer to audit contractor's invoices for overpayment); FAR 15.407-1(b)(7)(iii) (authorizing Contracting Officer to assess penalties for knowing submission of defective cost or pricing data resulting in overpayment).

In view of the obligations imposed on contractors and the remedies provided to the Government in these FAR provisions, it is the Section's view there is no need to specifically create additional suspension and debarment triggers to maintain the integrity of the procurement process with respect to overpayments. Although the Proposed Rule includes such an additional ground for suspension or debarment, it provides no predicate establishing either (i) the need for such a rule or (ii) the need to treat overpayments as anything other than a matter of contract administration.

First, this new basis for suspension or debarment comes with no explanation, and it is unclear how or why contractor notification of overpayments is related to the other issues of contractor integrity or compliance programs addressed elsewhere in the Proposed Rule, or why this rule is necessary to improve the procurement process at all. In addition, the Proposed Rule does not connect overpayments to the criminal law violations upon which the rest of the Proposed Rule is focused. Except for the brief statement that the new basis for suspension or

H-11

General Services Administration
January 18, 2008
Page 12

debarment was "requested by DoJ," the FAR Council has not indicated any reason to propose this severe sanction for overpayments. Furthermore, there is no demonstration that present FAR provisions requiring the disclosure of overpayments are ineffective, or that the FAR Council (or DoJ, for that matter) expects the additional threat of suspension or debarment to materially improve reporting of overpayments under the existing regulatory regime.

Second, there is no explanation why overpayments need to be treated as anything other than matters of contract administration, as they traditionally have been. To the extent the Proposed Rule may have been intended to focus upon disclosure of fraudulently-induced overpayments, the resulting language is much too broad and makes no distinction between the normal business of contract administration and criminal behavior. This question is of particular concern because, as noted above, the FAR Council looked at issues involving contract overpayments as recently as 2003 and determined at that time to treat overpayments strictly as a matter of contract administration, not suspension or debarment. The Section respectfully suggests that if the FAR Council is revisiting this determination, there should be an accompanying explanation and justification.

Ultimately, the Section believes that the Proposed Rule does not contain an adequate showing that the present procedure for contractor reporting of overpayments is ineffective or requires enhancement. Mandatory disclosure provisions have been in effect for more than five years, and the FAR Council and DoJ have not shown that the present reporting mechanisms do not adequately result in proper disclosures and resolutions of overpayments. The Section notes that the Proposed Rule provides no evidence, empirical or otherwise, to suggest that contractor overpayments are systemically unreported or that additional measures would improve the information reported to the Government. Accordingly, there is neither a demonstrated need for this provision of the Proposed Rule; nor any likely benefit from its implementation. Accordingly, in the Section's judgment, this provision of the Proposed Rule should be withdrawn.

C. The Mandatory Disclosure Provision Will Result In Increased Burdens On Contractors And The Government

The Proposed Rule will impose a highly burdensome obligation on contractors — to make their own assessments whether there has been a violation of federal criminal law that must be disclosed. This places responsibility on a contractor to make the decision whether a federal criminal violation or some lesser civil or administrative violation has occurred, and whether it is related in some manner to a federal contract or subcontract. Each element of that analysis is subject to discretionary judgments — deciding whether an act is criminal involves

General Services Administration
January 18, 2008
Page 13

assessment of available facts, weighing countervailing theories, determining whether all elements of a crime are present and what facts are sufficient to establish intent or reckless disregard versus negligence. While there will be obvious cases where only one conclusion is possible, the reality is that most cases that will require this analysis will not be clear, and the conclusion about criminality will not be obvious. Each will require careful assessment, and more importantly, each will expose contractors to possible suspension or debarment under the Proposed Rule if government investigators later disagree with a contractor's conclusion – however reasonable – that a criminal violation did not occur.

Under the current voluntary disclosure programs, a contractor has the flexibility to make assessments about whether violations of law constitute criminal conduct, and whether such potential criminal conduct could be addressed without initiating a formal voluntary disclosure. The contractor can assess the risks and benefits of disclosure through various alternatives, without risking further consequences from that decision alone. Under the Proposed Rule, where suspension or debarment awaits those whose judgments about criminality and reporting methods are challenged by the government, contractors that doubt whether conduct rises to the level of disclosure as criminal conduct would necessarily have to err on the side of reporting even the least suspicious of events, which would impose significant burdens on the contractor as well as on federal agencies.

Effectively requiring that every potential violation be reported also will tie up government resources unnecessarily. With a mandatory disclosure requirement and a contractor need to minimize risk of debarment, the government is at risk of being inundated with minor allegations that will have to be sorted through before the truly significant problems can be identified and addressed. In addition, the contractor and government expenses (both in terms of time and money) to implement such a sweeping disclosure program will increase with the need to investigate, disclose, and address every potential issue under the Proposed Rule. While the Section does not oppose the government expending resources where a true need is identified and benefits will be achieved, there is no indication that the mandatory disclosure requirement does either.

Finally, the new reporting regime would impair the procurement systems of the government. Assuming contractors err on the side of reporting even minor matters to reduce risk, the Inspector General will be required to investigate each such matter and then refer the matter to DoJ, under the same standard. This new reporting regime will deprive the Contracting Officer of his or her authority to manage many contract issues, even those matters for which there is only a slight chance of actual criminality. This has the potential to add months or even years to

General Services Administration
January 18, 2008
Page 14

the process of sorting out even the least significant of noncompliance issues, and to transfer responsibility for such routine compliance matters away from the contracting personnel who are most knowledgeable about the impact of compliance issues on program needs.

D.   **The Initial Regulatory Flexibility Analysis Does Not Fully Identify And Address The Burdens The Proposed Rule Will Impose On Small Business**

   1.   **The Proposed Rule's Disproportionate Impact on Small Business is Not Recognized**

The Section notes favorably that the Proposed Rule specifically exempts small businesses from the requirement to have a formal ethics awareness program and an internal control system, a provision appearing reasonable to the Section. The letter from the DoJ Criminal Division to the Administrator of the Office of Federal Procurement Policy (OFPP) dated May 23, 2007, makes note of this. Nevertheless, the Section notes that the Proposed Rule's primary enforcement mechanism – suspension or debarment – will necessarily have a disproportionate impact on small businesses. First, small businesses generally do not have the same financial, human, or other resources as large businesses to institute the substantial compliance programs compelled by the Proposed Rule. Further, unlike their large business counterparts, many small businesses serve in a less critical role in the procurement process and, thus, lack the leverage to negotiate agreements in lieu of debarment. The very real likelihood, therefore, is that small businesses will bear the brunt of the suspension/debarment remedy postulated in the Proposed Rule. Thus, the Proposed Rule's reliance upon suspension and debarment as an enforcement mechanism for implementation of much more substantial compliance and disclosure measures than they currently are required to maintain has the potential to disproportionately damage small business interests, a disparate outcome that is not reflected in the Regulatory Flexibility Analysis.

   2.   **Regulatory Flexibility Analysis Requirements**

Although the FAR Council conducted an initial regulatory flexibility analysis ("IRFA") in support of the Proposed Rule, as summarized at 72 Fed. Reg. 64020-21, the IRFA does not adequately address all of the factors required to be considered under the Regulatory Flexibility Act ("RFA"), 5 U.S.C. § 603. In particular, the IRFA:

   (i)   does not evaluate adequately the Rule's compliance costs or the number of small entities to which the rule will apply;

General Services Administration
January 18, 2008
Page 15

(ii) does not articulate the need for the Proposed Rule;

(iii) does not estimate adequately the projected reporting, recordkeeping and other compliance requirements of the rule; and

(iv) does not consider the extent to which the Proposed Rule overlaps other rules.

As a consequence, full consideration has not been given to the substantial impacts of the Proposed Rule on small businesses, as required by law. The Section believes that the IRFA is invalid for this reason and the Proposed Rule should be withdrawn pending further examination and explanation.

a. **The IRFA Does Not Adequately Evaluate The Proposed Rule's Compliance Costs Or Reasonably Estimate The Number Of Small Businesses Affected By The Proposed Rule**

The RFA was enacted to "require[] an agency promulgating a rule to consider the effect of the proposed regulation on small businesses and to design mechanisms to minimize any adverse consequences." *Southern Offshore Fishing Ass'n v. Daley*, 995 F. Supp. 1411, 1433 (M.D. Fla. 1998). To ensure that this goal is met, the RFA requires an agency to conduct an IRFA before it may issue a rule which is expected to have a "significant economic impact on a substantial number of small entities." 5 U.S.C. § 605(b).

The primary shortcoming with the IRFA for the Proposed Rule is the disconnect between the FAR Council's conclusion, on the one hand, that "[t]he changes may have a *significant economic impact on a substantial number of small entities* within the meaning of the Regulatory Flexibility Act," and its finding, on the other hand, that the Proposed Rule's mandatory reporting requirement is *not* expected "to be a significant burden on small businesses, because it *only impacts those small businesses that need to report* violations of Federal criminal law in connection with the award or performance of a Government contract." 72 Fed. Reg. at 64020-21 (emphasis added). The inconsistency in these two findings suggests that the IRFA focused *solely* on the burdens associated with *actually reporting* violations of law (which were deemed minimal) and did not address the significant costs and burdens required to establish and maintain the comprehensive compliance program needed to fully comply with the rule, even when a mandatory disclosure is ultimately determined not to be required.

As a result of this narrow focus, the FAR Council estimated that the new rule would affect *only 28 small businesses* in the course of a year pursuant to the

General Services Administration
January 18, 2008
Page 16

mandatory disclosure requirements of the proposed FAR 52.203-XX(b)(3). 72 Fed. Reg. at 64021. This number is strikingly low. The estimate considers only "the number of small business concerns that will be required to submit the report of violation of Federal criminal law with regard to a Government contract or subcontracts." *Id.* Thus, the IRFA does not address the extent to which small businesses will be required to expend financial and managerial resources to determine whether allegations or suspicions of wrongdoing are covered by the mandatory disclosure requirement or not. For example, the IRFA does not consider the substantial time and expense associated with a small business's determination of whether an allegation or suspicion of potential wrongdoing (i) rises to the level of "reasonable grounds" requiring disclosure, (ii) is a "violation of Federal criminal law," or (iii) is "in connection with the award or performance" of a federal contract.

The Section believes that there is a misconception inherent in the IRFA -- that small businesses will spend time and resources to comply with the proposed FAR 52.203-XX(b)(3) *only* when they actually have a reporting obligation. For every company that discloses a wrongdoing under the mandatory requirement, however, many more will confront situations involving allegations or suspicions of wrongdoing that do not ultimately require disclosure under the Proposed Rule. The company will be required to expend substantial human and financial resources to determine whether the alleged wrongdoing falls within the scope of the Proposed Rule even if it ultimately determines it does not. Perhaps most significantly, the limited resources of small businesses will necessarily be diverted to conducting internal investigations, often requiring the commitment of time by senior management and other employees and the significant expense of engaging outside legal counsel. Contractors are not experts in federal criminal law and will likely require the advice and assistance of legal counsel to determine if a "violation of Federal criminal law" is even at issue. Many small businesses may find the cost of outside legal advice and assistance to be unduly burdensome.

Thus, the conclusion in the IRFA that only an estimated 28 small businesses would be affected per year by the Proposed Rule is unreasonable because the subset of contractors on which the IRFA focused is too narrow. The Section believes the lack of consideration of the significant necessary effort prior to any reporting results in an underestimation of the magnitude of the business impact that the Proposed Rule would have on small business entities.

        b.   **There Is No Demonstrated Need for the Proposed Rule and the IRFA Does Not Articulate One**

The RFA requires that an IRFA include "a description of the reasons why action by the agency is being considered." 5 U.S.C. § 603(b)(1). In this case, and

General Services Administration
January 18, 2008
Page 17

as discussed above, the IRFA does not reflect a rational basis for the decision to undertake the proposed changes, other than the brief statement that "[t]his case is in response to a request to the Office of Federal Procurement Policy from the Department of Justice." 72 Fed. Reg. at 64019. There is no empirical or anecdotal evidence to explain why the mandatory disclosure requirement is required for the proper functioning of the procurement system.

The IRFA states, without explanation or justification, that in the absence of the proposed disclosure requirement, "only 1 percent of those contractors/subcontractors that are aware of a violation of Federal criminal law in regard to the contract or subcontract will voluntarily report such violation to the contracting officer." 72 Fed. Reg. at 64021. The one percent figure used in the IRFA suggests that the FAR Council believes that the mandatory disclosure requirement could lead to a 100-fold increase in the number of reported violations above those that are reported under the present voluntary disclosure system. Nothing in the IRFA, however, supports this estimate. Thus, there is no rational basis to support a claim that this disclosure requirement is needed for the effective functioning of the procurement system.

  c. **The Projected Recordkeeping And Compliance Requirements Are Far More Burdensome Than Reflected In The IRFA**

Under the RFA, an IRFA must include "a description of the projected reporting, recordkeeping and other compliance requirements of the Proposed Rule, including an estimate of the classes of small entities which will be subject to the requirement and the type of professional skills necessary for preparation of the report or record . . . ." 5 U.S.C. § 603(b)(4). The IRFA also does not reflect this RFA requirement.[5]

In analyzing the compliance requirements of the Proposed Rule, the IRFA only repeats the reporting requirement of the Proposed Rule and suggests that the report "would probably be prepared by company management, and would probably involve legal assistance to prepare." 72 Fed. Reg. at 64021. Pursuant to the requirements of the RFA, however, an analysis must be done of the recordkeeping or compliance burdens that the Proposed Rule would impose.

Considering the severe suspension/debarment sanction that a contractor may face under the Proposed Rule, contractors (with some exceptions for small businesses) will be required to establish comprehensive compliance programs and

---

[5] The Section notes that the underestimation of burden applies equally to the Paperwork Reduction Act analysis at 72 Fed. Reg. at 64020-21.

General Services Administration
January 18, 2008
Page 18

maintain extensive records any time they investigate allegations or suspicions of such violations. Even if a company determines that disclosure is not required, the contractor must still document its investigation to enable it to demonstrate later the *bona fides* of its investigation and explain why it did not believe that there had been a violation of federal criminal law that required disclosure. If the contractor fails to keep adequate records of its decision-making process, and it is later determined that the contractor was in fact required to disclose the purported wrongdoing, the contractor would be hampered in defending itself against a threatened suspension/debarment.

Thus, good business sense will require that contractors develop and keep far more extensive records to comply with the Proposed Rule than the reporting function set forth in the IRFA. Notwithstanding this practical implication of the Proposed Rule, the IRFA has not addressed these compliance and recordkeeping functions that the Proposed Rule will require, focusing on the limited instances in which an actual report to the Government disclosing wrongdoing is required. Because a report to the Government likely will be involved in only a minority of instances in which contractors investigate suspicions or allegations of wrongdoing, the compliance requirements addressed in the IRFA do not reflect the entirety of the compliance obligations imposed. In this regard, the Section views the IRFA as incomplete and lacking a reasonable estimation of the compliance requirements that contractors will face.

d. **The IRFA Does Not Consider Adequately The Overlap Or Conflict With Numerous Federal Laws**

Under the RFA, the FAR Council is required to "identify[y], to the extent practicable, all relevant Federal rules which may duplicate, overlap, or conflict with the proposed rule." 5 U.S.C. § 603(b)(5). In this case, the Council concluded that "[t]he rule does not duplicate, overlap, or conflict with any other Federal rules." 72 Fed. Reg. at 64021. In the Section's judgment, this conclusion is incorrect. As discussed more fully below, the IRFA does not address the inconsistency between the Proposed Rule and the Federal Sentencing Guidelines, existing suspension and debarment regulations, and the False Claims Act ("FCA"), 31 U.S.C. § 3729 *et seq.*

First, the Proposed Rule is inconsistent with the Federal Sentencing Guidelines. Despite the statement in the Preamble to the Proposed Rule that it was intended to harmonize, or "more closely match" with the Federal Sentencing Guidelines, the mandatory disclosure requirement not only deviates from the Guidelines, but it would preempt and nullify important mitigating consideration given in the Guidelines to the voluntary disclosure of corporate criminal action. *See* U.S. Guidelines Manual, § 8C2.5(g). Under the Proposed Rule's mandatory

General Services Administration
January 18, 2008
Page 19

disclosure scheme, a government contractor could not make a *voluntary* disclosure of the type contemplated by the mitigation provisions of the Guidelines, thereby eliminating a contractor's ability to fully participate in the Federal Sentencing Guideline process.

Second, the mandatory disclosure requirement is inconsistent with the mitigation considerations established in the FAR for debarment or suspension proceedings. Consistent with the Federal Sentencing Guidelines, the FAR suspension and debarment provisions require the Government to consider voluntary disclosures of contractor wrong-doing as a mitigating factor in any debarment proceeding (and may give consideration in a suspension proceeding). *See* FAR 9.406-1(a) (Debarment); FAR 9.407-1(b)(2) (Suspension). In requiring mandatory disclosure of criminal conduct, the Proposed Rule would eliminate a contractor's long-standing ability to receive mitigating credit for a voluntary disclosure in any resulting suspension or debarment proceeding.

Third, the mandatory disclosure requirement would eliminate an important incentive for voluntary disclosure under the FCA. Presently, a contractor that voluntarily discloses false claims can reduce its damage exposure from treble damages to double damages, and can avoid entirely substantial per-offense penalties. 31 U.S.C. § 3729(a). The Proposed Rule's mandatory disclosure scheme is inconsistent with those statutory provisions and government contractors would be effectively foreclosed from availing themselves of an important provision of the Act.

The IRFA, however, does not address these conflicts, and, as a consequence, the IRFA is incomplete and lacks a proper assessment of the likely impact of the rule on small businesses. In addition, the focus of the IRFA is too narrow, and the analysis relies on assumptions and estimates regarding the nature of the Proposed Rule's impact on small businesses that in the Section's opinion are unsupportable.

For these reasons, the Section believes that the Proposed Rule is not in accordance with the law and should be withdrawn so that the impacts on small businesses can be fully and adequately considered.

E. The Vagueness Of The Proposed Rule Will Cause Implementation Problems And Raises Possible Constitutional Concerns

The Proposed Rule provides unduly vague mandates for disclosure of matters with criminal penalties, under threat of suspension or debarment. A rule with insufficient standards as to what is considered a discloseable violation, or when that duty to disclose will arise, poses the risk of creating more harm than good. The Section believes that the Proposed Rule should be rewritten to define more clearly what is reportable and when the obligation to report is triggered.

Specifically, the Proposed Rule provides that:

> The Contractor shall notify, in writing, the agency Office of Inspector General, with a copy to the Contracting Officer, whenever the Contractor has reasonable grounds to believe that a principal, employee, agent or subcontractor of the Contractor has committed a violation of Federal criminal law in connection with the award or performance of this contract or any subcontract thereunder.

Proposed Rule at 52.203-XX(b)(3). Further, a contractor could be suspended or debarred for:

> Knowing failure to timely disclose -- (A) An overpayment on a Government contract; or (B) Violation of Federal criminal law in connection with the award or performance of any Government contract or subcontract.

Proposed Rule at 9.406 2(b)(1)(v) and 9.407-2(a)(7).

Both provisions use sweeping language with severe potential consequences, without providing sufficient clarity. For example:

- The Proposed Rule does not define what constitutes a possible criminal violation that would require mandatory disclosure. It is not clear whether the Proposed Rule intends to encompass all felonies and misdemeanors of any nature.

- The standard of "reasonable grounds to believe" a criminal violation has occurred is also too vague. Would a contractor be forced to disclose something that appears "reasonable" before it has had the opportunity to investigate an allegation made through an anonymous hotline complaint? Or does "reasonable" allow a company to conduct an investigation of the complaint to determine whether such an allegation had any substance? The Proposed Rule does not specify when in the commission, discovery and investigation continuum there would be sufficient knowledge to require a disclosure.

    ⇒ Where virtually any performance error has the potential for criminal consequences under the FCA or the False Statements Act, the line between disclosing every possible violation that

General Services Administration
January 18, 2008
Page 21

- someone might claim could be treated as a criminal violation — billing errors, misreported time, quality issues and the routine business of administering contracts — and disclosing truly criminal behavior is far from clear.

- Prosecutors and contractors will surely differ regarding what is a "reasonable" belief that a criminal violation has occurred, which creates the potential for misunderstandings and abuse.

- The Proposed Rule is silent as to who within the contractor entity would have to have knowledge sufficient to establish the "knowing" standard for a contractor. Would a contractor be subject to punishment for nondisclosure where only a lower-level employee has reasonable knowledge that someone else has violated criminal law? To punish the contractor — a corporate body — the Proposed Rule at least should require specific knowledge of a particular criminal violation by someone at a significant managerial level, before a contractor could be punished for a "knowing" failure to disclose.

- Another potential source of confusion is the interplay of individual and corporate suspension and debarment remedies under the Proposed Rule. For example, if a lower-level employee does not disclose what turns out to be a reportable violation to his or her superiors, will he or she be exposed to individual debarment or suspension if the matter is discovered and reported by others? The Proposed Rule potentially could impose debarment on an employee who merely suspects something is wrong, but may not have the knowledge or training to ascertain whether the problem constitutes a covered "criminal violation." The sweeping disclosure and compliance obligations and the potential for remedies applied to individuals have great potential for misunderstanding.

- The Proposed Rule is silent about whether it is meant to cover past acts or only acts going forward from the effective date the Proposed Rule is incorporated into a contract. To impose a rule that would punish entities going forward for past acts would violate constitutional ex post facto prohibitions.

Accordingly, the Section respectfully suggests that the Proposed Rule will create substantial implementation concerns because of the vagueness of its requirements.

General Services Administration
January 18, 2008
Page 22

In addition, the vagueness of the Proposed Rule may deprive contractors and their employees of their due process rights.

F.   Any Final Rule Must Confirm A Reasonable Scope For "Mandatory Cooperation" With Government Investigations

The Proposed Rule mandates cooperation with the Government. In providing such "cooperation," companies and company employees must be permitted the opportunity to continue their own investigations and preparation of defenses to criminal allegations. The Proposed Rule should make clear that cooperation does not foreclose any contractor rights.

The charging guidelines contained in the Thompson Memorandum (January 2003) were revised in 2006 in recognition of the need to support the "sanctity of attorney-client privilege" and "encourage full and frank communication between corporate employees and their lawyers." *See, e.g.*, Department of Justice Press Release, "U.S. Deputy Attorney General Paul J. McNulty Revises Charging Guidelines for Prosecuting Corporate Fraud," December 12, 2007 (www.usdoj.gov/opa/pr/2006/December/06_odag828.html). Consistent with that announcement by the DoJ, the Proposed Rule should make clear that no waiver of the attorney-client privilege is either required or imputed from the making of a disclosure under the Proposed Rule, and that assertion of the privilege in subsequent proceedings is not a failure to cooperate in an investigation.

In light of the current state of the law on this topic, the Section believes the implication in the Federal Register notice that the privilege should be at risk at all under the Proposed Rule is simply inappropriate. *See* 72 Fed. Reg. at 64020. The attorney-client privilege is a fundamental right that is critical to companies' ability to effectively address compliance issues and should not lightly be dismissed, particularly in a broad-ranging regime that would effectively put at risk all privileged communications about any law that could affect the performance of a government contract.

Similarly, the ability of companies to pursue their own investigations should not be impaired. Generally, companies want to cooperate with proper government investigations into suspected criminal violations within their companies. Indeed, they have a fiduciary duty to do so to protect shareholder/owner interests. At the same time, and for the same reasons, companies need to be able to pursue their own investigations to determine if there are defenses to mitigate or explain the events that resulted in a disclosure of possible criminal activity. It is fundamental to our legal system that the investigation into and preparation of a defense should not be construed as a failure to cooperate.

General Services Administration
January 18, 2008
Page 23

Thus, the Proposed Rule should make clear that "cooperation" does not bar companies from conducting their own investigations, defending themselves and their employees, or indemnifying their employees' defense. Without this clarification, the Proposed Rule will have an undesirable chilling effect on company communications between company employees and counsel. *See* Department of Justice Memorandum, "Principles of Federal Prosecution of Business Organizations," by Deputy Attorney General Paul McNulty (Dec. 12, 2006).

G. The Proposed Rule Will Have A Chilling Effect On Internal Investigations

A further concern is the likely chilling effect of the Proposed Rule on company compliance programs. Communicating the obligation to disclose essentially every event that might be criminal, along with providing appropriate training and other compliance program enhancements, beyond what has already been implemented pursuant to existing FAR requirements, would quickly make clear that reporting even a suspicion will have immediate unpleasant consequences rather than creating an opportunity to improve processes and fix mistakes. This has substantial potential to decrease rather than enhance cooperation with company compliance efforts.

In addition, the likelihood of severe consequences will necessarily change the relationship of the company and its employees. Where the company is obligated to disclose every potentially criminal violation (particularly if it must do so before it has the opportunity to fully investigate and make an informed determination about criminality and responsibility), it will no longer have the benefit of cooperative work with its employees to identify and correct problems – every interview will have the potential of resulting in employees being reported as part of a mandatory disclosure of an apparent criminal violation, just to protect the company. Employee entitlement to counsel under state law or company bylaws, or at least warnings that they may need counsel and reminders that company counsel are not there to protect them, will make matters more cumbersome, slowing and even directly impairing the ability of a company to investigate compliance matters.

Further, where company investigations and reporting are required as a matter of law, the specter of state action arises — and if the company is deemed to be acting on behalf of the Government in investigating and disclosing criminal activity, it is possible that investigative targets would not only be entitled to counsel but also to *Miranda* warnings. The Section notes that a 1986 proposal from DoD to make fraud disclosures mandatory also foundered on state action grounds.

H-23

General Services Administration
January 18, 2008
Page 24

H. The Proposed Rule Does Not Properly Address the Exemption for Commercial Item Vendors and Overseas Contracts

Although the FAR Council has indicated that it does not intend for certain aspects of the Proposed Rule to apply to contracts or subcontracts for "commercial items," the Section is concerned that the rule, as currently drafted, does not clearly reflect that intent. As explained below, the Proposed Rule could be interpreted as subjecting commercial item contractors and subcontractors to the same substantive provisions of the Proposed Rule as non-commercial item contractors — including, most importantly, the provisions requiring contractors to maintain internal policies and controls and report suspected violations of law — because the provisions relating to suspension/ debarment do not exempt commercial item vendors.

Consistent with the approach taken in connection with the recently-issued rule regarding "Contractor Code of Business Ethics and Conduct," FAR Case 2006-007, the FAR Council has indicated that the Proposed Rule is not intended to apply to contracts for commercial items:

> The Councils do *not* recommend application of the *clause* to contracts for the acquisition of commercial items. Requiring commercial contractors to comply with the rule would not be consistent with Public Law 103-355 that requires the acquisition of commercial items to resemble customarily commercial marketplace practices to the maximum extent practicable. Commercial practice encourages, but does not require, contractor codes of business ethics conduct. In particular, the intent of FAR Part 12 is to minimize the number of Government-unique provisions and clauses. The *policy* at FAR 3.1002 of the proposed rule *does apply* to commercial contracts. All Government contractors must conduct themselves with the highest degree of integrity and honesty. However, consistent with the intent of Pub. L. 103-355 and FAR Part 12, the clause mandating specific requirements contractor compliance program and integrity reporting is not required in commercial contracts.

72 Fed. Reg. at 64020 (emphasis added); *see also* 72 Fed. Reg. 65873, 65876 (Nov. 23, 2007) (rejecting suggestions that current contractor ethics and compliance rule should apply to commercial item contractors).

The Section agrees that the Proposed Rule should not apply to contracts or subcontracts for commercial items. But, the rule as currently drafted does not

General Services Administration
January 18, 2008
Page 25

adequately reflect the stated intent to exempt commercial item contracts. First, the only exception for commercial item contracts is contained in proposed section 3.1004, which requires use of a mandatory contract clause in contracts "except when the contract . . . [w]ill be for the acquisition of a commercial item awarded under FAR Part 12 . . . ." 72 Fed. Reg. at 64022. The Proposed Rule would not exempt commercial item contracts from the provisions at proposed section 3.1002, which provides in part that "[a] contractor may be suspended and/or debarred for knowing failure to timely disclose a violation of Federal criminal law in connection with the award or performance of any Government contract performed by the contractor or a subcontract awarded thereunder . . . ." *Id.* Similarly, the Proposed Rule would not exempt commercial item contracts from proposed sections FAR 9.406-2 or FAR 9.407-2, which would subject contractors to suspension or debarment proceedings for "[k]nowing failure to timely disclose--(A) [a]n overpayment on a Government contract; or (B) [v]iolation of Federal criminal law in connection with the award or performance of any Government contract or subcontract." *Id.*

Because commercial item contracts would be explicitly exempt from the mandatory contract clause but would not be explicitly exempt from the provisions regarding suspension and debarment for failure to report suspected misconduct, the Proposed Rule as currently drafted could be interpreted as requiring commercial item contractors to maintain internal policies and controls and/or to report suspected misconduct. The Proposed Rule thus could be interpreted as requiring commercial item contractors and subcontractors to maintain the same mandatory policies, procedures, and internal controls for reporting suspected misconduct as non-commercial item contractors.

In addition, the Proposed Rule may not adequately exempt all acquisitions of commercial items, as it phrases the exemption as limited to FAR Part 12 procurements. *See* Proposed Rule 3.1004. Limited in this manner, the exemption does not include contractors that participate in other procurement methods used to acquire commercial items. By contrast, the Proposed Rule exempts all subcontracts for commercial items and is not limited to those awarded under FAR Part 12-type procedures. To be consistent, the Proposed Rule should make clear that the exemption for commercial item prime contracts covers *all* commercial item prime contracts, not just those awarded under FAR Part 12. *See* Proposed Rule 52.203XX(d).

To the extent that the Proposed Rule could be interpreted as requiring commercial item contractors or subcontractors to adopt specific compliance programs, report suspected misconduct, or both, such a requirement would be contrary to existing statutes and regulations regarding commercial item contracts,

General Services Administration
January 18, 2008
Page 26

which prohibit the use of government-unique terms and conditions and call for the use of terms and conditions that more closely resemble those customarily found in the commercial marketplace. In fact, the FAR Council expressly recognized that "[r]equiring commercial contractors to comply with the rule would not be consistent with Public Law 103-355 that requires the acquisition of commercial items to resemble customarily commercial marketplace practices to the maximum extent practicable." 72 Fed. Reg. at 64020.

The Section respectfully requests that the Proposed Rule be revised to clearly provide an exemption for commercial item contracts and subcontracts in the manner outlined above.

As a final point, the Section notes that the Proposed Rule excludes from its scope contracts performed overseas. Although the Section realizes that some U.S. laws are inapplicable and/or unenforceable overseas, there is no explanation provided as to why a basic policy of a code of ethics and business conduct should not apply to contracts performed overseas, and thus the Section is limited on its ability to comment on this provision.

I. **Adding Disclosure Obligations To Subcontracts Will Adversely Affect Contract Performance And Imposes Inappropriate Burdens On Prime Contractors**

Although contractors and subcontractors need cooperation in contract performance, the threat of debarment or suspension can sour such relationships quickly. The Proposed Rule will create a contractual relationship, via the flowdown of the proposed clause, under which prime contractors will have a contract obligation to ensure their subcontractors perform this aspect of their contract. In expressly contemplating application of the clause to the prime contractor's agreement with its subcontractor, the Proposed Rule mandates that the disclosures go directly to the Government and not through the prime contractor; otherwise, the balance of the contract clause becomes a subcontract performance obligation. This is a significant burden that appears not to have been considered in the drafting of the Proposed Rule.

The flowdown to subcontractors also helps crystallize a significant liability issue (although it is equally applicable with regard to disclosures regarding individuals) – while prosecutors may demand that every possible criminal wrongdoing be disclosed, contractors must worry about potential liability for disclosures concerning subcontractors that turn out to be in error. The consequences of any disclosure are assured to be substantial, even if criminal liability is never found, and the consequences for reasonable but erroneous

General Services Administration
January 18, 2008
Page 27

disclosures may not be significantly less. The FAR Council should consider whether damages assessed against contractors for erroneous reports would be allowable costs. The potential cost burden to the Government of increased indirect costs was not addressed and should be considered before implementing the Proposed Rule.

Also, it is unclear why the Proposed Rule requires disclosure of criminal actions by a prime contractor's principals, employees, or agents, but is less specific about subcontractor violations. To the extent disclosure obligations are imposed, the FAR Council should consider parallel coverage that refers to actions of the contractor's and subcontractor's principals, employees, and agents (at an appropriate managerial level) to limit potential confusion over the scope of the obligations.

Conclusion

As this letter indicates, there is substantial interest within the Section on the proposed rule "Contractor Compliance Program and Integrity Reporting." It is an important subject and deserves careful review and consideration by the FAR Council. The Section appreciates the opportunity to provide these comments and trusts they will be helpful to the FAR Council. The Section is available to provide additional information and assistance as the FAR Council may require.

Sincerely,

Patricia A. Meagher
Chair, Section of Public Contract Law

cc: Michael W. Mutek
Karen L. Manos
Donald G. Featherstun
Carol N. Park Conroy
John S. Pachter
Michael A. Hordell
Robert L. Schaefer
Council Members, Section of Public Contract Law
Chair(s) and Vice Chair(s) of the Professional Responsibility and Contracting Ethics Committee
Scott M. McCaleb
Kara M. Sacilotto

Federal Communications Commission.
Marlene H. Dortch,
Secretary.
[FR Doc. E8–11043 Filed 5–15–08; 8:45 am]
BILLING CODE 6712–01–P

DEPARTMENT OF DEFENSE

GENERAL SERVICES ADMINISTRATION

NATIONAL AERONAUTICS AND SPACE ADMINISTRATION

48 CFR Parts 3, 9, 12, and 52

[FAR Case 2007–006; Docket 2007–0001; Sequence 11]

RIN 9000–AK80

Federal Acquisition Regulation; FAR Case 2007–006, Contractor Compliance Program and Integrity Reporting (2nd Proposed Rule)

AGENCIES: Department of Defense (DoD), General Services Administration (GSA), and National Aeronautics and Space Administration (NASA).

ACTION: Proposed rule; additional changes proposed.

SUMMARY: The Civilian Agency Acquisition Council and the Defense Acquisition Regulations Council (Councils) are seeking comments on changes to the proposed rule, FAR Case 2007–006, Contractor Compliance Program and Integrity Reporting, published in the **Federal Register** at 72 FR 64019, November 14, 2007, for which the initial comment period has closed, that may be included in the final rule. The Councils do not contemplate publishing a final or interim rule until public comments are received and considered on the specific changes discussed further in this document.

DATES: Interested parties should submit written comments to the FAR Secretariat on or before July 15, 2008 to be considered in the formulation of a final rule.

ADDRESSES: Submit comments identified by FAR case 2007–006 by any of the following methods:
• *Regulations.gov: http://www.regulations.gov.*Submit comments via the Federal eRulemaking portal by inputting "FAR Case 2007–006" under the heading "Comment or Submission". Select the link "Send a Comment or Submission" that corresponds with FAR Case 2007–006. Follow the instructions provided to complete the "Public Comment and submission Form". Please include your name, company name (if any), and "FAR Case 2007–006" on your attached document.
• *Fax:* 202–501–4067.
• *Mail:* General Services Administration, Regulatory Secretariat (VPR), 1800 F Street, NW., Room 4041, Washington, DC 20405.

Instructions: Please submit comments only and cite FAR case 2007–006 in all correspondence related to this case. All comments received will be posted without change to *http://www.regulations.gov,* including any personal and/or business confidential information provided.

FOR FURTHER INFORMATION CONTACT: Ernest Woodson, Procurement Analyst, at (202) 501–3775 for clarification of content. For information pertaining to status or publication schedules, contact the FAR Secretariat at (202) 501–4755. Please cite FAR case 2007–006.

SUPPLEMENTARY INFORMATION:

A. Background

The Councils published FAR Case 2007–006, Contractor Compliance Program and Integrity Reporting, as a proposed rule in the **Federal Register** at 72 FR 64019, November 14, 2007. The proposed rule was published, at the request of the Department of Justice (DOJ), in order to—
• Require contractors to have a code of ethics and business conduct;
• Establish and maintain specific internal controls to detect and prevent improper conduct in connection with the award or performance of Government contracts or subcontracts; and
• Notify contracting officers without delay whenever they become aware of violations of Federal criminal law with regard to such contracts or subcontracts.

The proposed rule was a follow-on case to FAR Case 2006–007, published as a final rule in the **Federal Register** on November 23, 2007 (72 FR 65873).

Thirty three respondents commented on the proposed rule. The Councils currently are reviewing the comments and are considering changes to the proposed rule.
• The public and other interested parties have expressed concerns about—
○ The proposed exemption for contracts to be performed entirely outside the United States; and
○ The proposed exemption for contracts for the acquisition of commercial items.
• In addition, the Department of Justice (DOJ) proposes to add a requirement for contractors to report violations of the civil False Claims Act, and add knowing failure to timely report such violations as an additional cause for debarment or suspension to FAR Subpart 9.4.

Therefore, the Councils are seeking comments and recommendations regarding the changes to the proposed rule FAR text listed later in this notice. This notice includes only the sections of the proposed rule affected by these changes, summarized as follows:

(1) *Require inclusion of the clause FAR 52.203–13 in contracts and subcontracts that will be performed outside the United States (see FAR 3.1004 and 52.203–13(d) in the initial proposed rule).* This change would result in making the clause requirements for a contractor code of business ethics and conduct, business ethics awareness and compliance program, and internal control system applicable to contracts performed outside the United States.

The exemption from the requirement to include the clause 52.203–13 in contracts and subcontracts to be performed entirely outside the United States was a carry-over from the proposed and final rules under FAR Case 2006–007, which addressed both contractor code of business ethics and conduct and the use of fraud hotline posters. The final rule under FAR case 2006–007 relied heavily on the Defense Acquisition Regulations System (DFARS) coverage of contractor business ethics and hotline posters (see 48 CFR 203.70 and 48 CFR 252.203–7002). The DFARS clause on hotline posters does not apply to overseas contracts or to commercial items. There is no DFARS clause on contractor code of business ethics and conduct, just recommended guidelines. When the Councils added the clause at FAR 52.203–13 to contractually require a contractor code of business ethics and conduct, the same exemptions as applied to the hotline posters were perpetuated. The proposed rule under 2007–006, which was issued on an extremely expedited basis, did not propose change to the exemption for overseas contracts that was initiated under FAR case 2006–007. After publication of the proposed rule under 2007–006, DOJ and other respondents expressed concern about the overseas exemption.

The Councils note that the proposed rule did not exempt contracts that will be performed entirely outside the United States from all the requirements of the proposed rule. The proposed rule—
• Applied the proposed debarment/suspension for knowing failure to timely disclose an overpayment on a Government contract or violations of Federal criminal law in connection with the award or performance of any

Government contract or subcontract, to all contracts, whether domestic or overseas.
- Applied the policy demanding integrity and honesty (see FAR 3.1002) to all contractors.
- Only exempted contracts to be performed entirely outside the United States from inclusion of the clause.
- Had a clause requirement for an internal control system which mandated an internal reporting mechanism by which employees may report suspected instances of improper conduct, and instructions that encourage employees to make such reports on any of the contractor's contracts or subcontracts, whether overseas or domestic.

(2) *Require inclusion of the clause at FAR 52.203–13 in contracts (and subcontracts) for all acquisitions of a commercial item.* However, just like small businesses, a formal business ethics awareness and compliance program and internal control system are not required in contracts and subcontracts for the acquisition of commercial items. This would have the effect of applying to contracts for the acquisition of commercial items the requirements for—
- A written code of business ethics;
- Preventing and detecting criminal conduct; and
- Notifying, in writing, when the contractor has reasonable grounds to believe that violations of the civil False Claims Act or Federal criminal law have occurred in connection with the award or performance of this contract or any subcontract thereunder.

This is in some ways more fair to contractors providing commercial items, because even though the clause was not included in contracts for the acquisition of commercial items, the contractors were still subject under the initial proposed rule to debarment or suspension for knowing failure to notify the Government of violations of Federal criminal law in connection with the award or performance of the contract (or subcontract). Now the requirement to report violations is explicitly stated in the contract.

(3) *Add a new cause for suspension or debarment to the current lists at FAR 9.407–2 and 9.406–2, respectively.* For suspension, the new cause would be adequate evidence of a knowing failure to timely disclose the violation of the civil False Claims Act in connection with the award or performance of any Government contract, or subcontract thereunder. For debarment, the new cause would be a preponderance of the evidence of a knowing failure to timely disclose violation of the civil False Claims Act (31 U.S.C. 3729–3733) in connection with the award or performance of any Government contract, or subcontract thereunder. This would also be added as a required disclosure in the contract clause.

This is not a significant regulatory action and, therefore, was not subject to review under Section 6(b) of Executive Order 12866, Regulatory Planning and Review, dated September 30, 1993. This rule is not a major rule under 5 U.S.C. 804.

B. Regulatory Flexibility Act

The changes may have a significant economic impact on a substantial number of small entities within the meaning of the Regulatory Flexibility Act, 5 U.S.C. 601, et seq., because small businesses will be required to notify, in writing, the agency Office of the Inspector General, with a copy to the contracting officer, whenever the contractor has reasonable grounds to believe that a principal, employee, agent, or subcontractor of the contractor has committed a violation of the civil False Claims Act or a violation of Federal criminal law in connection with the award or performance of this contract or any subcontract thereunder.

An Initial Regulatory Flexibility Analysis (IRFA) was prepared in connection with the initial proposed rule. The analysis is summarized as follows:

> The IRFA reported that "the clause requirements for a formal awareness/training program and internal control system will not apply to small business concerns." (See 72 FR 64021.) That is still true. Only the requirements of paragraph (b) of the clause will apply (to have a written code of business ethics and to notify the agency Office of the Inspector General in writing, with a copy to the contracting officer whenever the Contractor has reasonable grounds to believe that a principal, employee, agency, or subcontractor of the contractor has committed a violation of the False Claims Act or a violation of Federal criminal law).
>
> The proposed changes that affect the IRFA are as follows:
> - Applies to contracts to be performed outside the United States.
> - Applies to contracts for the acquisition of commercial items (except 52.203–13(c)).
> - Requires reporting of violations of civil False Claims Act.
>
> The requirement in the proposed rule "to notify the agency inspector general and the contracting officer in writing whenever the contractor has reasonable grounds to believe that a principal, employee, agent, or subcontractor of the contractor has committed a violation of Federal criminal law in connection with the award or performance of any Government contract or subcontract" (72 FR 64020) was applicable to small, as well as large, businesses. The IRFA estimated that approximately 1,400 prime and subcontracts with small businesses would include the contract clause. We estimate that by including small businesses that offer commercial items or that perform contracts outside the United States, the number of small businesses impacted by the clause may increase by 50%. We estimate that the requirement to report violations of the civil False Claims Act may double the number of reports. The number of small businesses that would actually be required by the clause to submit a report would then be calculated as 84 (28 × 1.5 × 2). The number of small entities that are not impacted by the clause requirement but would report alleged violations of the civil False Claims Act was estimated to be 17. This estimate has doubled, because of the addition of mandatory reporting of violations of the civil False Claims Act. Therefore, the total number of small businesses submitting a report has increased from 45 to 118 (84+34).

The FAR Secretariat has submitted a copy of the amended IRFA to the Chief Counsel for Advocacy of the Small Business Administration. A copy of the IRFA may be obtained from the FAR Secretariat. The Councils will consider comments from small entities concerning the affected FAR parts 3, 9, 12, and 52 in accordance with 5 U.S.C. 610. Comments must be submitted separately and should cite 5 U.S.C 601, *et seq.* (FAR case 2007–006), in correspondence.

C. Paperwork Reduction Act

The Paperwork Reduction Act (Pub. L. 104–13) applies because the proposed rule contains information collection requirements. Accordingly, the FAR Secretariat will submit a request for approval of a revised information collection requirement concerning Contractor Compliance Program and Integrity Reporting to the Office of Management and Budget under 44 U.S.C. 3501, *et seq.* The estimated reporting burden for a violation remains *3* hours. Based on the revised number of impacted contractors and retaining the other figures used in the initial estimate, the annual reporting burden is revised as follows:

Respondents: 284.

Responses per respondent: 1.

Total annual responses: 284.

Preparation hours per response: 3.

Total response burden hours: 852.

Annual Reporting Burden

Public reporting burden for this collection of information is estimated to average *3* hours per response, including the time for reviewing instructions, searching existing data sources, gathering and maintaining the data needed, and completing and reviewing the collection of information.

D. Request for Comments Regarding Paperwork Burden

Submit comments, including suggestions for reducing this burden, not later than June 16, 2008 to: FAR Desk Officer, OMB, Room 10102, NEOB, Washington, DC 20503, and a copy to the General Services Administration, FAR Secretariat (VPR), 1800 F Street, NW., Room 4041, Washington, DC 20405. Please cite OMB Control Number 9000–00XX, Contractor Compliance Program and Integrity Reporting, in all correspondence.

Public comments are particularly invited on: Whether this collection of information is necessary for the proper performance of functions of the FAR, and will have practical utility; whether our estimate of the public burden of this collection of information is accurate, and based on valid assumptions and methodology; ways to enhance the quality, utility, and clarity of the information to be collected; and ways in which we can minimize the burden of the collection of information on those who are to respond, through the use of appropriate technological collection techniques or other forms of information technology.

Requester may obtain a copy of the justification from the General Services Administration, FAR Secretariat (VPR), Room 4041, Washington, DC 20405, telephone (202) 501–4755. Please cite OMB Control Number 9000–00XX, Contractor Compliance Program and Integrity Reporting, in all correspondence.

List of Subjects in 48 CFR Parts 3, 9, 12, and 52

Government procurement.

Dated: May 14, 2008.

Al Matera,

Director, Office of Acquisition Policy.

Therefore, DoD, GSA, and NASA propose amending 48 CFR parts 3, 9, 12, and 52 as set forth below:

1. The authority citation for 48 CFR parts 3, 9, 12, and 52 continues to read as follows:

Authority: 40 U.S.C. 121(c); 10 U.S.C. chapter 137; and 42 U.S.C. 2473(c).

PART 3—IMPROPER BUSINESS PRACTICES AND PERSONAL CONFLICTS OF INTEREST

2. Amend section 3.1002 by adding paragraph (c) to read as follows:

3.1002 Policy.

* * * * *

(c) A contractor may be suspended and/or debarred for knowing failure to timely disclose a violation of the civil False Claims Act or Federal criminal law in connection with the award or performance of any Government contract performed by the contractor or a subcontract awarded thereunder (see 9.406–2(b)(1)(v) and 9.407–2(a)(7)).

3. Revise paragraph (a) of section 3.1004 to read as follows:

3.1004 Contract clauses.

* * * * *

(a) Insert the clause at FAR 52.203–13, Contractor Code of Business Ethics and Conduct, in solicitations and contracts if the value of the contract is expected to exceed $5,000,000 and the performance period is 120 days or more.

* * * * *

PART 9—CONTRACTOR QUALIFICATIONS

4. Amend section 9.406–2 by revising the introductory text of paragraph (b)(1) and adding paragraph (b)(1)(v) to read as follows:

9.406–2 Causes for debarment.

* * * * *

(b)(1) A contractor, based upon a preponderance of the evidence, for any of the following—

* * * * *

(v) Knowing failure to timely disclose—

(A) An overpayment on a Government contract;

(B) Violation of the civil False Claims Act (31 U.S.C 3729–3733) in connection with the award or performance of any Government contract or subcontract; or

(C) Violation of Federal criminal law in connection with the award or performance of any Government contract or subcontract.

* * * * *

5. Amend section 9.407–2 by adding paragraph (a)(7) to read as follows:

9.407–2 Causes for suspension.

(a) * * *

(7) Knowing failure to timely disclose—

(i) An overpayment on a Government contract;

(ii) Violation of the civil False Claims Act (31 U.S.C 3729–3733) in connection with the award or performance of any Government contract or subcontract; or

(iii) Violation of Federal criminal law in connection with the award or performance of any Government contract or subcontract.

* * * * *

PART 12—ACQUISITION OF COMMERCIAL ITEMS

6. Amend section 12.301 by redesignating paragraph (d)(2) as (d)(3) and adding a new (d)(2) to read as follows:

12.301 Solicitation provisions and contract clauses for the acquisition of commercial items.

* * * * *

(d) * * *

(2) Insert the clause at 52.203–13, Contractor Code of Business Ethics and Conduct, as prescribed in 3.1004(a).

* * * * *

PART 52—SOLICITATION PROVISIONS AND CONTRACT CLAUSES

7. Amend section 52.203–13 by—

a. Revising the date of clause;

b. Adding paragraph (b)(3);

c. Revising the introductory text of paragraph (c) and (c)(2)(ii);

d. Adding paragraph (c)(2)(ii)(F); and

e. Revising paragraph (d).

52.203–13 Contractor Code of Business Ethics and Conduct.

* * * * *

Contractor Code of Business Ethics and Conduct

([Insert Abbreviated Month and Year of Publication in the Federal Register])

* * * * *

(b) * * *

(3) The Contractor shall notify, in writing, the agency Office of the Inspector General, with a copy to the Contracting Officer, whenever the Contractor has reasonable grounds to believe that a principal, employee, agent, or subcontractor of the Contractor has committed a violation of the civil False Claims Act or a violation of Federal criminal law in connection with the award or performance of this contract or any subcontract thereunder.

(c) *Business ethics awareness and compliance program and internal control system.* This paragraph (c) does not apply if the Contractor has represented itself as a small business concern pursuant to the award of this contract or if 52.212–4 appears in this contract.

* * * * *

(2) * * *

(ii) At a minimum, the Contractor's internal control system shall provide for the following:

* * * * *

(F) Timely reporting, in writing, to the agency Office of the Inspector General, with a copy to the Contracting Officer, whenever the Contractor has reasonable grounds to believe that a principal, employee, agent, or subcontractor of the Contractor has committed a violation of the civil False Claims Act (31 U.S.C 3729–3733) or a violation of Federal criminal law in connection with the award or performance of any Government contract performed by the Contractor or a subcontract thereunder.

* * * * *

(d) *Subcontracts.* (1) The Contractor shall include the substance of this clause, including this paragraph (d), in subcontracts that have a value in excess of $5,000,000 and a performance period of more than 120 days.

(2) In altering this clause to identify the appropriate parties, all reports of violation of the civil False Claims Act or violation of Federal criminal law shall be directed to the agency Office of the Inspector General, with a copy to the Contracting Officer.

(End of clause)

[FR Doc. E8–11137 Filed 5–15–08; 8:45 am]
BILLING CODE 6820–EP–P

DEPARTMENT OF THE INTERIOR

Fish and Wildlife Service

50 CFR Part 17

[FWS–R6–ES–2008–0001; 92220–1113–0000–C6]

RIN 1018–AU67

Endangered and Threatened Wildlife and Plants; Proposed Removal of Erigeron maguirei From the Federal List of Endangered and Threatened Plants; Availability of Post-Delisting Monitoring Plan

AGENCY: Fish and Wildlife Service, Interior.

ACTION: Proposed rule; notice of availability.

SUMMARY: We, the U.S. Fish and Wildlife Service (Service), under the Endangered Species Act of 1973, as amended (Act) (16 U.S.C. 1531 et seq.), propose to remove the plant *Erigeron maguirei* (commonly referred to as Maguire daisy) from the List of Endangered and Threatened Plants. The best scientific and commercial data available indicate that this species has recovered and no longer meets the definition of threatened or endangered under the Act. Our review of the status of this species shows that populations are stable, threats have been addressed, and adequate regulatory mechanisms ensure the species is not currently and is not likely to again become an endangered species within the foreseeable future in all or a significant portion of its range. We seek information, data, and comments from the public regarding *E. maguirei*, this proposal to delist, and the Post-Delisting Monitoring Plan. This proposed rule completes the 5-year status review initiated on April 7, 2006 (71 FR 17900).

DATES: We will accept comments received or postmarked on or before July 15, 2008. Public hearing requests must be received by June 30, 2008.

ADDRESSES: You may submit comments by one of the following methods:

• *Federal eRulemaking Portal: http://www.regulations.gov.* Follow the instructions for submitting comments.

• *U.S. mail or hand-delivery:* Public Comments Processing, Attn: RIN 1018–AU67; Division of Policy and Directives Management; U.S. Fish and Wildlife Service; 4401 N. Fairfax Drive, Suite 222; Arlington, VA 22203.

We will not accept e-mail or faxes. We will post all comments on *http://www.regulations.gov*. This generally means that we will post any personal information you provide us (see the Public Comments section below for more information).

FOR FURTHER INFORMATION CONTACT: Larry Crist, Field Supervisor, U.S. Fish and Wildlife Service, Utah Field Office, 2369 West Orton Circle, West Valley City, UT 84119, or telephone (801) 975–3330. Individuals who are hearing-impaired or speech-impaired may call the Federal Relay Service at (800) 877–8337 for TTY assistance.

SUPPLEMENTARY INFORMATION:

Public Comments Solicited

We intend that any final action resulting from this proposal will be as accurate and as effective as possible. Therefore, we hereby request data, comments, new information, or suggestions from the public, other concerned governmental agencies, the scientific community, Tribes, industry, or any other interested party concerning this proposed rule. We particularly seek comments concerning:

(1) Biological information concerning this species;

(2) Relevant data concerning any current or likely future threats (or lack thereof) to this species, including the extent and adequacy of Federal and State protection and management that would be provided to the *Erigeron maguirei* as a delisted species;

(3) Additional information concerning the range, distribution, population size, and population trends of this species, including the locations of any additional populations of this species;

(4) Current or planned activities in the subject area and their possible impacts on this species; and

(5) Our draft Post-Delisting Monitoring Plan.

You may submit your comments and materials concerning this proposed rule by one of the methods listed in the **ADDRESSES** section. We will not accept comments sent by e-mail or fax or to an address not listed in the **ADDRESSES** section.

If you submit a comment via *http://www.regulations.gov*, your entire comment—including any personal identifying information—will be posted on the Web site. If you submit a hardcopy comment that includes personal identifying information, you may request at the top of your document that we withhold this information from public review. However, we cannot guarantee that we will be able to do so. We will post all hardcopy comments on *http://www.regulations.gov*.

Comments and materials we receive, as well as supporting documentation we used in preparing this proposed rule, will be available for public inspection on *http://www.regulations.gov*, or by appointment during normal business hours at the Utah Field Office, 2369 West Orton Circle, West Valley City, UT 84119 (801/975–3330).

Public Hearing

The Act provides for one or more public hearings on this proposal, if requested. Requests must be received by June 30, 2008. Such requests must be made in writing and addressed to the Field Supervisor (see **FOR FURTHER INFORMATION CONTACT** section).

Previous Federal Action

Section 12 of the Act directed the Secretary of the Smithsonian Institution to prepare a report on those plants considered to be endangered, threatened, or extinct. On July 1, 1975, the Service published a notice in the **Federal Register** (40 FR 27824) accepting the Smithsonian report as a petition to list taxa named therein under section 4(c)(2) (now 4(b)(3)) of the Act) and announced our intention to review the status of those plants. *Erigeron maguirei* was included in that report (40 FR 27880, July 1, 1975). Maguire daisy is the common name for *Erigeron maguirei*, however we will use primarily the scientific name of this species throughout this proposed rule to clarify taxonomic issues or the legal status of the plant.

On June 16, 1976, we published a rule in the **Federal Register** (41 FR 24524) to designate approximately 1,700 vascular plant species, including *Erigeron maguirei*, as endangered pursuant to section 4 of the Act. The 1978 amendments to the Act required that all proposals over 2 years old be withdrawn. On December 10, 1979, we published a notice of withdrawal (44 FR 70796) of that portion of the June 16, 1976, proposal that had not been made final, which included *E maguirei*.

On December 15, 1980, we published a revised notice of review for native plants in the **Federal Register** designating *Erigeron maguirei* as a candidate species (45 FR 82480). Section 4(b)(3)(B) of the 1982

ATTACHMENT B

AMERICAN BAR ASSOCIATION

ABA Defending Liberty Pursuing Justice

Governmental Affairs Office
740 Fifteenth Street, NW
Washington, DC 20005-1022
(202) 662-1760
FAX: (202) 662-1762

June 20, 2008

General Services Administration
Regulatory Secretariat (VPR)
Attn: Ms. Laurieann Duarte
1800 F Street, N.W., Room 4041
Washington, D.C. 20405

Re: Preserving the Attorney-Client Privilege, the Work Product Doctrine, and Employee Legal Protections in Connection with FAR Case 2007-006, "Contractor Compliance Program and Integrity Reporting," 72 Fed. Reg. 64019 (November 14, 2007; Original Proposed Rule) and 73 Fed. Reg. 28407 (May 16, 2008; Second Proposed Rule)

Dear Ms. Duarte:

On behalf of the American Bar Association ("ABA") and its more than 413,000 members, I write to express our concerns over certain key provisions in the above referenced revised proposed FAR rule, "Contractor Compliance Program and Integrity Reporting," and to urge the Civilian Agency Acquisition Council and the Defense Acquisition Regulations Council ("Councils") to add language to the rule that would better protect companies' attorney-client privilege, work product, and employee legal rights. As Chair of the ABA Task Force on Attorney-Client Privilege, I have been authorized to express the ABA's views on these important issues.

Although the ABA has not taken a position on the overall proposed rule,[1] we urge the Councils to delete language in the revised proposed rule that requires contractors to disclose to the Office of Inspector General and the Contracting Officer when they have "reasonable grounds to believe" that a violation of federal criminal law or the civil False Claims Act has occurred. In addition, we urge the Councils to add language to the final FAR rule clarifying that federal officials may not pressure contractors to waive their attorney-client privilege or work product protections or take certain unfair punitive actions against their employees during any audit, investigation, or corrective action. Enclosed is specific proposed language that we believe would achieve these goals without impairing the effectiveness of the revised proposed rule in any way.

The Importance of the Attorney-Client Privilege, the Work Product Doctrine, and Employee Legal Rights

The attorney-client privilege enables both individual and organizational clients to communicate with their lawyers in confidence, and it encourages clients to seek out and obtain guidance in how to

---

[1] While the ABA has not taken a position on the overall proposed rule, the ABA Section of Public Contract Law filed comments expressing its views regarding the original proposed rule on January 18, 2008. The Section's comments were not reviewed or considered by the ABA House of Delegates or Board of Governors and therefore should not be construed as representing the views of the full ABA. Those comments are available at
http://www.abanet.org/contract/federal/regscomm/conflicts_003.pdf

June 20, 2008
Page 2

conform their conduct to the law. The privilege facilitates self-investigation into past conduct to identify shortcomings and remedy problems, to the benefit of corporate institutions, the investing community and society-at-large. The work product doctrine underpins our adversarial justice system and allows attorneys to prepare for litigation without fear that their work product and mental impressions will be revealed to adversaries.

The ABA strongly supports the preservation of the attorney-client privilege and the work product doctrine and opposes governmental policies, practices and procedures that have the effect of eroding the privilege or doctrine. In addition, the ABA believes that it is equally important to protect employees' constitutional and other legal rights—including the right to effective counsel and the right against self-incrimination—when a company or other organization is under investigation. Unfortunately, both the vague "reasonable grounds to believe" mandatory disclosure standard and the "full cooperation" requirement of the proposed rule threaten to undermine these fundamental rights in different ways.

Problems with the Proposed "Reasonable Grounds to Believe" Mandatory Disclosure Standard

The revised proposed FAR rule requires contractors to notify the Office of the Inspector General and the Contracting Officer of the relevant federal agency in writing "whenever the Contractor has reasonable grounds to believe that a principal, employee, agent, or subcontractor of the Contractor has committed a violation of the civil False Claims Act...or a violation of Federal criminal law in connection with the award or performance of any Government contract performed by the Contractor or a subcontract thereunder." *See* 73 Fed. Reg. 28409 (May 16, 2008). Although the term "reasonable grounds to believe" is not defined in the revised proposed rule, any knowing failure to timely disclose this information is cause for debarment or suspension of the contractor, a draconian penalty that could make the contractor ineligible to receive further government contracts.

The ABA is concerned that the vague nature of the "reasonable grounds to believe" disclosure standard in the revised proposed rule will undermine the confidential relationship between contractors and their attorneys. Under existing federal statutes and regulations governing federal procurement— as well as broad criminal statutes such as the False Claims Act and the False Statements Act— virtually any noncompliance in connection with a federal government contract *may*, depending on the circumstances, constitute a violation of federal criminal law. On the other hand, these same procurement rules are complex and often esoteric, giving rise to defenses against allegations of non-compliance or criminal conduct.

As a result, the revised proposed rule will often require contractors to seek and rely upon the legal advice of their counsel in order to make the judgments necessary to comply with the rule's notification requirement. At the same time, the rule will often require contractors to disclose the results of their counsel's legal advice—or the legal advice itself—resulting in waiver of the attorney-client privilege. In addition, once the contractor is forced to disclose its legal advice, the disclosure is likely to be followed by a demand from the Office of Inspector General for all underlying information, including information that is protected by the attorney-client privilege and/or the work product doctrine.

J-2

Even in those instances in which a contactor determines that disclosure is not required under the revised proposed FAR rule, the contractor still may be forced to waive its attorney-client privilege and work product protections if the government disagrees with the contractor's determination and decides to initiate a suspension or debarment action. In order to justify the "reasonableness" of its determination that certain conduct did not meet the reporting threshold of the law, the contractor may need to disclose the basis for its determination. In many such cases, the contractor may be required to disclose information protected by the attorney-client privilege or work product doctrine, including communications between company counsel and employees and the actual legal advice that the contractor received.

Compounding this problem is the procedural fact that a suspension may occur without any opportunity for a contractor to be notified in advance. Since the mere act of suspension can start a chain reaction of contract cancellations and consequent adverse impact on the value of the contractor's stock, the rule as proposed would subject a contractor to immense pressure to waive the privilege rather than risk being second guessed and penalized.

For all of these reasons, the vague "reasonable grounds to believe" disclosure standard in the revised proposed FAR rule is likely to seriously erode the contractor's attorney-client privilege and work product protections regardless of whether the contractor discloses or declines to disclose possible violations under the rule. Therefore, the ABA urges the Councils to delete the mandatory disclosure provisions from the proposed rule, as shown in the attached suggested amendments. If the Councils decide not to remove that requirement from the final FAR rule in its entirety, then the ABA recommends that the "reasonable grounds to believe" standard be replaced with an "actual knowledge that a civil False Claims Act or Federal criminal law violation has occurred" standard.

Problems with the "Full Cooperation" Requirement of the Proposed FAR Rule

Although the proposed FAR rule does not specifically require contractors to waive their attorney-client privilege, work product, or employee legal protections during investigations, the ABA is concerned that the rule's requirement that contractors establish an internal control system and give "full cooperation...(to) any Government agencies responsible for audit, investigation, or corrective actions" could be read to require waiver of these protections. *See* 72 Fed. Reg. 64023 (November 14, 2007). In addition, we are concerned that the "full cooperation" language in the proposed rule could embolden agencies to demand such waiver from companies.

The ABA believes that a broad interpretation of the "full cooperation" language in the proposed FAR rule, like the more explicit waiver policies adopted by the Justice Department, the Securities and Exchange Commission (SEC), and other agencies[2], could lead to a number of profoundly negative consequences.

---

[2] The Justice Department's cooperation standards—outlined in the 1999 "Holder Memorandum," 2003 "Thompson Memorandum," and 2006 "McNulty Memorandum"—pressure companies to waive attorney-client privilege and work product protections in many cases in return for receiving cooperation credit during investigations. The Justice Department standards also pressure companies to take certain punitive actions against their employees in many cases—such as not sharing information with them, terminating them, or in certain "rare" cases, not paying their attorneys fees—in return for such credit. Similar policies also have been adopted by the SEC, the EPA, HUD, and other agencies, and these materials are available at http://www.abanet.org/poladv/priorities/privilegewaiver/acprivilege.html.

June 20, 2008
Page 4

First, the ABA believes that this language in the proposed rule could lead to the routine compelled waiver of attorney-client privilege and work product protections. Although the proposed rule does not explicitly state that waiver is required in every situation, the sweeping "full cooperation" language in the proposal is likely to encourage federal agency staff, directly or indirectly, to pressure contractors to waive their privileges on a regular basis as a condition for receiving cooperation credit during investigations. From a practical standpoint, contractors will have no choice but to waive when encouraged or requested to do so because the risk of being labeled as "uncooperative" will have a profound effect not just on the federal agencies' enforcement action decisions, but on the contractor's public disclosure obligations, credit worthiness, stock price, and image. In this way, the broad "full cooperation" language of the proposed rule will likely exacerbate the "culture of waiver" problem caused by the existing Justice Department, SEC, and other federal agency policies.[3]

Second, the ABA is concerned that the broad "full cooperation" language in the proposed rule, like the similar policies adopted by the Justice Department and other federal agencies, will further weaken the attorney-client privilege between contractors and their lawyers, erode the work product doctrine, and undermine the contractors' internal compliance programs. By making the privilege uncertain in the corporate context, these policies discourage contractors from consulting with their lawyers, thereby impeding the lawyers' ability to effectively counsel compliance with the law. In addition, by creating an environment in which contractors are expected to waive their work product protections, these policies discourage the contractors from conducting internal investigations that are designed to quickly detect and remedy misconduct. The ABA believes that federal officials can obtain the information they need from a cooperating contractor without pressuring it to waive these protections. For all these reasons, the ABA believes that the proposed rule will undermine, rather than enhance, compliance with the law.

Third, the ABA is concerned that the broad "full cooperation" language of the proposed rule—like the cooperation standards adopted by the Justice Department, the SEC, and other federal agencies—could erode employees' constitutional and other legal rights by pressuring contractors to not pay their employees' legal fees during investigations in violation of the employees' Sixth Amendment right to counsel, to fire them for not waiving Fifth Amendment right against self-incrimination, or to take other punitive actions against the employees long before any guilt has been established.[4] By pressuring contractors to punish their employees long before any guilt has been shown, the proposed rule will weaken the presumption of innocence, overturn basic corporate governance principles, and violate the Constitution.

---

[3] According to a March 2006 survey of over 1,200 corporate counsels, almost 75% believe that a "culture of waiver" has evolved in which federal agencies believe that it is reasonable and appropriate for them to expect a company under investigation to broadly waive attorney-client or work product protections. The detailed survey results are available at http://www.acc.com/Surveys/attyclient2.pdf. Although the Justice Department revised its waiver policy in December 2006 as part of the "McNulty Memorandum," prosecutor demands for waiver have continued unabated. Numerous specific examples of post-McNulty demands for waiver are outlined in the September 2007 Report of former Delaware Chief Justice Norman Veasey, available at http://www.abanet.org/poladv/priorities/privilegewaiver/acprivilege.html

[4] For a full discussion of the Justice Department and other federal agency cooperation standards that erode employees' constitutional and other legal rights, please see the ABA's September 18, 2007 statement to the Senate Judiciary Committee, pgs. 11-15, available at http://www.abanet.org/poladv/priorities/privilegewaiver/20070918_mcnulty.pdf

June 20, 2008
Page 5

Finally, "full cooperation" may be interpreted by the government to include an admission of guilt or liability when in fact there may be substantial legal and factual reasons not to do so. Yet, for a contractor to try to raise potentially dispositive defenses may be regarded as less than "full cooperation" and thus subject the contractor to the extreme risks inherent in suspension and debarment.

The ABA Task Force on Attorney-Client Privilege has prepared suggested changes to the revised proposed FAR rule that would preserve fundamental attorney-client privilege, work product, and employee legal protections during investigations while ensuring federal agencies' continued ability to obtain the important factual information that they need to effectively enforce the law.

The proposed amendment to the proposed FAR rule enclosed herewith would accomplish these objectives by: (1) preventing federal agencies and their staff from seeking privilege waiver from contractors during audits, investigations, or corrective actions; (2) preserving the agencies' ability to request important factual information from contractors as a sign of full cooperation without implicating broader privilege waiver concerns; (3) clarifying that a waiver of privilege should not be considered when assessing whether the contractor provided full cooperation; and (4) recognizing that full cooperation credit can be given for providing factual information. The proposed amendment also would clarify that while federal agencies and their staff may consider a contractor's reasonable efforts to secure its employees' cooperation as a factor in determining whether the contractor has fully cooperated during an audit, investigation, or corrective action, the contractor should not be asked or expected to punish any employee who chooses to assert his or her legal rights.

We believe that the proposed amendment, if adopted by the Councils, would strike the proper balance between effective law enforcement and the preservation of essential attorney-client privilege, work product, and employee legal protections, and we urge you to consider it.

If you or your staff have any questions or need additional information about this vital issue, please ask your staff to contact me at (404) 527-4650 or Larson Frisby of the ABA Governmental Affairs Office at (202) 662-1098.

Thank you for considering the views of the American Bar Association on this subject, which is of such vital importance to our system of justice.

Sincerely,

R. William Ide, III, Chair
ABA Task Force on Attorney-Client Privilege

enclosure

cc: Patricia A. Meagher, Chair, ABA Section of Public Contract Law
    Thomas M. Susman, Director, ABA Governmental Affairs Office
    R. Larson Frisby, Senior Legislative Counsel, ABA Governmental Affairs Office

PROPOSED AMENDMENT TO REVISED PROPOSED FAR RULE TITLED "CONTRACTOR COMPLIANCE PROGRAM AND INTEGRITY REPORTING," FAR CASE 2007-006, 72 FED. REG. 64019 AND 73 FED. REG. 28407

PREPARED BY THE AMERICAN BAR ASSOCIATION TASK FORCE ON ATTORNEY-CLIENT PRIVILEGE

(Excerpts of the proposed FAR rule are reprinted below to provide context; proposed additions are underlined in blue; proposed deletions are struck through in red

JUNE 20, 2008

PART 3—IMPROPER BUSINESS PRACTICES AND PERSONAL CONFLICTS OF INTEREST

...3.1002 Policy.

~~(c) A contractor may be suspended and/or disbarred for knowing failure to timely disclose a violation of the civil False Claims Act or Federal criminal law in connection with the award or performance of any Government contract performed by the contractor or a subcontract awarded thereunder (see 9.406-2(b)(1)(v) and 9.407-2(a)(7)).~~

PART 9—CONTRACTOR QUALIFICATIONS

...4. Amend section 9.406—2 by revising the introductory text of paragraph (b)(1) and adding paragraph (b)(1)(v) to read as follows:

9.406—2 Causes for debarment

* * * * *

(b)(1) A contractor, based upon a preponderance of the evidence, for any of the following—

* * * * *

~~(v) Knowing failure to timely disclose—~~
~~(A) An overpayment on a Government contract; or~~
~~(B) Violation of the civil False Claims Act (31 U.S.C. 3729-3733) in connection with the award or performance of any Government contract or subcontract; or~~
~~(C) Violation of Federal criminal law in connection with the award or performance of any Government contract or subcontract.~~

...5. Amend section 9.407—2 by adding paragraph (a)(7) to read as follows:

9.407—2 Causes for suspension

(a)* * *

~~(7) Knowing failure to timely disclose—~~
   ~~(i) An overpayment on a Government contract; or~~
   ~~(ii) Violation of the civil False Claims Act (31 U.S.C. 3729-3733) in connection with the award or performance of any Government contract or subcontract; or~~
   ~~(iii) Violation of Federal criminal law in connection with the award or performance of any Government contract or subcontract.~~

PART 52—SOLICITATION PROVISIONS AND CONTRACT CLAUSES

7. Amend section 52.203—13 by—
   a. Revising the date of clause;
   ~~b. Adding paragraph (b)(3);~~
   c. Revising the introductory text of paragraph (c) and (c)(2)(ii);
   ~~d. Adding paragraph (c)(2)(ii)(F); and~~
   e. Revising paragraph (d).

52.203—13 Contractor Code of Business Ethics and Conduct

As prescribed in 3.1004, insert the following clause:

CONTRACTOR CODE OF BUSINESS ETHICS AND CONDUCT (DATE)

…(b) *Code of business ethics and conduct.* …

   ~~(3) The Contractor shall notify, in writing, the agency Office of the Inspector General, with a copy to the Contracting Officer, whenever the Contractor has reasonable grounds to believe that a principal, employee, agent, or subcontractor of the Contractor has committed a violation of the civil False Claims Act or a violation of Federal criminal law in connection with the award or performance of this contract or any subcontract thereunder…~~

…(c) *Business ethics awareness and compliance program and internal control system.* …The Contractor shall establish the following within 90 days after contract award, unless the contracting officer establishes a longer time period—

   …(2) An internal control system.

      …(ii) At a minimum, the Contractor's internal control system shall provide for the following:

         ~~…(F) Timely reporting in writing to the agency Office of the Inspector General, with a copy to the Contracting Officer, whenever the~~

2

J-7

~~Contractor has reasonable grounds to believe that a principal, employee, agent, or subcontractor of the Contractor has committed a violation of the civil False Claims Act (31 U.S.C. 3729-3733) or a violation of Federal criminal law in connection with the award or performance of any Government contract performed by the Contractor or a subcontract thereunder; and~~

…~~(G)~~(F) Full cooperation with any Government agencies responsible for audit, investigation, or corrective actions, <u>subject to the conditions established in subsection (iii) below.</u>

<u>(iii) Protection of Attorney-Client Privilege, Work Product, and Employee Legal Rights.</u>

<u>(A) Staff of Government agencies responsible for audit, investigation, or corrective actions ("Agency staff") shall not take any action or assert any position that directly or indirectly demands, requests or encourages a contractor or its attorneys to waive its attorney-client privilege or the protections of the work product doctrine.</u>

<u>(B) In assessing a contractor's cooperation, Agency staff shall not draw any inference from the contractor's preservation of its attorney-client privilege and the protections of the work product doctrine. At the same time, the voluntary decision by a contractor to waive the attorney-client privilege and/or the work product doctrine shall not be considered when assessing whether the contractor provided effective cooperation. Agency staff may consider, however, in assessing whether a contractor has provided effective cooperation, the degree to which the contractor has provided factual information to the Agency staff in a manner, to be worked out by the contractor and the Agency staff, that preserves the protections of the attorney-client privilege and work product doctrine to the fullest extent possible.</u>

<u>(C) Notwithstanding the general rule set forth in subsection (iii)(B) above, Agency staff may, after obtaining in advance the approval of their respective agency's Director of Enforcement or his/her designee, seek materials otherwise protected from disclosure by the attorney-client privilege or the work product doctrine if the contractor asserts, or indicates that it will assert, an advice of counsel defense with respect to the matters under investigation. Moreover, Agency staff also may seek materials respecting which there is a final judicial determination that the privilege or doctrine does not apply for any reason, such as the crime/fraud exception or a waiver. In circumstances described in this subsection (iii)(C), Agency staff shall limit their requests for disclosure only to those otherwise protected materials reasonably necessary and which are within the scope of the particular exception.</u>

<u>(D) Although Agency staff may consider whether a contractor has asked its current or former officers, directors, employees, or agents ("Employees") to</u>

cooperate with Agency staff and/or whether the contractor has made reasonable efforts to secure such cooperation as factors in determining the contractor's degree of cooperation, a contractor should not be asked or expected to take any of the following punitive actions against its Employees in return for cooperation credit:

(i) terminating or otherwise sanctioning an Employee who exercised his or her Fifth Amendment rights against self-incrimination in response to a government request for an interview, testimony, or other information;

(ii) declining to provide counsel to an Employee or pay for such counsel;

(iii) declining to enter into or ceasing to operate under a joint defense, information sharing and common interest agreement with an Employee or other represented party with whom the contractor believes it has a common interest in defending against the investigation; or

(iv) declining to share its records or other historical information relating to the matter under investigation with an Employee.

"(3) Paragraph (2) shall not apply in the case of an individual who fails to complete service agreed to by the individual—

"(A) by reason of the death of the individual; or
"(B) for a reason referred to in section 16133(b).

"(j) REGULATIONS.—(1) The Secretary of Defense, in coordination with the Secretary of Veterans Affairs, shall prescribe regulations for purposes of this section.

"(2) Such regulations shall specify—
"(A) the manner of authorizing the transfer of entitlements under this section;
"(B) the eligibility criteria in accordance with subsection (b); and
"(C) the manner and effect of an election to modify or revoke a transfer of entitlement under subsection (f)(2).

"(k) SECRETARY CONCERNED DEFINED.—For purposes of this section, the term 'Secretary concerned' has the meaning given in section 101(a)(9) in the case of a member of the armed forces.".

(d) CONFORMING AMENDMENTS.—Section 16133(a) of title 10, United States Code, is amended by striking "(1)" and all that follows through the period at the end of the subsection and inserting "on the date the person is separated from the Selected Reserve.".

(e) CLERICAL AMENDMENTS.—(1) The table of sections at the beginning of chapter 30 of title 38, United States Code, is amended by striking the item relating to section 3020 and inserting the following new item:

"3020. Authority to transfer unused education benefits to family members of career service members.".

(2) The table of sections at the beginning of chapter 1606 of title 10, United States Code, is amended by inserting after the item relating to section 16132 the following new item:

"16132a. Authority to transfer unused education benefits to family members.".

(3) The table of sections at the beginning of chapter 1607 of such title is amended by inserting after the item relating to section 16163 the following new item:

"16163a. Authority to transfer unused education benefits to family members.".

TITLE VI—ACCOUNTABILITY AND TRANSPARENCY IN GOVERNMENT CONTRACTING

CHAPTER 1—CLOSE THE CONTRACTOR FRAUD LOOPHOLE

SHORT TITLE

SEC. 6101. This chapter may be cited as the "Close the Contractor Fraud Loophole Act".

REVISION OF THE FEDERAL ACQUISITION REGULATION

SEC. 6102. The Federal Acquisition Regulation shall be amended within 180 days after the date of the enactment of this Act pursuant to FAR Case 2007–006 (as published at 72 Fed Reg. 64019, November 14, 2007) or any follow-on FAR case to include provisions that require timely notification by Federal contractors of violations of Federal criminal law or overpayments in connection with the award or performance of covered contracts or subcontracts, including those performed outside the United States and those for commercial items.

DEFINITION

SEC. 6103. In this chapter, the term "covered contract" means any contract in an amount greater than $5,000,000 and more than 120 days in duration.

41 USC 251 note.

CHAPTER 2—GOVERNMENT FUNDING TRANSPARENCY

Government Funding Transparency Act of 2008.

SHORT TITLE

SEC. 6201. This chapter may be cited as the "Government Funding Transparency Act of 2008".

31 USC 6101 note.

FINANCIAL DISCLOSURE REQUIREMENTS FOR CERTAIN RECIPIENTS OF FEDERAL AWARDS

SEC. 6202. (a) DISCLOSURE REQUIREMENTS.—Section 2(b)(1) of the Federal Funding Accountability and Transparency Act (Public Law 109–282; 31 U.S.C. 6101 note) is amended—
    (1) by striking "and" at the end of subparagraph (E);
    (2) by redesignating subparagraph (F) as subparagraph (G); and
    (3) by inserting after subparagraph (E) the following new subparagraph:
        "(F) the names and total compensation of the five most highly compensated officers of the entity if—
            "(i) the entity in the preceding fiscal year received—
                "(I) 80 percent or more of its annual gross revenues in Federal awards; and
                "(II) $25,000,000 or more in annual gross revenues from Federal awards; and
            "(ii) the public does not have access to information about the compensation of the senior executives of the entity through periodic reports filed under section 13(a) or 15(d) of the Securities Exchange Act of 1934 (15 U.S.C. 78m(a), 78o(d)) or section 6104 of the Internal Revenue Code of 1986.".
    (b) REGULATIONS REQUIRED.—The Director of the Office of Management and Budget shall promulgate regulations to implement the amendment made by this chapter. Such regulations shall include a definition of "total compensation" that is consistent with regulations of the Securities and Exchange Commission at section 402 of part 229 of title 17 of the Code of Federal Regulations (or any subsequent regulation).

31 USC 6101 note.

TITLE VII—MEDICAID PROVISIONS

SEC. 7001. (a) MORATORIA ON CERTAIN MEDICAID REGULATIONS.—
    (1) EXTENSION OF CERTAIN MORATORIA IN PUBLIC LAW 110–28.—Section 7002(a)(1) of the U.S. Troop Readiness, Veterans' Care, Katrina Recovery, and Iraq Accountability Appropriations Act, 2007 (Public Law 110–28) is amended—
        (A) by striking "prior to the date that is 1 year after the date of enactment of this Act" and inserting "prior to April 1, 2009";

121 Stat. 187.

U. S. Department of Justice

Civil Division

2007-006-22

Assistant Attorney General   Washington, D.C. 20530

July 15, 2008

General Services Administration
Regulatory Secretariat (VPR)
1800 F Street, NW
Room 4041
Washington, DC 20405

Subject: Comments on FAR Case 2007-006

Dear Sir or Madam:

We appreciate the work of the Department of Defense, General Services Administration, and National Aeronautics and Space Administration with the Civilian Agency Acquisition Council and the Defense Acquisition Regulations Council on the proposed changes to the Federal Acquisition Regulation (FAR) for establishing a contractor compliance program and a requirement for integrity reporting.

On January 14, 2008, the Assistant Attorney General for the Criminal Division, Alice S. Fisher, submitted comments on FAR Case 2007-006. Those comments recommended, among other items, that the proposed rule require that contractors report any violation of the civil False Claims Act (FCA), 31 U.S.C. § 3729 *et seq.* Additionally, Assistant Attorney General Fisher recommended that the knowing failure to report an FCA violation serve as grounds for suspension or debarment.

The Civil Division of the Department of Justice, which is responsible for the enforcement of the FCA, fully supports these recommendations. The FCA is the government's primary civil tool for redressing false claims for government funds. Since the FCA was amended in 1986, the government has recovered more than $20 billion on behalf of taxpayers. Thus, requiring the disclosure of FCA violations, and making the knowing failure to report such a violation a ground for suspension or debarment, is a natural addition to the existing provisions of the proposed rule that make the knowing failure to report an overpayment, or a criminal violation, a basis for suspension or debarment. This addition would ensure that a contractor whose underlying conduct falls short of a criminal violation, but is more than a mistake or negligence, cannot avoid the effect of the proposed rule by failing to disclose that it has received government funds to which it knows it is not entitled. The disclosure of such information will enhance the government's civil enforcement efforts, which are a critical component of the government's overall scheme for combating government contract fraud.

General Services Administration
Regulatory Secretariat (VPR)
Page 2

    Moreover, requiring the disclosure of FCA violations would complement the disclosure provisions of the FCA, which permit a court to reduce the government's recovery of damages where a person makes a timely disclosure and complies with other applicable requirements. Specifically, the FCA provides that a court may impose only double, rather than treble, damages if a person reports an FCA violation within 30 days of obtaining information about the violation, fully cooperates with the government's investigation, and was not previously aware of the existence of any such investigation. 31 U.S.C. § 3729(a). Adding the civil FCA to the mandatory disclosure provision in the FAR should enhance the effectiveness of these provisions because a person that meets these requirements would receive the dual benefit of qualifying to seek reduced damages under the FCA and avoiding the potential for suspension and debarment under the FAR.

    We urge the Councils to adopt as a final rule the proposal in FAR Case 2007-006.

                    Sincerely,

                      Gregory G. Katsas
                      Assistant Attorney General

COUNCIL OF DEFENSE AND SPACE INDUSTRY ASSOCIATIONS
4401 Wilson Boulevard, Suite 1110
Arlington, Virginia 22203
703- 875-8059

July 15, 2008

CODSIA Case No. 01-08

Ms. Laurieann Duarte
Acting Director
Regulatory Secretariat (VIR)
General Services Administration
1800 F Street, N.W.
Room 4041
Washington, DC 20405

Subject: FAR Case 2007–006
Contractor Compliance Program and Integrity Reporting

Dear Ms. Duarte:

The undersigned members of the Council of Defense and Space Industry Associations[1] (CODSIA) appreciate the opportunity to offer comments on changes to the second proposed rule, FAR Case 2007-006, Contractor Compliance Program and Integrity Reporting, published in the Federal Register on May 16, 2008. The proposed rule was first published in the Federal Register on November 14, 2007,[2] and CODSIA submitted comments on the original proposed rule on January 11, 2008.[3]

---

[1] Formed in 1964 by industry associations with common interests in federal procurement issues touching the defense and space industries, CODSIA consists of seven associations – the Aerospace Industries Association (AIA), American Shipbuilding Association (ASA), National Defense Industrial Association (NDIA), Professional Services Council (PSC), the American Council of Engineering Companies (ACEC), the Information Technology Association of America (ITAA) and the Chamber of Commerce of the United States of America. CODSIA's member associations represent virtually all of the major federal contractors in the defense and space industries, and each member association is composed of many smaller firms who are actively involved in the federal procurement process. CODSIA acts as an institutional focal point for coordination of its members' positions regarding policies, regulations, directives, and procedures that affect them.

[2] 72 Fed. Reg. 64019 (proposed Nov. 14, 2007) (to be codified at 48 C.F.R. pts. 3, 9, 42, and 52)).

[3] CODSIA's original comments can be found at
http://www.regulations.gov/fdmspublic/ContentViewer?objectId=0900006480399bba&disposition=attachment&contentType=crtext

CODSIA Comments on FAR Case 2007-006
July 15, 2008
Page 2

INTRODUCTION

As stated in its original comments on FAR Case 2007-006, CODSIA applauds the work of the Civilian Agency Acquisition Council and the Defense Acquisition Regulation Council (collectively, the "Councils") and fully supports their efforts to reduce fraud in government contracting. CODSIA acknowledges the importance of business ethics codes and internal controls in promoting contractor integrity. Indeed, CODSIA supports policies and programs that encourage contractors to ferret out and eliminate fraud.

CODSIA submits that the proposed rule, including the new changes thereto – however well intended – is both unnecessary and unsound for the reasons we stated in our January 11, 2008 submission as well as those set out here.[4]

As discussed in CODSIA's January 11, 2008 comments, the November 14, 2007 proposal to <u>require</u> contractors to report violations of federal criminal law in connection with the award or performance of any government contract or subcontract, and making a knowing failure to report such violations cause for suspension or debarment, will undermine attorney-client privilege and otherwise serve to make the intraorganizational detection and identification of misconduct more difficult.

CODSIA also opposes the May 16, 2008 proposed rule. This proposed FAR rule would <u>require</u> a contractor to report whenever it has "reasonable grounds" to believe that one of its employees or subcontractors may have violated the civil False Claims Act (FCA). The proposal would also allow for suspension or debarment for a knowing failure to timely report a violation of the civil FCA. In tying a reporting requirement to the FCA, the proposed rule sets out a vague, if not impossible, standard considering the complexities of the statute and the evolving case law in this area. Moreover, the proposal is unlikely to materially affect the behavior of those relatively few companies engaged in intentional misconduct – such companies would have factored in the severe penalties imposed by the civil FCA prior to engaging in the offending course of conduct. Instead, the proposal is more likely to result in the threat of suspension or debarment when the Government and a contractor honestly disagree on whether a dispute is purely contractual versus one that the Government alleges arises to the level of "reckless disregard" required under the civil FCA.

No Demonstrated Need for Mandatory Reporting

As with the original proposed rule, the May 16th proposed changes fail to articulate a discernible problem with the *status quo* and certainly no problem that would justify the significant initiative contemplated by the proposal. Notably, neither

---

[4] CODSIA acknowledges that Section 6101 of the fiscal year 2008 Emergency Supplemental Appropriations Act (P.L. 110-252) requires mandatory disclosure. It does not dictate, however, that *this* rule is to be implemented. We encourage the Councils to issue new rulemaking regarding the implementation of that law.

M-2

CODSIA Comments on FAR Case 2007-006
July 15, 2008
Page 3

the Department of Justice (DOJ) nor the Councils have cited data to show that voluntary disclosure programs are ineffective in uncovering violations of the civil FCA. In fact, the available data shows that current mechanisms for exposing fraud are working.[5]

The *qui tam* provisions of the civil FCA are a primary means of bringing allegations of false claims submitted to the Government to the attention of the DOJ. Under the *qui tam* provisions, private persons may sue persons who are alleged to have presented false claims to the Government or caused someone else to submit false claims to the government, provided that they first bring the information on which the suit is based to the attention of the DOJ. The requirement to bring the information first to DOJ assures that the DOJ is made aware of information it has not developed on its own[6], and it allows the DOJ to make a determination whether or not to pursue the case itself. The DOJ can, and often does, determine not to pursue a case that is not meritorious. In sum, the *qui tam* provisions already provide a well-developed procedure for assuring that cases involving false claims are brought to the attention of the DOJ.

Data relating to *qui tam* litigation shows that this is a powerful mechanism for achieving the government's goals. In a January 31, 2006 report, the Government Accountability Office (GAO) reported that, for the years 1987-2005, the Department of Justice received 8,869 FCA cases, of which 57.8% (5,129 cases) came from *qui tam* disclosures. During the same period, DOJ closed out 2,490 unsealed cases, including 819 procurement fraud cases (that is, procurement fraud cases constituted 32.8% of the closed cases). The GAO reported that almost two-thirds of the civil FCA recoveries (64% or $9.6 billion out of $15. billion) resulting from these closed cases was attributable to cases filed by *qui tam* relators.

Significantly, the data reported by GAO shows that the DOJ chose not to pursue the majority of procurement fraud cases brought to its attention by *qui tam* relators – DOJ pursued only 29% of such cases (237 out of 819 cases). GAO also reported that recoveries in cases not pursued by DOJ are much less than in those DOJ pursues.

These GAO data show that (1) *qui tam* relators aggressively reported instances of suspected fraud to the DOJ, and (2) DOJ pursues only 29% of the cases *qui tam*

---

[5] As reported in the article entitled "A Backlog of Cases Alleging Fraud" (Washington Post, July 2, 2008, A1) there is no need for mandatory reporting because the existing qui tam system of reporting fraud is already overloaded. "More than 900 cases alleging that government contractors and drug makers have defrauded taxpayers out of billions of dollars are languishing in a backlog that has built up over the past decade because the Justice Department cannot keep pace with the surge in charges brought by whistle-blowers, according to lawyers involved in the disputes." Because the government has been unable to adequately address these claims, contractors are tied up for years in costly and damaging inquiries that more often than not are rejected.

[6] A *qui tam* relator may not base such a suit on information publicly disclosed in investigations, unless the relator is an "original source" meaning the relator has direct and independent knowledge of the facts on which the suit is based.

relators brought to its attention. There is no indication that significant instances of fraud are not being brought to light. Accordingly, there is no demonstrated need to add mandatory reporting requirements for violations of the civil FCA.

No Demonstration the Proposed Rule Would Be Effective

Even if there were a demonstrated need to require reporting, there is no demonstration that the proposed rule requiring mandatory reporting of civil FCA violations would be effective in exposing more instances of contractor fraud. CODSIA posits that there are three categories of contractors who get swept up in civil FCA cases: (1) unscrupulous contractors who purposefully file false claims in order to defraud the government; (2) responsible contractors who discover after the fact that rogue employees have filed false claims; and (3) responsible contractors who, having filed claims in good faith, dispute the factual or legal basis for the FCA allegations. The proposed mandatory reporting requirement will not result in increased reports or decrease the instances of fraud for any of these groups.

The changes would not provide any improvement in bringing fraud to light as to the first group. Unscrupulous contractors who make calculated decisions to submit false claims with the purpose of defrauding the government are not likely to be deterred from doing so by a mandatory reporting requirement. Their calculated decisions to submit false claims already factor in the threat of severe sanctions, and these unscrupulous contractors are unlikely to be dissuaded from doing so by the specific threat of debarment for failing to put themselves on report. They will simply ignore the reporting requirement and actively work to conceal their fraud. It is more likely that fraud will be exposed by others rather than through a mandatory reporting requirement on the contractor.

The second group – responsible contractors who discover after the fact fraud by their employees – already have significant incentives to report the fraud voluntarily. Such contractors understand that, if they discover fraud by rogue employees, their corporate interests are best served by making a <u>voluntary</u> disclosure. These contractors recognize that a voluntary disclosure is the only practical means of assuring that the corporation will not be seen as being complicit with the rogue employees or condoning their actions. They understand that a failure to report such instances within a reasonable time after discovery would be direct evidence that the corporation chose to accept the benefits of the fraud. Accordingly, they know prompt action must be taken to disclose the fraud and disassociate the corporation from the wrongdoing. Thus, with the encouragement of an active and effective voluntary disclosure program, responsible contractors need no further incentive to make disclosures in such circumstances, and there is no benefit from requiring mandatory disclosure from them.

Requiring mandatory disclosure will also not affect the actions of contractors in the third category – contractors who file claims in good faith and who dispute the factual or legal basis of later filed civil FCA allegations. The proposed reporting

CODSIA Comments on FAR Case 2007-006
July 15, 2008
Page 5

requirement will not be an incentive to them because they believe in good faith they have not committed any violation.

The civil FCA presents many difficult legal and factual issues, such as whether a submission constitutes a "claim;" whether a statement is "false;" and whether the person making the statement or submitting the claim acted with requisite knowledge. Case law involving the civil FCA continues to evolve, and the law on several key elements of the statute sometimes differs from jurisdiction to jurisdiction. Moreover, FCA issues are often hotly contested over the course of years before a determination is made. Requiring contractors to report "violations" of the civil FCA before any legal determination is made as to the sufficiency of allegations would not promote the exposure of fraud. It would more likely be a disincentive for contractors to enter, or remain, in the government contract marketplace.

Indeed, for this latter category of contractors, the proposed changes will lead to charges that they should be debarred because they failed to report that which they believed was a proper claim. The newly proposed requirement to report violations of the civil FCA will shift the focus away from determining whether the underlying activity constituted a civil FCA violation to determining whether a report was made concerning disputed activity. Contractors may be suspended for failing to report, when later they are found not to have committed any civil FCA violation. Alternatively, contractors will clearly be incentivized to report to the contracting officer every single contract dispute as a potential civil FCA violation so as to avoid the threat of unwarranted suspension or debarment. The system will be overwhelmed, and its use of resources drawn from matters that legitimately require attention. Likewise, contracting officers will be likely to turn to the IG and DOJ for direction on every matter disclosed to them to avoid criticism, further overwhelming the contracting process with little likelihood of additional benefit.

Since the scope of the civil FCA is so broad, many contractors potentially fall into this category. The civil FCA has been interpreted as encompassing violations arising out of certifications that a product or service meets all contract requirements, and there is constant pressure to expand its scope. For example, in a recent case, *United States ex rel. Wilson v. Kellogg Brown & Root, Inc.* (4th Cir. No. 07-1516, May 16, 2008), *qui tam* relators contended that the contractor fraudulently induced the United States into awarding a contract by executing a standard form in which the contractor accepts "the terms and conditions" of the contract and "agrees to perform the same." The relators alleged the company had no intention of performing to the contract's requirements. Fortunately, the Fourth Circuit saw the peril in this attempt to expand the scope of the civil FCA, and the Court's summary provides a cautionary reminder of why mandatory reporting of civil FCA violations would be problematic for responsible contractors acting in good faith. The Court stated:

> Since initiating this litigation, Relators have consistently sought to shoehorn what is, in essence, a breach of contract action into a claim that is cognizable under the

False Claims Act. This misguided journey must come to an end. If every dispute involving contractual performance were to be transformed into a *qui tam* FCA suit, the prospect of litigation in government contracting would literally have no end.

These words are just as true in the context of reporting civil FCA violations; the Councils should be wary of creating a prospect of unending reporting obligations for responsible contractors operating in good faith.

CONCLUSION

In sum, CODSIA supports the Councils' efforts to promote honesty and integrity in contracting, including reinforcing the advantages of voluntary disclosure; however, CODSIA believes the proposed mandatory disclosure and full cooperation provisions included in both versions of the proposed rule are not the appropriate means to achieve such ends. Neither the Councils, DoJ nor DoD has demonstrated a need for this drastic departure from traditional voluntary programs, nor have they addressed the potential harm that may result from a policy that could overwhelm the process with matters better addressed through contract administration.

We appreciate the opportunity to submit these comments. If you have questions or need additional information, please contact CODSIA Project Officer Ruth Franklin of NDIA at (703) 247-2598 or at rfranklin@ndia.org.

Sincerely,

Peter Steffes
Vice President, Government Policy
National Defense Industrial Association

Alan Chvotkin
Executive Vice President & Counsel
Professional Services Council

A. R. "Trey" Hodgkins, III
Vice President of Federal Government
 Programs
Information Technology Association of
 America

Robert T. Marlow
Vice President, Acquisition Policy
Aerospace Industries Association

Richard L. Corrigan
Policy Committee Representative
American Council of Engineering
Companies

R. Bruce Josten
Executive Vice President for
 Government Affairs
U.S. Chamber of Commerce

Cynthia Brown
President
American Shipbuilding Association

AMERICAN BAR ASSOCIATION

Section of Public Contract Law
Writer's Address and Telephone

Suite 301
582 Market Street
San Francisco, CA 94104
Phone: (415) 362-6517
Fax: (415) 362-6519
pmeagher@rossimeagher.com

July 15, 2008

VIA FACSIMILE AND FIRST CLASS MAIL

General Services Administration
Regulatory Secretariat (VIR)
Attn: Ms. Laurieann Duarte
1800 F Street, N.W.
Washington, DC 20405

Re: **FAR Case 2007-006, Contractor Compliance Program And Integrity Reporting (Second Proposed Rule), 73 Fed. Reg. 28407 (May 16, 2008).**

Dear Ms. Duarte:

On behalf of the Section of Public Contract Law of the American Bar Association ("the Section"), I am submitting supplemental comments on the above-referenced proposed rule ("Second Proposed Rule"). The Section consists of attorneys and associated professionals in private practice, industry, and government service. The Section's governing Council and substantive committees contain members representing these three segments to ensure that all points of view are considered. By presenting their consensus view, the Section seeks to improve the process of public contracting for needed supplies, services, and public works.[1]

The Section is authorized to submit comments on acquisition regulations under special authority granted by the Association's Board of Governors. The views expressed herein have not been approved by the House of Delegates or the Board of

---

[1] Mary Ellen Coster Williams, a Delegate representing the Section of Public Contract Law in the ABA House of Delegates, and Sharon Larkin, a member of the Section's Council, did not participate in the consideration of these comments and abstained from voting to approve and send this letter.

General Services Administration
July 15, 2008
Page 2

Governors of the American Bar Association and, therefore, should not be construed as representing the policy of the American Bar Association.[2]

COMMENTS

A.   **Introduction**

The Second Proposed Rule represents a substantial modification of a rule first proposed on November 14, 2007 (72 Fed. Reg. 64019) ("First Proposed Rule"). The Section submitted comments on the First Proposed Rule on January 18, 2008. *See* Attachment A. The Second Proposed Rule does not address or take into account those comments, but rather than repeat them, the Section urges the Councils to consider those comments together with the supplemental comments provided here. In addition, the ABA Task Force on Attorney-Client Privilege submitted comments on the Second Proposed Rule on June 20, 2008. *See* Attachment B. The Section incorporates those comments by reference.

The focus of these supplemental comments is on the Second Proposed Rule's expansion of the First Proposed Rule to (1) require a contractor to report instances where it has "reasonable grounds to believe" that a violation of the civil False Claims Act ("FCA") by a principal, employee, agent, or subcontractor of the contractor has occurred in connection with the award or performance of its contracts or subcontracts, and (2) add to the grounds for suspension and debarment the contractor's "knowing failure to timely disclose" any possible violation of the civil FCA. 73 Fed. Reg. at 28409 (May 16, 2008). As discussed below, the addition of mandatory disclosure requirements for potential civil FCA violations (1) appears to be an afterthought not supported by any of the justifications advanced by the Department of Justice ("DoJ") for the First Proposed Rule; (2) would put contractors in the untenable position of guessing, under penalty of suspension or debarment if they guess wrong, which situations the Government or a *qui tam* relator might subsequently assert constitute a civil FCA violation; and (3) would unfairly subject contractors to potential *qui tam* suits if they err on the side of disclosure. The Section believes that such uses of the Government's suspension and debarment authority are unfair and would constitute an abuse of that authority.

---

[2] This letter is available in pdf format at http://www.abanet.org/contract/regscomm/home.html under the topic "Ethics."

General Services Administration
July 15, 2008
Page 3

B. **The Second Proposed Rule's Extension of Mandatory Disclosure Requirements To Potential Civil FCA Violations Appears To Be An Afterthought Not Supported By The Justifications For The Rule.**

The First Proposed Rule resulted from a request by the DoJ that was conveyed in a May 23, 2007, letter from the Assistant Attorney General for the Criminal Division, Alice Fisher, to the Administrator of the Office of Federal Procurement Policy ("DoJ Letter"). The DoJ Letter did not mention the civil FCA, and the mandatory disclosure rule that she sought was limited to potential violations of federal criminal law (and overpayments). More importantly, the justifications offered by DoJ for adopting a mandatory disclosure rule for potential criminal violations do not apply to the civil FCA, and the rule is not necessary to alert the Government to potential civil FCA violations.

As an initial matter, DoJ's professed concern with the alleged decline in the number of voluntary disclosures pursuant to the Department of Defense ("DoD") Voluntary Disclosure Program has no bearing on enforcement of the civil FCA. That statute, unlike federal criminal statutes, contains a private enforcement mechanism — the provision for civil FCA suits to be instituted and prosecuted by private persons referred to as *qui tam* relators. *See* 31 U.S.C. § 3730(b). The FCA's *qui tam* provisions have resulted in hundreds of civil FCA suits being filed by *qui tam* relators each year alleging millions of dollars of overcharges and other civil FCA violations by defense, healthcare, and other government contractors and subcontractors. Indeed, so many *qui tam* suits have been filed that a "backlog" has developed. *See* "A Backlog of Cases Alleging Fraud," *The Washington Post*, July 2, 2008. Accordingly, the alleged decline in contractor use of the DoD Voluntary Disclosure Program — whatever its relevance for the enforcement of federal criminal laws — has had absolutely no effect on the enforcement of the civil FCA.

DoJ's other purported justification for the First Proposed Rule — that it would bring contractors into line with other industries currently required by statute or regulation to report potential violations of certain federal criminal laws — is also inapplicable to the civil FCA. No statute or regulation currently requires any entity to report potential violations of the civil FCA to the Government. Thus, rather than being "careful not to ask contractors to do anything that is not already expected of their counterparts in other industries, and ... avoiding imposing any unnecessary burdens on small businesses or creating any expensive paperwork requirements," DoJ Letter at 1, the Second Proposed Rule would do precisely that.

Although the preamble to the Second Proposed Rule states that DoJ proposed the expansion of the Rule to cover potential civil FCA violations, it offers

General Services Administration
July 15, 2008
Page 4

no justification for this significant expansion, and neither did DoJ.[3] Indeed, the proposed expansion of the mandatory disclosure rule to potential civil FCA violation appears to have been an afterthought on DoJ's part. The Section believes that this expansion would have significant adverse effects on contractors and the integrity of the suspension and debarment process.

C. **The Second Proposed Rule Would Put Contractors In The Untenable Position Of Guessing, Under Penalty Of Suspension Or Debarment, Which Situations *Might* Constitute A Potential Civil FCA Violation.**

The FCA imposes civil liability on persons who "knowingly" present "false claims" to the United States, 31 U.S.C. § 3729(a)(i), or who "knowingly" make or use a false statement or record to get a claim paid or approved by the Government. 31 U.S.C. § 3729(a)(2). The elements of a civil FCA violation thus include, at a minimum, a "claim," "falsity," and "knowledge." The courts have interpreted the civil FCA also to require a showing of materiality, *i.e.*, that the alleged falsity affected or would have affected the Government's decision to pay the claim. *See, e.g., Harrison v. Westinghouse Savannah River Co.*, 176 F.3d 776, 785 (4th Cir. 1999) ("Liability under each of the provisions of the False Claims Act is subject to the further, judicially imposed requirement that the false statement or claim be material."). In addition, the United States Supreme Court recently held that a *qui tam* relator alleging that a subcontractor had violated the civil FCA by making or using a false statement or record to get a claim paid by the Government must show that the subcontractor *intended* that the false statement or record be material to the Government's decision to pay or approve a false claim. *Allison Engine Co., Inc. v. United States ex rel. Sanders*, 128 S. Ct. 2123, 2008 WL 2329722 (June 9, 2008). Given the multiple elements required to establish a civil FCA violation, and the numerous and sometimes conflicting court decisions interpreting those elements, it is unreasonable and oppressive to demand that contractors undertake to determine whether there are "reasonable grounds to believe" that one or more of its employees, principals, or agents may have violated the civil FCA.[4]

---

[3] DoJ's comments on the First Proposed Rule state only that "[s]ince the proposed regulation already includes the knowing failure to disclose an overpayment as well as violations of federal criminal law as a basis for suspension and debarment, it would be an obvious omission to not include the FCA." As explained in this letter, the omission of the FCA is appropriate.

[4] Even DoJ recognized in its May 2007 letter that "to limit the scope of the [proposed rule], it may be necessary to include guidance that defines terms such as reasonable grounds." No such guidance, however, was included in the First or Second Proposed Rule.

General Services Administration
July 15, 2008
Page 5

Further, many civil FCA actions arising out of federal procurements hinge on questions of contract interpretation. In many such cases, although the Government or a *qui tam* relator might state a potential cause of action, the contractor's actions ultimately are vindicated by a ruling that there was no violation of the civil FCA. *See, e.g., United States ex rel. Wilson v. Kellogg Brown & Root, Inc.* 525 F.3d 370 (4th Cir. 2008). Yet, the Second Proposed Rule would penalize contractors for failing to disclose actions that could well result in an ultimate finding of no liability.

The task of discerning a possible civil FCA violation would be compounded where the contractor is required to determine whether there are reasonable grounds to believe that a *subcontractor* may have violated the FCA. It could be extremely difficult for a contractor to obtain access to the facts necessary to assess whether a subcontractor "knowingly" made or used an allegedly false record or whether the subcontractor made or used an allegedly false record with the intent to materially affect the Government's decision to pay or approve a claim. *Allison Engine, supra.* This task will be even more difficult with respect to foreign and commercial item subcontractors, both of which the Second Proposed Rule proposed to add to the coverage of the mandatory disclosure rule.

The civil FCA *qui tam* provisions would further exacerbate the challenges and uncertainties that a mandatory disclosure requirement for potential FCA violations would create for contractors. These *qui tam* provisions allow private entities to allege, on behalf of the United States, facts that can give rise to an FCA violation. The size of the potential awards to *qui tam* relators incentivizes them to develop novel theories of liability under the FCA. *Cf. Hughes Aircraft Co. v. United States ex rel. Schumer*, 520 U.S. 939, 949 (1997) ("As a class of plaintiffs, *qui tam* relators are different in kind than the Government. They are motivated primarily by prospects of monetary reward rather than public good.... *Qui tam* relators are thus less likely than is the Government to forego an action based on a mere technical nonconformance with reporting requirements that involve[] no harm to the public fisc."). The Second Proposed Rule would, as a practical matter, require contractors to guess what theories of liability a *qui tam* relator might conceivably argue and whether those arguments would survive a motion to dismiss. A contractor that guesses incorrectly could be subject to potential suspension or debarment for failure to timely disclose a situation where a *qui tam* relator might allege a potential civil FCA violation. Under these circumstances, contractors would be pressured to err on the side of disclosure, with substantial risks, described below.

General Services Administration
July 15, 2008
Page 6

D. **The Second Proposed Rule Would Unfairly Subject Contractors Who Err On The Side of Disclosure To *Qui Tam* Suits Based Upon Their Disclosures.**

A contractor making a mandatory disclosure of a potential civil FCA violation pursuant to the Second Proposed Rule would face the risk of *causing* the filing of a *qui tam* suit based upon its disclosure. The civil FCA contains a provision — commonly referred to as the "public disclosure bar" — that deprives the court of jurisdiction over a *qui tam* suit if the allegations in the suit are based upon public disclosures. 31 U.S.C. § 3730(e)(4). Most courts, however, do not recognize disclosures to an agency Inspector General or contracting officer as a "public disclosure" that bars the *qui tam* suit. Therefore, a contractor making a mandatory disclosure would not be protected by the civil FCA's "public disclosure" bar unless the disclosures were subsequently published in the media, a lawsuit, or an administrative or congressional hearing or audit report. Relators who had access to the disclosures other than through these sources could file a *qui tam* complaint based upon the contractor's disclosures.

This risk will be magnified if the proposed amendments to the FCA currently pending in the House and Senate become law. Both the Senate amendments (S.2041) and the House amendments (H.4854) would strip defendants of their current ability to raise the public disclosure jurisdictional bar as a defense in a *qui tam* suit. Instead, DoJ would be able to file a motion to dismiss based on the public disclosure bar, or the court might also dismiss *sua sponte*. Because DoJ lacks the incentive to file such motions, relators would be able to file *qui tam* suits based upon public disclosures, including mandatory disclosures reported in the media or in a government report. Moreover, the amendments would overturn the long line of decisions that preclude government employees from acting as *qui tam* relators. This change would allow the very government officials to whom the mandatory disclosures were made to bring a *qui tam* suit against the contractor based upon its mandated disclosures.

E. **Threats of Suspension and Debarment Should Not be Used to Enforce Mandatory Disclosure of Possible Civil FCA Violations.**

For the reasons set forth above, use of the FAR suspension and debarment authority to compel contractors to disclose possible civil FCA violations is not warranted. Suspension and debarment are remedies designed to protect the Government from doing business with contractors that are not presently responsible — that is, that lack the integrity or systems adequate to ensure that they conduct business in an ethical and compliant manner. A contractor's reasonable determination that conduct does not justify a possible civil FCA action, *e.g.*, that its

General Services Administration
July 15, 2008
Page 7

conduct was permitted under the contract, that the questioned conduct was not material, or that it was not undertaken with the requisite level of intent, should not be taken as reflecting a lack of business integrity or adequate compliance systems. Moreover, exposing contractors (and their employees and subcontractors) to potential *qui tam* suits based upon mandatory disclosures is not consistent with the goals of the FAR's suspension and debarment provisions. There is no need or justification for employing the suspension and debarment authority to assist relators in identifying and prosecuting *qui tam* suits.

CONCLUSION

As indicated in the Section's comments on the First Proposed Rule, there is substantial interest within the Section in the Proposed Contractor Compliance Program and Integrity Reporting rule. The Section is concerned that the Second Proposed Rule fails to address or take into account many of the issues identified in the Section's comments to the First Proposed Rule. These concerns now include the extension of mandatory disclosure obligations to cover possible civil FCA violations. We urge the Councils to eliminate the requirement that contractors disclose potential civil FCA violations or face potential suspension and debarment if they do not.

The Section appreciates the opportunity to provide these comments and is available to provide additional information and assistance as the Councils may require.

Sincerely,

Patricia A Meagher

Patricia A. Meagher
Chair, Section of Public Contract Law

cc: Michael W. Mutek
Karen L. Manos
Donald G. Featherstun
Carol N. Park-Conroy
John S. Pachter
Michael A. Hordell
Robert L. Schaefer
Council Members, Section of Public Contract Law
Chair(s) and Vice Chair(s) of the Procurement Fraud Committee
Chair(s) and Vice Chair(s) of the Suspension and Debarment Committee

General Services Administration
July 15, 2008
Page 8

      Scott M. McCaleb
      Kara M. Sacilotto

DEFENSE CONTRACT AUDIT AGENCY
DEPARTMENT OF DEFENSE

IN REPLY REFER TO

SUBJECT: DCAA Formal Request for Information on ▮▮▮▮ Control Environment for ▮▮▮▮

Dear ▮▮▮,

As discussed on ▮▮▮▮, we are providing our formal request for information regarding ▮▮▮ Control Environment. Obtaining an understanding of the management control environment at every major contractor is an essential part of our annual audit plan.

This request for information is based on the DCAA Internal Control Matrix identifying the key internal controls required for assessment of the Control Environment. We have categorized our request for data as listed in the matrix. The list below is based on a reduced scope and limited to ▮▮▮ control environment for Contractor Fiscal Year (FY) ▮▮▮.

We ask that the information identified in each item below be consolidated and presented to us for discussion and sampling at a meeting, at a time and place of your choice, within the next two weeks. The information in this letter will need to be provided annually during the first quarter of each year. For this reason we suggest you keep this information current and up to date on an ongoing basis.

INTEGRITY AND ETHICAL VALUES

1. We are required to evaluate ▮▮▮ policies, procedures, training, and compliance with policies and procedures related to conveying integrity and ethical values.

Our examination of ▮▮▮ Integrity and Ethical Values will consist of the following:

a. Verifying the existence of ▮▮▮ written codes of conduct/ethics. We will selectively test the codes of conduct to determine if they adequately cover expected standards of

Subject: DCAA Formal Request for Information on
Control Environment for Fiscal Year ▓

conduct affecting significant internal and external business and employee relationships. Please provide ▓ most recent codes of conduct/ethics for our discussions.

b. Verifying that ▓ policies and procedures provide for an ethics training program for all employees. We will selectively test this control by evaluating completed training records for the last 12 months in accordance with FAR 52.203-13(c)(1). Therefore, please provide a list of ethics training ▓ provided its employees during the last 12 months, agendas for the training provided, and a list of employees who attended the training.

c. Verifying that the written codes of conduct (i) are periodically communicated to all employees, (ii) are formally acknowledged, and (iii) cite consequences for violations. We will selectively test this control by evaluating records of the acknowledged communications and documentation of management actions related to monitoring compliance as well as actions related to violations that have occurred within the last 12 months. Please provide ▓ most current written code of conduct; the policies/procedures related to communication, acknowledgement, and consequences for violating the code; a list of employees who acknowledged receipt of the code during the past 12 months.

d. Verifying that ▓ performs periodic reviews of the company business practices, procedures, and internal controls for compliance with standards of conduct as stated in FAR 52.203-13(c)(2)(ii)(C) and provides appropriate disclosure to the government of information needed to fulfill its responsibilities. We define adequate disclosure as disclosure to DCAA and the ACO of all findings that significantly impact government contracts within 5-10 days of identification; disclosure of the corrective actions in process or planned by the company; and disclosure of adjustments to government contract costs and improvements to underlying business systems. Please provide a list of violations to the code of conduct/ethics which occurred in the past 12 months.

2. We will evaluate ▓ self-governance activities, as well as the reporting to and cooperation with the Government.

Our examination of ▓ self-governance activities will consist of the following procedures:

a. Verifying that ▓ has a system to identify/report noncompliances with codes of conduct and pursue corrective actions. ▓ should have a mechanism, such as a hotline, by which employees may report suspected instances of improper conduct in accordance with FAR 52.203-13(c)(2)(ii)(D). Please provide documentation of ▓ mechanism (e.g. hotline program, ombudsman program, etc.) for employees' use in identifying and reporting noncompliances. Further, provide a list of reported noncompliances during the past 12 months.

Subject: DCAA Formal Request for Information on
Control Environment for Fiscal Year

    b. We will determine the extent to which ▮ participates in self-governance programs, such as Coordinated Audit Planning, Defense Industry Initiative, DoD Hotlines, or any procedure for reporting suspected irregularities. Please provide ▮ policies/procedures related to self-governance programs, specifically identifying the nature and extent of the programs.

    c. Verifying ▮ reporting to Government officials. We will review ▮ policies and procedures and determine if they provide for timely reporting to appropriate Government officials of any suspected violation of law in connection with Government contracts or any other irregularities in connection with such contracts in accordance with FAR 52.203-13(b)(3) and FAR 52.203-13(c)(2)(ii)(F). Please provide ▮ policies/procedures detailing the steps for timely reporting to appropriate Government officials of any suspected violation of law in connection with Government contracts.

    d. Verifying that ▮ policies and procedures provide for cooperation with any Government agencies responsible for an investigation involving any suspected violation of law per FAR 52.203-13(c)(2)(ii)(G). Please provide us with a company-wide list of any current open investigations.

    e. Verifying that ▮ has properly displayed the DoD Hotline Poster prepared by the DoD Office of the Inspector General in accordance with FAR 52.203-14. Provide a list of areas in which the DoD Hotline Poster is placed within ▮ facilities (please specify contractor site/locations).

3. We will evaluate ▮ management intervention and/or overrides.

    Our examination of ▮ management intervention and/or overrides will consist of the following:

    a. We will determine whether ▮ policies and procedures address the situations and frequency of management intervention, require documentation and approval of intervention, and the strict prohibition of any management overrides. Please provide ▮ policies and procedures related to management intervention, the required documentation and approval of intervention, and required documentation of the intervention. Please provide a listing of labor and material transfers for the last 12 months.

    b. We will selectively evaluate documentation of management interventions or overrides and assess compliance with ▮ policies and procedures.

4. We will evaluate ▮ internal and external audit functions and efforts related to its current accounting system.

    Our examination of ▮ internal and external audit functions will consist of the following:

Subject: DCAA Formal Request for Information on
Control Environment for Fiscal Year

   a. We will determine whether ▮ system of management controls provides for internal and/or external audits. Please provide a listing showing all of the management reviews and internal audits conducted in the last 12 months.

   b. Provide us with the external CPA's report of material weaknesses of internal controls and/or management letter for the most recently audited year.

      I. If there were any identified weaknesses of internal control, demonstrate that the appropriate corrective action has been taken to correct the item.

      II. We require documentation to verify that the external CPA does not provide accounting services to ▮.

5. We will review ▮ annual report (or 10K report) for SEC registrants for an internal control report, if applicable. Please provide a copy of the annual report and internal control report and brief us on significant disclosures/issues that impact or could possibly impact government contracts/costs. The internal control report should include an assessment of the effectiveness of the internal control structure and procedures for financial reporting and the independent auditor must attest to and report on the ▮ assessment.

   a. If applicable, we will determine whether ▮ has taken corrective actions in response to any identified internal control weaknesses.

ADVANCE AGREEMENTS

6. Please provide the policy and procedure for ensuring compliance with and for periodically reviewing advance agreements.

7. Provide a listing of all current advance agreements between ▮ and the government. The listing should identify the agreement number (if applicable), subject, applicability, effective date, and duration (reference FAR 31.109(b)).

   Should you have any questions about the information requested, please feel free to call

DRAFT PROCEDURE FOR COMPLIANCE WITH THE FAR MANDATORY DISCLOSURE RULE (TEMPLATE FOR NOTICE TO EMPLOYEES OF INTERNAL REPORTING OBLIGATION)

I. **BACKGROUND AND PURPOSE**

The Federal Acquisition Regulation Mandatory Disclosure Rule (the "Rule") became effective on December 12, 2008. The Rule requires that contractors and subcontractors make a timely disclosure to the Agency Office of Inspector General whenever, in connection with a Federal contract, they become aware of "credible evidence" of a violation of Federal criminal law involving fraud, conflict of interest, bribery, or gratuity, or a violation of the civil False Claims Act. FAR 52.203-13(b)(3). The Rule further requires that contractors and subcontractors make a timely disclosure to the Government when they become aware of significant Government overpayment on a contract. FAR 9.406-2(b)(1)(vi). [*Consider whether to define significant overpayment more specifically by reference to a dollar threshold or some other characterization, either here or in the example section later in this template.*]

The internal reporting procedure facilitates ABC Company's (the "Company") compliance with the Rule. The procedure covers a broader range of potential conduct than does the Rule. This allows the Company to receive internal reports, investigate all reports, and determine whether "credible evidence" exists that warrants disclosure under the Rule.

The internal reporting procedure is in addition to any existing contractual, statutory, and/or regulatory reporting requirements. The Company and its employees are still required to fully comply with all existing policies, procedures, and reporting requirements. [*Identify policies, procedures and/or reporting requirements relevant to your Company.*]

Noncompliance with the Rule may result in suspension or debarment.

II. **INTERNAL REPORTING PROCEDURE**

All Company employees must comply with this internal reporting procedure and the Company's Code of Conduct.

All Company employees must report knowledge or suspicion of potential wrongdoing or a significant Government overpayment to a manager, Ethics Officer, Human Resources representative, the Company's legal department or the Company's anonymous hot line at 1-800-XXX-XXXX. [*Include additional reporting resources relevant to your Company.*] Any person receiving such reports should advise the reporting individual to retain all records (electronic, hard copy, emails, etc.) relating to the allegations.

All Company employees must fully cooperate with any Company internal investigations of any reported allegations.

The Company prohibits retaliation against any employee for reporting potential wrongdoing or for cooperating in the conduct of an investigation. Any retaliation against an employee may lead to disciplinary action, up to and including the termination of employment.

III.   EVENTS THAT MUST BE REPORTED INTERNALLY

      A.   Activities Involving Contract Fraud
      B.   Activities Involving Conflicts of Interest
      C.   Activities Involving Bribery
      D.   Activities Involving Gratuities
      E.   False Statement(s) or Claims to the Government
      F.   Significant Government Overpayments

IV.   EXAMPLES OF POTENTIALLY REPORTABLE EVENTS

The following are examples of conduct that, depending on the circumstances, could be covered by the Rule and should be reported. The list is *not* comprehensive and provides *examples* only:

Activities Involving Contract Fraud:

- Charging for goods that were not received.

- *Include examples relevant to your Company's operations.*

Activities Involving Conflicts of Interest:

- Awarding a federal subcontract to a company owned by the spouse of a person involved in the award decision.

- *Include examples relevant to your Company's operations.*

Activities Involving Bribery:

- Providing a Government official something of value to increase the chances that she will award a contract to the company.

- *Include examples relevant to your Company's operations.*

Activities Involving Gratuities:

- Providing anything of significant value to a Government official.

- *Include examples relevant to your Company's operations.*

False Statement or Claims to the Government:

- Submitting a proposal that contains material misstatements in response to a RFP.

- *Include examples relevant to your Company's operations.*

Government Overpayments:

The following are examples of overpayments that, depending on the circumstances, could be covered by the Rule and should be reported. The list is *not* comprehensive and provides *examples* only:

- Overpayments resulting from duplicate invoices.

- *Include examples relevant to your Company's operations.*

Overpayments resulting from the following types of payments are exempted by the FAR Mandatory Disclosure Rule and need not be reported through this process:

- Progress payments
- Interim payments
- Provisional payments
- Advance payments
- Other payments encompassed by FAR 32.001

V. INVESTIGATION OF INTERNALLY REPORTED EVENTS

The Company will review or investigate all internally reported allegations. Multiple organizations within the Company may be involved in the internal investigation process, *i.e.*, the Legal Department, Internal Audit, Human Resources, Quality Assurance, etc.

An internal investigation conducted by or at the direction of the Company's legal department will fall under the protection of the "Attorney-Client Privilege." Not all internal investigations will be conducted under the Attorney-Client Privilege. This determination will be made by the Company's legal department and management.

VI. QUESTIONS AND COMMENTS

All questions should be directed to [*insert proper contact information*].

**DEFENSE INDUSTRY INITIATIVE
ON BUSINESS ETHICS AND CONDUCT**
ESTABLISHED 1986

Internally Reportable Events

Background and Purpose: It is Company policy to comply with all applicable federal, state, and local laws, regulations, contract terms and conditions, and related Company policies governing our business operations (collectively referred to as "governing authorities"). One way the Company monitors compliance with such governing authorities is to review and investigate possible noncompliance with those authorities. We rely on our managers, employees, and agents to raise concerns internally so that the Company can evaluate possible noncompliance and, where appropriate, adopt responsive corrective action. Corrective action can take many forms, including enhanced employee training, adopting or changing company policies and procedures, employee discipline, termination of consulting or subcontract agreements, or restitution or refund of contract overpayments. Further, certain types of violations involving our federal government contracts[1] and subcontracts must be reported to the federal government when they involve the award, performance, or closeout of a government contract or subcontract. In addition, in other circumstances, the Company may choose to report to the federal government even in the absence of an explicit requirement to do so.

While it is impossible to list each and every possible violation of governing authorities that the Company expects its managers, employees, and agents to disclose internally to the Company, the Company has endeavored to identify certain categories and specific examples of the types of possible violations that may be encountered and thus are required to be disclosed internally. Again, this list is not exhaustive, and, if in doubt, we encourage reporting of any compliance matter of concern internally so that the Company's assigned subject matter experts can perform a thorough review, bringing to bear the full resources of the Company available for this purpose. Violations involving the Company, its principals, managers, employees, agents, vendors, subcontractors, teaming partners, and others with whom it does business must be reported internally through Company channels.

Reports. The Company has many channels available to receive reports of possible violations, including: the Compliance Officer; the Compliance "hotline"; members of the Compliance Department; [the Audit Committee of the Board of Directors]; members of the Legal Department; Internal Audit; and managers. Company managers who

---

[1] All references to "government contracts" apply equally to government subcontracts.

**DEFENSE INDUSTRY INITIATIVE
ON BUSINESS ETHICS AND CONDUCT**
ESTABLISHED 1986

receive reports covered by this policy are required to timely notify the Compliance Officer so that the matter can be tracked and a thorough review conducted.

Types of Internally Reportable Events

For ease of reference, reportable events are grouped into categories below; however, infractions can occur during any phase of the procurement process and should be reported internally, no matter when they might have occurred.

I. *Contract Award*

- a false statement – orally or in writing – made to the government, directly or indirectly, including false certifications and representations, in a proposal or during an oral presentation to the government, etc. *E.g.*,
    - misstatements of Company or employee qualifications or performance results
    - false independent price certification
    - concealment of a material fact

- bribery of or providing a prohibited payment or gratuity to a government official or his/her family/household member (exceptions: gifts or things of value permitted under law and company policy)
- employment discussions between a government employee and the Company giving rise to a conflict of interest
- knowing failure to disclose required information, such as cost, pricing, or other information requiring such disclosure, *e.g.*, cost or pricing data under the Truth in Negotiations Act; organizational conflict of interest information; commercial sales practices under GSA Schedule requirements, etc.
- unlawfully obtaining government source selection information or contractor bid or proposal information prior to award of a contract to which the protected information relates

II. *Contract Performance*

- mischarging under a government contract, *e.g.*, knowingly charging the wrong contract or work order number for labor or materials, over charging
- failure to perform required processes or tests required by the contract, or falsification of test results
- failure to deliver products or services that conform to contract requirements, in the absence of authorized customer approval. *E.g.*,
    - overbilling or billing for work not performed

- failure to adhere to country of origin requirements (*e.g.*, Trade Agreements Act or Buy American Act)
- using used parts when new parts are required
- using substandard parts

- a false statement – orally or in writing – made to the government, directly or indirectly, concerning contract performance. *E.g.*,
    - misstatements of contract performance associated with award fee or milestone payments
    - concealment of a material fact

- false or fraudulent claims, *e.g.*, invoices for payment containing overstatements of progress payment requests or for incurred costs, inclusion of unallowable costs in indirect cost rate submissions, etc.
- falsification or unauthorized destruction of Company books and records, *e.g.*, financial, quality, testing, billing, etc.

III. *Contract Closeout*

- false statements – orally or in writing – made to the government, directly or indirectly, concerning contract claims or entitlement
- false or fraudulent claims, *e.g.*, invoices for payment containing overstated progress payment requests or for incurred costs, inclusion of unallowable costs in indirect cost rate submissions, etc.
- falsification or unauthorized destruction of Company books and records

IV. *Other, when related to the award, performance, or closeout of a government contract*

- Performance of prohibited activities by a former government employee on behalf of the Company contrary to post-employment restrictions
- Offering or accepting illegal kickbacks in connection with government subcontracts, at any tier
- Retaliation against an employee who raises an issue involving Company noncompliance with any governing authority
- Falsification or unauthorized destruction of Company books and records
- [a scheme, agreement, or conspiracy to defraud the government with respect to any claim for payment or property]
- [obstruction of a federal audit]

THE NEW FAR DISCLOSURE RULE

James Graham

THE STATEMENTS IN THIS PRESENTATION DO NOT REPRESENT
THE VIEWS OF THE U.S. DEPARTMENT OF JUSTICE

WHAT THE RULE DOES NOT DO

According to the comments by one practitioner,

- "fundamentally shifts the focus of the acquisition system from the management of acquisitions and contracts for the purpose of achieving agency missions to law enforcement"
- "de facto management of the federal acquisition system has effectively shifted to agency inspectors general and the Department of Justice"
- "compliance may be more important than the quality, value and timeliness of products or services delivered"

WHAT THE RULE DOES DO

- Requires that large contractors have real compliance programs
- As part of those programs contractors are expected to cooperate with the government in fraud and corruption investigations arising in their contracts
- All contractors are expected to disclose to the CO and the IG if they become aware fraud or corruption in their contracts with the federal government.
- Provides extra incentive for contractors to report significant overpayments to the CO

The Key FAR Provisions on Disclosure

3.1003 Requirements
****

2) Whether or not the clause at 52.203-13 is applicable, a contractor may be suspended and/or debarred for <u>knowing</u> failure by a <u>principal</u> to <u>timely</u> disclose to the Government, in connection with the award, performance, or closeout of a Government contract performed by the contractor or a subcontract awarded thereunder, <u>credible evidence of a violation</u> of Federal criminal law involving fraud, conflict of interest, bribery, or gratuity violations found in Title 18 of the United States Code or a violation of the civil False Claims Act. Knowing failure to timely disclose credible evidence of any of the above violations remains a cause for suspension and/or debarment until three years after final payment on a contract (see 9.406-2(b)(1)(vi) and 9.407-2(a)(8)).

The Key FAR Provisions on Disclosure (cont'd)

9.406-2 Causes for debarment

(b)(1) A contractor, based upon a preponderance of the evidence, for any of the following--

* * * * *

(vi) Knowing failure by a principal, until 3 years after final payment on any Government contract awarded to the contractor, to timely disclose to the Government, in connection with the award, performance, or closeout of the contract or a subcontract thereunder, credible evidence of--

(A) Violation of Federal criminal law involving fraud, conflict of interest, bribery, or gratuity violations found in Title 18 of the United States Code;

(B) Violation of the civil False Claims Act (31 U.S.C. 3729-3733); or

(C) Significant overpayment(s) on the contract, other than overpayments resulting from contract financing payments as defined in 32.001.

The Key FAR Provisions on Disclosure (cont'd)

52.203-13 Contractor Code of Business Ethics and Conduct

(a) Definitions

****

Full cooperation – (1) Means disclosure to the Government of the information sufficient for law enforcement to identify the nature and extent of the offense and the individuals responsible for the conduct. It includes providing timely and complete response to Government auditors' and investigators' request for documents and access to employees with information;

(2) Does not foreclose any Contractor rights arising in law, the FAR, or the terms of the contract. It does not require—

(i) A Contractor to waive its attorney-client privilege or the protections afforded by the attorney work product doctrine; or

(ii) Any officer, director, owner, or employee of the Contractor, including a sole proprietor, to waive his or her attorney client privilege or Fifth Amendment rights; and

(3) Does not restrict a Contractor from--

(i) Conducting an internal investigation; or

(ii) Defending a proceeding or dispute arising under the contract or related to a potential or disclosed violation.

****

Principal means an officer, director, owner, partner, or a person having primary management or supervisory responsibilities within a business entity (e.g., general manager; plant manager; head of a subsidiary, division, or business segment; and similar positions).

WHAT HAVE THE FAR COUNCILS SAID ABOUT IMPLEMENTATION

What to Disclose?

- Disclosure to the government of the information sufficient for law enforcement to identify the nature and extent of the offense and the individuals responsible for the conduct. See FAR 52.203-13
- A description of the overpayment including the circumstances of the overpayment, affected contract number and delivery order number, affected line item or subline item and contractor point of contact. See FAR 52.232-25

WHAT HAVE THE FAR COUNCILS SAID ABOUT IMPLEMENTATION (cont'd)

Time for Internal Investigation?

The Councils have replaced "reasonable grounds to believe" with "credible evidence". DoJ Criminal Division recommended use of this standard after discussions with industry representatives. This term indicates a higher standard, implying that the contractor will have the opportunity to take some time for preliminary examination of the evidence to determine its credibility before deciding to disclose to the Government. FR 67073

WHAT HAVE THE FAR COUNCILS SAID ABOUT IMPLEMENTATION (cont'd)

Does the Rule Require Contractor Investigation?

Although the rule allows contractors time to take reasonable steps to determine that evidence of wrongdoing is credible, it does not direct contractors to carry out any particular level of internal investigation. FR 67086

****

The Government does not direct companies to investigate. In the normal course of business, a company that is concerned about ethical behavior will take reasonable steps to determine the credibility of allegations of misconduct within the firm. It is left to the discretion of the company what these reasonable steps may entail. FR 67087

WHAT HAVE THE FAR COUNCILS SAID ABOUT IMPLEMENTATION (cont'd)

How Far Back?

The Councils do not agree with the respondents who think that disclosure under the internal control system or as a potential cause for suspension/debarment should only apply to conduct occurring after the date the rule is effective or the clause is included in the contract, or the internal control system is established. The laws against these violations were already in place before the rule became effective or any of these other occurrences. FR 67073-74

****

To some extent, the effective date of the rule actually trumps the other events, because the failure to timely disclose as a cause for suspension/debarment is independent of the inclusion of the contract clause in the contract or the establishment of an internal control system. FR 67075

WHAT HAVE THE FAR COUNCILS SAID ABOUT IMPLEMENTATION (cont'd)

What Does Timely Mean?

First, the Councils note that the new statute uses the term "timely" in setting forth disclosure requirements …….. because it implies that the contractor will have the opportunity to take some time for preliminary examination of the evidence to determine its credibility before deciding to disclose to the Government. This does not impose upon the contractor an obligation to carry out a complex investigation, but only to take reasonable steps that the contractor considers sufficient to determine that the evidence is credible. FR 67074

WHAT HAVE THE FAR COUNCILS SAID ABOUT IMPLEMENTATION (cont'd)

Risk of Prosecution?

Existing DoJ guidelines addressing corporate prosecution standards, while certainly not providing amnesty, suggest that if a company discloses such violations, the prosecution will be of the individuals responsible for the violation, not the entire organization. FR67071

WHAT HAVE THE FAR COUNCILS SAID ABOUT IMPLEMENTATION (cont'd)

Risk of Debarment?

It is unlikely that any contractor would be suspended or debarred absent the determination that a violation had actually occurred. Present responsibility is the ultimate basis of suspension or debarment. FR67078

WHAT HAVE THE FAR COUNCILS SAID ABOUT IMPLEMENTATION (cont'd)

Who Has Knowledge - Principal?

The Councils note that this definition should be interpreted broadly, and could include compliance officers or directors of internal audit, as well as other positions of responsibility. FR 67079

WHAT HAVE THE FAR COUNCILS SAID ABOUT IMPLEMENTATION (cont'd)

Application of the False Claims Act?

The Councils do not agree that the requirements of the civil FCA cannot be reasonably ascertained and understood by contractors.

****

Genuine disputes over the proper application of the civil FCA may be considered in evaluating whether the contractor knowingly failed to disclose a violation of the civil FCA. FR 67081

WHAT HAVE THE FAR COUNCILS SAID ABOUT IMPLEMENTATION (cont'd)

New Duty to Report Overpayments?

The Councils dispute the allegation that "contractors currently have no obligation to report overpayments". ******* it is within the discretion of the suspension and debarment official to determine whether an overpayment is significant and whether suspension or debarment would be the appropriate outcome for failure to report such overpayment. FR 67080

What are the Requirements for Disclosure of Overpayments?

52.232-25 Prompt Payment.
* * * * *
   PROMPT PAYMENT (OCT 2008)
* * * * *
   (d) <u>Overpayments</u>. If the Contractor becomes aware of a duplicate contract financing or invoice payment or that the Government has otherwise overpaid on a contract financing or invoice payment, the Contractor shall--
   (1) Remit the overpayment amount to the payment office cited in the contract along with a description of the overpayment including the
      (i) Circumstances of the overpayment (e.g., duplicate payment, erroneous payment, liquidation errors, date(s) of overpayment);
      (ii) Affected contract number and delivery order number if applicable;
      (iii) Affected contract line item or subline item, if applicable; and
      (iv) Contractor point of contact.
   (2) Provide a copy of the remittance and supporting documentation to the Contracting Officer.

(End of clause)

73 Federal Register 54006-7 (September 17, 2008)

Issues for Contractors

- When I become aware of an allegation, do I conduct an internal investigation before deciding whether to disclose?
- How conservative do I want to be on disclosures—only clear instances of a violation?
- Do I help myself by hiring outside counsel to conduct an internal investigation? To render an opinion on whether there is credible evidence?
- What do I tell my employees in the process of conducting an internal investigation?
- Can the matter be disclosed to the CO as an overpayment only and meet the disclosure to the IG requirements? Any risks?

Issues for the Government

- How much to rely on a contractor's internal investigation in deciding whether to initiate an investigation?
- How to distinguish between an actionable fraud and a matter for the CO without conducting an investigation?
- How can the investigative and decision process be expedited to encourage contractor disclosure?
- How can the government reward contractors who disclose to encourage contractor disclosure?

GSA Office of Inspector General

Office of Inspector General
For the General Services Administration
GSA

FAR Contractor Reporting Form

No electronic submissions using this form will be possible until Dec 12th at 9:00am EST

To implement the December 12th, 2008 FAR amendment this form is to allow the Contractor to notify, in writing, the agency (GSA) Office of the Inspector General, whenever the contractor has credible evidence that a principal, employee, agent, or subcontractor of the Contractor has committed a violation of the civil False Claims Act or a violation of Federal criminal law involving fraud conflict of interest, bribery, or gratuity violations in connection with the award, performance, or closeout of a contract or any related subcontract. The individual completing this form must be an officer or manager empowered to speak for the company by filing this report. When you submit this electronic form an email will automatically be generated to send you a tracking number and a copy of what you have submitted so you may also forward it to the Contracting Officer. The information you are providing is not deemed to be submitted until you have received that confirmation email. If you wish to provide information that does not fall within these guidelines, please visit the Inspector General Hotline.

Your Company Information (All mandatory fields are denoted with a *)

Your First Name*:
Your Last Name*:
Your Title*:
Your Business Email*:
Confirm Your Business Email*:
Company Name*:
Business Address1*:
Business Address2:
Business City*:
Business State / Province*:
Business Zip or Postal Code*:
Business Country*:
Business Phone Number*:
Business Fax Number:

Relationship

My company is the: Prime

I am reporting on: My Company

Contract Information

Contract No:
DUNS or TINS:

http://oig.gsa.gov/integrityreport.htm (1 of 3) [12/4/2008 8:59:09 AM]

R-20

GSA Office of Inspector General

GSA Contracting Officer Name: [   ]

GSA Component / Region: [Administrator] / [1 - Boston, MA]

If other, please specify: [   ]

Description of Services/Supplies/System:
[   ]

Incident

Estimated Amount of Loss: [   ]

Loss Description: [   ]

Incident Date: [01] / [01] / [   ]

Date contractor learned of potential violation: [01] / [01] / [   ]

Has an investigation been conducted? ○ Yes ○ No

Attributes

Does the incident you are reporting include any of the following attributes:
(check all that apply)

- ☐ Duration of the activity longer than 3 months
- ☐ Multiple individuals involved
- ☐ Actual or potential security compromise
- ☐ Actual or potential employee/public safety/health threat
- ☐ Actual or potential misuse of personally identifiable information
- ☐ Actual or potential national security threat

Comments

Please provide a complete description of the facts and circumstances surrounding the reported activities, including the evidence forming the basis of this report, the names of the individuals involved, dates, location, how the matter was discovered, potential witnesses and their involvement and any corrective action taken by the company.

NOTE: Please include the names, email contact, and phone numbers of all individuals involved and/or potential witnesses.

[   ]

Please list any other entities you are notifying:
[   ]

Attachments

[   ] [Browse...]

[Add File]

Certification

GSA Office of Inspector General

I certify that the information contained herein is true and correct to the best of my knowledge.

NAME: [   ]

Validation

Please enter the number from the image into the adjacent field:

[CAPTCHA image] [   ] I cannot read the image.

No electronic submissions using this form will be possible until [xx:xx] to [xx:xx] EST

[Clear] [Submit]

Copyright 2008 GSA OIG

Home Offices Contact US Publications FOIA Employment Privacy Statement

R-21

Where to send IG Disclosures?

www.ignet.gov